Praise for *Don't Divorce*

"Modern culture urges us to put convenience ahead of commitment. Diane Medved knows better. *Don't Divorce* makes a brave stand on behalf of the institution of marriage and offers a sensitive, practical handbook for couples making the same brave stand in their own lives."

> **—ARTHUR BROOKS**, president, American Enterprise Institute

"*Don't Divorce* is about fighting through challenges that occur in every relationship—married or unmarried. It's about not giving up and getting to renewed, even stronger, love and understanding. A must-read, in other words, for everyone who cares about love and friendship, about overcoming temporary issues that obscure relationships worth fighting to preserve."

> **—LANNY J. DAVIS**, attorney, crisis management specialist, and columnist for *The Hill*

"In a hard situation, divorce can seem like the sensible solution, but marriage is a journey, not a destination. As Diane Medved shows in this indispensable book, the stakes are so high for so many people that it's worth fighting for your marriage."

> **—J. C. WATTS JR.**, former U.S. congressman and author of *Dig Deep: 7 Truths to Finding the Strength Within*

"In every decade there are a few truly great and inspiring books, and *Don't Divorce* is one of them. Rife with clarity, warmth, and wit, it is a must-read for anyone in a marriage punctuated by disappointment, heartbreak, or damaged love."

> **—RABBI HANOCH TELLER**, author of *Heroic Children: Untold Stories of the Unconquerable*

"Dr. Diane Medved presents a brave and brilliant case against divorce that few contemplating divorce ever consider. Her unflinching candor and immensely readable style make for a book you won't forget—and could dramatically enhance your life."

—**RABBI DANIEL AND SUSAN LAPIN,** hosts of *Ancient Jewish Wisdom* TV show and authors of *Madam, I'm Adam: Decoding the Marriage Secrets of Eden*

"In a throw-away society that prefers discarding to repairing, Diane Medved offers a powerful and much-needed corrective. *Don't Divorce* dissects grounds for divorce then offers the enthusiastic case for improving your marriage, with plenty of vivid examples and a wealth of wisdom about true contentment."

—**RABBI BENJAMIN BLECH,** professor of Talmud, Yeshiva University

Don't Divorce

DON'T
DIVORCE

*Powerful Arguments for Saving and
Revitalizing Your Marriage*

Diane Medved, Ph.D.

REGNERY
PUBLISHING
A Division of Salem Media Group

Regnery® is a registered trademark of Salem Communications Holding Corporation

Cataloging-in-Publication data on file with the Library of Congress

ISBN: 978-1-62157-521-4

Published in the United States by
Regnery Publishing
A Division of Salem Media Group
300 New Jersey Ave NW
Washington, DC 20001
www.Regnery.com

Manufactured in the United States of America

10 9 8 7 6 5 4 3 2 1

Books are available in quantity for promotional or premium use. For information on discounts and terms, please visit our website: www.Regnery.com.

Distributed to the trade by
Perseus Distribution
www.perseusdistribution.com

*For my late parents, Stanley and Genevieve Edwards,
whose marriage of fifty-nine years was a model of kindness
and romance, and for my own romantic soul mate, Michael,
who teaches me about generosity and fills me with awe.*

CONTENTS

Why You Need to Read This Book

MARRIAGE AND DIVORCE AT WAR

I f you're married, you're at war—not against your spouse, but against the menace of divorce.

You may not recognize the nature of the struggle; marriage and divorce simply seem like two coexisting possibilities for relationships. But in reality, they're two irreconcilable ideas.

Marriage and divorce battle in every corner of our culture, one side with hearts and flowers and pledges of forever, and the other with casual porn, meetup apps, specialty lawyers, and friends who've slogged through it themselves. Stealth efforts are undermining your vows and imperiling your children's future.

This book lays out strategies to help you fight these threats to your marriage—and win.

If you're on the verge of surrendering, you need ammunition to combat these subversive squadrons. You need to overcome the propaganda insisting that divorce will solve your problems and bring liberation.

Marriage used to be the primary gateway to adulthood, which started immediately following adolescence. But now young people first pursue gap years, graduate degrees, and career exploration. In 1960, before the impact of feminists and Boomers, the median age of women's first marriage was just over twenty, and men tied the knot at just over twenty-two.[1] Since then, as increasing numbers of twenty-somethings put it off, the median age of first marriage moved all the way to twenty-seven for women, and twenty-nine for men. Marriage used to be a launch into responsibility, but now it's what you do after a few live-in relationships and career ascent, when the clock's ticking and you better hurry up and start your family.

Three trends in particular affect your perception of marriage every day. First, fewer couples overall are married, and almost everyone's circle of friends and relatives includes a greater mix of single, cohabiting, married, and divorced people.[2] Second, religion, traditionally a major support for marriage, is fading in importance to Americans.[3] And the third anti-marriage trend comes directly through our laptops, where Facebook and other social media offer the community, titillation, and entertainment we used to rely on spouses to provide and share.

THE BOOK I HAD TO WRITE

Two decades ago I wrote *The Case Against Divorce*, which began with a confession: "This is not the book I set out to write."

In my psychology practice at the time, I specialized in helping unmarried couples decide whether or not to wed. I'd also developed a program to help married couples evaluate the decision to have children. Marriage and childbearing were options, and since divorce was easy and everywhere, I assumed that when the relationship got tough, divorce was just another choice to be reasoned through.

So after writing books on the marriage and childbearing decisions, I turned my attention to divorce, the next important choice that could be better made in an organized, thoughtful way. Wouldn't any distressed couple benefit from well-designed tools to assess the pros and cons?

A publisher agreed, and I wasted no time talking to divorced people to see what they went through. I began by asking if they regretted their divorces. The nearly unanimous response was that divorce ultimately made the respondent stronger, and as a result, he or she had come to a better place. Then I asked my second question—and my third, fourth, and fifth: "What happened to cause the divorce?" "What is your relationship with your ex like?" "How did the divorce affect each of your kids?" "What's your experience in the dating world?" "How have your finances changed?" "Looking back now, do you think you might have been able to make it work?" To quote from my book:

> Often in a rush of tears, they described the suffering and anguish they had endured—nights of fantasies about the husband or wife who left, days of guilt after abandoning a once-devoted mate. They talked about the nuts-and-bolts of daily life, of uprooting, of shifting to an apartment and splitting possessions, of balancing parental duties with now-pressing work demands. They spoke of changing relationships with their children, who moved from innocent babes to confidants to arbitrators and sometimes to scapegoats.
>
> And they mourned a part of themselves never to be recaptured. The part they had once invested in a marital or family unit that was now destroyed.... [4]

These answers floored me, and I found myself forced to re-evaluate my plan. Instead of helping people decide whether to stay in a marriage or leave it, I needed to sound a warning. In most cases, divorce was a catastrophe, leaving permanent scars on children, family, and the partners themselves—a cure worse than the disease.

My book got a lot of attention, much of it hostile. It flew in the face of the conventional wisdom that self-fulfillment takes precedence over outdated commitments. All I did was present facts that few people consider in the heat of anger but that could save them from disaster. I tried to show them how they hurt those they love and what they do to their own characters and future, how the divorce industry sweeps them along toward a decree, and how the profiteers of loneliness add to the heartache.

I thought I was being helpful, but suddenly I was the enemy of "liberation," accused of dragging a free-at-last generation back into marital slavery. Divorce had been transformed from a tragedy into a prize, and I quickly learned that it was a business in which a multitude of enterprises were invested.

But even though the media thrive on shock and novelty, most Americans retain solid family values. Even hippies and outliers want their kids to have a strong, supportive relationship. Whatever your politics, when it comes to personal choices, nearly everyone sees marriage and committed caring as ideal.

Suddenly I was overwhelmed with calls from readers who hoped I could help them. Most had spouses threatening to leave and craved validation that their relationships should be revived rather than abandoned. Many of these people felt powerless or wallowed in blame (their own or from others) for standing in the way of their partner's happiness. They'd been to therapists who'd heard the departing spouse's complaints and responded logically, "Well, then you ought to leave." The therapist would then turn to the desperate remaining partner and say sympathetically, "It takes two people for a marriage, and your spouse doesn't want to be there."

There's a pattern here: One person's not happy or sees an opportunity with someone else. The other one is rejected, with no recourse except for "mopping up" therapy and the consolation of friends.

I'm thinking of Jacquie, who thought she had a secure, happy marriage to Kevin. She taught part-time at a preschool, securing reduced tuition for their daughter and son, and was taking college classes for her teaching credential. She was the mom who brought decorated cupcakes for holidays; she was the teacher who decorated the classroom with kids' photos and her own drawings of book characters. And she was the wife who arranged her schedule to be home to greet her husband when he arrived.

Until the afternoon he told her about his other relationship and started to pack, blindsiding Jacquie and blasting apart her world. She had no clue. He'd been emailing, texting, and ultimately hooking up with a client, and she'd missed it all, blithely trusting him, immersed in the sweet innocence of her child-centered world.

"Isn't there anything I can do?" she pleaded when he told her. "You're just going to leave our family and go off?" That was exactly the plan. I call it "chop and run," a common and cruel tactic, very effective because the chopper can escape discussion, tears, and negotiation. He was out, and his blameless, loving wife, who'd done nothing but provide a wholesome, happy home, was suddenly thrust into single parenthood. Kevin paid the bills and gave Jacquie the house and tore her heart out every time he came to the door with the kids—especially when she could see his new love interest waiting in the car. That divorce served no purpose other than fulfilling Kevin's selfish quest for excitement.

All their friends treated the split matter-of-factly. "Kevin dumped you for a girlfriend? Gosh, Jacquie, that's awful. What a turd. You need anything? Maybe our kids can get together next week." Yep, that was as much as they could do. In our no-fault culture, fulfilling one's desires is legitimate. Just go for it; this is your only life. Outsiders didn't want to get involved in Jacquie's and Kevin's "personal business." Maybe Jacquie didn't give Kevin what he needed.

Except that she did. He'd never complained or asked her to behave differently. Their disagreements were few and quickly resolved, mainly because Jacquie willingly adjusted to please him. Kevin wasn't looking for someone new, but when the opportunity arose, he just responded to the advances made. And while he loved his kids, his need to be there for them didn't seem as urgent as grabbing the brass ring dangling in front of him. They'd be all right. After all, Jacquie was such a great mom.

This "great mom" was devastated. She'd been living in a fantasy world and didn't even know it. She was rejected because of Kevin's narcissism and desire for fresh sex and adoration, but also because he knew he could take off to pursue excitement and nobody would censure him. Everybody would be an "adult." The lawyers would meet, they'd sign the papers, and that would be it. As long as he acceded to Jacquie's demand for custody and financial support, he could move on and see his kids on Saturdays—he could "have it all."

Since I wrote *The Case Against Divorce*, the purpose of marriage has changed. Marriage can hardly be called an "institution" anymore, a term that suggests a solidity and centrality it no longer has. Two decades of observing, treating, and sympathizing with people victimized by our indifference to both marriage and divorce have brought me to a new conclusion: this is the book I *had* to write.

In these pages you'll meet real people with real-life experiences. They may have put aside their crushing memories. They may even deny them. They may be living fabulous lives. Making lemonade out of lemons just requires sweetener to tame the bitterness, and that comes naturally to psychologically healthy people. You have to get behind people's public facades before you find them defending serious till-death-do-us-part marriage. Otherwise you get just the do-it-yourself morality that produces broken hearts, broken marriages, and broken spirits.

DON'T DIVORCE!

Everyone has the potential for joy. People shattered by betrayal, who feel they can never again approach the person they trusted with their soul, people in the depths of depression, crushed and broken, who see little light or hope, still hold that potential. While you're still married, recognize the commitment you made and its significance to yourself, your partner, your children, and the many others with a stake in your union.

To save a marriage, *your* marriage, you also need to know what you're up against and how to combat the forces pushing you or someone you love toward divorce. You need fortification.

You are half of your marriage, yet in our no-judgment culture, it seems you're not as important as the partner who wants out. No-fault, speedy divorce saves legal expenses and spares families the spectacle of shaming a spouse, but it also weakens the power of right and wrong to hold together marriages. You are right to uphold your vows, and unless abuse or unaddressed addiction puts someone's safety at risk, you are right to do everything possible to correct the problems that threaten them.

You married with the intention of spending the rest of your life with your partner, of fashioning a durable, supportive, and rewarding bond. But changes undermined your commitment, and now you need to strengthen and reclaim it.

·   Don't divorce! Mending the marriage is *good for you and for your partner*. Overcoming your problems will teach you how to prevent future problems in your marriage and with others. Facing your issues rather than running from them will provide *insight about yourself*, your needs, and areas where you need to improve. Elevating your communication and accommodating another will immediately *improve your daily existence*.

On the other hand, divorce *harms* your self-esteem, your present and future health, and your standard of living. And it does the same to your ex and your children. You're going to expend psychic energy anyway—it can go toward dismantling your marriage and the family you've formed or toward addressing and healing your divisions. Of the two choices, divorce is more likely to bring loneliness and uncertainty, while upgrading your marriage offers a future shared with the one most invested in you already.

Above all, your children will benefit throughout their lives from the "two-parent advantage." They'll learn from your example of conflict resolution, observing that rifts between people can be overcome. At the same time, your children will suffer if you divorce. Your separation will have permanent psychological effects, perhaps crippling their own romantic relationships. Shared custody requires of young children a demanding dual identity. If your children are grown, your divorce mars their happy recollections and changes their relationship with each of you.

Your marriage is more significant than you realize, affecting many beyond your nuclear family. In a divorce, parents and in-laws lose someone they accepted into their lives and hearts. Their role as grandparents shifts when your home tears in two—logistics become difficult, people take sides, and relations become awkward. Sometimes grandparents must become substitute parents.

By healing your marriage you hold together family and friendships with lifelong histories. Demonstrating that "blood is thicker than water" (and more durable than vows), each side tends to rally round its own in a divorce, withdrawing from, and perhaps vilifying, the ex. Friends and colleagues get pulled into the fray, and their comments, emotions, and gossip become part of the atmosphere of your life. You can shrug it off, but the mere news of your divorce affects each person it touches.

Your success or failure reverberates in your community and beyond. If you weather the storms in your marriage, you inspire your friends with your commitment, confirming that their relationships can also endure. But if you split, the environment for your friends' marriages becomes less hospitable. An unexpected breakup sends the message that marriages that look strong "can turn on a dime." Acquaintances, their confidence in relationships shaken, say to themselves, "You never know what goes on behind closed doors."

The culture you inhabit becomes less predictable with the fragmentation of its members. Organizations in which you participate as a family and couple must cope with the complexity of two households and sets of directives instead of one. Economic setbacks from divorce might reduce the support your family can give to religious and civic organizations.

In other words, you should do everything you can to refurbish your marriage for the sake of yourself, your spouse, the partnership you forged, your children, and every person or institution your marriage affects.

We like to believe marriage is wonderful and fulfilling, cozy and insular. But wonderful and fulfilling are generalizations, and cozy and insular are falsehoods. Your marriage matters to many people, and it matters to God.

YOU CAN'T ERASE DIVORCE

I've been married to my husband, Michael, for more than three decades. Together we have raised our three gratifyingly functional children, with whom we have close relationships that light up our lives. But I speak with some authority about this subject because I did go through a youthful divorce. There were few assets and no children involved, and I was able to sever that relationship completely. I have no ongoing communication with my ex, who is remarried with children in another state, but I assure you that no matter how far you move on after divorce, you can't take it back. It remains a painful line on your résumé that you can't delete.

When some old photo or song reminds me of my former partner, I'm filled with sadness, a sense of failure and embarrassment. Divorce doesn't jibe with the way I want to see myself. I feel guilty for causing pain to my ex and my family, and recalling the swirling anger of that phase elicits discomfort and even shame. I am not proud of "surviving" divorce. Even after all this time, it's not just another fact of life or milepost. Yes, I benefitted ultimately. But I don't want my children to view their mother's path as one to emulate. I wish I didn't even have to confess this failure to you.

I got off relatively easy. There wasn't much to divide, and my ex was cooperative. Some might dismiss the episode with the trendy term "starter marriage." The question of divorce changes radically when children are in the picture. You can't completely end your children's connection to their other parent unless you've been abandoned, which is even more difficult. That wasn't my situation. And my divorce occurred when American divorce was at its highest rate, its stigma dead, and women thriving in high-powered fields. Divorce was nobody's fault anymore, so being "judgmental" when someone opted out became politically incorrect.

I don't blame the culture for my divorce, though, because every marriage, and every divorce, is the story of two people and their determination to bridge problems. Each spouse must first accept responsibility for some part of the crisis. Jacquie, the perfect wife gob-smacked when her husband chopped and ran, was victimized by a jerk who was far more selfish than he seemed. But even she admits she took for granted the health of the relationship, not bothering regularly to connect on a deeper level with her husband. She didn't go out of her way to ask about his interests and aspirations.

Each partner is culpable in part for the marital breakdown, and each can spearhead recovery as well. You're not yet ruefully looking back on your divorce but are still part of a marriage that, precarious as it might feel, can still be saved. Look squarely in the mirror, because some part of the problem is you, even if it's the way you *react* to your spouse.

A willing wife can influence a withdrawn or refusing husband by abruptly and radically changing a pattern of responses. Perhaps he *is* stubborn or crabby or easy to roil. If you toss it right back at him and then some, he won't become any *less* obnoxious. You'll have to try something different, even if it's the opposite of your inclination. Perhaps an insightful friend or therapist can help you craft the response that will surprise and therefore motivate your spouse to take a look at you and the issues. But it has to be more than a one-time try. Effective unilateral strategies require consistent and unwavering practice. The first step in renewing your marriage has to be yours.

EACH DIVORCE IS DIFFERENT

I've got a problem—I don't know you. If I did, I'd be able to listen to your story and talk to you about your own prospects for healing your marriage, about why you need to "suffer" in the short term to prosper in the long, about the forces in your environment that are pushing you or your partner to consider divorce.

As it is, I have to write for everyone considering a divorce, and that covers a wide range of circumstances. To address the most people with the most cogent arguments, I have to make some assumptions, and they won't fit everyone. Rather than make you stumble over endless *he or shes* and *his or herses*, I often use a pronoun of the gender that fits the most common scenario. In nearly every such case, the opposite gender would fit just as well. In addition, as you would expect, I've changed the names and identifying details of the persons and cases I describe to protect their privacy.

Whatever the details of your story, I assume that at least one person in your marriage has raised the issue of divorce. If it's you, you're probably reading this book because you're unsure; you don't know if that's really a good idea. And I hope I can convince you it isn't, because although your marriage may be boring or sexless or simply filled with irritation and annoyance, these problems are all reparable. Or perhaps you're reading this book because your partner asked you to. It may be hard to do, but please read with an open mind. While reading, notice when your body is tensing up, when you want to throw down the book, when you'd like to yell at me. These are the moments you may be subconsciously acknowledging I'm right. Respect your own reactions. No matter how strong your desire for divorce at the moment, please consider that *you could be making a mistake*, especially if your partner is committed to you and wants to make your marriage satisfying for both of you.

If your mate is the one raising the issue of divorce and you're looking for some way to convince him or her to refocus on the marriage and stay with you, you'll find some excellent reasons here. You're going to need some strength to stand up for yourself, because the assumption in our culture is "Gee, if he isn't in love with me anymore, then we don't have a marriage." You *do* have a marriage, and the notion that both partners must stay "in love" for the entire duration of their life together is wrong. Don't accept that. The trouble with emotions is that they change, sometimes very suddenly. If he loved you once and now says he's no longer "in love" with you, there's a deeper conversation the two of you need to have.

If your spouse is the one who wants to leave, you might consider asking him or her the following questions. What can I or we do to make our marriage more satisfying to you? Is your career future the one you'd like to have for yourself? Do you no longer find me attractive? Are you attracted to someone else? What can I improve about my habits or behavior that would show you I value you? How long have you felt discontent? What were and are the triggers for those feelings?

I will remind you many times that in divorce, emotions trump logic. Making sense, having ironclad arguments for staying together, and using the "adult" approach of calm, non-judgmental reason work only in a small number of cases. So if you want to stop this divorce, you'll need to appeal on an emotional level. You'll need to figure out your partner's feelings about the relationship you've got, where he wants to go, and what's bugging him.

In marriage, there's a continuum from dire misery to ecstasy. Think about moving your marriage just a notch at a time from its present precarious point toward the happy end of the continuum. If you aim for small, incremental changes and ask your partner to acknowledge small improvements, you can start a trend, consistently increasing the number of favorable emotions, gestures, and interchanges. Don't see changing your minds about whether to divorce as the "hump" to get over, the big relief that lets you stay married. To keep divorce from becoming a recurring issue, keep the momentum moving, inching across the continuum, increasing the percentage of your time together that's close and mutually supportive.

Section One

Beware the Perils
for Marriage

CHAPTER 1

Stop the Divorce Momentum

You're in a bad marriage, so bad that you want a divorce. Or your spouse wants one, even if you don't. Maybe it's your son or daughter or your best friend. Maybe you're close to leaving, or you and your spouse have drifted so far apart there hardly seems any point to continuing. Maybe the spark—the desire, sexual or otherwise, that you used to have for one another—is no longer there. You're in pain; your life is breaking into pieces. Perhaps it's a relief not to be together.

You're holding this book because, however bad things have gotten, at least a part of you wants to save the situation—or your partner or someone else you care about does. This book is for people looking at a relationship already in shambles.

The first task is to stop the momentum of your divorce. Once you use the "D-word," verbally acknowledging that divorce is coming, it becomes a self-fulfilling prophecy.

But you can stop it. If your partner is pushing for divorce but you have doubts, you can act *right now* to throw on the brakes. Even if you are the one who wants a divorce, you owe yourself and your partner—and if you

3

have children, you owe *them* especially—a sober examination of what you're doing. You need to jump off the conveyor belt toward divorce and make at least one more effort to save your marriage. You've already invested time, experiences, and emotion—probably several years' worth—in your marriage, so a pause for a fair assessment is, in comparison, minor. And yet committing to an open-minded consideration of the value of your marriage could be life-changing, and will certainly be life-*improving*.

Doing the smart, sensible, and decent thing—turning for a while toward your marriage instead of toward the door—will allow you and your partner to get back on the same page considering the potential for a rewarding and supportive relationship. You are already married; it is *breaking up* the marriage that requires active change. Even if you've emotionally checked out, you're still there physically, and the emotional impact is yet to come for your children, family, and friends.

On the other hand, if you have decided irrevocably on an exit, if counseling and reading this book and even simply communicating about your marriage and feelings with your spouse are just boxes to check off before you depart, be honest about it. Don't put your partner on another emotional rollercoaster with no possibility of success. Don't be cruel. But at the same time acknowledge that cutting off any chance to reconcile circumscribes your children's future and sets off ripples of instability that will harm many others.

FIRST, HOLD THOSE EMOTIONS

If you're willing to think this divorce through, you need to change your mindset. *Divorce is driven by emotions, not logic.* So you need to radically change the *feel* of your relationship, immediately.

If you're experiencing physical or mental abuse, you must act immediately to end the danger and gain safety. But you may be suffering from something less lethal, though possibly very intense—feelings of betrayal, anger, frustration, conflict, disgust, hurt, rejection, or hate. These are great motivators to change, and change can save your marriage.

Most decisions to divorce arise from emotions, but emotions, though valid and powerful, are often self-destructive. If you want to salvage your marriage—and even if you don't, if you simply want to act in your own best interest—you've got to notice and accept your emotions and put them in an accessible mental box. With your feelings set aside, you can more objectively assess your history, what's happening at the moment, and the potential for yourself, your spouse, your children, and the others you love. If you let emotions overcome these other realities, you could make an enormous, life-scarring mistake.

To put your emotions into that container, stop the internal conversation. Change the subject, focus on someone who needs your help, leave the premises. Otherwise emotions, building on themselves, become overwhelming. Summarizing the psychological research, Carol Tavris reports that anger escalates. If you're in an argument, it tends to amplify; if you're rehashing your own internal rage, that will expand too, magnifying your pain. It's better to cut off escalating anger by any means available, distraction probably being the handiest. If you keep retorting, you'll fuel a crescendo of rage.[1]

"Turn away from bad and do good," says Psalm Thirty-Four—good advice for purging the anger and resentment from your relationship. To do that, you must first control your *thoughts*. Stop replaying vignettes and conversations in your head.

Second, "turn away from bad" by refusing to *talk* about your spouse or your problems.[2] Stop bad-mouthing your partner, even to sympathetic listeners. By refraining, you'll prevent your problems from gaining strength by moving from the realm of thought into the physical world of sound. Thinking is a non-tangible reality—a spiritual reality, if you will—but speech, well that's something more consequential. Speech is what makes human beings unique on earth. It allows us not only to communicate facts but also to express intangibles to others. Our words can make us godly or bring us down into the gutter. Critical or reproachful words affect not only you but those who hear them. So when you fall into lamenting and complaining, distract yourself and redirect the conversation. Reserve your speech for subjects that are uplifting and productive.

The third way to "turn away from bad" is to avoid writing about it. Don't create a permanent record of your hurt and anger in letters, emails, tweets, and videos. Writing about your emotions might be therapeutic later on, but concretizing your feelings while you're suffering might now or later prove hurtful. As you evaluate the idea of divorce, you'll make more progress if you turn your attention to your strengths, your possibilities, and the value of the people you love.

"Turn away from bad and do good." You've got to turn away from divorce to even attempt to give your marriage a fair evaluation. *Sincerely*—not simply as a check-the-box exercise on your way out. Putting aside your feelings for now doesn't mean all the pain and problems that brought you to this place will disappear, but you can't stop the bleeding without a tourniquet.

If you're determined to leave (and this is not an abuse situation), then you have already put your emotions about your marriage on hold. You have sealed them away so your guilt and sentiments don't impede your exit. You've "hardened your heart," to use a biblical reference. You may behave civilly, but you have erected a cruel barrier to the pain and hurt of the one left behind. The spouse executing a "chop-and-run" divorce has severed the emotional connection that once bound the family. If that's you, you're probably reading this under protest. I know you, and I've spent much of my career helping the one you've emotionally abandoned. You may not even approve of your own behavior, but you'll put that out of your mind because you're heading somewhere else, and your spouse and family are just not part of that new scenario.

This book is not about improving your marriage. I'm not going to give you conflict resolution lessons or teach you how to communicate. It's an anti-divorce book. If you're racing down the crowded road to divorce, I'm telling you to slam on the brakes so that you and your spouse can commit to solving your problems. Identifying and healing your divisions may take a therapist, and it may take time. There are shelves of books in your library with advice and programs to heal a wounded marriage. But right now you have to decide to direct the energy you'd expend on tearing away from your spouse to strengthening the bond you already forged. Turn away from the bad and do good.

WHY STAY MARRIED?

Why should you stay married? Because you already have a tie to your partner. You can go through the agony of breaking that tie and become a better person, or you can uphold your wedding vow and *still* become that better person, with (or perhaps without) the support of the one you chose. You may need some space initially to calm the situation and allow anger or hurt to fade. But that space—a breather, a truce, even a temporary separation—may be all you need. Proceeding to divorce will hurt both of you and all those to whom your marriage means something.

You should stay married not for the sake of the children but for the sake of the *family*. Importantly, you should stay married because in the long run working through this rough patch and emerging with new resolve and skills will benefit *you*.

WHEN YOU SHOULD—AND MUST—LEAVE: PHYSICAL OR SEVERE EMOTIONAL ABUSE

Some marriages cannot or should not continue. There are gray areas, situations that may feel unbearable but objectively cause no physical harm or untenable mental damage. But some relationships, descending into sarcasm, criticism, punishment, and anger, become crushingly painful and even violent and abusive. The Centers for Disease Control and Prevention, in their 2010 National Intimate Partner and Sexual Violence Survey, found that a third of all women reported experiencing rape, domestic violence, or stalking, at some time in their lives.[3]

These are not the relationships I address in this book. If you're being abused, physically or emotionally, through unrelenting anger or punishment, it doesn't matter if you do see hope for the relationship. Contact the National Domestic Violence Hotline or a similar local resource to discuss the best exit strategy. Leaving can trigger a violent response. If you're in this situation, prudence could save your life.

In cases of physical abuse especially, no matter how much you want to stay in your marriage, you must protect yourself and your children. If you feel abused or powerless, you need to remove yourself physically, at least temporarily, from danger. You could be right that someday the relationship can be repaired, but the priority must be your safety and that of your children. And before any reconciliation, you need to be absolutely sure you won't become vulnerable to abuse again. No contract, commitment, marriage, or attachment supersedes safety and sanity.

Many women stay in abusive relationships because of fear or guilt. They come to believe the demeaning words with which their abusers exercise control. They may be ashamed or embarrassed; they may have no one they can call upon for help, especially if their abuser isolates them from outside relationships. Even if they're rescued by the police or another agency, women in abusive marriages often decline to press charges out of fear of their partner's retribution or a mistaken but very real sense of self-blame.

The situation may improve for a while, but the problem compounds the longer the victim of abuse remains, feeling hopeful but also responsible for perpetrating the situation. Her fear of and hate for the abuser (sometimes alternating with doubt, comfort, or love) coexist with self-hatred—for having those feelings or for allowing the marriage to continue. She may feel paralyzed, with no means to extricate herself from the nightmare. Some women (and 95 percent of domestic violence victims are women) suffer in a "cycle of violence," anticipating, dealing with, and recovering from abusive outbursts. These are often described as phases, including the buildup of tension, explosion, the abuser's remorse, and a "honeymoon" in which he seemingly makes up for the aggression—until the tension starts to build again.

Every city has a domestic abuse hotline. A call to 911, whether you're in a dire emergency or not, will connect you to someone who can help. If you feel endangered or threatened or frightened, you must call, no matter the hour, to describe your situation and receive instructions on what to do to immediately remove yourself and your children from a potentially harmful situation.

This seems obvious, but too often imperiled women and teens deny the risk they're facing because they're frightened of the changes and anger their leaving may spur. You may have the noble idea that marriage is for life, and that spouses fight, and that you can handle this. You may tell yourself that he always calms down eventually and you just have to let this pass, or that it's because he was drinking or on medication or high. There are a thousand rationalizations for avoiding confrontation and for avoiding the truth about a dangerous situation.

As much as I want to help people keep rocky marriages together, I must emphasize that *some* marriages need to end. How do you know if you're in one? A marriage needs to end if a partner habitually humiliates, punishes, and belittles the other and refuses to change or get help, even if between those bouts he apologizes or seems loving; if lashing out or intimidation becomes expected or routine; if one partner is afraid and knows her spouse won't change. If one spouse starts to suffocate and wither, the relationship is less a marriage than a punishment. This is no way to live. The aggressor needs to confront his abusive behavior and release control, but many pathologically controlling spouses simply won't. These are the cases of truly necessary divorce.

Divorce may be necessary in other cases as well: lopsided relationships, in which one partner has effectively removed himself from the duo; betrayal with no remorse or desire to restore trust; and chop-and-run rejection, when a partner exercises one of Paul Simon's "fifty ways to leave your lover." And there are cases of addiction in which the addict places his or her need for a "fix" above the relationship and cannot or will not change. In some cases, there might be a sliver of genuine hope for improvement, though you might have to fashion for yourself a marriage on a new basis.

In any case, you know there are serious problems in your marriage. Let's look at how you can evaluate your situation.

THINKING ABOUT DIVORCE NEEDN'T MAKE IT SO

What happens to spouses who think about divorce? In 2015, researchers at Brigham Young University questioned three thousand spouses between the ages of twenty-five and fifty about the extent of their "ideation" about divorce.[4] Three-quarters of the respondents didn't think about it at all in the half-year prior to reporting, while the remaining quarter reported either expressed or unexpressed thoughts at one or many points in their marriages. Of the quarter that thought about divorce, 43 percent said they didn't really want a divorce and were willing to work hard on the marriage. Another 23 percent of those who had thought about divorce were willing to work hard on their marriages if their spouse would make some changes. A mere 5 percent of those with divorce on their minds said they were done with their marriages. Thinking about divorce, then, doesn't indicate that one's marriage is doomed.

As we've seen, it may be prudent and appropriate to consider divorce. Forty-three percent of the respondents who had thought about divorce faced serious problems of infidelity, abuse, or addiction, so weighing the possibility of divorce made sense and might even spur restorative action. The remaining 57 percent of the divorce-thinkers reported "less intensive

problems," "things like growing apart or losing connection, losing romantic feelings, not paying enough attention to the marriage, and money disagreements."

Though it's reassuring to hear that thoughts about divorce aren't that
widespread and that they don't usually bring about an actual divorce, I
wonder if that's the whole story. Perhaps committed partners don't want to
admit having entertained an exit fantasy in a moment of frustration. Among
the quarter of respondents who had divorce thoughts, 57 percent were what
the authors of the study called "soft thinkers," those without any real threat
to their marriages.

It seems to me that emphasis in the media and the "divorce industry"—
therapists, support groups, life coaches, singles websites, and social Internet
sites—on narcissism puts divorce front and center for everyone. How can
you not think about divorce when the word is screamed from every tabloid
in the grocery checkout line and every magazine in the dentist's office? How
can you not think about divorce when Internet newsfeeds planted before
your eyes tell you this or that Hollywood star is in splitsville? You may not
think your own marriage is in trouble, but if you do have a spat, how can
you avoid the fleeting thought of "I'm outta here"? At the moment of conflict
you're disgusted, but underneath you know you don't mean it; you don't
really want a divorce. But the word is everywhere, and in the normal course
of marital friction, wouldn't it be weird if that word didn't occasionally flit
through your mind? Even those with strong commitments are bombarded
daily with messages undermining marital security. No one is immune and
everyone knows someone who's divorced. Divorce is out there, taken for
granted, and the only way to put up a barrier against the influence of divorce
in your own relationship is to purposefully build it.

THE EROSION OF COMMITMENT

Extraordinary effort *should* go into resuscitating a drifting or dying
love, but friends, relatives, co-workers, bosses, movie stars, and politicians
suggest the opposite. If your relationship is on the rocks, you ought to stand
up for yourself and get what you want, because no one wants an uncomfortable marriage. Media and people you know tell you that your feelings and
your psychological needs must come first. In a bad situation, you might let

your spouse down gently, and stick around long enough to tend to the children, but don't prolong unhappiness just because you were once in love and got married.

Instead of fighting your spouse and instead of "fighting for" your marriage, you need to fight these messages. Don't buy it when they tell you people change and the relationship you once had is gone. Don't swallow the line that nobody's right or wrong, or that divorce isn't about fault but about reality. On your wedding day, were you thinking that if you ever wanted out, you'd go? If you did, then you're probably the one who's wanting to leave now, though you still need to know what you're in for. And you need to hear the other side, the balance to all the voices that have brought our culture so much unnecessary misery, so much instability and hesitancy and equivocation—the ones who say, "Take care of yourself and get out." The other message—the one that's true—is take care of yourself and *don't* get out.

Right now, if your marriage is suffering—from neglect and withdrawal or from anger and conflict—you're likely craving relief. Understandable. But running out is not the only way to stop the pain. You can regain your equilibrium and then with determination work toward love. Choosing to rebuild your marriage will reward you in health, money, and time, and will save you from mental and spiritual degradation. It will spare a lot of other people harm in deep and subtle ways. If you and your spouse stop the divorce, you can develop new skills and bonds that will ultimately elevate you, individually and as a couple.

It's not always possible to restore a marriage. But it's always worth a try.

THE NEW MARRIAGE: DEVALUED OR ELEVATED?

Is it true that marriage just isn't that important anymore, that being married or being divorced, being a jerk or an exemplary mom or "family man," all earn just about the same detached reaction?

That seems to be the case. Fewer people are getting married, and those who do tie the knot do it later in life.[5] When we're repeatedly told (falsely) that half of marriages crack up, divorce seems normal. Women have babies out of wedlock. It's common for entertainers and women in their forties to

get pregnant, sometimes through a sperm bank, without any man in the
picture for the long term. These developments suggest marriage has become
an optional accessory rather than a nearly universal expectation.

On the other hand, many argue that marriage matters a lot. Same-sex
couples' demand for legal recognition of their unions rests on the premise
that marriage is necessary for personal fulfillment. Why wage the long and
costly battle to legalize gay marriage if it's unimportant? As the Supreme
Court noted in *Obergefell v. Hodges*, the 2015 decision declaring same-sex
marriage legal in all fifty states, same-sex couples, "far from seeking to
devalue marriage, seek it for themselves because of their respect—and
need—for its privileges and responsibilities."[6]

So which is it? Is marriage an emotionally expressive ritual in which
two persons proclaim their love and an intent for the future with a big party
and lots of gifts? Or is it so serious and essential that denying it harms those
excluded? Of course, it's both. We'll see that thwarting your divorce depends
on the meaning *you* give your vows and how *you* choose to value your
marital commitment. That's what will make or break your marriage—and
your divorce.

What were your expectations when you married, and what are they
now? What did you see as your and your mate's roles in your relationship
in the short and long run? The assumption is that you believed your marriage
was forever. But your background and how you relate to your partner might
have affected how ironclad that "forever" might be.

When you got really angry, were you completely resolved to work it out?
Did you still believe your marriage was permanent? If divorce is now a possibility, at what point did you start to doubt the endurance of your vow?

Some people hold that marriage is indissoluble. You've heard the quip,
"murder maybe, divorce never." These couples might "have a fight," but
that never endangers their underlying bond. Did you ever meet someone
who holds that marriage lasts until death, no matter what? Someone who
would stay married even in unsatisfactory circumstances? There are such
people, and there used to be a lot more of them.

According to her biographers, Lady Bird Johnson took a lot of abuse
from her husband.[7] Lyndon demeaned her in public and demanded her
service rudely and crudely while carrying on numerous affairs. She always
took it with grace, but why? For Mrs. Johnson's generation, divorce was a

failure and even a disgrace. A role model for the nation, the First Lady was expected to exemplify virtue. Of course, those were times when a more homogeneous society wielded the power of disapproval. Scandal had consequences. Unsavory acts were hidden.

That kind of loyalty now seems passé, almost self-destructive, but even in the era of feminism, Hillary Clinton responded to her husband's hurtful and humiliating behavior in much the same way. Mrs. Clinton and Mrs. Johnson chose to stay married to men who treated them outrageously. Who can say they would have been happier or more successful if they had acted differently?

WHAT IS MARRIAGE ABOUT?

One theme emerges in every decision about marriage and divorce: *emotions trump logic*. In a clash between emotions and common sense or morality, emotions almost always win. Marriage no longer embodies self-imposed obligations and social expectations but is contingent on the emotion of love. Since emotions are unpredictable, senseless, and upside-down, marriage is too.

That change in the character of marriage has made it tough to persuade people to stay married. Persuading is an exercise in logic, but marriage and divorce center on emotions. Nevertheless, I'm determined to use logic to reach your emotions. I hope that the facts I present will trigger your instinct to protect your children or awaken a closely-held ideal. If that happens, I can tap into your feelings about your spouse, your family, and yourself.

But even an airtight argument backed by irrefutable statistics won't turn around someone committed with all his *heart* to divorce. If emotion-driven "head over heels" love is the standard for marriage, then "head over heart" commitment when emotions have changed is a hard sell, particularly in a culture that celebrates following one's heart as the highest good.

It wasn't always that way. Marriage in other cultures and earlier epochs was based on all sorts of helpful, wise, and sometimes oppressive criteria, but feelings weren't among them. When it's easier to form relationships, it becomes easier to end them. Individuals' casual attitudes toward hooking up, living together, marrying or not when a child comes along, and divorce all devalue what used to be a very serious and permanent vow. In *The Book of Marriage*: *The Wisest Answers to the Toughest Questions*, Dana Mack and David Blankenhorn look at a wide range of sources for marital definitions.[8] After consulting the Bible and Qur'an, Shakespeare, *Pride and Prejudice*, John Locke, and an array of modern psychologists, novelists, and poets, they define the bond as "a social institution sanctioned by custom or law." Their survey of marriage through the millennia suggests that while it is an enduring and fundamental feature of every human culture, its details have varied widely.

In her historical study *What Is Marriage For?* E. J. Graff finds that marriage has been primarily about money, sex, babies, kin, order (who's allowed into what status), and "heart." Even before same-sex marriage was the law of the land, Graff argued that "western marriage today is a home for the heart: entering, furnishing and exiting that home is your business alone. Today's marriage—from whatever angle you look—is justified by the happiness of the pair." We have "endorsed what some of us think of as the most *spiritual* purpose of marriage, the refreshing of the human spirit."[9]

Defining marriage as a "home for the heart" encourages divorce. If feelings can come, they can go. To the hokey heart horde, commitment is a feeling that "I want to be with you." When that desire fades, commitment disappears. The new marriage vow is an expression of the emotion of love, a declaration of intent that love continue into the future, rooted in a series of "right nows." But as soon as one partner discovers that the zing isn't there—well, so long.

Marriage is a two-person commitment. Divorce is unilateral.

The *New York Times* columnist David Brooks identified three types of modern marriage.[10] In the first, the partners' psychological make-up is seen as life-long and unchangeable. What you marry is what you get. Your happiness, then, depends on the mate-selection process—choose someone with a good temperament and free from psychological problems, and (if you're healthy as well) you'll have excellent chances for a life of harmony, come what may.

The second type of marriage centers on romance. It begins with passion—the "hopelessly falling in love" that unites movie couples in a magnetic embrace—which eventually melts into an enduring bond of love.

Brooks's third type of marriage transcends psychological compatibility and passion. Religious people see their role as fulfilling God's will for man on earth. Secularists see moral good in the formation of families as the grounding for communities and nations. In this third type of marriage, rooted in a broader purpose beyond the partners, the family transmits values and provides a secure base for each member's highest productivity and potential.

While most strong marriages include elements of all three types, Brooks suggests, the partners' immediate perspectives and present desires are replacing the objective view of the third type. And that's my point exactly—marriage no longer serves a long-term purpose but is a means of immediate self-fulfillment.

If you want a more dependable marriage you need a larger context to endow it with gravity and value. If your marriage matters to God or to your children, if it is to be an example to your friends or to serve a greater good, then personal issues must bow to a motivation to overcome them. That ultimately brings both your marriage and the institution itself greater durability and strength.

Your own definition of marriage and your partner's definition are what matter. And you get to choose what that is. Perhaps you believe that your marriage vows are permanent, binding until one of you dies. Or perhaps you believe they're valid only as long as the emotions behind them last. It makes a difference which view you hold. If you and your partner value your marriage, you've got a better chance to put it back together. If one of you has changed his or her views, you have a more difficult problem to surmount, though one still well worth the effort to address.

I want to persuade you (and your partner as well) to try thinking of your marriage as a durable commitment to each other, to your family, and to the values that define you. That commitment will be the backbone of your relationship, enabling you to sort through and solve your problems. When you ultimately refresh your marriage, you'll have new skills ready for future challenges. But if you quit your marriage and step onto the relationship carousel Andrew Cherlin calls the "marriage-go-round,"[11] your painted horse will carry you and your old patterns of behavior into your next relationship.

Even with earnest effort, stopping your divorce might prove impossible, but if you don't muster everything in your power to prevent a breakup, then you lose the enormous investment you've already made in your marriage, hurting yourself and many others in the process.

IN THE MAKING FOR A GENERATION

While your current situation is attributable in part to you and your decisions, external forces also shaped your circumstances. Once you recognize the influences working on you, perhaps you'll cast them off and determine your own course. As you consider how you conceptualize your marriage, take into account the broader context in which you originally made your commitment and every day redefine it.

What moved our culture so radically and rapidly from marriage as the inviolate foundation of everything—families, communities, professions, even our national identity—to the prevailing view that marriage is worthwhile only if it meets our personal needs right now? Answer: the values of our movers and shakers. Early American culture was more homogeneous and almost universally Christian. The people growing our cities and writing our headlines came to our shores to embrace opportunities that were possible only in the famous melting pot of assimilation. American law codified Judeo-Christian morality. Traditional marriage wasn't debated or questioned; it was sanctified. The Christians and Jews who settled America shared biblical values that established the permanence and benefit to society of marriage as the only sanctioned setting for procreation and childrearing. As of July 2015, 83 percent of Americans self-identify as Christian.[12] As recently as 2008, Barack Obama, running for president, stated his support for traditional families: "I believe that marriage is a union of a man and a woman," adding, "Now for me as a Christian, it's also a sacred union. You know, God's in the mix."[13] That's ancient history to millennials, children of the Baby Boomers. As they grew up, gay relationships came out of the closet, and sexuality and gender identity became widely discussed topics. With blogs, cable TV, and social media, little is private or taboo. Online sexuality is so ubiquitous that browsing Internet porn is just a normal pastime.

Meanwhile, women "leaned in" to prominent corporate positions, crashing through former limits. Men's protective, solicitous attitude toward "ladies" gave way to workplace competition. Now even a compliment can be considered a "micro-aggression." The change in how men view female coworkers affected marriage.

Traditionally, the purpose of marriage was family, not feelings. By making children's biological parents responsible for them, marriage offered children the best chance to thrive. No one loves a child as much as his own parents, and wedlock—with an emphasis on *lock*—produced generational survival and continuity. The romantic feelings of the persons united in marriage usually mattered, but sometimes not. Arranged marriages, common in other cultures and found in subcultures even in America, established alliances between clans and families that enhanced societal stability.[14]

The Supreme Court's decree in *Obergefell v. Hodges* that the sex of the spouses is irrelevant to marriage established that, as a matter of constitutional principle, the emotional fulfillment of the spouses, rather than the raising of children, is the purpose of marriage. In the past, marriage determined the "legitimacy" of offspring, a role that gave it public importance. With the antiquated issue of "legitimacy" for children pitched—40 percent of babies are born to unwed mothers—no one but the two spouses has an interest in protecting the marital bond, which is now merely a personal expression of devotion.

For the most part, married couples do have children, for whom they intend to create a permanent bond and a stable home. In fact, part of what made gay marriage plausible were advances in reproductive technology that allow same-sex couples to scale previous barriers to bearing children. Thanks to surrogate wombs and sperm donors, many duos are living the stable, dedicated family lives to which heterosexual couples have always aspired.

But changing the definition of marriage to eliminate the *assumption* of children changes the mindset of every bride and groom. There was once not only an expectation but an obligation to "be fruitful and multiply" and to escort one's offspring into adulthood to replicate the family structure. Now that feelings are officially the basis for marriage, any such "duty" sounds absurd. The two partners' level of satisfaction is the sole measure of the health of their union. Emotions rule.

OUT WITH THE OLD

Obergefell was but the cherry-on-the-sundae of a new definition of marriage in the making for a generation. The transformation began in the early 1960s, when feminism changed everyone's expectations regarding men's and women's roles, in the family and in paid jobs and careers. The "sexual revolution" that accompanied feminism eliminated marriage's function of channeling sex toward the socially beneficial end of responsible childrearing.

The story of Elizabeth, a Baby Boomer, is typical. "When I was a kid," she recalls, "I learned from looking around that smart women could choose from a handful of occupations. You could be a teacher, nurse, librarian, or secretary. Or you could do one better and go to college and get your M.R.S. to a securely-employed man and raise the kids."

By the time she got to high school, Betty Friedan's *The Feminine Mystique* (1963) was assigned reading, and Elizabeth and her peers radically revised their views. By the time she finished college, she agreed with Gloria Steinem that "a woman without a man is like a fish without a bicycle." She got an IUD and explored her sexuality. Feeling no pressure to marry, especially after her parents divorced, she moved in with a boyfriend. To Elizabeth and her friends, marriage was just a piece of paper, nice to have when you wanted to settle down and have kids but otherwise just a bow to values that had oppressed women and restrained expressions of love.

Current public debate about marriage seems to have split into two camps. Traditional marriage is either permanent and defined by God, *or* it's outmoded because it isn't permanent or defined by God. Most young Americans feel not even a residual sense that sex is legitimate only within marriage and embrace their nuptials as an emotional commitment open to continual reassessment.

NEW ROLES, NEW MARRIAGE

Expectations about marriage changed drastically as women entered and excelled in formerly male-dominated careers. Once upon a time, if a wife worked outside the home you could assume her husband was absent or unable "to provide." The traditional family's division of labor seemed to work pretty well (except when it didn't). But the women's movement transformed universally-accepted American family roles, sometimes even insisting that males and females were not different.

When women broke through glass ceilings, feminists were surprised that men didn't rush to clean up the shards. Or to fill childrearing roles or even keep their houses clean. A few men adapted, and younger ones grew up learning to be more helpful and verbally supportive. But the ones who changed were *women*, who "fulfilled their potentials" in careers and *also* with their children. Lean in, ladies, because you need strength to carry more responsibilities. "Work-home balance" eluded women pulled to take advantage of career possibilities without sacrificing the rewards of motherhood.

You could argue that the change in women's roles was good, bad, inconsequential, or disastrous, but it complicated relationships. Partners became equally brazen and equally demanding of satisfaction. There were no universal assumptions; each relationship made its own rules, and without aligned expectations, mismatches between spouses came easily.

This history contributes to your marital troubles right now. In *What Our Mothers Didn't Tell Us*, my friend Danielle Crittenden writes about the pressures that the feminist-approved version of marriage adds to an already-dancing connubial duo. She regularly receives boos when presenting her politically incorrect belief that "much of the current crisis in marriage could be the consequence of the equality that we have now acquired. With both husbands and wives attempting to occupy exactly the same roles, a frantic struggle erupted over the demands of work and family," she writes. "And as a result of this preoccupation with the balance of power, a great many modern women—and men—find themselves unable or unwilling to make even very commonplace accommodations to married life."[15]

One of my friends expresses her guilt over enjoying the traditional roles she shares with her husband. She cares for her two children; he earns six figures as a college vice president. After earning her own doctorate, she spends her days volunteering in her son's sixth-grade classroom and accompanying her three-year-old to My Gym. "When people ask what I 'do' I always say 'I have a Ph.D. in public health,' rather than 'I'm a stay-at-home mom,'" she confesses.

I say it's time we honor parenthood and stop implying that family interests away from the job market are a "waste" of time or of an advanced degree. Your marriage is floundering in a new and amorphous wedded world. The combination of your background and your personality and philosophy has determined your own expectations for your marriage.

Your marriage is probably staggering because your or your partner's expectations about your relationship have been repeatedly ignored, disregarded, ridiculed, or betrayed. Or maybe it's just that your expectations were never fulfilled. That's why you must think about what your expectations for your relationship *were* and, with your marital experience, what they presently *are*. Here's a comparison of traditional marriage, pre-feminism, with the currently

dominant version of marriage. To gain insight on your expectations, plot where
your own expectations fall. The purpose is to pinpoint the source of your disappointments, so you can decide whether to keep or revise your expectations.

MARRIAGE: TRADITIONAL VERSUS REDEFINED

TRADITIONAL MARRIAGE	REDEFINED MARRIAGE
Marriage is revered and expected	Marriage is personally desired by many; societal expectation is absent or determined by one's subculture
Marriage is the only acceptable context for sex	Premarital sexual behavior is expected; postmarital sex is negotiable
Marriage unites one male and one female	Marriage unites any two adults
Wedding involves religion	Religious themes are often peripheral or absent
Partners come from similar backgrounds	Partners' backgrounds are irrelevant
The purpose of marriage is to raise a family	The purpose of marriage is to express and receive love
Marriage lasts until death	Marriage lasts until one partner's love ends
Marriage is sexually monogamous and sexually exclusive	Marriage is usually sexually exclusive, but the couple may define it otherwise
A couple unites in name and finances	Names and finances remain separate
Childrearing is primarily the mother's responsibility	Childrearing is shared and each parent's degree of responsibility is negotiated
Ideally, husband can financially support the family	Ideally, both spouses work in fulfilling careers; one parent may take career hiatus for childcare

NOTHING BINDS COUPLES IN THE MARRIAGE-OPTIONAL WORLD

The marital world of today offers advantages and disadvantages. One
crucial disadvantage is that with marriage and having children now optional,
every day you face the decision to stay or leave. In the old days, the stigma
and ostracism of divorce motivated couples to stay together. Some who were
unhappy stayed together and remained unhappy. But others—probably in
the vast majority of cases—were motivated by that stigma to "get through
the rough patch," confront and overcome their problems, or at least live
constructively and satisfactorily together.

No one should live with ongoing anger, hurt, or unhappiness. No one who's married should leave without first trying to address those problems and restore the marriage.

What holds unhappy couples together now? Not much, really. Marriage is no longer "wedlock." Family members fear sounding judgmental. Friends are expected to "empower" you by reinforcing whatever you seem to want. The culture has become a Greek chorus echoing your sentiments. To evaluate your situation fairly, you need to hear the other side, that marriage is a commitment for life, and that enduring anguish and discomfort may be necessary.

In a happy marriage, one's spouse provides that opposing or balancing voice that helps you see the entire picture. Unfortunately, the spouse who is supposed to *complement* you may seem more like an *adversary*. Even now, however, you might find that his or her opposition can ultimately help and uplift you.

I'll say it again: *emotions trump logic.* How you feel is going to propel your action much more than objective facts or well thought-out beliefs. Emotions are tricky—their intensity overcomes and subdues logic. You know you ought to fight them. When emotions kick in, the natural response is to discount anything that conflicts with them. "I'm not going to take feeling this way!" If you can, catch yourself; when you feel your heart beating faster and your anger rising, take a deep breath and regain control. Notice the triggers of your emotions, so you can figure out how to avoid or disarm them. Allowing feelings free rein is self-destructive. How you feel certainly influences decisions you make about your behavior and your marriage, but a smart assessment of long-term outcomes is the better basis for action.

CHAPTER 2

The Three Divorce Magnets

Y ou're surrounded by attitudes about marriage and divorce so seldom
contradicted that you probably assume they're true. But these attitudes
undermine your marriage. And right now, as you're in the midst of a
difficult time, these attitudes are tugging you toward divorce and out of your
marriage. I call them divorce magnets, and there are three that are particularly
dangerous.

DIVORCE MAGNET NO. 1: AN ENTICINGLY
PERMISSIVE CULTURE

Divorce used to carry a stigma. When wedding vows were iron-clad
commitments, divorce was considered a failure, inviting responses we now
would call "shaming." Now it's usually harder to get out of a business deal
than a marriage.

Guilt and embarrassment can be useful as a tool for self-betterment.
Sometimes social discomfort keeps us from acting in a way that may feel
good now but would be disastrous in the long run.

The stigma of divorce kept many marriages together because we care what other people think of us. Consider how excruciatingly diligent we are in crafting the images we put forth for others' scrutiny. With Facebook, Instagram, Twitter, and other social media, we manipulate how viewers and followers perceive us, spinning our experience with grandiose titles and descriptors, crafting a professional persona that never fails. These facades may conceal insecurities and flaws, and project our most optimistic aspirations. And if repeated often enough they may become a faux reality.

We care what other people think about our looks, our accomplishments, and our associations, but worry little that we'll be tarnished by the failure of our marriages. In fact, acknowledging that you're "going through a divorce" wins a comforting embrace, a caring reassurance of your value. Reaction to divorce has completely flipped from scolding social censure to an outpouring of concern and empathy.

In fact, you'll get a lot more sympathy by splitting than by announcing that you're working to mend your marriage. Friends assume a divorce leaves you shattered and bereft, requiring their piteous hugs, while restoring your marriage implies that you're bold and hardy. Most people prefer the warm embrace of sympathy, especially when the alternative is a difficult process with an angry or hurt spouse.

"Going through a divorce" also lets you get away with slacking. That might not be a reason to divorce, but the over-the-top accommodations we make for divorce illustrate the complete reversal in the way we treat marital breakups. If you miss a deadline or take a long lunch while "going through a divorce," your excuse is obvious. The assumption is you're emotionally strained, and since emotions trump logic (and heartache supersedes duty), your huge emotional event is met with unlimited forbearance.

So if you're suffering with a tough phase in your marriage, the embrace of tenderly supportive friends and family who take your side and give you a pass on responsibility is more appealing than the difficult work required to solve your marital problems.

DIVORCE MAGNET NO. 2: SEX IS EVERYWHERE (EXCEPT IN MARRIAGE)

When you don't like your spouse; when you're angry or betrayed or verbally abused, any sex in your marriage is either completely selfish or manipulative. In most marriages on the verge of divorce, there is *no* sex. None. In that case, sex is everywhere except in the one place it should be. It's available and exciting, and having it with anyone but your partner has a lot of perks. It shows your partner you don't need him or her. It affirms your desirability. It takes your mind off your problems. It's exhilarating and makes you feel alive. It also might be risky, which increases its allure.

The one thing nonmarital sex *isn't* is an expression of your bond to the one person to whom you've pledged your fidelity and love. Right now that love doesn't feel very good or doesn't seem to exist at all, so the lure of convenient sexual outlets exerts a powerful pull in any direction except toward your spouse. And Tinder is there to help. The popular meet-up app lets you survey potential partners who are close by, offering instant gratification if both parties want it. You get first name, age, photos, and maybe a blurb. Swipe right. You've got someone who finds you attractive literally at your fingertips. With no embarrassment, you can choose someone for a casual encounter. Or not, so swipe left, but it's nothing personal. Fantasizing about someone, based almost exclusively on his or her looks, becomes entertainment, something to do while in line at the bank.[1] It loosens allegiance to one partner, because somebody else is always available.

Tinder is a low-investment and often low-return boredom solution, but as such it's a reminder of sex, physicality, and available partners other than your spouse. *Business Insider* reports that 12 percent of those using the app are in a relationship.[2] It's been so long since the culture at large reproved nonmarital sex that the usual progression for newly-dating singles is sex after two or three dates, followed by cohabitation and, optionally, marriage, before or after children arrive.

Between 60 and 80 percent of college students have had a sexual "hookup,"[3] and easy sex in the general culture pressures couples with sexual problems to take advantage of opportunities that can provide the outlet and excitement their marriage lacks. And once outside sex occurs, the marriage in trouble moves to another plane of distress. Anger, hurt, and distance all increase when a partner in an already-teetering marriage succumbs to sexual temptation. Unsuspecting workers, drivers, TV viewers, Internet users—everyone—constantly encounter invitations to stray. Come-ons may be subtle or screaming, but most importantly, they're ubiquitous. Motor down a thoroughfare and billboards splashed with "T&A" vie for your attention. Buy a few groceries and those tabloids at eye level show you the before and after of some star who started out voluptuous in a revealing evening gown or bikini and became in the companion photo either fat or drugged-out gaunt. One constant in those publications is the cover cleavage. That's how they sell magazines—it may be anti-feminist, but men pick up the issue out of lust and women because they want to be that starlet or because they hate her. Either way, the comparison of that babe or hunk with your mate is probably poor, driving dissatisfaction. And a plethora of beautiful, come-hither bodies offers the illusion that sex is awaiting you.

While the hookup culture offers uncommitted sex with a real live person, pornography offers the thrills without the bother of a personal encounter. Pornography is as close as your phone or laptop, and younger men think nothing of accessing it—despite evidence that private viewing hurts relationships. A representative study in 2014 by the Barna Group for a Christian organization found that "eight out of ten (79%) men [in the general U.S. population] between the ages of 18 and 30 view pornography at least monthly," as do "two-thirds (67%) of men between the ages of 31 and 49" and half of men between fifty and sixty-eight. "Three out of ten men (29%) view pornography daily," even though many realize it's a problem. Asked if they're addicted to porn, "one-third (33%) of men between the ages of 18 and 30 either think that they are addicted or are unsure if they are addicted," and "18% of *all* men either think that they are addicted or are unsure if they are addicted to pornography, which equates to 21 million men."[4]

Robert started his porn habit before he got married. "All my friends just accepted it as something to do," he explains. After his marriage, he cut down because he knew Angie disdained it, but after their first baby took her attention, he'd steal time for it when she was preoccupied or out of the house. "I never thought of those actresses as real, or of viewing porn as anything serious," he says, but he did enjoy it, and sometimes he'd make excuses not to go to his parents' house with her just so he could indulge. From there it progressed into a pattern. "I'd finish my job [as an air conditioning technician] and watch a little on my phone in the truck before heading back." He'd get home and say hi, play with his daughter, and have dinner. He'd watch a movie with Angie, and she'd fall asleep, "then I'd have some more time on my computer in my office in the basement."

This went on for three years, even as Robert and Angie added a new baby boy to the family. "I never talked about it to Angie, but I just thought she knew," he shrugged. Their sex life was sporadic but satisfactory. Robert thought of his porn as a distraction that was fun, unlike the responsibilities he was increasingly shouldering as Angie went back to work. Childcare was expensive, the logistics of getting the kids to school and daycare difficult, and the financial stress of something always needing fixing made his secret outlet all the more attractive.

But Angie really had no clue he was spending so much time with porn videos. He excluded her from his private escape, and the more he indulged, the less he was inclined to mention it. It got to the point that Robert started thinking of his family time as an obligation, and he only relaxed when noshing chips while finding new sources of porn. His inability to talk to Angie about it became a wedge between them. Instead of sharing every aspect of his life with his wife, Robert harbored his secret. "Yeah, I felt excited by it, but at the same time embarrassed and guilty."

Robert was only thirty-five but overweight. Returning home tired most evenings, he would play with the kids, who were pure cuddly joy. They squealed with delight at his character voices while reading them bedtime stories. Angie, exhausted but glad to see Robert laughing as he connected with their children, wanted the kids to enjoy their daddy. If it weren't for the heart attack, Robert might have continued drifting away from Angie emotionally, but after that scary ride to the hospital in an ambulance, seeing her tears and complete devotion, he took stock.

Reeling from the shocking reminder of his own mortality, Robert decided he didn't want to spend what time he had left as the person he'd become. He quit porn completely, focusing on gratitude for his wife and family. He enrolled in a weight-loss program, went back to church, and took online courses toward the bachelor's degree he never finished. He realized he needed to communicate better, not only with Angie but also with his parents, his coworkers, and friends, so he found a therapist. Hearing that I was writing about our culture of easy sex, Robert wanted to tell me his story. "It's easier than you know to become dependent on porn," he warns. "It's just a personally selfish activity—a way for someone with low self-esteem to both feel better and wallow in it."

Studies show that men and women tend to use porn differently. Men tend to use porn in isolation, not with their partners, behavior that is correlated with *lowered* quality of relationships.[5] The types of porn preferred by men and women differ as well, with men more often seeking videos focusing on acts without context or personalities. Women more often select porn with a story, context, and suggestions of individual characterizations. Other studies show that men consume more porn than women do, that they consume it more frequently, and that the higher a husband's use, the more disapproval he receives from his wife.[6] The most damaging effect of pornography is the separation that arises when porn becomes the domain of one spouse to the exclusion of the other, especially if the second partner feels it is demeaning or detracts from their marital closeness.

The redefinition of porn as "normal" changed the dynamic of marriage. The husband who once hid his *Playboy* magazines under the mattress because ogling other women was disloyal acknowledged a higher standard even in transgressing it. The mainstreaming of pornography has disconnected sex from marriage. Purely physical, orgasmic hookups are now as legitimate an environment for sex as a stable and emotionally intimate relationship.

Setting an impossibly high bar for sexual performance, the writhing actors in porn videos make one's real partner seem like a sloppy second. But more importantly, pornography conveys permission to objectify other human beings. The more you watch, the more those types of relationships infiltrate your thoughts, consciously and subconsciously. Your mind becomes desensitized to wild appetites and capabilities that may not have a place in your marriage. The advertisers who pay hundreds of thousands of dollars to capture your eyes for sixty seconds know that every minute you watch has its effect. The orgasm-focused physical interactions in porn can't help but penetrate your soul. Do you think that's good or bad for your marriage? Does it strengthen your connection to your mate or weaken it?

Pornography undermines commitment to an existing relationship in both the short and long term, according to a series of five studies by Brigham Young University researchers. And the more porn the subjects consumed, especially men, the less commitment they demonstrated.[7]

Other studies show that viewing porn nudges spouses toward cheating.[8] Consumption of pornography turns out to be "a robust predictor of infidelity." It doesn't matter how strong or long-lasting one's current relationship has been, writes Dr. Peg Streep. "[E]ven though one's own pasture may be plenty green enough, just the thought of a greener one can be enough to send one roving."[9]

Looking at the issue from another angle, other researchers find that using porn weakens couples' loyalty. A comparison of the strength and fidelity of relationships with and without porn confirms its deleterious effect. Couples who view porn together reported much greater satisfaction with their sexual relationship than partners who used porn alone. But couples who *never* used porn reported significantly better communication and higher dedication to each other, and they were much less likely to be unfaithful than porn users. Rather than benefitting the couple, porn, even when a joint activity, can detract from closeness and provide a source of external distraction and possibility.[10]

A husband's use of pornography is deeply distressing to his wife, and it depresses the frequency of and satisfaction with marital sex. As one wife told researchers, "I am no longer sexually attractive or desirable to him. He's more attracted to the women depicted in his movies, magazines, and websites than he is to me, and I feel completely unable to compete...." More than half of cybersex participants no longer desired marital sex, and those who continued in marital relations were distant and objectified their mates. Several studies found women considered their husbands' Internet porn use infidelity.[11]

While there's controversy over whether frequent Internet porn use is an addiction or a compulsion, in either case a goal in treatment would be to eliminate its lure and redirect sexual activity to the marriage. A useful tactic, often developed in therapy, is to avoid the triggers that lead to porn use. Viewing porn can be replaced with a more acceptable activity that brings reward, like Robert finishing his college degree and spending more time with his kids. Also, he vowed to be transparent, realizing that anything he couldn't comfortably discuss with Angie would be bad for him.

In 1998 after Dr. Nicholas Terrett's drug sildenafil citrate received FDA approval to market in the U.S. as Viagra, a drug to address erectile dysfunction, observers hailed a new era of sexual liberation. Known as "the little blue pill" for its distinctively intense color, Pfizer's popular medication soon gained popularity via TV shows, movies, and commercials, including an advertisement by former GOP presidential nominee Bob Dole, who was involved in its clinical trials and pronounced it "a great drug."[12]

I'm driving to the gym and I hear an ad on talk radio (I'm a devotee of *The Michael Medved Show*). Doctor So-and-So is giving a seminar, and he's got a program to help you feel better, lose that weight, regain the sexual stamina of your youth. And your wife will love it too. Doctor So-and-So has lots of competition, and each ad includes the words "testosterone" and "estrogen" and "erectile dysfunction" and "lasting longer," inviting worry about the up-and-coming energy in your own marriage. If you don't have a partner interested in your reinvigorated pursuits, you're missing out.

Is it a coincidence that at the same time that sexuality spilled out into the public square its sanctity within marriage suffered? Filling radio, television, and film with talk about sex cheapens it. When marriage was the only acceptable setting for sex, when couples realized their union could produce a child, the significance of their congress transcended momentary physical pleasure. In the Jewish tradition, "set aside" or "separate" is the definition of "holy," and "holy matrimony" not only forms a pair elevated above all others (with approval from God) but offers a means for human beings actually to emulate God by creating and nurturing the next generation.

I'm suggesting that our sex-permeated culture pecks away at the shell protecting marital intimacy, each crude joke, each glimpse of porn, and each Viagra commercial eroding a bit of its "holiness." Casual acceptance of all things sexual into your consciousness nearly all the time diminishes the likelihood that you'll be turned on in your marriage, stealing some of the anticipation and excitement you might enjoy if you focused your sexuality on your mate. You can't avoid all of it, but you can opt out of a lot. Keeping your eye on the prize of increased closeness in your marriage helps filter out demeaning and desensitizing influences so you can treasure the relationship in which you've invested so much.

DIVORCE MAGNET NO. 3: WORKPLACE PRIORITY AND PROXIMITY

When Facebook COO Sheryl Sandberg, whose husband had passed away suddenly in May 2015, addressed the graduating class at UC Berkeley a year later, she didn't talk about her famous book *Lean In*, which urged women to press forward toward leadership. She didn't talk about her work at Facebook or her previous stint at Google or her career at Harvard. Instead she spoke about recovering from grief and how she burst free from the psychologist Martin Seligman's "three P's"—personalization, pervasiveness, and permanence—which can block positive thinking and mire people in their failures. Good advice. In a languishing or difficult marriage, it's useful to understand how we sabotage our own progress by taking on fault (personalizing), generalizing the problem (pervasiveness), and wallowing in and projecting the situation forward (permanence).

But what I found fascinating about Ms. Sandberg's speech was that it was clear that her heart's most beloved treasure is her marriage and family. For all the top-notch education she received and all the grooming and striving and connecting that brought her to the zenith of the business world, the core of her emotion was reserved for her husband. Marriage is precious and worth preserving.

She asked her audience what their priorities would be if they learned they had just a few days to live, a thought stimulated by the suddenness of her husband's demise. "Live with the understanding of how precious every single day would be. How precious every day actually is." She said capturing joy and expressing gratitude are the source of her resilience—"gratitude for the kindness of my friends, the love of my family, the laughter of my children."[13]

These intimate, family interactions mean so much more than an impressive corporate title or leading a cadre of women to prominence in a field formerly dominated by men. Few people would put on their tombstones "most dedicated employee," but "loving mother" and "devoted husband" are honored tributes.

What's all this got to do with divorce? When we teach young adults that women fulfill their potential through successful careers but fail to balance that with any mention of successful marriages, their priorities become skewed, and marriage falls into second place. Earning a baccalaureate ostensibly prepares graduates to succeed in life, but no collegiate institution teaches students that their most meaningful accomplishments will pertain to their families and marriages, even though plenty of academic research shows this.

For example, a 2012 study of twenty-five thousand graduates of Harvard Business School—the crème de la crème, the highly trained, driven achievers whose education puts them in immediate demand for top-notch positions—found that recent graduates defined success as accomplishment in their career, but twenty to forty years after attaining their Harvard MBA, their definitions of success centered around family and personal fulfillment.

"For me, at age twenty-five, success was defined by career success," responded a woman in her forties. "Now I think of success much differently: Raising happy, productive children, contributing to the world around me, and pursuing work that is meaningful to me." The researchers noted, "When we asked respondents to rate the importance of nine career and life dimensions, nearly 100%, regardless of gender, said that 'quality of personal and family relationships' was 'very' or 'extremely' important."[14]

If that's the case, why can't colleges erect a second pedestal elevating marriage next to the one for career fame and academic supremacy? Why do we celebrate those who strive for professional success but condone failure or lack of tenacity in marriage? The difference in the way we treat work and marriage excuses neglect of relationships and ultimately foments divorce.

I remember taking feminist-oriented courses in graduate school in which the "problem" of "having it all" was a theme. We analyzed the issue only from the perspective of an achieving woman professional who must balance leadership in her career, time with her children and husband, and pursuing her personal rewards (exercise, hobbies, travel). By "balance," we really meant establishing a hierarchy of values. A woman should achieve in the marketplace first, establishing her legitimacy and competence. Only then should she turn to the other two areas, "off-clock" obligations and interests that should be scheduled around the demands of work.

Anne-Marie Slaughter addressed this problem in a famous article in the *Atlantic*, "Why Women Still Can't Have It All,"[15] the response to which inspired her book *Unfinished Business*.[16] She came to realize that neglect of the traditionally feminine realm of marriage and family is the root problem in our culture, and if its importance were recognized, much anxiety—for both women and men—about forfeiting professional advancement and giving home life priority would disappear.[17] Such recognition would also reward keeping marriage and family intact. If having a strong marriage received the same societal approval as becoming a CEO, more husbands and wives would give their marriages at least as much effort as they give their careers.

And then there's the more sordid downside of the workplace—affairs. If the priority of career over family introduces emotional distance between spouses, the daily physical proximity to colleagues of the opposite sex can pose serious temptations to infidelity. Wouldn't it be great if every worker focused on the tasks at hand and maintained only professional relationships with co-workers and superiors, if every encounter with a new colleague were entirely pure and physical appearance were irrelevant? Are you chuckling yet?

"From flirting to flings, men and women are looking for romance in the workplace—and many are finding it!" writes MSNBC.com health editor Charlene Laino about a survey of thirty-one thousand persons on "office sex and romance," co-commissioned by *Elle* magazine.

The survey found plenty of threats to monogamy in the workplace:

- 92 percent of respondents said a co-worker they found attractive had flirted with them
- 62 percent admitted at least one office affair (while 14 percent said they would never date someone from work)
- 42 percent were married or in a relationship at the time of an office affair
- 41 percent had sex on the job, and 16 percent used a boss's office; 7 percent got caught in the act, but 87 percent got away with no consequence
- 19 percent had serious employment consequences, but just 3 percent lost their jobs
- 9 percent of married philanderers said their affair led to divorce or separation, while half reported no marital consequences
- Finally, 25 percent of women said they benefitted at work because a supervisor found them attractive, though 13 percent reported they lost a promotion because they were seen as sexually threatening[18]

Family law attorney Christina Pesoli has summarized the ways a "harmless intrigue" at work undermines marriage:

- Your outside interest is fueled by energy robbed from your marriage
- Your outside interest will weaken your marriage. Your "good mood" is really just your inflated ego, not a boon to your wife
- Your wife is at a competitive disadvantage (because she doesn't know there's competition, she can't offer a good defense)

- Your wife looks way better (and you look way worse) than you realize. It's easy to look great for little snippets of time with someone exciting
- Your actions will lead to a physical affair, even though you say it won't

Her advice? "You need to decide if you (a) want to be married, or (b) want to be divorced. In case that's not clear enough, let me dumb it down a little further: you need to either (a) break it off with your flirt buddy, or (b) get a divorce."[19]

The more women and men mingle, the more likely they'll be attracted to one another and the more likely they'll have affairs. There, I said it. As politically incorrect as it is, it's the truth. Anyone who thinks co-workers will ignore chemistry and stay professional and all-business is in denial. It's a jungle out there, and if you have to live in the jungle, you need the mosquito netting of polite reserve and decorum with the opposite sex. You may need more than that—a machete or perhaps an elephant gun—if any of the fauna get aggressive. Common sense and respect for human nature are the best defense for your marriage. The blatant truth is that propriety is passé. Standards of familiarity and formality that once defined boundaries have slipped so far that addressing a customer as Mr. or Mrs. So-and-So is often received as snotty or rude. "Hello, Diane, I'm Sam. How's your day going?"—breezily asks the operator at the phone number for an online retailer who got my order wrong. Well, I don't really want to tell you, Sam.

We can't put society in reverse, but formalities can help put enough distance between strangers to let them think more carefully about blurring the lines separating co-worker, coffee-break sharer, lunch companion, and after-work tryst. Try addressing others by their titles. If someone looks surprised, just say, "I'm practicing showing respect for people around me." Your listener's quizzical look will instantly switch to knowing admiration. "Respect" is politically correct (and just plain correct).

CHAPTER 3

The Danger of Detaching Marriage from Parenthood

We devalue anything that could curb our independence. We shack up, put off marriage, and defer the responsibilities of parenthood. It seems like ancient history when youths fell in love and quickly legitimized their desire by "popping the question." The latest figures from the Centers for Disease Control and Prevention show that 74 percent of men and 70 percent of women think it's acceptable for unmarried couples to live together.[1]

In a 1955 hit record, Frank Sinatra sang that love and marriage "go together like a horse and carriage."

> Love and marriage, love and marriage,
> It's an institute you can't disparage.
> Ask the local gentry
> And they will say it's elementary.
> Try, try, try to separate them.
> It's an illusion
> Try, try, try, and you will only come
> To this conclusion.[2]

Reflecting the once-universal assumption that love's natural destination is marriage—"You can't have one without the other"—the song today sounds as obsolete as, well, a horse and carriage. It resurfaced thirty years later as the theme song of the television series *Married...with Children*, an endearingly crass parody of oh-so-happy-family sitcoms like *Family Ties*, *Full House*, and the *Cosby Show*.

Featuring the ineffectual shoe salesman Al Bundy, his bonbon-noshing wife, their ditzy daughter, and socially inept son, *Married...with Children* shared one theme with the wholesome family shows it spoofed: marriage as a commitment that overrides everything else. "Bundys are losers, not quitters," patriarch Al declared. And despite crude insults, near-constant failures, and obnoxious behavior, Al insists the family unit rules: "Love, hate...look, we're a family—what's the difference?"

That dedication to a collection of people indivisibly united by the concept of family (love, hate—what's the difference?) inoculates against divorce. I wouldn't hold up Al, Peggy, Kelly, and Bud Bundy as exemplars of family relations, but their trudging forward together shows how placing family cohesion above slights and failures can result in a long-term success. When the TV tribe needed pumping-up, they stood in a circle with their hands in the center, raising them to the cheer "Whoa Bundy!"[3]

For a family to achieve unity, a couple must enter their marriage with the understanding that they're starting a family, not just forming a relationship. Let's compare two couples and consider which has the better long-term prognosis.

Emily and Jack, both thirty, have lived together for six years and assume they'll be a couple forever. When they met, Emily had just finished her bachelor's in anthropology, and Jack had purchased a math tutoring franchise. Now Emily teaches preschool, and Jack has grown his business. Overwhelmed with deadlines and urgencies, they can't foresee the need or the time to have children.

Cicely and William, twenty-five and twenty-six, grew up within a couple miles of each other. Though they met in high school, they got together as freshmen in the local university. They kept dating as William finished law school and Cicely earned a master's in accounting. As soon as William passed the bar and found a job, they announced their engagement, eager to start a family. When babies arrive, Cicely plans to continue her career part-time from home.

The differences between the two couples? Both have long-term relationships. But two distinctions separate them—Jack and Emily live together, and their careers take precedence in their future plans. Cicely and William held off moving in until after marriage, which they view as the foundation for raising children together.

COHABITATION AND DIVORCE

When you enter marriage with a dedicatedly long-term view, disagreements and problems become glitches in a lifelong project. A long-term view of the relationship is more difficult if you're just living together, which signals at least one party's desire for wiggle room. Living together before marriage may seem like a prudent way to test compatibility—a trial run with minimal consequences if it fails. But it reinforces a belief that you can back out of a relationship. If everything keeps humming along, you might get married, but just having that cohabitation experience lowers the chances you'll make it for the long haul.

A 2009 study published in the *Journal of Family Psychology* found that couples living together before engagement (43.1 percent of the study sample) "reported lower marital satisfaction, dedication, and confidence as well as more negative communication and greater potential for divorce than those who cohabited only after engagement (16.4%) or not at all until marriage (40.5%)."[4] Why does shacking up increase chances of divorce? One of the study's authors, Galena Rhoades, suggests, "Cohabiting to test a relationship turns out to be associated with the most problems in relationships. Perhaps if a person is feeling a need to test the relationship, he or she already knows some important information about how a relationship may go over time." Don't ignore your intuition. The researchers also observed that some live-in relationships "slide into marriage" just because it's easy, the "logical next step," rather than "because they really decided they wanted a future together."[5] The vision of "a future together" makes the difference. Especially when the couple sees raising a family—not just "having children"—as the agenda.

Of course, the "chicken and egg" question arises. It could be that couples who strongly honor commitment anyway are more inclined toward the formality of marriage and the adventure of parenthood. Those with doubts about the permanence of this coupling or wariness about relationships in general tend instead to live together in a sort of self-fulfilling prophecy. Data from the Centers for Disease Control and Prevention from 2010 show that a third of cohabiting women (ages fifteen to forty-four) in their first pairings were still shacking up three years later. In that same time frame, 27 percent broke up and 40 percent wed.[6]

Living together has become the "new normal" for those who fall in love and think there's potential. With its widespread acceptance, more couples who choose it do make their eventual marriages work. Statistics from the CDC National Survey of Family Growth through 2013 show 57 percent of women and 53 percent of men between the ages of eighteen and forty-four have cohabited at some point.

Looking more closely at these data, the University of North Carolina researcher Arielle Kuperberg found that the age of first pairing—whether it's living together or getting married—is the best predictor of a later breakup. Waiting until at least age twenty-three to form either type of union mitigated the risk of divorce once wed. Naturally, maturity is key to marital success.

Another factor countering ominous predictions for couples who marry after living together is the growing disapproval of divorce. Asked by the CDC to respond to the statement "Divorce is usually the best solution when a couple can't seem to work out their marriage problems," 62 percent of women and 60 percent of men disagreed or strongly disagreed.[7] Aversion to divorce is a great deterrent, but it's also a deterrent to marriage, and it probably contributes to rising first-marriage ages.

There are probably several reasons why, despite its prevalence, people feel so strongly about avoiding divorce. Professor Wendy Manning of Bowling Green State University says, "Marriage is becoming so selective that maybe people think if you achieve this status, you don't want to end it."[8] I'd suggest that children of divorce, scarred and scared by their early experiences, are determined not to replicate what they saw their families endure. They'd rather live together first, taking more time to establish their own careers, which in turn causes reluctance to brake momentum. They're pairing off later anyway, so when they do enter marriage, they're less likely to want children or end up having fewer. Fifteen percent of women aged forty to forty-four were childless in 2015.[9]

It's a conflict. Afraid of making a mistake and needing more degrees, internships, and experience to compete for good jobs, young people prolong their educations and put off marriage, turning it into what Catherine Rampell calls "a capstone rather than a cornerstone."[10] The average age of first marriage zoomed to twenty-eight for men and almost twenty-seven for women in 2010, a big contrast with 1970, when average ages were twenty-four for men and just over twenty-two for women.[11]

THE "FAMILY PROJECT" OF RAISING CHILDREN

These developments strip marriage of the multigenerational purpose that requires flexibility and accommodation of others' needs—precisely the traits that ward off marital conflict and divorce. To be sure, couples without children can expand their interests and skills, but the direction of that growth is much more of their choosing. Children are a couple's wild card. Each child is unique, with his or her own requirements for attention, many of which call for uncomfortable and inconvenient adaptations.

The qualities that caring for a baby, a child, and an adolescent force upon parents—patience, long-term perspective, putting another person's needs first—improve all of your relationships, particularly your marriage. Parenthood also teaches characteristics that, as you exercise them with your child, strengthen the partnership with your spouse. If you're determined that your child will grow up in a secure home with his biological parents, each step along a linear progression of time and events constitutes that long-term commitment. Breaking up with your spouse would cause the project to fail.

Two adults alone needn't use the linear thinking required in parenthood—selecting a two-wheeler bike that will last, choosing a house that can accommodate growing kids, saving for college. But children's evolving needs broaden the domestic enterprise, imbuing the spouses with an understanding that the relationship must endure at least until children launch.

Divorce ruins the project of raising happy children in a functioning family, inflicting pain and disruption on everyone. But if spouses see themselves not just as married-with-children but as builders of a *family*, they look beyond immediate feelings and desires. Any parent can tell you that she's often had to control anger, give up pleasures, and take care of a child before herself. The reward for these sacrifices is a bond with the child that outweighs everything. Most parents will admit they've grown and improved *because* of the demands of parenthood, even rising to practice the virtues they hope to instill (lest they be called hypocrites!).

When you're living by individual instead of family values, the criterion for obtaining what you want is that you want it. Ben liked to go on gambling junkets to Vegas by himself for a week at a time. He'd sit at the blackjack table using his card-counting strategy. He was successful some of the time, and then he'd play again, betting half his winnings. He went to strip shows and gorged at the buffets and called his wife, Fran, every other day.

She, meanwhile, spent the time knocking around the outlet mall, finding baby gifts, scoring designer shirts on sale for her grown daughters, discovering treasures at Home Goods. When Ben was home, he'd return from his stock trading job by two in the afternoon, eat in front of their sixty-inch TV, watch a movie with Fran, and start snoring before it ended. When he told Fran he was bored with their marriage, she suggested they get counseling. He realized there that he was happiest at the blackjack table and resented coming home to an environment about as far from a casino's stimulation as it could be. Fran tried to ratchet up their sex life with novelty and even props, but Ben realized he thought of her as depressingly matronly, and after eight meetings with the counselor he thanked her for his clarity and moved out.

Fran and Ben no longer had daughters at home to raise, and so their joint purpose slid off the table. Their project was over, according to Ben, so he was free to pursue his decadent and stimulating Vegas life. The outcome might have changed if they'd attempted to share interests throughout their marriage, but instead they'd practiced going their own ways.

In a family project, each member is the cheerleader and support system for the rest, and individual problems become family problems—the group works together to accommodate one or the other's particular needs while staying configured as a unit. "Whoa Bundy!"

NO KIDS, MORE DIVORCE

What about couples who marry with no possibility of a long-term "family project"? Many couples find each other beyond childbearing age, perhaps with grown children from a previous marriage. Child-free unions are valuable and cause for celebration, of course, but assume a different role for society. They're paramount to *the partners*, and they deserve every effort to preserve them. But they start off with a greater risk of divorce.

Sometimes couples desperately want a family but suffer the heartbreak of infertility. You'd think these partners should be the *most* committed to a long-term, family-oriented future. But the stressful, often prolonged medical procedures of fertility treatments strain relationships for a sizeable number of people: 10 percent of all women between fifteen and forty-four suffer from "impaired fecundity," the inability to conceive and carry a child to term. Even after treatments, 6 percent of all women remain infertile.[12]

A 2014 study of 47,515 Danish women in fertility treatment found that couples unsuccessful in overcoming infertility had *three times* the risk of divorce. "We knew that fertility treatment is tough both physically and mentally. It's very consuming and you think about it constantly," said the study's lead author. "But we were surprised to see that the effect lasted this long—up to 12 years after treatment we could see an increased risk of divorce if the couple did not have a baby."[13]

Lone Schmidt of the University of Copenhagen, who interviewed 2,250 couples for her own research, commented on the marital toll of infertility, "The reason why it is such a great challenge is also that it opens the question of whether you should stay with your partner or try to find someone else—especially if you know which of the two partners cannot produce babies."[14]

Interestingly, in Jewish law, a couple who bear no offspring after ten years of trying are eligible for divorce, should they both desire it, so that each has a second chance to find a partner with whom conception could occur. For Jewish couples in this position, a marriage without children is a sad hardship, a daily reminder of failure. Children are considered a source of joy in Jewish culture, fulfillment of the commandment "be fruitful and multiply." With the array of fertility treatments available nowadays, few take this divorce option, but it illustrates the Jewish fusion of marriage to parenthood as a lifelong project, which, if rendered impossible, even justifies starting over.

RISKY REMARRIAGE

Divorce throws parents with children back on the singles market. Forty percent of marriages in 2013 included a remarrying partner (in 20 percent it was one of the parties, and in 20 percent it was both). Women are less enthusiastic about remarrying, 54 percent saying they'd prefer to pass (as opposed to just 30 percent of men). If you include those who say they are unsure, 42 percent of women and 65 percent of men are open to remarriage.

I'm suspicious of figures, supposedly derived from census data, that suggest second and third marriages are far more divorce-prone than first marriages. One widely-quoted *Psychology Today* article goes so far as to say that 69 percent of second marriages and 73 percent of third marriages end in divorce. By way of comparison, real census statistics show that 30 percent of first marriages fail.[15] Don't take such pronouncements at face value. Official British figures reveal a divorce rate for remarriages even lower than that for first marriages, and some data from the United States indicate that the prognosis for second marriages without children involved is the same as or better than for first-timers. The average first marriage that ends in divorce lasts 9.2 years. People in unsuccessful remarriages know it sooner; the average second marriage that ends in divorce lasts 6.3 years.[16]

The factor that complicates and imperils a second or subsequent marriage is *children*. If yours is a blended family, put your marriage first and steel yourself for some conflict. After a childless first marriage to a woman who left him, Gideon remarried in his mid-thirties, and with his younger bride soon had two sons. Conflicts over finances and in-laws soon impinged. Carolyn's retired parents moved into the same block so they could babysit while Carolyn returned to work. That seemed like a good idea at first, but they quickly inserted themselves in Gideon's home, criticizing his TV viewing, straightening the house, and insisting they were "more experienced" in handling the boys. It didn't help that they had the wherewithal to buy the kids cute clothes from Hannah Anderson, sponsor the baseball team, and bring them whatever new toys they wanted.

Carolyn told Gideon he should be grateful for their generosity. She enjoyed having her mom and dad around; they made her life easier and they usually were right in their advice about the boys. But the one lesson Gideon learned from his first divorce was to assert himself when he and his wife differed. They went to counseling, where Carolyn said Gideon was being territorial and selfish. Gideon felt justified in wanting to head his own household.

Caught in the middle of his parents' dispute, the elder son, now twelve, developed trichotillomania, the compulsion to pull out his hair. It was clear

Carolyn and Gideon's conflict had escalated, and Carolyn blamed her husband for his unwillingness to "just chill" and let her parents ease their financial crunch. "The only way I can work is if they take care of the boys," she insisted. Gideon felt his in-laws were the problem and that his resentment wouldn't stop unless they stayed away.

It was an ultimatum that Carolyn couldn't accept. Her parents bought her a home "as an investment," and she and the boys moved a mile away, so the kids wouldn't have to change schools. There was no screaming, and signing the shared custody agreement was sad but amicable.

Soon Gideon was spending time with Shelly, a single mom he met at church. She had three kids, two boys thirteen and fifteen and an eleven-year-old girl. "I was attracted to her immediately. We laughed a lot," Gideon recalls. "She had a great voice and we'd take out our guitars and sing together; her kids basically were doing their own things with friends or in the other room." Shelly and Gideon spent plenty of time texting and talking on the phone; she'd make dinner for her family and invite Gideon, and they enjoyed private time when Gideon's sons were with Carolyn.

Living together was out of the question; logistics precluded it. So Shelly and Gideon married in their church, their five children serving as attendants. Gideon rented out his house and moved in with Shelly. The four boys got the master bedroom, Shelly's daughter and the newlyweds each had their own.

Hearing Gideon recall it, the family never emulsified. "I don't feel so bad about this divorce," he says. "You know that blended families have a lot of problems." The boys hated sharing a room, arguing about whose music could be played and which would be louder. Shelly considered the boys' constant fighting a "zoo" and would escape by taking her daughter shopping. Shelly's children saw Gideon as an interloper; after all, he moved into *their* home.

The light-hearted times Gideon and Shelly had shared were replaced with quelling arguments among the kids, which left each of them annoyed with the other. On the days Gideon's sons weren't there—half the time—his stepdaughter increasingly "got sick," requiring her mother's attention. "The stress level in our house was always sky-high," Gideon remembers, "and trying to keep the kids in line, get them to school, shuttle back and forth to Carolyn's, and just hold things together finally got to me. I knew Shelly's kids wanted me out, and after two years, they got what they wanted." Shelly and Gideon were more relieved than hurt when he moved out. They'd never achieved the civility, much less the unity, they sought for their families.

Blended families face problems that first-marriage biological families avoid—rivalries for attention, contentious adjustments, and lack of history that allows the new parent to understand stepchildren's personalities and behaviors. And of course, each age has its own developmental tasks, which become more difficult when overlaid with accepting new siblings and shifting between biological parents.

The legacy of first divorces for subsequent blended families tends to be a second divorce. Say "blended family," and the Brady Bunch comes to mind. But Mike and Carol Brady (whose television family was absurdly idealized in any case) were both widowed, not divorced; there were no exes in the background to complicate family relations.

Bestowing the title "family" on any combination of adults and children, whether or not they're related by blood or marriage, degrades the authority of parents in marital households. That authority faces enough threats as it is in a blended family, where kids are already tempted to respond "You're not my mother!" or "My step-siblings don't have to!" Tests of authority leave everyone frazzled and weaken marriage and newly fashioned bonds.

The decline of the family in general means you need to shore up the authority of your own family. One way is to distinguish your family from all the rest by prefacing parental statements with "In *our* family...." "In *our* family, we speak with kindness and respect." "In *our* family, we have rules about asking before borrowing." You're different—in other families language might be harsh, but that's not acceptable in *your* family. In other families, children talk back to their parents, but that's not acceptable in *your* family.

Maggie Scarf analyzes the hurdles for blended families in *The Remarriage Blueprint: How Remarried Couples and Their Families Succeed or Fail*.[17] Revisiting couples she interviewed a dozen years before, she evaluates their marriages and compares them with those of couples she interviewed more recently. She identifies five major challenges that remarried couples and their families confront:

1. Coping with "Insider/outsider forces," the dynamic that marginalizes or includes family members;
2. Dealing with the tough histories children bring to the new family combination;
3. Parenting, given the oppositional nature of two families' styles and alliances;
4. Integrating differing family cultures; and
5. Designing a boundary around the new family "with a hole" that allows absent biological parents and important others access

Every family has its own way of maintaining harmony, but adding these additional tasks to the usual array of habits, desires, and unforeseeables loads emerging relationships with baggage so heavy that the majority of blended-family remarriages sink.

If you're considering divorce and hope to remarry one day, you should realize that your chances of success in that second marriage go way down just because you've been married before. If you have children, realize that the odds are against your forming a permanently blended family—at least *two thirds of those who try fail.*

If you're presently in a difficult blended family, rather than giving up, try to identify what's making your life miserable—peel the onion and isolate the negatives from the positives. You can reinforce your underlying bond by magnifying daily pleasures and talking about them. Ask each family member to jot down each day on a large chalkboard in a central location a positive experience, a good feeling, or something he appreciates. Make the most of the good stuff.

Simultaneously, you can address each source of irritation and conflict. A family counselor may be required, but often by teasing out and dissecting conflicts the parties can compromise or agree to disagree. Bringing resentments and jealousies (for example) out into the open diffuses them to some extent. Just remember that you don't have to give up on the whole enterprise if it's possible to correct individual problems one at a time.

CHAPTER 4

The Divorce Industry: Friends and Helpers You Never Wanted to Know

I f you're teetering about whether to stick it out in your marriage or bolt, you're likely to meet an array of folks whose livelihoods depend on your opting out. Some of them even make their money by pushing you there.

Don't get me wrong. I'm not condemning those who make a living off other people's divorces. To the contrary, the right therapist can be essential to understanding, working through, and recovering from your suffering. Whether you want to come to your own epiphany or prefer direct guidance, there's a therapist to match your goals and personality. Cognitive behavior therapy, the modality I favor, examines patterns of thinking and seeks to replace unproductive viewpoints and habits with more accurate and useful tactics.

In this chapter you'll read about the six methods of obtaining a divorce—do-it-yourself, litigation, mediation, collaborative divorce, attorney settlement, and a settlement conference—and the different professionals who might be involved in each. If you ever obtain a decree, you will encounter the legal system and its myriad requirements.

The Divorce Industry includes not only legal and psychological professionals but also those who help dismantle your single family home and establish two separate ones—movers, furniture dealers, Craigslist resellers, storage unit palaces. The logistics of shuttling children between their "binuclear" households, as Constance Ahrons calls them in *The Good Divorce*, require apps, babysitters, car commutes, and bus or subway rides. And it gets even more complicated with second and third divorces.

Family disjunction entails lots of moving parts and arouses complex emotions that businesses rightly address. I salute entrepreneurs who see a need and meet it, smoothing in some way the bumpy and discombobulating reversals of our disorderly lives. But it's worth remembering that you control your personal decisions. If you find reliance on a lot of outsiders disconcerting, you can work all the harder to shore up your marriage against the sweeping flow of divorce.

ROOTING FOR YOU: THE NEW FIELD OF "LIFE COACHING"

Until about a decade ago, if you suffered from angst or anger or depression or just about anything you wished would go away, you could turn to a variety of mental health experts. The most-trained (and most expensive) was a psychiatrist (an M.D. certified in that specialty), who could dispense medications to treat the most debilitating symptoms. If medication wasn't required you might choose a psychologist (like me), who had a doctoral degree and lengthy practicum as well as state licensure. Or you may have found relief with a marriage and family counselor or licensed social worker, with master's degrees, practica, and licensure as well.

Then, seemingly out of left field—to adopt baseball terminology—came the "life coach." The services of Vikki G. Brock, a certified life coach since 1998, trace their origins to Werner Erhard's "est" seminars of the 1970s and Big Sur's Esalen Institute in the 1960s.[1] One of Erhard's followers, Thomas Leonard, developed a business offering an array of goal-oriented advice and coined the term "coaching." By the early 1990s, training programs for life coaches had sprung up, and today they proliferate online.

We all know what a baseball coach does. He organizes and evaluates his team and places players where they're best used. He instructs players on improving their game, and as a game progresses, he calls up the players most suited to tasks of the moment. But life is not a game, so what's a life coach?

A report on this burgeoning field by the industry analysts IBIS World counted 12,043 life coach businesses in the United States employing 17,944 persons as of February 2016. That's 17,944 American entrepreneurs who a decade ago weren't out looking for people in transition like you to help.

And what does a life coach do? According to IBIS, "This industry includes practitioners that primarily help clients set and achieve personal goals. Such goals can pertain to a client's job, personal life or interpersonal relationships. This industry does not include psychologists, mental health counselors or business analysts."[2]

That's about right. A new cadre of (unlicensed and self-regulated) advisors now joins mental health professionals serving people who are wavering at a consequential crossroads. The proliferation of helpers reflects the increasing fragility of marriage, and the plethora of professionals focusing on personal rather than family or marital goals could be adding to that instability.

In fact, for as little as $69.99, you can become certified online yourself.[3] And most of the two dozen coach certification sites I surveyed touted coaching fees ranging from one hundred dollars per hour to as much as a thousand dollars per hour for corporate or "executive" coaching, all payable by the client directly. No Medicaid, Medicare, health insurance plans, or Obamacare. That's because coaching is not mental health care, and if it veers into, say, anxiety or some psychological problem, your coach is probably unqualified to handle it.

Genevieve Smith checked out the coaching world for an article in *Harper's* magazine, sitting in on a well-regarded training course. Her description of touchy-feely exercises to encourage brainstorming reminded me of the consciousness-raising groups of the 1960s, and she mentions that many coaching techniques were inspired by the psychologist Milton Erickson's "powerful questions": What was it like? What do you want? What's available to you? What are you missing out on?

Aaron, a social worker therapist in Smith's coach-training class, explained why he was paying the more than five thousand dollar tuition for that program's certification: marketing. "Imagine if I went up to you and said, 'Hey, I'm a therapist, and I think you'd be really great in my therapy practice.' It's much easier to say, 'I'm in a coach-certification program, and I'd love to try this with you.'"[4]

Smith's conclusion? Most of the cheerleading and encouragement in a coach's repertoire could be provided free by an insightful friend. After all, what are friends for? To boost your ego, to say how right you are and that you shouldn't put up with it. To fortify you to stand up and follow your heart.

But having someone boost your ego and tell you how right you are won't necessarily redeem your marriage. Certainly being a doormat isn't ideal either, but when you're having conflicts in your marriage it's less helpful to the relationship to be right than it is to be merciful. Viewing the situation from your partner's perspective is more conducive to bridging discord than listening to someone cheer and echo your own perspective.

Your coach or therapist wants to see you happy and yet profits when you're not. No doubt advisors chose their careers because they want to help people while upholding the highest of ethics. Perhaps the most meaningful reward for their efforts is your improvement and gratitude. And yet, there's that conflict of interest. If after your first pre-divorce consultation you and your spouse make up and pledge changes that close your divisions, is your helper going to say, "Great! Don't come back!"? Or will it be, "Let's keep your next appointment to help troubleshoot those inevitable snags"? (Implication: "There will be snags. You need me.")

Each therapist and coach and psychologist comes with a bias, and I've observed that most are biased toward *you*. Meaning, when you're expressing pain you attribute to a spouse or frustration with his or her behavior or anguish over betrayal, the therapist wants to help you feel better. And often the swiftest way is to cut off the source of pain, frustration, or anguish by leaving the relationship, especially if you yourself say you want out. Despite the name "marriage and family counseling," most therapists focus on righting the *individual* client and sending him in the direction he seeks rather than preserving a marriage or family.

Clients can be wily. They spin stories to support their own perspectives, and the therapist usually doesn't hear the other side. Clients can (often unknowingly) manipulate their therapists, who, after all, can base their responses only on what the clients tell them. A savvy therapist recognizes this and knows how to diplomatically turn these tactics into useful insights and the basis for new strategies. Even so, the therapist, in the end, wants you to feel better, and that often results in a bias toward divorce.

And it may be that the client comes to the therapist to find justification for a decision already made. In such cases, therapy is nearly always "successful." It gets the client where he wants to go. But what if the other partner wants the counseling to heal the marriage? Sorry, no magic wand. "Unless both partners sincerely desire to attempt a repair of the relationship, couples often emerge from this attempt angrier than when they began" observes Sam Margulies, a divorce mediator.[5] Agreeing to counseling to prove the marriage is hopeless usually backfires, leaving the "deceived" spouse hungry for retribution.

Jed Diamond, a marriage and family therapist for more than forty years, admits, "Like most therapists (and most people these days), I've been married and divorced before. I told myself that my own divorce didn't bias me towards divorce as a solution to a couple's problems, but I realized that it did. It's difficult to accept that we may have made a mistake in our own relationships.... So if our client says, 'I'm no longer "in love" with you, I want to leave,' we unconsciously lean towards that solution."[6]

Every therapist is human and views events with a bias, but these observations by experienced counselors suggest that some don't recognize their biases. Consider the circumstances—the client sitting in your office is providing all the information and paying your fee, so *of course* you're motivated to help him reach his goals. A good therapist points out when a client's desires may be counterproductive or even harmful, but in our culture of stigma-free divorce, jumping ship seems a lot easier than bailing water, plugging the holes, and possibly going down anyway.

DIVORCE RECOVERY GROUPS

Look, if you must divorce, it's a lifesaver to have so many members of the Divorce Industry who can pluck you from the swirling tide of self-pity, blame, and sadness. Group therapy, even just having a place to vent and hear others' stories, is for many the most effective means of healing and moving on. Many of these groups are organized by ministries. Church Initiative, in Wake Forest, North Carolina, sponsors lay-led groups called Divorce Care and Divorce Care for Kids[7] at local churches around the country.

Participants meet in discussion groups and receive other means of support, such as spiritual guidance and daily encouraging emails.

Other services, like the online network Divorce Source (proclaiming "a passion for a better divorce"), are run as for-profit businesses, selling books, legal forms, and software. It offers referrals, free to clients; professionals pay a "membership fee" that gives them additional online exposure. The Divorce Industry kicks in the minute you realize you're unhappy and extends into single life.

Like many Divorce Industry professionals, Elise Pettus got into the business after going through her own divorce, founding Untied to help women "demystify the often-baffling process of divorce." When her husband left, she recalls, "I was so stunned, so collapsed by grief, but I thought, thank God for the Internet. I'm going to find these really intelligent women I can ask, 'What kind of lawyer do I call? Do I need a lawyer? Did your kids turn out OK? Did you regret keeping the house?'" She hosts groups of women in the newly renovated home she expected to share with her husband and children. Untied serves mainly well-to-do New Yorkers who pay ninety-seven dollars annually to get together to hear speakers and enjoy food and wine. "Wine is important early in the divorce process," Ms. Pettus remarks. Now she's in a new relationship but has branched out, putting "resingled" men and women together at dinners for twelve, an endeavor she calls the Good Part.[8]

Do these groups, by their very availability, encourage divorce? Unintentionally, yes. If you're sitting on a subway and see ads for divorce recovery get-togethers, you mentally file that resource away. Even if you're nowhere near divorcing, reading such announcements adds to your perception that divorce is everywhere. These dedicated and altruistic organizations may provide invaluable services when needed, and there's an especially compelling case for supporting people whose marriages have ended through no fault of their own. But when Elise Pettus's clients are featured in the *New York Times* Sunday Styles section enjoying animated conversation and a gourmet repast, divorce doesn't seem particularly tragic.

HELP YOURSELF TO DIVORCE

If you're not ready to venture out to divorcé dinners or to start group or individual counseling, you can choose from thousands of self-help books that will support, abet, and instruct you in your divorce. They address specific causes, such as depression, affairs, poor communication, boredom, unsatisfying sexuality, and anger. I highly recommend reading the ones that intrigue and apply to you before further discussing divorce with your partner. Ban the D word while you explore from every direction ways to restore a stable, functioning relationship.

Most self-help volumes buoy those already embroiled in or emerging from divorce, but several are aimed at spouses still struggling to decide the best course. Even books purporting to offer objective evaluation tools squeeze in subtle messages, almost always in favor of divorce. Perhaps the most helpful tool would be answers by divorced people years afterward to the question, "If you knew then what you know now, would you have preferred to *fix* your marital problems and *spare* yourself and your children the divorce?"

Could it be that the terrible consequences of divorce reported in news and research are (mostly) accurate—and at the same time that people who endure divorce make the most of surviving it? More to the point if you're still in a marriage: Can't spouses stay married and *still* grow? Why can't they use their trouble as a motivator to work on both themselves *and* their relationships at the same time? Start your reading with books on saving your marriage, especially those that emphasize changing *yourself* and the patterns and responses you display to your partner. Obviously, it's the combination of the two of you that makes your marriage. But by intentionally changing your half, even if your partner remains the same, you'll move your marriage off its present course. Sooner or later, your partner will have to respond, changing both of you. He may not respond the way you want, but that puts you in a different spot, a new pivot-point.

WOO-HOO! LET'S PARTY!

The stigma of divorce is long gone, and now the media portray Splitsville as joyous liberation. If memories of your wedding are tainted, replace them with a celebration of your divorce. Of course, the facilitators of the fun have a stake in your breakup. Every time you see a Facebook post about a divorce celebration, your brain gets a little more desensitized, and you become a little more accepting. You're thinking, "Yeah, divorce isn't so bad. It can even be a party!"

Time magazine reports, "Party planners and manufacturers of party supplies are raking it in selling everything from 'decapitated groom' cake toppers to black 'just divorced' sashes to nights on the town complete with VIP club entrance and limo transportation."[9] Las Vegas, Nevada, capital of Elvis Impersonator weddings and quickie decrees, boasts scads of businesses specializing in shindigs to celebrate that final filing. Sin City Parties urges its customers to live it up: "Why not, we are sure you spent a fortune on your wedding planner! Don't you deserve the same level of celebration now, or even more so?"[10] Down the street, Sapphire, "the world's largest gentlemen's club," invites you to celebrate your divorce in its "carefree world of long legs, perfect breasts, g-strings, Jack Daniels and Budweiser."[11]

Vegas VIP, a "luxury travel club," offers everything you need to make the evening memorable:

> Ramp up your divorce party décor with a great selection of divorce theme party decorations and accessories from our Divorced Diva line. Adorn your space with color-coordinated doormats, party balloons and silly signs like Ring for Sale. Get your guests to join in the celebratory spirit with wacky wearables like Divorced Diva Tiaras and Divorced Diva Boas. Organize some entertainment with the help of our satirical Pin the Tail on the Ex game and fun, Ex-Husband Pull-String Divorced Diva Piñata. It even has a special space where you can stick his photo.[12]

Bashing that piñata with your ex-husband's poster-sized smiling mug surely brings out the best in you. Think of what your children learn about the seriousness of your marriage when they see you sending out the "I'm Not With Stupid Anymore" dinner party invitations available on Café Press![13] And if the sentiment's there but the schedule full, your friends can send a divorce card. Maybe this: two female alligators talking. First alligator: "Nice purse!" Second alligator: "Thanks. It's my ex-husband." Or this: woman saying, "We divorced on religious grounds. He thought he was God. I didn't."

Many of them, however, seem pathetic and sad, like this one: a drawing of blindfolded Lady Liberty holding a giant sword saying, "Nothing says love like a restraining order." Or this one—front of card: "My ex was the center of my Universe." Inside of card: "And by that I mean a place of darkness that sucks the life out of everything."

Cards convey emotions, and overwhelmingly, divorcées and their friends seem depressed. Yes, being in a torturous marriage may be even more depressing, and escaping from pain like that may be blessed relief. But we're talking about *greeting cards* here. Even after the divorce, a survey of the cards *somebody* is buying suggests that finalizing the divorce is just a marker along a much longer pot-holed road of misery.

I'm not maligning those who throw divorce parties or send divorce cards. I'm merely pointing out that divorce is so common and free from sanction that entrepreneurs take advantage of that lucrative opportunity. This seemingly universal acceptance of divorce nudges someone like you, suffering in a relationship, toward leaving. The implication is that should you depart, your friends' support, the innumerable ranks of fellow travelers, and a panoply of service providers will ease your transition back to single life. And if you're so inclined, when you get that decree, throw yourself a bash and, like one New Yorker, barbeque your wedding dress (with a hot dog on top, representing her cheating former spouse).[14] Join the fun!

YOUR VIRTUAL DIVORCE

Through social media like Facebook, Twitter, Instagram, and LinkedIn, you have probably shared the history of your marriage, day by day, with a plethora of friends and followers. But divorce is all about disconnecting, and changing your status is only one update you'll want to make. The Divorce Industry has expanded to help you with that.

Wiping Facebook of evidence that you were attached is as simple as clicking on a new feature called "the breakup flow," which untags photos and removes mentions from your posts and newsfeed. Apparently Facebook has a "compassion team" that researched the gentlest ways to erase someone, consulting the Greater Good Science Center at UC Berkeley. Another quick delete for relationships on Facebook is KillSwitch, a ninety-nine-cent app that donates a portion of proceeds to—natch!—the American Heart Association of New York, healer of broken hearts. The pictures it pulls remain available on a hidden file.

Cleansing your page doesn't always free your mind, though. The sociologist Anabel Quan-Haase of the University of Western Ontario asked 107 students how a recent breakup had played out on Facebook. "[A]bout 62 percent of the users said they spent a lot of time reanalyzing wall posts and messages from the ex. About the same percentage said that updating their relationship on Facebook caused a flood of concerned and even tactless responses from family and friends."[15] Then you've also got to cleanse Instagram, Twitter, and any other social media where your past lurks.

In checking out divorce-related internet sites, I was disturbed to see how many suggest that breaking another person's heart is no big deal—and even funny. It's true that many of the blogs and vendors of breakup goods and services cater to doomed couples who aren't married. But these apathetic let-downs reverberate among friends and acquaintances, influencing even married people. The message is that everybody's in flux, change is inevitable, and no relationship is immune. In our callous "swipe left" world, impersonal dumping seems casual and easy.

The Breakup Shop is one such site. People who would never go to this website, by the way, might still encounter one of the many articles written about it.[16] These stories grab readers because the site is intended to be outrageous, but publishing descriptions of them doesn't seem particularly outrageous—"Cute idea for making a buck," we think.

If it's too traumatic to break the news in the old-fashioned way—in person, in a note, or by telephone—you can employ the Breakup Shop, an app that sends the type of breakup message you choose and lets you earn "trophies" for all the breakups you accumulate. It's a business model that monetizes broken hearts. "The Breakup Shop believes everyone deserves to be single," says its website. "Let us handle the messy work of the breakup so you can spend more time swiping right.... Recently single? You are now."

If you can wait up to three days, for ten dollars the Breakup Shop will send a text on your behalf: "What's worse then [sic] getting dumped over the phone? A breakup text. Show them you really don't care." Gee, if you're that kind of person, why not just go dark ("ghosting") for free? Ten dollars can also buy you an email with "helpful" links to Ben and Jerry's and Netflix, and there's a "mean option to include a photo attachment of you with a new significant other, if its [sic] that kind of breakup...."

Twenty dollars gets you snail mail: "Add a touch of class to your low-blow with our standard breakup letter. Includes our return address in case you don't want your ex to know where you live now." Apparently the option for a thirty-dollar personal phone call has been withdrawn. But you can still buy the eighty-dollar Breakup Gift Pack, which includes chocolate chip cookies, two wine glasses, a Netflix credit, sympathy letter, and either the movie *The Notebook* or a video game. All in a white cardboard crate with a handle: "The Breakup Gift Pack box can also be repurposed as a 'memory oven.' Empty the box and stuff it full of your ex's photos, jewelry, underwear, or whatever and set it ablaze (in a safe location of course.)"

Seems entirely like a bad joke, except they'll take your money and actually do the dastardly deed. "We see it as a tongue-in-cheek entity," Mackenzie Keast, one of two brothers who started the Breakup Shop told the *New York Times*. "Attitudes are changing. It doesn't have to be this lonely, miserable, emotional experience. It can be a means to moving on to the next potential partner."[17] That's not what he told Emanuel Maiberg, who paid thirty dollars for a breakup phone call to his girlfriend of five years and writes, "I asked several times if the whole thing was a joke or if they were serious about it as a business. The brothers said they're serious, and that they believe they can scale it up by automating part of the service."[18]

Plenty of other startups want some of your breakup shards, such as Never Liked It Anyway, a web outlet that specializes in recycling unwanted romantic detritus (rings, wedding dresses, music, gifts). The only difference between selling items here and elsewhere seems to be the opportunity to vent and the voyeuristic appeal of a backstory.

If you want an app to help you mop up emotionally, there's Rx Breakup, "a 30-day guide that delivers professionally developed self-help techniques in the tone of a trusted girlfriend."[19] Another app, Mend, offers subscription breakup advice and a podcast.[20] And plenty of blogs and websites also offer solace after a split, like Divorce360.com, Soyouvebeendumped.com and Splitsville.com.[21]

Your takeaway is to realize the invasive ways divorce and dumping permeate the media, making bust-ups normal, everyday occurrences. It seems unimaginable, but it was only a few years ago that Facebook became the first thing we checked in the morning. It was just the blink of an eye ago that our phones became the bearers of our feelings, our connections, our

photos, our queries—basically everything on our minds. Scads of hookup
and matching sites bring people together, and that means a lot of mismatches
that require post-mortem burial. "I've come to think millennial romances
are defined not by their casual beginnings but their disastrous ends," writes
thirty-year-old Maureen O'Connor. "We aren't the hookup generation;
we're the breakup generation."[22]

IN THE TRENCHES:
THE LEGAL DIVORCE INDUSTRY

You don't like your ex anymore; you're fighting or you're anxious or
you're hurt, enough to seriously plan getting out. That's when you come face
to face with the titans of the Divorce Industry, lawyers and their entourages.
And they're pretty intimidating.

I've been thinking for years about how marriage and divorce are evolving—or devolving—noting how drastically and swiftly the redefinition and
reconfiguration of both affect couples. I have a yellowed clipping from the
Wall Street Journal of February 12, 2003, titled "How to Plan the Perfect
Divorce." It's not about preparing the kids. It's not about lining up a friend's
couch to surf after your getaway. It's not about the emotional fallout about
to descend. It's about hiring a divorce planner.

You know, like a wedding planner, but at the other end of the marriage.

A divorce planner knows the law and financial options and can advise
on disentangling and dividing assets. Since money is probably the most
contentious aspect of divorce, an experienced planner might be the authority both parties can accept—or reject. "In an era when many people feel as
if they need a personal trainer to go to the gym and a therapist to get out of
bed, it's not much of a stretch to see where demand for divorce planners is
coming from," the article reads. "But it shows just how much divorce itself
has become an industry."

Back in 2003, organizations that trained divorce planners, like certification programs for life coaches, competed for students. Now it seems the
specialty has sorted itself out, and the generally accepted title is Certified
Divorce Financial Analyst. The Institute for Divorce Financial Analysts'
certification program requires two years' experience in the financial or legal
field and completion of four training "modules" ($450 each) capped by two

exams ($150 each). But other titles, such as Certified Financial Divorce Specialist, compete for customers,[23] and the Association of Divorce Financial Planners helps members promote their business.[24]

Your divorce planner will probably serve on a team aiming to make sure you and your parting spouse feel you received equitable shares of your holdings. As that fading *Wall Street Journal* article reports, "Divorce planners have joined the swelling ranks of investigators, forensic accountants and lawyers that couples now employ in what some call 'the exit process.'"

That process can go in many directions. My dear friend Lucy was traumatized when she was dumped by Eric, her husband of thirty-two years, but once she was convinced he would never return, she wanted to finalize the split quickly. I accompanied her as moral support when she interviewed two highly-recommended attorneys with very different approaches. First we went to the offices of a "family law" (i.e., divorce) lawyer known for her vigorous defense of women's interests. I call her Sekhmet after the Egyptian lion-headed war goddess (also known for healing), whose name means "powerful one." Renowned for her mastery of the courtroom, Sekhmet pursues a traditional "litigated divorce," preparing a case with the client, working with the ex's attorney, and ending up with a ruling by a judge. Litigated divorces don't usually go all the way to court; about 95 percent of them result in an out-of-court settlement.[25]

A tall, sturdy woman who greeted us with a firm handshake, Sekhmet was imposing in her tailored brown tweed dress and coiled scarf. Just the person you'd want in a tough negotiation. She was businesslike and to-the-point, asking about Eric's departure, their assets, and his likely requests and tactics, all the while assessing Lucy's grasp of the facts and communication style. Sekhmet ended the interview by laying out the possibilities and telling us her office would be in touch later that day.

Corinne, the receptionist, provided the warm-fuzzy component to the practice. Upon our arrival she cooed sympathy, bringing bottled water and offering a cookie. I could see how clients would feel well served here. Sekhmet exuded experience and competence, while Corinne filled in with encouragement.

In the car after our appointment, Lucy started to cry. This was the first time reality had smacked her in the head. She hadn't believed her husband could or would do this to her until she had to pay for a lawyer's consultation.

He'd moved out six months before, but she hadn't taken the pillow off his TV-watching chair. She slept on only half of the king-sized bed. She hadn't touched the clothes he said she could give away that still hung in the closet.

Lucy finally confronted moving on that afternoon with Sekhmet, the fearsome woman warrior. She realized that her husband was no longer on her side. After fathering her children, after thirty-two years of birthdays, holidays, and vacations, and after countless evenings sitting next to each other in front the television, her partner in life was now her adversary in a lawsuit.

Our second appointment was with a highly regarded expert in collaborative divorce. I'll call him Joseph, after the biblical brother sold into slavery who rose to be viceroy of Egypt. Despite the family acrimony, he was able to forgive his brethren and unite the twelve tribes. While Sekhmet emphasized strength and leadership, Joseph's goal was agreement and harmony.

Not only was he highly recommended by a lawyer friend, but his online reviews glowed. Nowadays, referrals are nice to have, but client reviews give a much fuller picture. These rating resources are themselves part of the divorce industry. Due diligence requires online investigation when choosing someone whose skill and expertise may determine your and your children's futures, but it's often difficult to evaluate the testimonials, honors, and reviews on display, which may be orchestrated by the attorneys themselves. In the midst of emotional turmoil, spending hours checking the veracity of each rating is a burden. In the end, you've got to weigh the whole of your research and pick at least two or three lawyers to interview.

Be sure to find out if the attorney charges for the initial interview. In my own survey of online evaluations, I came across a commenter complaining that a lawyer let her talk for an hour and a half, charging her by the clock, and then in the end said his approach (it happened to be collaborative) was unlikely to yield her the best outcome. She thought the attorney should have cut short her venting as soon as he suspected he wasn't the man for the job.

In addition to his favorable client reviews, Joseph had the highest Avvo rating,[26] appeared in the "best lawyer" lists, and was a peer-rated "Super Lawyer." He participated in professional associations such as the American Academy of Matrimonial Lawyers and the Academy of Professional Family Mediators.

Joseph's reception staff, like Sekhmet's, was warm and soothing. I can imagine that the anxious people coming through his door could use some patience and accommodation. When Joseph welcomed us into his private office, he offered Lucy tea and then rose to brew it himself, giving her an impression of attentiveness that would be confirmed throughout the divorce process. "Whenever Joseph saw I was anxious, he'd recognize it, and offer a countering move," Lucy recalled. "One time he suggested taking a few deep breaths, and he breathed with me. Another time, in the midst of a tense negotiation, he called a time out, as if it were for himself, and then we walked around the block together. That let me get through the emotions without breaking down in front of my ex."

Once Lucy succinctly laid out the basics of her situation, Joseph described her options for pursuing a divorce. The approach of Joseph's "collaborative practice" differs from Sekhmet's and the other four ways of handling divorce, which he explained. Here's what I gleaned. The default setting for divorce is litigation. That's what you'll get unless you actually choose a different route. Litigation may be the appropriate course in a contentious situation, but it's the most expensive and emotionally trying option. The litigants hand the decision over to the judge, who in the interest of fairness and compromise usually gives neither side all of what it wants.

The other five options, Joseph explained, involve some level of agreement between the former spouses. In a "kitchen table divorce," the spouses come up with their own plan. "This gives you total control," Joseph said, "and it's the cheapest," because you can use forms from websites like Legal-Zoom and Nolo for an uncontested, uncomplicated settlement that you can file yourself.[27] "But you have the least professional support," Joseph added. A do-it-yourself divorce might be right for a short marriage with no children and few assets to separate. To insure everything's proper, each party could hire a lawyer by the hour to review the documents.

The other out-of-court option involves the spouses, their lawyers, and a variety of support professionals—perhaps a financial advisor, a child psychologist, and a "divorce coach"—who together produce a settlement that both sides accept. Of course, the more hours of professional services provided, the higher the expense. But avoiding court, with its protocols, delays, and filings, may be the biggest saving.

Joseph moved on to the third option, mediation, in which a neutral mediator hired by the couple (or their lawyers) "keeps the conversation on track." The mediator can't give legal advice, so the parties consult attorneys as the process unfolds. Mediation sessions are confidential, and depending on what both parties want, may or may not include the spouses' lawyers. "Compliance is higher if the parties agree to the conditions," Joseph noted. He said mediation is successful 85 percent of the time; when it fails, you have to start over.

Then he described the type of resolution process he uses, collaborative divorce. Each side has an attorney, whose goal is to reach agreement, "not to later go to court." The lawyers who engage in this type of process receive special training to "focus on what's important to the parties." As in mediation, the content of collaborative meetings is confidential, and all the information used for decision-making is provided by the divorcing partners.

Of course, that leaves room for fudging. If one partner wants to hide assets or credit cards or purchases, he or she may not be a good candidate for this method, as it relies on a level of supervised trust. Supervised, as the lawyers know what to ask for and have an idea what to expect.

It's more expensive than mediation, Joseph explained, because "the professionals need to prepare to be able to work together," and his practice relies on a team approach, working with both a financial coach and divorce coach. Each team member's job is to oversee his area of expertise to minimize hold-ups.

The remaining two options are more likely to require a court decision if they're ultimately unsuccessful. "Attorney settlement" leaves the two attorneys to represent their clients and come to an agreement, without the spouses present. Joseph says in such situations "the clients' values are not always forefront, as the attorneys are also considering the court's values." He says that the cost of attorney settlement is comparable to that of collaborative divorce.

The final option is what Joseph called a "settlement conference," in which both sides—attorneys and clients—are separated. This arrangement might be required when one party is manipulative or when a history of abuse makes joint negotiation uncomfortable. A neutral go-between carries communication from one side to the other. "There's formalized information-getting," Joseph explained. "It's very expensive, and usually ends up being a preparation for court."

Most lawyers charge between $250 and $450 per hour, and each spouse usually engages separate representation, so the costs of divorce mount quickly. Even a paralegal's time is likely to be billed at fifty to a hundred dollars per hour.[28] You might be able to arrange a flat fee for a relatively simple, uncontested divorce, but the likelihood of knowing the total cost in advance diminishes as the case becomes more complex. And divorce cases do tend to be more, not less, complex than expected. Many attorneys require a retainer, an up-front fee, to ensure that they get paid if the divorce divides and depletes the couple's funds.

Its high cost makes the legal segment of the divorce industry more a deterrent than an attraction to divorce. Couples usually engage their services only after the *Sturm und Drang* result in a firm decision to split. If the prospect of lawsuits, halving your accounts, and making custody plans fills you with fear and anxiety, as it should, this might be a good time to take steps to avoid them. Better to do everything you can to solve your problems—improve communication and diffuse hostilities—even if therapy is costly, than to enter the legal funnel toward divorce.

Lucy's decree took about ten months. Her husband dragged his feet in providing some of the financial paperwork he promised. He attended a convention for two weeks. Each delay left Lucy frustrated, but she was glad Eric agreed to a collaborative process instead of the more rancorous litigation scenario. Their kids were grown, but they had a home they'd built together. Lucy hadn't worked for a decade, and she doubted she'd find another magazine editing position that paid enough to be worthwhile. Their problems were complicated by her husband losing his job and finding a replacement at only two-thirds of his prior salary.

Eric finally gathered all his records, and Lucy received a foot-high stack of files from the forensic CPA. "The financial advisor was good and thorough," Lucy recalled. "Everything was transparent. I found out Eric had seven charge cards I didn't know about. I found line items for phone charges that shocked me."

After the accountant and Joseph hammered out Lucy's demands, she and Eric met alone with the divorce coach, who prepared them for the collaborative proceedings. "She explained how we should behave in the meetings, how we should comport ourselves," Lucy said.

Finally the first bi-monthly conference with the two attorneys, two coaches, and the couple coalesced. Lucy met Eric's attorney. "I felt so sorry for her," Lucy sighed. "She was a genuinely nice person, so sympathetic to me. She said, 'I'm so sorry you have to be going through this.' I thought to myself, Eric has chosen a woman he can intimidate."

"Everyone was so aware of how hard it was for me," Lucy remembered. "I felt very supported by everyone except Eric. Throughout the negotiations, Eric acted like he wanted to be anywhere else. He'd arrive late and bolt at the end. No 'good-bye,' just outta there."

Each meeting had an agenda and goals. "The whole experience was transparent, and it was helpful to have professionals there, guiding us. At one point Joseph took me outside and said, 'Lucy, you have to take a stand and tell Eric what you really want.'" Lucy quivers at the thought. "I was so nervous that Joseph and I went into another office and role-played what I should say." At one point, Eric wanted to delay the next meeting so he could go on vacation. "Joseph put his foot down and said that would be prolonging my pain, and Eric backed off," Lucy said.

When the last of the forms had been signed, Lucy felt a mix of relief, sadness, and accomplishment. "At that last meeting, Eric shook hands with his attorney and my attorney. I was thinking it was business, so I stuck out my hand, too. Eric shook it, but didn't say 'thank you.'"

She remembered feeling she deserved a reward for completing the process. "I went across the street, where there was a party store," she smiled. "I bought myself a vase and wanted a particular balloon on display. The clerk said they were out of uninflated ones, but when I told her what I'd just been through, she gave the one they had to me free, saying 'Have a nice life.'"

I include these descriptions of the divorce process so you know what you're in for under the best circumstances. Every divorce is different. Some are acrimonious and result in permanent alienation. In others, the spouses plod through the steps, and the process ends up more sad than complicated. But the divorce process is never easy—not even the kitchen table variety, where you're just splitting up wedding gifts. It's always a reminder of hopes dashed, the uncertainty of emotions, and the (often volitional) fickleness of commitment.

Why Not Divorce: Reasons to Avoid a Split

CHAPTER 5

Hazardous to Your Health

Divorce for many seems like liberation. If your marriage has grown stale and lifeless, a chance to start over and find someone new sounds appealing, even compelling. At least until you consider all the ways that divorce hurts you and the people you care about, especially your children.

If you're thinking, "I deserve to be happy. My life is ticking away in this unsatisfying relationship, and I'm wasting precious time I could be spending with someone better," you're pretty typical. That "YOLO" (you only live once) mentality gets plenty of people in trouble, and it could lead you to the biggest mistake of your life.

The good news if you divorce is that you'll have lots of music to listen to—especially if you like country-western. Nothing seems to inspire song-writers like the pain of splitting up. Your divorce playlist will have to include Tammy Wynette's classic "D-I-V-O-R-C-E":

Our little boy is four years old and quite a little man
So we spell out the words we don't want him to understand,

Like T-O-Y or maybe S-U-R P-R-I-S-E.
But the words we're hiding from him now
Tear the heart right out of me.
Our D-I-V-O-R-C-E becomes final today.
Me and little J-O-E will be goin' away.
I love you both and this will be pure H-E double-L for me.
Oh, I wish that we could stop this D-I-V-O-R-C-E.

Reba McEntire's and Kenny Chesney's duet "Every Other Weekend," about a couple's regular rendezvous to swap their kids, evokes the pain of a sundered family, even with joint custody:

Every other Friday
It's toys and clothes in backpacks.
Is everybody in okay?
Let's go see Dad.
Same time in the same spot,
Corner of the same old parking lot,
Half the hugs and kisses there are always sad.
We trade a couple words and looks
And kids again
Every other weekend.

And what do we learn from our musical interlude? That divorce breaks your heart, costs a bundle, and makes you angry, and that songs about this suffering resonate with enough people to put them in the top-forty charts.

But you already knew that. What you may dismiss while concentrating on the liberation and new beginnings that make divorce appealing are its long-term wounds. Researchers have identified myriad harms, but in the next three chapters I'm going to focus on what it does to your health, finances, and emotions.

We intuitively expect divorce to damage health, and sure enough, loads of studies demonstrate that it does. "Going through a divorce" suggests little sleep, crying jags, anxiety attacks, antagonism toward your soon-to-be ex, big lawyer bills, faking sanity for the kids, and the physical ordeal of packing up and moving out. "Going through a divorce" tells a sad tale of two people who once loved each other turning their backs on that shared past. It implies a winner and a loser, one person crushed and rejected and another callously striding off lustily into the sunset, probably toward a beckoning lover.

Aside from the punishing physical effects of little sleep, poor diet, anguish, and stress, divorce invites dire diseases and can even hasten death. Yes, divorce enables you to select your partner for the next dance, but he could be the Grim Reaper.

Two gigantic meta-analyses from 2012, synthesizing information about millions of people, found a substantially greater chance of death among divorcees than among persons in other marital groups. Researchers from the University of Arizona, working from thirty-two studies covering 6.5 million people, found that divorcées had a 23 percent greater chance of dying during the survey periods; for men the risk was even greater, 31 percent.[1] The second study, from McGill University, included every piece of research ever done on the topic, covering *six hundred million* subjects. You read that right—six hundred million—and the results were even more emphatic: divorced people had a 30 percent higher chance of dying (from all causes) than their married or single counterparts during the survey periods, and the mortality risk for divorced *men* was a whopping 37 percent higher than for other men.[2]

If such statistics give you palpitations, divorcing is worse for your ticker, especially if you're female. A 2015 study from Duke University followed a representative sample of 15,827 people between the ages of forty-five and eighty, about a third of whom had experienced divorce. After controlling for age, race and ethnicity, obesity, high blood pressure, smoking, alcohol consumption, and other risk factors, once-divorced women had a 24 percent higher risk of heart of attack than the never-divorced. And twice-divorced women had a 77 percent higher risk of heart attack than the continuously married. Men divorced once had the same risk as their married counterparts, but with a second divorce, their risk was 30 percent greater.[3]

And when a heart attack strikes, divorced people are more likely to die from it. A 2016 British study of twenty-five thousand patients' medical records found that, controlling for age and sex, divorced heart attack victims were 21 percent less likely to survive than married patients and 7 percent less likely to make it than single victims. Divorced survivors required one more day in the hospital than the non-divorced before they were well enough to go home.[4]

In fact, the tense, hurtful, and angry process of divorce produces "a whole package of awful events," says Linda Waite of the University of Chicago, the author of a 2009 study following 8,652 people over time. Those who went through spousal death or divorce "reported about 20% more chronic health problems like heart disease, diabetes and cancer, compared with those who had been continuously married." And the vulnerability lasts. "The study showed that most married people who became single never fully recovered from the physical declines associated with marital loss," Dr. Waite writes, even if they remarried.[5]

One physical effect of divorce might be welcome—losing weight. Lawrence, a thirty-four-year-old, was admittedly spoiled by his wife, Anna. While not verbally expressive, she showed her love by cooking. And Lawrence ate it up. She made eggs Benedict with hollandaise and lasagna oozing with mozzarella. She made fried chicken, and she could bake—flourless chocolate cake, cinnamon babka, and cream cheese Danish.

What Anna couldn't communicate was that she wanted Lawrence to respect and appreciate her. He was happy in his career heading a children's soccer association, attending matches, getting together with colleagues, and occasionally traveling to give speeches or awards. Anna, a painter who worked at home, wanted Lawrence to choose their five-year-old daughter, Sophia, over his usual Sunday activity practicing with a garage bluegrass band. He played banjo like Earl Scruggs, and the group would gear up for a yearly festival in July. By the time he got home every Sunday, Lawrence was pooped.

But there'd be a nice bowl of risotto.

They entered counseling, but it was unsuccessful. Lawrence claimed he "tried everything the therapist said," but Anna wanted out. Lawrence was forty pounds heavier than on their wedding day eleven years before. Moving out was tough, especially because he missed seeing his adorable Sophia in the mornings and at bedtime, which had been his main points of contact. He felt like a college student setting up in an apartment with just a few pieces Anna could spare.

But at the same time, most of his life continued in its previous pattern. He'd go to work, play banjo, listen to music, and drop by to see his daughter. It dawned on him that when he got through with the divorce, he could start dating.

When a colleague saw him at a talk three months later, he did a double-take. "What happened to *you?*" Lawrence grinned. "It's called the Divorce Diet. It's real simple. You consume only two things: beer and ice cream." And that's what Lawrence had in his fridge. India pale ale and rum raisin Häagen-Dazs. But he started lifting weights and he was looking good. Maybe his arteries weren't so pleased, but Lawrence was young enough not to notice.

Leaving aside his character flaws and insensitivity, Lawrence is pretty typical of guys who get divorced when it comes to diet. A British study compared the health of 5,788 middle-aged couples at two points, 3.6 years apart, including their consumption of eleven fruits and twenty-six vegetables (more veggies in greater variety are healthier). Women continued eating the same way whether they stayed married or became widowed, divorced, or separated, but separated and divorced men's diets went seriously downhill.[6]

Divorce often causes sleepless nights, and if insomnia persists it can jack up your blood pressure. The psychologist David Sbarra led a University of Arizona study that followed 138 people who had separated or divorced sixteen weeks before, monitoring their sleep and blood pressure. Sleep problems are "probably pretty normal" after separation, Dr. Sbarra says, but he found that if it continued ten weeks, blood pressure began to rise. When that happens, Dr. Sbarra warns, "there seems to be a cumulative bad effect." He adds that "sleep problems that persist for an extended period may mean that people are potentially becoming depressed, that they're struggling with getting their life going again, and it is these people that are particularly susceptible to health problems."[7]

One of the more unusual health problems that divorce can trigger is Munchausen syndrome by proxy (MSBP), in which a parent, usually a mother (who was likely abused as a child herself), fakes her young child's physical illness to get sympathy and attention, to manipulate her ex, or because she just can't face or accept the divorce. Though I'm a psychologist, I had never come across MSBP (also called "Fictitious Disorder Syndrome") until I read Edward Farber's *Raising the Kid You Love with the Ex You Hate.*[8] Patients with this disorder have been known to deceive doctors by adding blood to a urine test, heating a thermometer, giving drugs to make a child vomit or have diarrhea, and making up lab results. It's both a mental illness and child abuse.[9] What a pathetic reaction to divorce. But rejection and disruption can cause some serious and in this case bizarre repercussions.

CHAPTER 6

"I Got the Shaft": The Financial Cost of Divorce

Financially, divorce is a lose-lose proposition.

Returning to our post-divorce playlist for just a minute, you might find this selection illuminating. These words of warning come from Jimmy Reed in a 1982 hit song:

> She got the gold mine,
> I got the shaft!
> They split it right down the middle,
> And then they give her the better half.
> Well, it all sounds sorta funny,
> But it hurts too much to laugh.
> She got the gold mine, I got the shaft!

When researchers probe the leading cause of arguments that lead to divorce, money is always number one. A 2012 study of longitudinal data on 4,574 couples from the National Survey of Families and Households found that financial disagreements were the strongest predictors of divorce.[1]

Interestingly, if you're wearing a big rock on your finger, your marriage is more likely to end in divorce. A 2015 Emory University study found an inverse correlation between the amount spent on the ring and ceremony and the length of the marriage. Grooms who spent between two and four thousand dollars on the ring were 1.3 times as likely to divorce as guys who paid between five hundred and two thousand dollars, and couples whose weddings cost more than twenty thousand dollars divorced 3.5 times as often as those who spent five to ten thousand dollars.[2]

Arguments about finances could come from a clash in the way each of you relates to money. According to a representative 2015 Harris poll, among married or cohabiting persons who reported relationship stress, money led the list of causes (35 percent), followed by annoying habits (25 percent). Even if finances didn't inflame the couple, spouses didn't sync when labeling themselves the "savers" or "spenders" of the duo. Thirty-four percent claimed they were the "savers," while only 13 percent admitted they were the "spenders." And nearly half of the respondents said they differed from their spouses in the way they spend.[3] If you're diverging about money before you separate, when you're forced to divide your assets, the scene may be less than copacetic.

I have already described the variety of professionals queued up to help you through your divorce—empathetically, ethically, properly, and kindheartedly, while sucking your bank account dry. Each one of these professionals—attorneys, divorce coaches, forensic accountants, child psychiatrists, private detectives, therapists, mediators, paralegals, auditors, appraisers, and more—charges his respective and respectable fee. Sometimes you'll need a matched set—two lawyers or two accountants, for example—and sometimes a judge may require you to hire more professionals than you'd expected. The more stuff you've accumulated and the more contentious the parting, the more it'll cost you.

PUT IT IN PERSPECTIVE: CELEBRITY SETTLEMENTS

When a rich celebrity wants out, the fortune dispensed to an ex-spouse is merely collateral damage. Unfortunately, reading about these enormous awards affects your own view, even as you're waving it off with "Oh, that's not reality, that's Hollywood." Their breakup battles seem like fantasy, but even though actors and producers receive astronomical paychecks, the suffering of these spouses and their children is as real as anyone else's. Their divorce awards may seem beyond comprehension, but news coverage of each of these splits, simply *because* of the sums and famous personalities involved, reinforces the perception that divorce is everywhere and worth multi-millions of dollars to attain. The headlines on the supermarket tabloids seep into your soul and have an effect.

Think about the impression the following figures, gleaned from my survey of six websites covering the most expensive business or Hollywood divorces, makes on you. I offer them here to highlight the way influential media sell their products at the expense of our values.

Former Governor of California Arnold Schwarzenegger's sordid affair with the family housekeeper, carried on under the nose of his TV reporter wife, Maria Shriver, is speculated to have cost him approximately $200 million.[4]

Newspaper mogul Rupert Murdoch—now married to Mick Jagger's ex, Jerry Hall—famously paid record amounts to dissolve two of his four marriages. In 1999, after thirty-two years of marriage and three children, he paid Anna Maria Torv $1.7 billion, at that time the highest settlement recorded. Seventeen days later he married intern-translator Wendy Deng, thirty-eight years his junior. The union dissolved after fourteen years and two daughters in a reported $1.8 billion settlement.[5]

The year 2011 wasn't so great for actor-director Mel Gibson. Shortly after his wife of thirty-one years and mother of his seven children, Robyn Denise Moore, won a divorce settlement of $425 million, audio of a racist rave against his girlfriend Oksana Grigorieva, mother of his toddler daughter, Lucia, went viral.[6]

When Kelsey Grammer, of *Frasier* fame, and his actress wife, Camille, split in early 2011 after thirteen years of marriage, she got half of their sixty million dollar pot.[7]

Sir Paul McCartney divorced the skier-model Heather Mills in 2008 after four years of marriage and a daughter, Beatrice, paying a $48 million settlement.[8]

Harrison Ford finalized his divorce from the *ET* screenwriter Melissa Mathison in 2004 after twenty-one years of marriage and two children, paying a sum reported at between $85 and $112 million.[9]

Singer Madonna was the rare wife whose fortune exceeded her husband's at divorce. After eight years and two children (one adopted) with singer Guy Ritchie, the pop idol paid "between $76 and $92 million" when her marriage didn't meet her expectations.[10]

I'm sure every famous pair's split has its own sad tale, but let's concentrate on the exchange of funds. In the nine "community property" states, including California, where most entertainment couples live, assets must be split equally. When the love in a relationship vanishes, the generosity that once motivated a wealthy celebrity to throw a lavish wedding and share his income often gives way to a bitter determination to withhold it, increasing acrimony and vindictiveness. The gripping but nasty details of high-stakes divorces splashed all over the tabloids lining every supermarket check-out line send two messages: (1) No marriage, not even the fairy-tale romances of stars and magnates, is immune to divorce, and (2) Given the size of these settlements, getting out of an unhappy marriage is worth paying everything you own.

"RIPPING YOUR HEART OUT THROUGH YOUR WALLET"

The late actor-comedian Robin Williams, who parted with $20 million in two divorce settlements, left us with a vivid description of the cost of a marital break-up: "Divorce is expensive. I used to joke they were going to call it 'all the money,' but they changed it to 'alimony.' It's ripping your heart out through your wallet."[11]

The image of "ripping your heart out through your wallet" combines the emotional agony of the parting with the pain of carving up the assets you have worked to build. The financial impact of divorce is not only the loss of assets by one party or the other; it's the crude and cruel reduction of emotion, history, and hopes into numbers on a legal pad. A wife who has borne children—perhaps even at risk to her life—doesn't get her stretch-mark-free body back. A partner who built up a business and must sell it comes away with half its sale price but none of the sweat equity of planning, expanding, and strengthening its brand.

Underlying the dollars-and-cents cost of divorce is distress that your onetime partner in building your family's wealth has become the force demolishing it. If you're now feeling distant from or disgusted by your spouse, once you start negotiating for your share, those feelings amplify and harden, even if you ardently desire "good divorce" amicability.

If one of you was more clearly the "breadwinner," the lower-earning spouse becomes the *inferior* spouse when the wealth is split. Offering a settlement, alimony, and even child support seems like an act of generosity to the richer one, as you count and divvy remuneration for work in the marketplace. On the other hand, the value of running a household, raising children, and other intangible but essential contributions to the couple and family, which can't be quantified, may be forgotten or appear worthless.

Juls Carter, a financial advisor for RBC Wealth Management in Seattle, notes that one partner in the marriage usually manages the family finances. "If that's the person pushing for the divorce," she tells me, "the other person often feels he has no control, and becomes suspicious that the departing spouse isn't fairly dividing the assets." She often sees "anger from the rejected one, who feels all this thrust upon him against his will. He's the victim of a process ripping away half of his world." A tug-of-war over money complicates the divorce, infusing distrust and sometimes extra cost, with demands for audit by a forensic accountant.

Often there's a sudden awakening by the spouse who trusted the other with the finances. "I've seen cases where one is surprised by debts he didn't know about, especially credit cards that deplete joint savings, reducing the amount the left-behind spouse receives," Carter explains. "Suddenly this person who was your ally is the enemy."

Most couples, however, work sedulously to smooth the division of their assets. "In my own case last year," Carter confides, "my ex and I were pretty equal in the amounts we contributed to the marriage." They strove to save the marriage for the sake of their six-year-old daughter. Two years of pastoral counseling failed after a blow-up. "Once he understood that we couldn't put the marriage back together, we could move forward into 'OK, now we've got to get some papers signed.'" She poignantly describes the period in which she prepared to leave: "I was an actress for six months. I wasn't going to move out until I had everything lined up, so our daughter's life would be least disrupted. That meant that I had to hold back my feelings and act like everything was just fine around her. That was the hardest part of the whole process."

The contraction of your standard of living and your horizons that often accompany divorce exacerbates the anguish you're already feeling. As the divorce rate was peaking in the early 1980s, the experts debated about how much women suffer financially from divorce. Lenore Weitzman got in hot water for asserting in her 1985 book *The Divorce Revolution* that women's standard of living drops by a whopping 73 percent while men's increases by 42 percent.[12] That didn't sit well with divorce-boosters (i.e., the already-exes), and in 1996 a re-analysis of her data, which had been collected in 1977, substantially lowered those figures. Nevertheless, women's standard of living *still* plummeted by 27 percent, while men's rose by 10 percent.[13] You might say yes, but that was then, this is now. Opportunities for women have opened up further, and employers have become more family-friendly since 1996. Even so, women who divorce still find their fortunes notably reduced, and now *men do as well.*

Noting that "[s]tudy after study has shown that divorced women fare poorly economically in both absolute terms and when compared with divorced men," researchers at the University of Michigan evaluated two "waves" of data from the National Survey of Families and Households (1988 and 1992–1994). "The Michigan study confirmed that staying married would have prevented [the] monetary decline" of the women studied and that women's "economic well-being" nosedives after divorce.[14]

An economist found in 2005 that "divorce reduces a person's wealth by about three-quarters compared to that of a single person, while being married almost doubles comparative wealth." In other words, a married person's monetary worth is double a single person's—but a divorced person's worth is just a quarter of *that*. The differences are mind-boggling. Bank accounts start declining a few years before the actual divorce, and by the time of the decree, there's much less than before the union deteriorated. "If you really want to increase your wealth, get married and stay married," says the study author. "On the other hand, divorce can devastate your wealth."[15]

For women with children, marriage improves financial prospects, whether they marry a minimum-wage restaurant worker or a CEO. The work of Robert Lerman of the Urban Institute suggests that because of economies of scale, at every point on the income continuum marriage produces a higher standard of living than living alone or as a single mom. "Even after taking account of much of the observed and unobserved difference among mothers, being in a married state appears to add substantially to living standards, not only relative to single parents living alone but also compared to mothers in cohabiting relationships or single parents living with other adult relatives." By contrast, divorce shatters the platform of support, casting women into an economic crevasse.[16]

A business-section headline in my Seattle newspaper laments a situation that Juls Carter sees frequently: "Mercer Island woman finds out she's financially lost after divorce." Pam Charney, fifty-seven, applied to the paper for a free "financial makeover" after her divorce six months before. "Like a lost sailor who couldn't read a nautical chart, she was unaware of her financial condition and unfamiliar with the mechanics of money management."[17] Maybe so, but she was in a good position without debt and flush with the proceeds from the sale of the family home. Most people's ledgers are more complicated—or they choose to make them that way in the retaliatory spiral of divorce.

Carter tells me about an organized wife fed up with her flighty, sometimes addicted husband. "She just wanted to be finished with him," but he drew out the process by disappearing for several days at a time, moving back into her house saying he had nowhere else to go, and then playing her friends against her in retribution for being dumped. Disentangling their lives took two hellish years, during which their two young children were confused and at times distraught.

"The husband's antics made designing and then signing a financial agreement so much more difficult, which might have been his desire," Carter recalls. "He didn't want to go and didn't want her to stop loving him—even though he kept doing things to push her away and undermine any affection she once had." Divorce often brings out the worst in people, especially when one party is scorned, and withholding money or prolonging the process are favorite weapons.

CHAPTER 7

Bad for Your Spirit

Your health, your finances, and especially your psyche suffer when you divorce—and the marks are indelible. Emotional disorders often play out in the body, affecting it for months or years, and sometimes forever.

The author of *Splitopia*, Wendy Paris, makes a valiant effort to justify her book's subtitle, *Dispatches from Today's Good Divorce and How to Part Well*. But it's hard to find anything "good" or "well" in her own experiences and the cases she describes. The anxiety of her split brought on internal bleeding and a hospital stay. When she discovered her ex was seeing someone else, she fell apart:

> I was heading for a crisis. I could feel it coming on. I thought about people I'd spoken to who'd had real breakdowns. A man in Ohio had told me about a crushing depression after his wife left. His dog of sixteen years died the following week. He couldn't sleep, couldn't rise in the morning.... Finally a therapist prescribed an antidepressant and group therapy.

So Ms. Paris decided to try a support group. But as she listened to other people's stories, her thoughts returned to her ex. "I knew he was heading to a romantic date in the city, perhaps to take her to another party with our mutual friends, then return to her place to have sex, sleep in. He'd bring her coffee as he'd once brought it to me."

The memes of the mind are relentless and brutal. They recycle in sinister circles, engraving the agony. Wendy Paris was the one instigating the divorce, and yet she could not let go.

> I felt like one of the harrier, more aggressive primates, like an orangutan perhaps—raging, free-ranging fury. I went down to the pier to lope through the grass like an orangutan, thinking maybe that would exorcise my anger, this ripped-to-shreds feeling, this desire to rip something else apart. It was Orangutan Therapy I'd just invented, a version of scream therapy.
>
> It didn't work. I felt like an orangutan who needed a nap.[1]

I should note that Ms. Paris eventually got through her intense, animalistic phase, and she advises her readers about what to expect and how to make the most of life post-divorce. But alarming and disabling emotional obstacles like hers are to be avoided, not chosen.

Ending a marriage may trigger feelings of bereavement. If a partner leaves to pursue an exciting affair that subsumes everything in a glitter of sexual ecstasy, the one left behind gets to wallow in grief and rejection alone—unless she's overwhelmed taking care of upset children, shuttling them everywhere herself, and keeping the home running, all the while running up a tab of rage against the jerk who pitched his family like a bag of trash.

Then there's nighttime. You can't escape the quiet hours when everyone else is asleep and you should be too, except that you're playing that morbid meme in your brain. Maybe you're answering all his exit lines, wondering if you might have said something to change his mind. Or you're worrying about the finances, how you'll pay the bills you never had to pay yourself. You can sit up watching comedies, but then there's the scene where the couple catch each other's eyes as one is darting from the elevator and—whoops—you're choking on tears again.

Now, you might say that staying in your marriage wouldn't be much better. You might feel "dead inside," as many report before bolting. You might be on edge, pondering if being free of your spouse will allow you some peace as the memories of nights like tonight begin to recede.

But remember two things. First, we carry our problems with us. You can't just dump them at the threshold as you cross into singledom. You're the same person with the same cast of characters in your life, even if they've rearranged and deranged you. Unless you work on the problems that brought you to divorce, they'll continue to plague you and your children, if not your partner now that he or she is separate. But your partner is never separate if you've got children to bind you. Divorce hurts you emotionally, and slapping on some iodine and Band-Aids can't heal a broken spirit.

Second, being single brings its own demands and problems. If you ever hope to find a stepparent for your child as well as a truly loving marriage for yourself, you'll have to navigate a minefield of emotions for yourself and your family. The logistics alone become a tiresome chore. If your children are grown, you may be freed from many responsibilities, but you're alone both in daily living and when picking through the "goods" in the marriage marketplace, most of whom have their own families and problems and emotions from their complicated pasts.

Men and women may respond differently to the emotional pain of divorce. A 2003 study identified three ways in which men's mourning over divorce differs from women's—*when* (men begin to mourn later), their *focus* (on losing home and children rather than the wife), and *how* (men mourn through actions rather than words or emotional displays). Men's less demonstrative way of grieving doesn't mean their pain is less acute.[2] There's no escaping some degree of mourning, even if you're the one initiating the split.

And of course, divorce is depressing. Sixty percent of those with a history of clinical depression suffer a debilitating bout of it when they divorce, though only 10 percent of those who have never experienced depression begin their first bout with the decree.[3]

Situational depression can creep up with the most excusable of symptoms. You become absent-minded, misplacing your car keys. You forget to eat, since your stomach's tied up in knots. You have no patience, snapping when someone's in your way. You have a tough time falling asleep or staying asleep. Or perhaps you sleep the day away and find yourself staring at the computer screen thoughtlessly. Any of these irritating symptoms may mean little by itself, but combined they may signal depression.

Women are more susceptible than men. When Nicole forgot to pick up her son at preschool, she was embarrassed, but when it happened a second time, she got worried. With her mediation coming up, she needed to gather her receipts, but she couldn't bring herself to get started. She hated her new apartment, with half the furniture from her house and a neighbor who kept banging his car door into hers. Some days everything was an irritant, and some days everything was meaningless.

She worked at a real estate office, opening the place at seven in the morning so she could pick up her son at 3:30, but what was the point of sitting in that place so long every day? What was the point when her husband had just decided one day to take a job writing code for a competitor sixty miles away and didn't want her to move with him?

Riddled with hurt and confusion and saddled with more tasks than ever, Nicole fell apart. She'd start crying suddenly when she'd hear a snippet of a song or for no reason. Just sobbing. She'd try to pull it together around four-year-old Jacob, but sometimes couldn't even muster the try. "Mommy, I'll protect you," Jacob offered when he caught her weeping one morning. That made her cry some more.

Nicole's mom started picking up Jacob from preschool, and she brought homemade tacos and salad. That helped feed Jacob, but Nicole didn't find anything appetizing. Finally her father insisted she see a doctor. Thin and wan with bags under her eyes, she didn't bother to return phone calls. Her dad made the appointment and drove her to the doctor. Nicole knew she was depressed but felt she just needed to wade through it. She couldn't see the effect it was having on her health and on Jacob, who felt helpless and protective at the same time.

Luckily, Nicole had watchful and caring parents who spoke with the doctor and filled her prescription. Depression can be light or debilitating. Mental health professionals can recognize the symptoms of clinical depression, which include depressed mood, loss of interest in pleasure, changes in weight, sleep irregularities, agitation or withdrawal, loss of energy, depressive or suicidal thoughts, and difficulty concentrating, each symptom occurring frequently or for a prolonged period.[4]

Depression can result from or contribute to divorce, but proper treatment is essential. Widespread but uninformed views to the contrary, depression is not a personal weakness.[5] Given the success rate for medications for depression, it's clear that physical, chemical changes directly affect depression.

In marriage, it's not depression that causes problems but the behaviors that result if it goes untreated or is poorly contained. Most medications require several weeks to kick in, and some have side effects, but the unreported story is how beneficial these drugs usually are.[6]

DIVORCE AND YOUR VALUES

Marriage, the most intimate and consequential human relationship, establishes elaborate connections of law, kinship, and affection. Divorce pulls all that apart. No wonder the wounds are so deep and take so long to heal. In my practice, I usually find that it takes half as long as the relationship's duration for exes to reach *indifference*, midway between desire and love at one end and revilement and hatred at the other, the point where peace can return. That's a lengthy process, made more difficult by every instance of contact between the spouses.

Divorce hurts you emotionally, no doubt, but it also hurts *who you are*. Actually, that's a good question to ask: *Who do you think you are?*

Are you an honest person? Are you a sensitive person? Are you one who is considerate of others' feelings? Do you see yourself as responsible? Are you an open, transparent soul? Are you reliable? Are you kind? If you're like most people, you answer "yes" to these questions. You honor the Ten Commandments and obey the law. You pay your taxes and vote.

But what kind of employee are you? What kind of parent? What kind of spouse? These are the roles in which you actualize these abstract virtues. If you're an honest person, then you behave honestly, not fudging or stretching the truth, and certainly never saying anything you know to be untrue. Admittedly, everyone tells a fib now and then. Asked their age or weight, most women demur...or underestimate. Telling a story, we might exaggerate for effect—like the fisherman describing the one that got away. The "poker face" is a practiced bluff, a hiding of feelings. Is that dishonesty?

Some people are very uncomfortable telling a lie. Their faces flush. They stutter. They squirm. The ends of their mouths curl.

If your marriage is fading, you might distance yourself from your spouse and employ the dishonesty of omission. You might not mention whom you had lunch with. You might not bring up your plans for the day your partner's got a conference. If you and your spouse are distant, you might start acting less like the person you want to be and more like "that guy" who's mean or snarky or disrespectful. The one who seems like a misogynist or a shrew, a bully or a bitch.

And of course in cases of infidelity, there's outright lying, destroying trust, which is the basis of marriage. Adulterers sneak around, check their pockets and purses, erase things from their cell phones. Sometimes that excitement and the creativity in eluding detection make the affair more attractive. But what does it do to your soul? An anonymous essay offers one woman's answer:

> The first time you cheat is filled with nervous energies and hesitant movements. It's exhilarating and scary and new.
>
> The second time is intoxicating. So is the third. It's passionate and off-limits and for some reason, that makes it all that better.
>
> The fourth time is when the guilt starts to kick in. It's gone from excitement and passion to secret texts and sex in the backseat of a car in an empty high school parking lot.
>
> The fifth time is the first time you say it's the last time. It's the first time you say this, so you believe it.
>
> The sixth time is when you begin to understand just how little power you have over your own actions. It's when you realize just how bad a situation you've gotten yourself into.
>
> The seventh time is when you realize that there's no point keeping track. You're officially doing something you swore you'd never do. You're cheating.[7]

One of the comments posted in response to that essay is especially insightful:

When the guilt kicks in, this means eroticism has peaked and is now in decline. Shame and fear replace that erotic intoxication with the frenzy of naughty coupling in transgression. Being wrong becomes being right. Your ethical compass is destroyed. You lie more easily to all.

This is when the couple start saying "I love you" all through secret dinners and sex. Love you love you love you. There is no other discourse just the vacuous chanting of this self-justifying mantra. Self-damaging behavior grows as you lie, not only to others, but to yourself. Your self-deception eases the guilt and over-rates the intimacy. Your integrity is destroyed. With honesty already gone, time to quit and rebuild your life. Start with your moral compass so you may become whole again, one person.

In divorce, your moral compass goes akimbo. Even if fidelity is not the issue, you start speaking in terms and tones you'd never use around others, even people who know you intimately, like your sister or your best friend. Your irritation descends into disgust or anger, and your effect in the marriage becomes unfriendly and standoffish. It gets even worse when you actually separate. The desire to secure your share of the assets can quickly lead you to even lower levels of turpitude.

Jeff Landers, a divorce planner, describes the dirty tricks many husbands employ to deprive their wives and children of their wealth.[8] "Conflicting out" attorneys is the way a husband will make sure his wife doesn't hire any of the most aggressive lawyers in town. All he has to do is make appointments with the top guns, telling them his side of the dispute. He hires only one, but all the rest are disqualified from representing the wife because the earlier consultation with the husband raised a conflict of interest.

A nasty husband can "stall and delay" by repeatedly rescheduling court dates and appointments, adding to his wife's expenses and attorneys' fees in the hope of pressing her to accept a less favorable settlement just to finish the deal. On the other hand, a husband might do the opposite, pushing for a hasty settlement before she finds out what he's hiding.

Landers warns that a scoundrel who has handled the family finances solo might "ensure that only he can access family funds," which lets him "cut off his wife's credit cards and move funds out of family accounts." This is common in cases of physical abuse, where a retaliatory husband deprives his wife of the cash to hire her own attorney or even to sustain herself. Some men defy the law, retaining assets or failing to pay alimony or child support, "and they force their wives to try to extract the promised payments at considerable legal cost long after the divorce is over.... [E]ven when a woman follows requirements to the letter, and even for a well-meaning judge, deception on the part of an ex-husband can be difficult to decipher or prove." So the jerks prevail.

You might assume that these heels behaved just as badly during the marriage, that their trickery caused or contributed to the divorce. That's undoubtedly true in some cases, but the desire to stockpile riches brings out the worst side of men who might have channeled that competitive urge into benign interests like sports or business or even into beneficial efforts like conquering homelessness or religious outreach. Divorce can turn a man into a ruthless predator by making his wife and family his adversaries.

Are you that guy?

Eugene seemed so pious, attending church every day, teaching Bible classes, donating to charity. An epidemiologist at a university, married twenty years with two teenagers, he came across as quiet and unassuming. But that was the exterior. His private life in the man-cave of his home's basement featured hours watching porn and smoking marijuana. Occasionally, he'd employ call girls.

Which one was the "real" Eugene? He would say he was a decent man who helped a lot of people. His "bad habits" harmed no one but himself. "Appreciating" women was a hobby that didn't affect the way he treated the women he knew. And when his shocked wife, Mary, caught him watching obscene videos on his laptop, even she was in denial. "That's not the Eugene I know. He wouldn't miss church. He had dinner with me and our kids several times a week. Who *is* this person?" A hypocrite. A liar and denier.

Confronted with his wildly divergent public and private lives and Mary's ultimatum, Eugene chose to reform. With therapy, he started understanding the dichotomy in his life and his need for religious rigor rather than rebellion in porn, prostitutes, and pot. He decided to spend his free time in the presence of others, replacing porn with two hours at the gym followed by a movie with Mary. He quit his marijuana habit and lined up twice-weekly Bible studies with his pastor. The couple's reintegration took eighteen months, during which Mary was skeptical and cautious. But their home life continued, and Eugene found he was sleeping better. Their kids never suspected the details—they thought Dad's increased energy was the result of working out and eating better.

The thing Eugene had going for him was that his underlying values were solid. He hated the side of himself that kept secrets from his family, and he wanted to be close to God. He now says that being discovered was "a gift. I needed a swift kick to get me in the right direction, and I'm only grateful that Mary stuck by me. I'll never take that for granted."

Divorce lowers your moral level even if during and after the divorce process you behave honorably. Divorce forces you to disconnect from one you vowed to love forever. In itself, that is failure, even if you see it as necessary. If you want to lead a life of which you can be proud, a divorce is a smirch on your résumé. Divorce injects sadness, remorse, and embarrassment into your life. The circumstances certainly matter, but divorce is never pleasant or cherished. On the other hand, overcoming marital problems is an achievement. If you can rekindle the feelings that inspired your vow, you can overcome the distress that is causing you to consider divorce.

So you have a choice. You can join the hedonistic culture that tweets what it feels, no matter whom it might hurt, and treats sex, the most intimate of encounters, as lightly as tapping an app. Or you can take the long view and seek deeper happiness. Dennis Prager, an insightful author and radio host, distinguishes between happiness and fun. Fun is short term, often physical, and inconsequential. Happiness, on the other hand, is enduring and based on virtue—gratitude, loyalty, faith. You even have a moral *obligation* to the people you care about to be happy, because your attitude affects them directly.[9]

What kind of person do you strive to be? Reviving your marriage encourages the long-term view, preserving the history you've shared with your spouse, and creating footing for an improved future. Divorce, on the other hand, dishonors the vow you made, cuts off a substantial portion of your life, harms your children and others, and thrusts you into an unknown future with the same problems and personality that brought you to your divorce.

Look frankly at the potential for your marriage and determine what the honorable, the laudable course would be. Perhaps the best question is, what is the moral example you'd like to model to your children?

CHAPTER 8

A Crucial Difference: Divorce With and Without Children

D ivorce is tough and painful for any couple. But divorces of couples without children, while just as distressing to the spouses, have fewer consequences for fewer people than divorces that involve children. This crucial distinction is reason to resist divorce tenaciously if you have children.

Consider the case of Gerald and Pat, who got together in high school and never dated anyone else. They were so easy together, dating with a group of peers. Gerald, a couple years ahead of Pat, went to community college, joining her at the local university when she finished high school. Pat turned down a bid to rush the most popular sorority because she didn't want to divert any attention from Gerald. They never fought and in their free time shared hiking and museums and free concerts. By the time Pat was a sophomore and Gerald a senior, a wedding seemed like the natural next step. "What were we waiting for?" Pat recalls thinking. "I was still living at home, and so was he. We felt we should finally become adults, and the way to do that was to get married."

After graduating, Gerald got a job supervising the mailings of a non-profit organization. When he came home he liked to watch TV and relax while Pat was absorbed with her homework. She got a job as a research assistant and applied to a five-year program for a Ph.D. in economics. Pat remembers those exciting years as "split between the library and my research office."

Meanwhile, Gerald was content. He liked the people at work and thought his relationship with Pat was rewarding. But Pat was being drawn into a challenging world of intellectual stimulation. She presented her work at professional conferences, occasionally wrote commentaries for the local paper, and was asked to advise a political campaign.

It was a case of two people with agreeable personalities diverging in their aspirations and drive. When, after five years of marriage, Pat tried to push Gerald to "make something of himself," their relationship cracked. Gerald felt Pat should accept him for who he was, just as he'd always done for her. He wanted her to consider his less stressful job with lower pay as important to their marriage as her own.

Eventually, Pat left. She felt awful abandoning Gerald after so many years. They'd grown up together but into very different people. Gerald wanted to go to counseling so Pat would understand that they could be different and continue their pleasant life. But Pat came to feel she was wasting her potential. She wanted an intellectual peer whose energy and ambition matched her own.

Did that marriage have to die? You can think about that. But ask yourself this: What if Gerald and Pat had had children? What if they shared parenting of a five-year-old and a three-year-old, and Gerald had taken on more than half of the childcare while Pat ascended in her academic career?

The childless Gerald and Pat, still in their twenties, could split up and conclude the relationship. Gerald could find someone who appreciated his easygoing, low-pressure style, and Pat could pursue the fast-paced life she craved. The parting would include hurt for Gerald and sadness for Pat and would require her to close herself to her husband's pleas. Their families would be perplexed, their longtime friends incredulous. It wouldn't be easy, but it could be final.

The journalist Pamela Paul has coined a term for a young-in-life divorced relationship without children: "starter marriage."[1] Just a mistake. No big deal. Interviewing sixty friends of friends about their marriages of five years or less, she concluded that waiting until maturity to wed is a good idea, that young brides and grooms lured into fancy weddings are often unequipped to navigate the realities of married life.

With two little ones, Gerald and Pat would have been linked forever, their offspring thrown into the confusion that children of divorce endure—stepparents and stepsiblings, twice the familial complexity, their attention and identities split between Mom's side and Dad's side. The children would have been the collateral damage from Pat's quest for intellectual stimulation.

All marriages deserve the best effort of both partners to rebuild. But what's crucial to recognize is that *relationships that have produced children can never truly end*; a complete split from your children's other parent cannot occur until death. This is reality. If the children are grown at the time of the divorce, perhaps the connection between former spouses can be less frequent, but it will always exist, and as long as the exes live, occasions or questions related to their children will revive bittersweet memories, if not troubles and heartaches.

Divorce inevitably complicates children's relationship with each parent, even when parents maintain their unwavering love for those children. If a vindictive spouse turns child custody into a weapon, one parent can lose the children he loves because of legal restrictions, the child's changed reaction to him, or simply a decrease in the time the parent has to shape and share childhood. And the impact of parental divorce extends to the circles of family and friends beyond the children, the consequences lingering long after the lives of the divorcing couple.

Divorce with no kids can be as simple as a one-time division of assets—as emotionally devastating and prolonged as that might become. A divorce with children entails that division of assets *plus* a division of time and money extending into the future. The calendar is remorseless—holidays and milestones will require continuing discussions and planning with your ex, while your children learn that the old assumptions about family celebrations—where, when, with whom—have been wiped away, replaced by incessant negotiations.

THE WEIGHTIEST FACTOR

In evaluating when a couple should give up trying to save their marriage, the welfare of their children ought to carry more weight than almost any other factor. I say "almost" to account for life-threatening circumstances like abuse and addiction. But even when a couple have deeply divisive problems or must cope with mental illness, addiction, or outrageous behavior, they should do everything they can to overcome those obstacles—as serious and far-ranging as they are—because their children's future is at stake.

The central importance of children in divorce has led some marriage advocates to suggest that, except in abuse cases, a divorce shouldn't be granted to those with kids in the home unless both partners agree to it.[2] The unilateral power that "no fault" divorce now gives to the bolting spouse leaves the one who wants to preserve the family with no recourse. In this way, *our culture favors divorce.*

You may be thinking, "Shouldn't my happiness count too?" That's what Jennifer was thinking. Her husband was demanding, and she was tired of his snappy expectations and bursts of anger when she didn't meet his requirements. "Why did you let me run out of shampoo?" he'd ask accusingly if he found the bottle empty. God forbid she touch the radio when he was driving or the TV remote when he was home. She was completely responsible for the kids and for keeping the house spotless. No negotiation. He worked long hours in tech security, he paid the bills, and when he got home, he wanted things just so.

Getting Andrew to change would be a large order, and he'd have to cooperate. Even if he agreed to try, she doubted he'd actually change his behavior. She couldn't envision being with him another ten years—the amount of time their two kids would be at home—much less anything beyond that. Why should she endure his berating and commanding, and—just as important—why should her kids have to watch their mom suffer? Andrew loved the children, but he couldn't see he was as much a role model when he exploded at her as when he played piggyback with them.

The only time Jennifer felt at ease was in her art studio when Andrew was out of the house. She had Saturdays when he worked, and three evenings a week when he volunteered on a political campaign. Friends and outsiders didn't see his temper; only his mother knew his oppressive side.

"My kids deserve a calm home, and to see parents who are not only respectful of each other, but loving," Jennifer insisted. "Yes, it would be great if they had both a mother and a father around, but should I walk on eggshells whenever he's home only for that?"

Jennifer's need for respect and her concern about her kids emulating her dysfunctional husband were legitimate, of course. At this point, after ten years of marriage, the problem was not only Andrew's unfair anger but also Jennifer's adapting to it by holding back her hurt and frustration. Though she wanted out, she just couldn't disrupt her children's lives.

Jennifer navigated her husband's moods to give her kids security, sacrificing her comfort for theirs. She felt a responsibility to them that superseded all else. "Staying together for the sake of the children" sounds antiquated and unfair, and if that's all you do, it might even appear masochistic. Staying together and *improving the relationship* for the sake of the children, however, is a noble and worthwhile goal. You don't have to sacrifice your happiness if you resuscitate the love you once felt for your spouse and the satisfaction you found in your marriage and even make them grow.

Once you had children, you and your mate became a team for life. Certainly for your children's lives, and you have the option and power to solidify that team for your life as well. The process of strengthening or even forming your team may be daunting, yes. Your sole motivation at first might be your love for your children. But with daily effort to provide those children a secure two-parent home, feelings can change, especially under the guidance of a professional counselor or therapist.

Involving a therapist was essential to Jennifer confronting the resentment she'd built up, and hidden, in her marriage. At first she went alone to sessions, where she received support for her needs and learned strategies to shape her marriage. Later she was able to communicate them to Andrew in the therapist's presence.

Andrew was shocked to hear Jennifer's assertions, despite the many times and many ways she had tried to tell him before. Because he was paying for therapy and was in the presence of an authority figure, he finally listened. At first he reacted poorly, but with a third party refereeing the discussion, he couldn't resort to his usual pushy, angry silencing tactic. He understood that this time he faced an ultimatum: behave differently or lose your family. Andrew didn't like "the women" ganging up on him. He wanted a different therapist! He wanted another opinion! But after the therapist validated his feelings, he calmed down, eventually realizing that he was a major source of anxiety for the rest of his family. That epiphany

allowed Andrew, Jennifer, and the therapist over time to craft constructive
strategies to monitor and change the couple's interactions.

IS THE MARRIAGE WORTH MORE WITH KIDS?

To underscore, kids make an enormous difference. Couples with children have the most compelling reason to stay together—the welfare of others who exist because of but beyond their two-person relationship. Couples with no children also have compelling reasons to stay together, but the consequences of divorce are far fewer and less enduring than when you alter children's lives permanently.

Am I saying that a marriage with children is worth more than one without them? *No*, each marriage is precious and identity-defining. Each marriage brings love and caring to two people and stability to a community. Each marriage forms a home that shapes the lives of everyone in it and changes the lives of those surrounding it.

But I'm not talking about marriage. *I'm talking about divorce.*

A divorce that involves children has far-ranging consequences not just for the couple, but for everyone who cares *about* those children and who cares *for* those children. The consequences to the children themselves cannot be fully measured (many of them we'll discuss) and continue throughout their lives.

Even in the most congenial separation arrangements, children lose a sense of place. If they are still at home, they lose the sense of security that being raised by their two biological parents—or the two people who took their biological parents' place—provides. Children do adapt, in varying degrees, but they are always affected, even and especially by the mere idea that the two people who brought them into the world or into their home to raise together are now abandoning their primary pledge.

The children learn that they are secondary, even if they hear repeatedly from each parent how loved and adored they are, how craved and missed. Children learn that their parents place their own choices above the children's.

You might argue: Haven't children always been secondary to adults? Haven't children always had to do what their parents instructed—from being "seen and not heard" to standing when an elder approaches? Perhaps, but that's not the model for childhood now. Respecting elders is an essential value that children must learn to become caring, upstanding people. But in their younger years, as they learn to trust the world and gain confidence to venture forth, they need a firm foundation that assures them that the world is trustworthy and that their attempts to shape it can bring success. When parents divorce, children must adapt to a new reality. Actually, if custody is awarded jointly, they must adapt to *two differing* realities. Two households, with two sets of rules and two casts of characters. Every study of the effect of divorce on children reveals pervasive and harmful consequences.

Does this upset you? If you love your children, of course it does.

And most Americans agree with you. The 2015 American Family Survey of three thousand persons found that fewer than a quarter of them (21 percent) think divorce should be easier to obtain, but a miniscule 11 percent, across political affiliations, feel that way when there are children still at home.[3]

If you're the spouse most desiring the divorce, you might focus, depending on your reasons and situation, on where you're going and how your current mate is hindering you. Perhaps you justify your desire to leave by insisting that you deserve to be happy, that you have one life and so should do with it what you want. But what damage will you inflict on your children in the process? They have no say in this disruption to their world. Do *they* deserve to be happy? Should the balance between their wellbeing and your desires really tilt toward you?

This needn't be an "either-or" question of leaving an untenable relationship or remaining and suffering for the sake of the children. There's another option: deciding that maintaining your family is paramount and working to *change* the negative aspects of your marriage. There is an infinite number of points on the continuum from ideal to unbearable marriages. The happiest marriages go through moments, days, weeks, or even months when the relationship is under strain. But relationships do rebound. Skills can be learned and interpersonal dynamics rearranged with time, willingness, effort, and communication.

If you're the spouse being rejected, the knowledge that your children now face a mountain of new and unforeseen problems breaks your already burdened heart. You must repress your emotions in the presence of your children just to function and provide for their needs.

In either case, if you love your children, you must make them your foremost concern. If you saw them drowning in a lake, would you jump in to save them? You now need to jump in to save your children, even if you are risking your life. And you're *not* risking your life. You may risk your happiness for now, but if you divorce, you throw them into the lake. Right now, jump in. You need to *save their lives*.

CHAPTER 9

If You Love Your Children

A LIFETIME OF REPERCUSSIONS

G o to any library, and you'll find shelves of volumes there to help you make divorce easier on your children. They'll tell you the gentlest ways to break the news, offer tips on controlling your emotions around the kids, and describe the kindliest kinds of custody. But every one of them warns that your divorce inevitably and permanently hurts your children.

The renowned British psychologist Penelope Leach, for example, maintains a dispassionate tone in *When Parents Part: How Mothers and Fathers Can Help Their Children Deal with Separation and Divorce*[1] but can't avoid the sad observation, "Nothing you can do will prevent parental separation from hurting your children. We know how lastingly important family breakdown and parental separation is for children." Summarizing the research in four bullet points, she writes:

• Separation/divorce makes children miserable

- Children tend to take guilty responsibility upon themselves for parents' breakup
- Children tend to feel shut out by separating parents
- Split loyalty is agony[2]

Dr. Leach tries to minimize the agony, addressing a staggering number of ominous truths about children's experience at every age. Regarding shared care for a three- or four-month-old infant, she cautions, "while such a young baby may not be visibly upset, there is a serious risk that frequent separations will disrupt her primary attachment to her mother and its security."[3]

Citing research about preschoolers,[4] Dr. Leach writes, "The extreme attachment distress of regularly separated toddlers could be seen in their relationships with the primary parent. Some became very upset, crying or clinging to the parent; others became aggressive, hitting, biting or kicking. A few developed eating problems such as food refusal or gagging."[5]

As for older children, "If sadness is the predominant emotion in most rising five- to seven-year-olds whose parents separate, anger often overwhelms it in this older (8–11 years) age group.... However angry your child may be, though, anger will not be his or her only reaction to the family upheaval."[6] She suggests that parents of elementary children confide their situation to the parents of their childdren's best friends. Is this something you look forward to doing?

Costs of a split increase for children in their middle school years. "Although your thirteen-year-old's concern about the situation may be less obvious than your nine-year-old's, it will probably be even more intense and potentially more hazardous."[7]

Dr. Leach lets high schoolers express their own distress about their parents' divorces, quoting an eighteen-year-old boy: "When they told me they were splitting up and selling the house...they seemed to think I wouldn't care. No, worse than that, they seemed to think it was none of my business. I actually think that's why I made such a mess of everything."[8] In other words, teenagers have the capacity to express their sorrow and anger in frighteningly destructive or *self*-destructive ways.

Let's say while coping with the repercussions of the divorce (which never end), you or your ex meets someone new. Dr. Leach has some sobering words for you: "[M]ost children whose parents have divorced are not at all glad to have a step-parent. Many have found it impossible to accept that their parents' separation is permanent, and though the divorce has been finalized, they often go on for years dreaming of a reconciliation."[9]

Perhaps the children have been watching *The Parent Trap*, a movie (two movies, actually—an original version from 1961 and a remake from 1998) in which identical twins, separated as infants by their parents' divorce and meeting coincidentally at camp, switch places so each can know her non-custodial parent. In fulfillment of the fantasies of most children of divorce, when the plan is discovered, the estranged parents reunite. Everyone enjoys *The Parent Trap*, but what child would want to see a movie where the twins have to return to their single parents' homes alone? That's no happy ending.

After dispensing her practical suggestions, Dr. Leach makes her most important observation: "This is the first generation of parents in a position to realize that from birth, or even before, a child's attachment, first to the mother (or her substitute) and soon also to the father, is responsible not only for his health and happiness today—which is obvious—but also for his entire growth and development as a person, brain and body, now and forever, which is not obvious at all." In other words, your divorce is not just about ending your marriage; it shapes the emotional, behavioral, and psychological future of your children. "Whether the offspring of separating parents is six months or six, sixteen, or twenty-six years old," she writes, "having the family split up and mother and father living separately from each other and interacting with her only one at a time will always be emotionally as well as practically disruptive, miserable, bewildering, and sad."

Dr. Leach makes another crucial point: "Considering that about half of all children live through and with family breakdown, it's astonishing how little it is acknowledged. If half the children in your child's school year faced a physical disaster, such as losing a limb, everyone would be talking about it all the time."

But splitting parents seek refuge in the myth of their children's natural resilience, a selfish comfort that excuses the damage they inflict. Writes Dr. Leach: "Children adapt to new circumstances and relationships—what choice do they have?—but even when they seem to have healed there will be scars remaining."

Separation and divorce must be available as a "relationship safety valve," Dr. Leach acknowledges, but she worries that "the well-being of the children...is being put at unnecessary risk by the way that safety valve is deployed." She urges parents to put their children first, viewing the breakup from the child's perspective. Even those who seek relief from a bad marriage should make their children's welfare their priority in any decision-making.

HIDE YOUR EMOTIONS, EVEN IF YOU'RE HUMAN

In contrast to Penelope Leach's candid and realistic assessment of what divorce will do to your children, Edward Farber, Ph.D., urges divorcing parents set aside their feelings and commit to "co-parenting" because every child needs two parents. In *Raising the Kid You Love With the Ex You Hate*, he acknowledges that emotions can be raw: "Do not refer to your ex as a son-of-a-bitch, bastard, Mr. Smith, Ms. Smith, that whore or 'your father' with a sneer in your voice."[10] But he nevertheless urges divorcing parents to follow his "rules" for post-divorce interaction: (1) Your child needs both parents; (2) Reduce parental conflict after the separation; (3) Both parents make decisions.

To which I respond, "Easier said than done." Why? Because conflicts are inevitable, and in such situations, people are looking for some authority to whom they can point and say, "See? You're supposed to be reasonable—even this book says so—and you're *not!*"

The conflicts that made it impossible for the two of you to continue to raise your children together could easily remain, and with divorce you're free to fully vent and execute your wont. Even if a problem spouse enters therapy and improves, you can't escape the scars from past differences and reminders of dysfunction. You might respond that these scars and reminders could affect a revitalized marriage, and yes, that's true, but choosing to maintain your marriage keeps you and your spouse focused on the future together in an ongoing relationship.

Divorce isn't just a logical "next step" in an uncomfortable marriage. No matter what, it's an emotions-dominated disentangling that by definition divides your child's life into two competing universes.

I want to underscore that the experience of divorce is not primarily procedural or orderly or legal. It is primarily *emotional*. Good luck telling partners to restrain their emotions and approach the welfare of their children with clarity and calm, as Dr. Farber does here: "When principles of co-parenting conflict, compromise cannot be reached, and a negative impact on the child is being evidenced, creative, alternative solutions have to be found.... " Notice the passive voice—who is going to find those "creative, alternative solutions" and sell them to the separated spouses?

Farber offers case studies to illustrate how others handled conflicts over parenting. Richard and Monica clashed over whether their son should take Christian confirmation or bar mitzvah classes, both of which would infringe on his weekend time with one of his parents. They compromised with a tutor and a modified bar mitzvah celebration. Farber's moral: "You no longer control the values, schooling or religious and moral upbringing of your child all the time. These are shared in a business partnership with someone you once loved but now do not."

How does that prospect make you feel? If you divorce, you might as well start a Pinterest page of recipes for ongoing frustration. Not every family has religious conflicts, of course, and plenty of children survive their estranged parents' clashes over their upbringings, growing up to become productive though scarred adults. But right now you still have control over whether your children join that emotionally handicapped class. Now, by staying married, you can prevent disputes arising from separate homes and separate lifestyles and spare your child the permanent mark they leave even on youngsters who overcome their effects later on.

STAY TOGETHER IN "LOW CONFLICT" FOR THE KIDS?

After the divorce rate ballooned to its peak of 35 percent of all marriages in 1981, researchers started to analyze the no-fault, no-stigma revolution. They found that children who suffered the collateral damage considered necessary for their parents' self-fulfillment carried the effects of divorce into young adulthood. Educators and psychologists (including me) began to wonder if the new non-judgmental approach to divorce led to greater damage for children.

Andrew Cherlin, encouraging parents to jump off the new "marriage-go-round" of relationships, reveals the emotional toll of domestic disruptions on kids and urges parents to stick together, whether they're married or not. "Stable households, whether headed by one or two parents, do not require that children adjust repeatedly to the loss of parents and parent figures or to the introduction of cohabiting partners and step-parents and the new children these partnerships sometimes bring."[11]

One divorce sets off a chain of events that sabotage children's security and long-term mental health. When studied throughout the 1990s, children of divorce displayed myriad maladies—psychological, behavioral, and physical. A major longitudinal study led by Judith Wallerstein revealed that "the major impact of divorce...rises in adulthood as serious romantic relationships move center stage. When it comes time to choose a life mate and build a new family, the effects of divorce crescendo." Her periodic interviews with children from early childhood through adulthood suggest that all the penalties and pains suffered at the time of divorce are but a mild preview of its life-long consequences.[12]

Sarah McLanahan of Harvard and Gary Sandefur of the University of Massachusetts spent ten years combing several national longitudinal studies for information on how living in a single-parent home affects children of divorce. Their findings weren't exactly what divorce advocates wanted to hear: "Children who grow up in a household with only one biological parent are worse off, on average, than children who grow up in a household with both of their biological parents, regardless of the parents' race or educational background, regardless of whether the parents are married when the child is born, and regardless of whether the resident parent remarries."[13]

This spate of bad news about the permanent effect of divorce made many people, especially those who'd been sucked into the divorce vortex, defensive. The toothpaste was out of the tube. Once the media de-stigmatized divorce, few wanted to retroactively condemn those who had bolted. Surely there were cases where exiting a bad situation was as beneficial to children as it was to the parents? Barbara Dafoe Whitehead describes the "waves" of research that set out to prove various socially acceptable positions. A first wave of analysis followed the peak divorce years with a decade of "speculative lines of argument." One compared the new prevalence of divorce to the centuries when a father's death commonly removed him from the home.[14] Today's children of divorce were merely coping with a new version of a historical problem.

Another "line of argument" took a much brighter view—that divorce could be a fresh start for both unhitched parents and their children, spurring self-development and the acquisition of useful skills. A happier mother would breed a happier child who could overcome the disadvantages of lacking a second parent, while the economic damage of divorce would be offset by women blooming in new opportunities in the workplace, aided by expanded childcare options.

But this first wave of thinking was followed by a second wave—well-designed studies, including several that followed divorcing families over long periods, that put the lie to hopes that divorce was a net positive for children. No study showed children unscathed by divorce, and no research found that single-parent, joint-custody, or "blended" families offered children advantages comparable to those of families with two married parents. As David Blankenhorn wrote, "Marriage does many fine things for human beings, but this one is probably the finest: It gives me as a child the mother and the father who made me."[15]

Given how many people were suffering from their own, their parents', or their friends' and co-workers' divorces and how many others were supporting and bucking-up people suffering from divorce, many wanted some indication that all this misery could be worth it. Also, a burgeoning divorce industry sought to deflect threats to its business. Divorce needed to remain freely accessible to fuel the economy, sell tabloids, and supply clients (including children) for the growing ranks of therapists, marriage counselors, psychiatrists, and "life coaches."

One way to bolster divorcing parents was to suggest that, on balance, divorce leaves some children better off than they would have been if their parents had stayed married. You hear this line all the time. So researchers classified troubled marriages to find which were more and less likely to harm children.

According to Paul Amato and Alan Booth's twelve-year longitudinal study of the quality of the pre-divorce home environment, in "high conflict" marriages (marked by abuse or intense fighting), a child is less harmed by divorce and usually benefits from the relief a divorce affords.[16] Freed from the tense environment, a child can compensate for, though never regain, the two-married-parents advantage. But high-conflict cases account for only 15 to 25 percent of divorces.

The vast majority of divorces dissolve "low-conflict" marriages, in which children usually don't even realize there's a problem. "Low-conflict" may mean the couple goes through "rough patches" of anger or resentment, or one partner feels unhappy or unfulfilled. Academics agree these marriages could continue, and with intervention could substantially improve, sparing children permanent damage. Constance Ahrons found from her longitudinal research that two-thirds of divorces involve these potentially reparable marriages.[17]

Dr. Amato's study of two thousand married people and seven hundred children led him to conclude that "For 55 percent to 60 percent of couples, these are not bad marriages. They are just not ecstatic marriages." When they fall apart, they're especially harmful. Children from low-conflict homes are more at risk of serious problems even than those who escaped high-conflict situations. "These low-conflict divorces are very disturbing for children," Dr. Amato cautions. "The first time they discover something is wrong is when they come home to find Dad has moved out."[18]

Even Divorcesource.com—the people with "a passion for a better divorce"—recognizes that "children from low-conflict marriages tend to see their parents' divorce as a personal tragedy and appear to experience inordinate adversity, both psychologically and socially, including their own ability to form quality intimate relationships."

The message is that maintaining or, better yet, improving a dissatisfying but low-conflict marriage can save your child. Boredom, lack of affection, differing interests, and occasional clashes might make a new start attractive to you, but you can't back away from the multitude of new problems you'll confront with your child.

ALWAYS A CHILD OF DIVORCE: ADULTS LOOK BACK

Adult children of divorce usually wouldn't call their lives a comedy, and yet their experience is common enough that Stuart Zicherman decided to mine its comic potential in the 2013 movie *A.C.O.D.* (that stands for "adult children of divorce"). Starring some of my favorite actors (Catherine O'Hara, Amy Poehler, Jane Lynch), *A.C.O.D.* is the loopy tale of the adult children of two whacky divorced people, their new families, their old families, and the protagonist's discovery that his boyhood "therapy" was part of the research for a book called *Children of Divorce*. Played by Adam Scott, he scours its pages and finds he's "Rick," deemed "a total disaster," a description with which he takes issue. His brother's wedding occasions a resumption of the family fray, and his parents pick up the fight where they left off. "You have just turned a nine-year marriage into a hundred-year war," their son tells them.

Even when parents can relate civilly, their divorce intrudes into their children's lives for what seems like a hundred years. Younger kids attract concern and protection during a divorce, but once they're eighteen, it's assumed they'll handle the divorce with maturity. In most cases, children of divorce do adapt; they have no choice. Many succeed far beyond mere functionality, but there's no escaping history. Even the most successful adults continue to deal with the ramifications of their parents' split and carry its emotional toll.

The siblings Patti, Sam, Matthew, and Janice were all under ten when their parents divorced at the peak of the trend. The girls often spent nights with their mom, while the boys stayed with their dad, then they'd switch. Patti, now a high school math teacher, remembers lots of time waiting in the car. "I kind of resented the fact that we were like ping-pong balls hit from one side of the table to the other," she says now. "I saw divorce as this huge logistical mess, and when I was with either of my parents, Janice and I were like an adjunct to their schedules."

The shared-custody childhood affected each sibling's marital behavior differently. "I didn't want to ever get married," Patti chuckles, "because when the divorce came I'd be a slave to the calendar and car." As an adult, she lived with three different guys, for several years each, in the "serial monogamy" so common among her friends. Now, at forty, Patti regrets never marrying and might resort to a sperm bank so she won't miss out on motherhood.

Patti tells me that Sam, Matthew, and Janice all veered from the conventional marital path. "Sam became an anthropologist and married a Bolivian woman, whom he basically impregnated and left," she reports. Back in the United States, he lives with a woman who has two teenagers from a previous marriage, who stay mostly with their dad.

"Matthew," Patti recalls, "was always trying to patch up the animosity between my parents. He had a real sense of compassion, and we weren't surprised when he became a priest." And Janice? "She has three children, two from short-lived marriages and a two-year-old with her present boyfriend. She went to business school and now is the CFO of a rather well-known tech company, so she can afford having a live-in for her kids."

What struck me was that in the original family of four siblings, none was married and raising children in a two-parent home. Each one seemed skittish about committing wholly to another person—which my research suggests is the most common psychological response to parental divorce. Perhaps it's the insecurity and disorientation of the "two worlds" life to which children of divorce become subjected.

That's the theory of Elizabeth Marquardt, a sociologist whose three-year study of 1,500 randomly selected young adults is the subject of her book *Between Two Worlds*.[19] Half the subjects were raised in intact families; the other half's parents divorced before they were fourteen years old. All completed a lengthy survey about the way they now view their parents, their parents' divorce, and their own evolving reactions to both. Marquardt reveals an array of disturbing psychological and emotional consequences persisting for decades after the divorce. The author writes that she herself still grapples with the effects of her parents' divorce, which occurred when she was a toddler.

The major psychological harm of divorce Marquardt identifies is the "divided self." The child takes on differing personae to fit in with environments that never merge. "Almost two thirds of children of divorce who stay in contact with both parents say they felt like they grew up in two families, not one," Marquardt reports. "[G]rowing up in two worlds creates endless and often painful complications for a child. But one of the first and most troubling consequences is that resembling a parent is no longer the mark of being an insider, a part of a larger family to which the child and other family members belong." To the contrary, "we became insiders and outsiders in each of our parents' worlds. We were outsiders when we looked or acted like our other parent or when we shared experiences in one world that people in the other knew little or nothing about." The stress of changing status in each of two homes with differing identities and norms creates a permanent tension, a constant confusion that requires ongoing reorientation.

Marquardt explains that a married couple in disagreement wants to resolve any differences in individual "worlds" so they can live in harmony.

So they work through problems, and the child sees conflict resolved *by the parents*. But divorced parents don't need to live together at all, so they don't need to work together or mesh their two divergent worlds. When their goals or rules clash, fording the churning conflicts between them becomes the daunting task of the *child*. "The most important models for our own budding identities—our mother and our father—no longer had the job of rubbing the rough edges of their own worlds together in an attempt to hand us something reasonably whole.... Instead, the rough edges of their worlds rub together in only one place—within the inner life of their child."

To cope with this burden, those remarkably "resilient" children adopt strategies and undertake roles that children in intact families do not. According to Marquardt's research, they often watch each parent to discern behavior that will allow them to be accepted in each one's environment. They frequently become "little adults," rushed into mature behavior. Family roles flip inside out. While parents in intact families protectively surround their children, divorced parents become the focal points of their separate emerging worlds, around which children must revolve. Many of the children Marquardt studied became protective of their parents, feeling that they had to reassure their parents of their love. A common method was making a big deal of the parent's birthday.

The story of Harlan, whom I met when he was twenty-eight, illustrates this point. His parents had split for good when he was twelve. There had been several earlier separations; his mother wasn't quiet in lamenting the outside relationships Harlan's dad pursued. With one older brother struggling with Asperger's syndrome, and two even older in college, Harlan was left with the task of comforting his mom, and he was solicitous and selfless. He cleaned up after his brother and kept him occupied when he saw his mom was emotionally teetering. When his mom needed to vent, he was the one she talked to, though Harlan didn't like hearing her depressive complaints about his dad. Even when his parents finally divorced a couple years later, he continued to be the good kid. Though his grades suffered, Harlan was bright enough to get by with little study. His family came first.

When Harlan was in his late twenties and most of his peers were pairing off, he'd date a girl for a while, she'd fall in love with him (after all, he was always attentive and a great listener), and then he'd find some imperfection and let her down easy with an excuse. This played out repeatedly with one lovely, heartbroken girl after another. Over the years, Harlan was there to take his mom to doctor's appointments and arrange get-togethers for her with the siblings. He was the glue holding the family together. He was dating a girl at the time his mom's cancer finally ended her life and he became free to live his own life. He married that girl, and it still means a lot to him that before she passed away, his mom got to meet his wife.

Despite having two homes, the children of divorce in Marquardt's study felt lonesome. "If there is any single experience that unites children of divorce it is our feelings of loneliness as children," she reports. Her respondents were three times as likely as children from intact families to agree that "I was alone a lot as a child." Divorce often leaves children on their own. The demands of maintaining separate households can make parents less available to children, as can court restrictions and hassles of transportation. When a divorced parent re-enters the singles' world, "dating relationships are not usually welcoming of children, especially in the early stages," Marquardt notes.

But loneliness may be the least of a child's problems after divorce. There's kidnapping, for example. The possibility of one parent absconding with his child without permission is now in the mix of considerations surrounding the disposition of children, along with rules for "custody" and "visitation," words Marquardt associates with criminals and prisons. In one of the most touching sections of her book, she recounts her own experience at age thirteen. Her mother warned her to guard her younger brother from kidnapping by her stepfather, who drove a white van. Marquardt loved her stepfather, but now she was told to be wary and protect her brother from him.

"No white van ever appeared. Instead just a few months later we learned of my stepfather's suicide. Kidnapping fears gave way to waves of grief. For years, though, if I was walking down a street and saw a white van I would feel a mixture of foreboding and excitement, a desperate desire to see Rob again coupled with a nagging sense of fear."

Presented with differing sets of directives, children become insecure. They're left to establish their own set of morals and values, gleaned from the sometimes conflicting examples in each of their environments, becoming what Marquardt calls "early moral forgers." Some become moral chameleons, conforming to the expectations of their current environment. Some take their religious, academic, or athletic standards to extremes. Some manipulate the system, playing parents against each other, or disregard or rebel against what their parents require. Marquardt's children of divorce were far likelier than those from intact families to say their values diverge from their parents'.

Marquardt's findings prompt divorced parents to ask, "What arrangement *is* best for children of divorce?" Her answer: "Everything I have discovered in my research and my life leads me to conclude that, overwhelmingly, the best possible scenario for children is to live in one home with their mother and father." She acknowledges that high levels of hostility and certainly violence may warrant divorce. "However," she cautions, "most marriages that end in divorce these days—two thirds of them—are low-conflict. These troubled marriages offer the best hope for being saved and strengthened for the sake of the children."

There's that unpopular phrase, "for the sake of the children." Staying married "for the sake of the children" is passé; it went out when "self-fulfillment" beat out "duty." Toughing out trouble contradicts the accepted view that children fare poorly when their parents are unhappy. Trudging forward "for the sake of the children" demonstrates doubt in children's resilience, their ability to adapt to change. But as we've seen, voluminous research demonstrates the multitude of disadvantages children suffer because of the dissolution of their parents' marriages. Staying together for their welfare is perhaps the most important stand a married couple can take for their children's futures.

Elisabeth Joy LaMotte, a licensed social worker, based her book *Overcoming Your Parents' Divorce: 5 Steps to a Happy Relationship* on the assumption that her readers' romantic lives have been horribly messed up by their parents' divorces.[20] After all, a whole segment of the divorce industry makes its living mopping up the relationships of adults still contaminated by it.

The foremost troublemaker for these offspring as they grow up, LaMotte suggests, is a fear of commitment expressed in romantic choices. She's got some cute terms, like "choosing candy bars over apples," quick-fix partners who aren't really good for you. Or "renting over buying," never making a long-term investment in someone. Ms. LaMotte's solution is to analyze your parents' experiences and feelings surrounding their divorce using your adult maturity, gleaning the sources of your self-defeating behaviors in order to correct them.[21] Ultimately, she found that fully understanding the divorce from each party's perspective can moderate commitment phobia and let the adult move on.

But if you haven't yet divorced, and are therefore in a position to *spare* your children a lifetime of self-defeating behavior and marital mishaps, wouldn't you do that for them? Not by gritting your teeth and suffering in a static state for their sake, but for your own sake, by re-grounding the marriage that brought them into the world.

WHAT DIVORCE DOES TO KIDS' FUTURES

Elizabeth Marquardt's research illustrated some of the psychological harm children of divorce suffer. But beyond that, parental divorce affects their health, academic performance, careers, and economic success.

In their 2011 article, "Reconsidering the 'Good Divorce,'"[22] Paul Amato, Jennifer Kane, and Spencer James summarize the research:

> Given that children thrive on stability,[23] the cumulative effect of multiple changes concentrated within a short time increases children's risk for a variety of problems. Even among children who do not develop clinically significant disorders, parental divorce can generate long-term feelings of unhappiness, confusion, and pain—despite parents' best efforts to be supportive.[24]

Here are a few specifics on how divorce harms children:

More likely to smoke: Men whose parents divorced before they were eighteen are 39 percent more likely to smoke. Women whose parents divorced before they were eighteen are 29 percent more likely to smoke. That's *after* controlling for the factors that usually correlate with smoking, like lower education, low income, anxiety and depression, and childhood traumas, such as parental addictions or childhood physical, sexual, or emotional abuse.[25]

More susceptible to illness: Parental separation significantly correlates with children's illness.[26]

Lag in math and social skills: A large study following children from kindergarten through fifth grade found in 2011 that children whose parents divorced fell behind their classmates in math and social skills and were more likely to suffer anxiety, stress, and low self-esteem.[27]

More likely to drop out of high school: A Canadian study following 9,403 children born in 1984 found that the ones whose parents divorced before they were eighteen were significantly less likely to finish high school, and the younger they were when their parents parted, the less likely they were to complete school.[28]

More likely to be juvenile delinquents: In a test of whether juvenile delinquency comes from genes ("nature") or experiencing parents' divorce ("nurture"), a Minnesota study of 406 biologically unrelated and 204 biologically related families with adolescents "strongly supported" the conclusion that divorce is the more powerful influence.[29]

More likely to live in poverty: Thirty-four percent of American children lived in a single-parent household in 2014.[30] According to the work of McLanahan and Sandefur, income for non-poor mothers and children declines by 50 percent after divorce. "And these children experience ongoing economic instability, as single mothers go in and out of the labor force and as they form and dissolve new intimate relationships."[31]

More likely to divorce: A 2005 book by Nicholas Wolfinger, *Understanding the Divorce Cycle: The Children of Divorce in Their Own Marriages*, examined two large data pools and found divorce cycles intergenerationally: "Many families have more than one child; having grown up in divorced families, these children will be more likely to end their own marriages."[32]

More likely to attempt suicide: An analysis of census data for forty-nine thousand people shows that after controlling for major variables, parental divorce increases the likelihood of a suicide attempt by 14 percent. This pales with the influence of parental alcoholism, however, which, with or without divorce, increases chances of a suicide attempt by a whopping 85 percent.[33]

Less likely to move up the income ladder: "Divorce is particularly harmful for children's mobility," a large, long-term study found in 2010. Of children starting out in the lowest third of incomes, "only 26 percent with divorced parents move up to the middle or top third as adults, compared to 50 percent of children with continuously married parents."[34]

The list of harmful consequences of divorce for children goes on and on, but I must temper all this bad news. Many of the studies rely on data from twenty and thirty years ago and need updating. It's more common now for divorced partners to find creative ways to split time, and more therapists and lawyers are fostering workable relationships between former spouses.

But financially, divorce always brings a huge hit, and lower-income families are smacked with a double-whammy. "When a marriage ends, the same processes that worked to build family wealth now work in reverse to drain the savings account," write Linda Waite and Maggie Gallagher in *The Case for Marriage.* "Two households need more money than one to have the same standard of living—about *one third more income just to break even in terms of lifestyle.*"[35]

A SENSE OF PLACE

Divorce forces middle- and lower-income families to split their limited assets, so both parties and their children end up with much less. If there's a family home, for example, the couple usually must sell it and divide the proceeds, leaving each spouse with a check for half and no place to live. First you tell the children that their parents are going their separate ways, and then you take away even the piece of real estate that defined their united family. A house instills a sense of place and security. Now your children must mourn its loss while adapting to not one but *two* smaller abodes.

Children almost always have happy memories of the house where they grew up, even if it was the scene of parental discord. Given that two-thirds of divorcing couples leave "low-conflict" situations, most children think of their home with fondness. Even in unhappy homes, children find their special places of refuge, their snug comfort zones within the larger home. One twelve-year-old girl would sit in her mom's walk-in closet, reassured by the fragrance of the mother's perfume. A nine-year-old boy made himself a burrow in the backyard, covering it with plywood and a layer of fallen leaves. Even for smaller children, their own bedroom or perhaps just their bed, with the familiar view to which they awaken, reminds them of their parents' care. The divorce sale closes the precious chapter when Mom and Dad lived at home. You can tell the kids that you're still a family, that your love for them is stronger than ever, but selling their home—their secure place—undermines those assurances.

An adult might view four or five years in a particular house as a brief interlude, but for a young child, four or five years are an enormous portion of his life. Adults need to be sensitive to this significance for their children. You may see your home simply as an asset to divide into halves, but its sale throws your children into a transition that would be traumatic even without a divorce. Any happy memories from their family home become tainted by its association with the pain and disruption of divorce. Amid the hassle and commotion of moving to a new place, few adults have the time or inclination to mourn the old—even as their children grieve.

I'll never forget my client Amanda, married seven years and then "discarded" by her lawyer husband, who found a lover. Their son, Jesse, was six and in first grade. Amanda had been a stay-at-home mom, and her husband's settlement provided her the house, child support, and alimony. She could have stayed in the only home Jesse knew—where he had friends living on their street and he could play with the dogs next door. But she imagined her husband bringing the woman now replacing her to their home, and even his audacious use of their bedroom for his sordid rendezvous, and it drove her crazy. The housing market was reviving, and though she now owned the home outright, she felt compelled to move.

Amanda hired a realtor friend, who recommended a couple of updates—fresh paint, flowers in front—and Amanda complied. Then she faced sorting through her household goods and choosing what to pack. This was mental torture. Many of her favorite possessions were wedding gifts, but she repeated to herself, "I have to move on." Jesse came into the dining room, where Amanda had made piles of items—one for the thrift store, one to distribute to friends, one to keep.

"Why are you giving away my Pooh Bear plate?" he wanted to know. "I love that plate!"

Amanda remembered how at three and four Jesse wouldn't eat anything green unless it was on the Pooh plate. "You're a big boy now and can use big boy plates like Mommy does."

"I'm not too big for my Pooh plate!" Jesse protested. Then he looked at the other piles. He remembered the large platter from Thanksgiving. "I get the drumstick off that plate! You can't give that away."

"It's just too heavy to take," Amanda replied.

"No it's not. I'll carry it." And so she had to justify the "give-away" piles to her dismayed son because almost everything had been part of the secure home Jesse wanted to keep.

When she tearfully described this episode in my office months later, I understood her sadness. Now she was in a rental home, much smaller, much less to her taste. By this time, there was nothing to do but make the best of her downsizing and the divorce. Jesse's new room had a sports theme, with soccer and baseballs, but after spending Friday and Saturday nights with his dad, on Sunday nights he sometimes woke up disoriented.

Amanda now regretted the move. The real estate market took off after her sale, and she would have gotten much more had she not been in such an emotions-fueled rush. But more importantly, she now realized the cost of her move to Jesse. He would have faced the weekend shuttle to and from his dad's in any case, but moving to the rental home made every night an adjustment. Beyond that, he wasn't near his friends, whose parents were comfortable guardians while he was at their homes. Amanda had to drive him to school, and he took a bus back. But now she was looking for a part-time job. Her relocation made logistics more difficult, but surpassing any inconvenience was seeing Jesse feel isolated and confused.

To minimize disruption for their children, some divorced parents have self-sacrificially taken the disruption onto themselves with some creative domestic arrangements. Here's the lead from a *Wall Street Journal* article I've been saving since 2003: "The custody arrangement in Linda Stewart's divorce has brought some of the usual difficulties that accompany the dissolution of a marriage with children—among them a new routine of bouncing back and forth between two different homes. But it's the parents, not the children, who are doing the bouncing."[36]

Linda and her ex-husband each spent a week in the long-time family home in Michigan. On his off weeks, the dad would stay in a motel. A *motel*. On her off weeks, Linda rented an apartment in a farmhouse nearby. The parents acknowledged that the arrangement, which they vowed to continue until their youngest child attended college, was trying. "'If this is hard on me, what is it like on children forced to pack up, to study at a different table, and not have their friends come over?' Ms. Stewart says."

This arrangement picked up the name "birdnesting," after the avian practice of leaving the hatchlings in the nest while the parents fly off to catch the worm. As more couples try collaborative and mediated divorces, they seek less adversarial ways to care for their offspring. In some cases, the estranged parents even remain under the same roof with the children, though in separate ends of the house.

Hollywood types like *Mad Men's* Anne Dudek and her ex-husband, Matthew Heller, as well as the glamorous Gwyneth Paltrow and her former mate, Chris Martin, experimented with birdnesting and earned the practice attention from the press.[37] But because it's expensive and requires an extraordinary degree of cooperation, few couples can keep it going for the envisioned long haul. In most cases it functions as a bridge to selling the family home or the remarriage of one of the parties.

Nevertheless, some parents are determined to make it work. In 2005, the *San Francisco Chronicle* profiled Rob and Julie Chrisman, who had been birdnesting with their two children for four years, since the end of their eleven-year marriage.[38] Their lawyer had drawn up a contract covering every facet of their house-sharing, from expenses to hygiene.

"People say, 'What a great thing to do for your kids, but I could never do it,'" Julie Chrisman noted. And their children realized how exceptional their residence plan was. Thirteen-year-old Robbie mentioned their neighbors "who got divorced and really hate each other and everything," recalling that the mom in that family got a restraining order after the dad sneaked in to make the kids pancakes. Ten-year-old Marie said that she missed having married parents when she visited friends in intact homes and saw their harmonious families together. And yet Rob and Julie placed their children before themselves. "Our personal lives got left behind," Rob notes. Julie adds, "If I wanted to get married again, I wouldn't have done it this way."

There are potential downsides for kids, too. In acrimonious divorces, the constant issues in sharing a home might fan flames of anger. And if they get along well, parents who inhabit the home at the same time might raise kids' false hopes for reconciliation. Another concern is that children who "own" their home while parents clearly cater to their needs might gain a sense of entitlement.

If the cost of three houses is prohibitive, another kids-first living option is to set up their own places near to each other—sometimes as close as across a hallway. Research on California divorced couples in the mid-1980s found that the farther apart parents live, the more infrequent the non-residential parent's contact with his child.[39] So parents who want to maximize their involvement willingly pay extra for proximity.

After Seth Levy got divorced from Gina, he stretched his paycheck as a bank officer to buy a home on the same Cleveland Street as the fancier place he'd shared with her. Even though he resented that Gina got the family home, Seth decided his primary commitment was to his three sons. He wanted them to feel they had a refuge nearby, open to them at any hour. Seth didn't approve of Gina's new spouse or the religious direction they'd taken, and he wanted to grab every opportunity to influence the boys.

The oldest son, fifteen-year-old Connor, more serious and reserved, took advantage of that propinquity. He'd come over nearly every afternoon to do his homework in Seth's quiet dining room, away from his boisterous brothers.

Seth had a strategy. Whenever Connor came over, he'd have snacks and sometimes pizza or ice cream. Seth would be sure to sit down with his son and catch up on the day's events, and share a personal anecdote. Seth still spoke on the phone nightly with the other two, but the time with Connor not only inspired the boy's religious interests, but also conveyed to his brothers that Dad was always available.

Even if parents stay in the same neighborhood, living in two homes isn't easy for the kids. Hannah Jones Lawrence, now in her late twenties and a branding officer at a website for millennials, recalls shuttling between her mom's apartment at West End Avenue and Ninety-Third Street and her dad's on West Eighty-Sixth in New York. "Sometimes I actually can't believe I had the schedule that I did," she says. "On Mondays and Wednesdays I'd be at my mom's house, on Tuesdays and Thursdays I'd be with my dad at his house, and if it was his weekend, I'd spend Friday and Saturday with him and go back to my mom's on Sunday." Sounds like a typical fifty-fifty agreement, what parents often fight to achieve in custody battles. But while it reassured Ms. Lawrence of her parents' presence, ultimately she protested. As she was finishing high school, she told her parents, "I'm done. Please don't make me do this anymore."[40]

Cristina Gitti and Matteo Bologna went a step further than sharing a common neighborhood—they lived on separate floors of the brownstone they'd bought years before. When married, the couple and their two daughters had lived together on the top floor, while the other two levels were rented out. At the split, Ms. Gitti remained there, while her ex-husband took over the garden level. Four years into the arrangement, the girls, twelve and eight, were carrying their backpacks between the two apartments, movements made smoother by a requirement that visits by the parent not on duty be preceded by a phone call.[41]

So the big question is, if parents can get along well enough to coordinate these complicated and expensive living arrangements, why can't they get along well enough to rejuvenate their relationships? Shouldn't they be motivated by parental protectiveness and finances to take back the love that brought them to marriage?

"CHILDREN'S RESILIENCE": A RUTHLESS EXCUSE

There were so many books about helping children through their parents' divorce on my local public library's shelves that I whipped out my cellphone to digitally capture them. They wouldn't fit in even two or three photos—I needed four shots to capture all the titles. But for all the variety, there is one theme that appears in virtually every book I perused, regardless of the author's style, professional background, or philosophy: divorce will inevitably hurt your children, but *kids are resilient.*

Who would dispute that someone who endures the explosion of his family and thereafter does his best to recover can be called "resilient"? Trouble is, the term implies an effortless bounce, a rubbery ability to spring back into one's prior shape. That doesn't happen with children or adults going through divorce. They may survive, but they are *never* the same.

"Our six-year data on children after divorce, which found three quarters developing within the normal range, stand as a tribute to the resilience of boys and girls," says E. Mavis Hetherington, describing her landmark longitudinal study of divorce.[42] In fact, she offers "The Resiliency Lesson" as the ultimate, comforting finding of her twenty-five years of research, observing, "There seems to be a strong 'self-righting' tendency in development, a striving to adapt and cope positively with the challenges that confront us, including those of divorce.... After all, adaptability is central to human survival."

What's the choice? Survive or...not?

Yes, three-quarters of the people directly affected by divorce whom Dr. Hetherington studied later fell "within the normal range" on her measures of well-being. And yet in the same paragraph she writes, "Looking back, many parents and adult offspring describe divorce as the most painful event in their lives...." Can anyone expect to pop back from catastrophe unchanged?

The "positive psychology" guru Dr. Martin Seligman of the University of Pennsylvania heads the Penn Resiliency Program (PRP), touted as "the most widely researched depression-prevention program in the world." It seems, however, that resiliency is only one of the "coping skills" necessary for student well-being. The PRP also teaches optimism, realism, flexibility, assertiveness, creative brainstorming, decision-making, and relaxation.[43]

In other words, if you impose divorce on your children and then excuse the resulting damage with "kids are resilient," you're making two big and unfounded assumptions: (1) that all children possess the wide range of skills they'll need to recover, and (2) that your child will be able to summon those skills each time she encounters a setback in the divorce process.

But what if your child *hasn't* developed this complicated mash of useful habits? Some people have these skills and others don't. Some people are raised in homes where the mood is gloomy and pessimistic, others are born with a melancholy temperament, and still others have adapted to a somber culture. Do we assume these children, too, are "resilient"? To say "kids are resilient" is to ignore the crucial reality that many kids are not. Which is why there's a need for Dr. Seligman's program.

The good news is that kids can learn; the PRP has evidence that well-being can be taught, changing negative patterns into positive ones. But even for kids equipped with a healthy, upbeat attitude and skills to ward off depression, divorce is a bummer. That's because the *reality* of divorce is unavoidably negative. It's one thing to spin things for the best; it's another to live in fantasyland.

I put myself through graduate school by working at the Center for the Study of Evaluation at UCLA, where I helped develop a curriculum for fourth-graders called Heart Smart Adventures. Our goal was to boost "self-esteem," the big educational buzzword at the time. Heart Smart Adventures received its funding because children lacked the skills we were hoping to teach. So the question arises—if kids need to be *taught* self-esteem, if they need to be *taught* the many values and skills of the PRP, why do we assume that when hit with the most enormous, out-of-their-control, life-changing disruption of their lives, any and all kids can summon up their resilience and quickly rebound?

Resilience is a wonderful virtue to have, but as Dr. Anthony Scioli points out, the *foundation* of resilience is hope.[44] And hope, says Dr. Scioli, requires "attachments" or relationships.[45] When parents split, no matter how strongly they insist that their allegiance and love for the child will never change, the child *observes* the opposite of these assurances. The child sees Mommy and Daddy, heretofore the dual pillars and security of his life, demonstrating that *their* attachment has failed. No matter how clever your script—gently announcing that "Mommy and Daddy can't get along and so will be living separately" or that "Mommy and Daddy no longer love each other but will always love you" or that "Mommy and Daddy want to have their own homes"—conveys the same terrifying message: Mommy used to love Daddy, but now she has stopped loving Daddy. Next, she could stop loving *me*.

It's a lesson repeated in every interchange of the divorce process—as you move out, as you divide your possessions and sever ties, as you exchange custody of your children for the weekend. They will encounter hundreds of reminders that their parents don't love each other; hundreds of moments of anger, sadness, and worse. They'll watch the hardening of their parents' hearts toward each other. Even if they're able to maintain a close relationship with each of you, they've got a front-row seat when at least one of their parents shows callousness or businesslike indifference to the other parent they love.

To have hope, Dr. Scioli says, a child also needs to feel control over his world, a sense of mastery.[46] But when his parents split, his predictable day-to-day routine is shattered. A hundred unfamiliarities—not knowing where to find the toothbrush, awakening to an unfamiliar view, choosing items to fill an overnight bag—remind him of his parents' broken love. Each encounter with the new duality of his life—keeping a pair of pajamas at each house, hearing a strange-sounding alarm clock, lying in a bed facing a different direction—damages his hope and long-term resilience.

Divorce is probably the *least* empowering situation a child can endure. He hears reassurance, yet experiences the opposite. He's told "We'll always be family," yet understands that "no matter how much you want us to stay together, or fix our problems, we won't." Mom says, "You're strong; you're handling this just wonderfully," but the reality is *feeling* sad, weak, and disregarded. It's a dissonance that adds to the pain.

So bucking up your child with "positive" messages could backfire: "Gee, Mom thinks I'm strong. I better keep up the act so I don't disappoint her."

The third condition for hope, writes Dr. Scioli, is "a belief that you aren't trapped in a bad situation, and have a way out." In the distress of divorce, your kids would have to "hold on to positive thoughts and feelings, while processing something negative," a feat even adults have a tough time accomplishing. Children under age eighteen have *no* "way out" when their parents place them in a new double lifestyle.

Constance Ahrons's sequel to *The Good Divorce*, *We're Still Family*, includes a chapter called "Fostering Resilience," in which she notes that in divorce, parents' needs and desires trump those of their children. "Except in the most highly conflicted and abusive marital situations, children want to live with *both* of their parents."[47] She suggests that parents "foster" resilience by setting up a supportive co-parenting relationship—in other words, mimic as closely as possible a two-parent family. Second best, when the exes need to minimize contact to avoid conflict, is "parallel parenting," in which each parent provides a separate positive relationship. It's "more difficult for both children and their parents" but "a better solution than the loss of one parent." Third choice would be the common situation where only one parent, usually the mother, provides "the guidance of a strong, responsive and nurturing parent." But what if the mom, under a host of new stresses, can't be as strong, responsive, and nurturing as she would like? Last resort is to enlist grandparents, friends, and step-parents as the "buffers."

My question is whether the presence of someone to "buffer" the pain actually makes a child resilient. Dictionaries define resilience as an "ability" or a "capacity" to regain an original shape, snap back, or recover from misfortune, adversity, or illness. This implies that resilience comes from *within* the person; it exists prior to the adversity requiring it. Children and adolescents, who are just *shaping* their life views and skill in responding to events, can't be expected simply to bounce back after the end of the life they've known.

It's true that children are born with temperaments[48] and "capacities," and some may cope with parental divorce just fine. Within any family, children will handle the crisis differently, depending on the roles they've played in the family before and their personalities. Every child *will* eventually navigate the facts of his life with varying degrees of competence, but when you call this survival "resilience," you're dismissing with a euphemism the inevitable devastation you cause your defenseless child.

I've tried to "peel the onion" of children's resilience so you can appreciate the tenderness of your own child's psyche. Your divorce doesn't tap some previously unseen reservoir of resilience. Children are knocked about so much by the wounds and uncertainties of divorce that they may *lose* the ability to bounce back. Even if you unreasonably insist that *all* children rebound from the blows of divorce, *why would you demand that of your child*? Resilience requires hope, energy, and optimism; dismantling children's worlds, studies show,[49] leads a considerable number of them to the opposite result, depression.

PARENTS' DIVORCE? IT'S DEPRESSING

In a politically correct effort to shield personal decisions from "judgment," academics conduct a lot of research hoping to show that divorce doesn't harm children. At least in the long run. At least when the exes get along. At least if they've been in a "high conflict" home. At least....

Unfortunately, the data have been analyzed from several angles, and the conclusion is always the same: however you measure success and satisfaction, children of divorce fare worse than children who grow up in intact families. No doubt, the majority of children whose parents split function well. Many are even inspired by the divorce to excel. These "normally developing" children, the ones forging their own happy lives and solid marriages, do so *despite* their backgrounds. They're able to understand and overcome the difficulties and sadness and bad memories, but no matter what, the difficulties and sadness and bad memories stay with them.

A favorite cliché in books about divorce is "When life hands you lemons, make lemonade." In *Overcoming Your Parents' Divorce*, Elisabeth Joy

LaMotte even tries to convince still-suffering adults that there's a "possible upside to fearing intimacy and delaying long-term commitment." Yep. Add a lot of sugar.

You're reading this book because "life" has not yet plucked that sour citrus from your tree. You're in a position to keep your children's world intact. You have the power to retain for your children their most fundamental advantage in life. There's no more powerful way to ensure your children's welfare.

Would you say the kids from broken marriages who end up successful *benefited* from divorce? Are there any divorces that allow the child to keep all the advantages he had, or would have had, in his original two-parent home? In high-conflict situations or in cases of addiction or abuse, yes, the child is certainly better off in safety with the non-abusive, non-addicted parent. But *any* child of divorce suffers disadvantages compared with his peers in never-disrupted two-parent homes.

Judith Wallerstein reached some disheartening conclusions in her twenty-five-year study of 131 children, fifty-nine of their mothers, and forty-eight of their fathers. Her work has been criticized because the families she followed weren't nationally representative, but her rich data still offer touching and important lessons. "The life histories of this first generation to grow up in a divorce culture tell us truths we dare not ignore," she admonishes. "Their message is poignant, clear, and contrary to what so many want to believe." When parents announce their divorce, children become "frightened and angry, terrified of being abandoned by both parents and responsible for the divorce." In periodic interviews, the vast majority of the children told Dr. Wallerstein that "their world increasingly resembled what they feared most," later becoming a "family" with "porous walls that include new lovers, live-in partners and stepparents. Not one of these relationships was easy for anyone." You can nearly hear her sigh as she writes, "But it's in adulthood that children of divorce suffer the most. The impact of divorce hits them most cruelly as they go in search of love, sexual intimacy, and commitment."

Research spanning three decades confirms that parents' divorce increases the likelihood of teen depression. Some studies point to the contributing effect of financial decline, as the child moves from a two-parent into a single-parent household. Others note that when younger children must handle the divided life of joint custody, they're more likely to suffer depression in their teen years. In fact, a 2004 American Psychological Association summary of the research notes, "While it is often difficult to isolate the myriad of factors that impact children of divorce, research has established that they are at a higher risk for adjustment problems than children from intact families. For example, divorced children experience less financial security, lower academic achievement, more alcohol and cigarette use, and lower rates of employment as young adults."[50]

YOUR HALF OF YOUR CHILDREN'S DOUBLE LIVES

While kids feel torn inhabiting two worlds, parents suffer too. The state of Washington's Parenting Act of 1987 replaced post-divorce "custody" and "visitation" with a progressive framework of "parenting functions" and "residential schedules," customized with a "parenting plan" for each divorce, intended to minimize conflict. A study commissioned by the state supreme court ten years later, gathering through focus groups the testimony of parents who live under the Parenting Act, illuminates what post-divorce life is like for parents.[51]

If you're a divorced parent in Washington, your life is governed by a court-decreed schedule. Imagine a court limiting the time you can spend with your children and stipulating the days of the week and "special occasions" you can share. The parents who participated in the 1997 study had not only signed on to their parenting plans but, in varying degrees, had helped to design them. And yet they live with ongoing frustration and emotional pain.

I thought it would be instructive for you, a parent wondering if you should divorce, to ponder what's ahead by reading about the experiences of divorced moms and dads. Should you decide to split, you will soon meet "the system." Dr. Diane Lye, the author of the Washington State study, notes, "For parents, dealing with 'the system' is extremely stressful," as one woman recalls, laughing at her earlier naïveté:

> One day I got this letter—more of a form really. Well every time anything came from the courts I was a mess right away—thinking it was my ex—you know—trying to mess with me. So when

I opened it up I couldn't make sense of it—something about a
dissolution of marriage and seeing a court commissioner. I
freaked. What was all that stuff about marriage? I wanted a
divorce. And I didn't know who a court commissioner was. I
decided I'd better go down there and try and sort it out. So I
called work and told them I wouldn't be in the next day—the
whole nine yards. Then that evening, I got to thinking, and I
realized it was just my appointment to go and get the papers
signed. But that's what it's like—you're in such a state that you
can't think straight and there is all this paper.

As part of the process, divorcing spouses receive a packet of information, including the parenting plan form. The do-it-yourselfers usually assume
it is just another paper to complete rather than a lifetime proposal. One
woman just filled it out on her kitchen table. Those with attorneys tended
to be clueless as to the best schedule to request.

And if you ask for help, your lawyer's fees mount. "Focus group participants [in the Washington State study] who had worked with an attorney
often reported that their legal bills had been very high," Dr. Lye relates.
"Several reported [in 1999] figures of $10,000 to $15,000, and many parents reported that they had sold property, including real estate, cars, and
boats, to cover legal expenses. One parent observed: 'I spent my kids' college
tuition on legal fees.'" Two fathers went bankrupt.

Beyond the lawyers, the court often required additional expenses,
"including the costs of parenting classes, mediation, parenting evaluations,
and supervised residential time." Participants mentioned cost as reasons for
settling or "not fighting" for the parenting plans they wanted, and some
fantasized about returning for a better judgment, "But most parents held
such negative views of the civil justice system they said they would never go
back to the courts."

Parents recalled bargaining for time with their children, especially trading more time with the kids for additional support. Most of the couples
ended up with the "every other weekend" deal, where a "primary residential
parent" (the new term for "custodial parent") has the children during the
week and every other weekend; the "nonprimary residential parent" gets

the "off" weekend and one day during the week. Would you like that arrangement with your kids?

Neither do the parents who live it. Some comments:

> Let's be honest. We all want more time with our kids. But you can't have it all. That's part of getting divorced. You have to be practical.

> Even that Wednesday visit is too much really. They're exhausted by it, and I see it the next day. They're always wiped out after his weekends. So I really think every other weekend is about the best you can do.

> Every other weekend sucks. You spend all your time in the car and that's not really being in your kid's life. It's just a visit.

> Of course I fought. When my lawyer said I could get every other weekend, I said, "No—she can get every other weekend— they can live with me."

Though "very few" Washington parents had plans that divided children's time fifty-fifty, some parents wanted it:

> The restrictions on [getting] 50/50 are unfair. They say you can only do it if there is no conflict. But there's always conflict when a marriage ends. And that means one parent can veto 50/50. Women have no incentive to even try—because the court will most likely favor the mother.

And some did not:

> I don't want 50/50—my son needs a place to be and his mom does a good job. But you can't be a real parent every other weekend.

Primary residential parents tended to make most decisions regarding the children, and that too provoked disagreement.

He was never interested. I tried to get him to come and check out day cares with me. He said, "You decide." Now suddenly he's gonna be interested?

[Mutual decision-making] is a joke. Sometimes she tells me afterwards.

That was the only thing we fought over. The kids are living with me, and I didn't want the decision thing coming back to bite me. I didn't want to be beholden to him. So I have sole decision-making.

And once the parenting plan is finalized and signed, you're left with the reality of living with it every single day. Dr. Lye found parents fell into one of four styles of adherence to requirements: flexible followers, close followers, strict followers, and resisters. Laid-back parents with a good relationship could handle more flexibility. And then there are the other three-fourths, whose lives are...complicated.

She doesn't mean to screw up. It's just so complicated and we're busy. She's always calling me about where they're supposed to be. I'm glad it's all written down.

Oh she sticks to that thing. A couple of weeks ago I had some free tickets to the [Mariners]. Good seats, an afternoon game. So I called her up to see if I could take them. I said we could swap my Sunday afternoon for hers—I know better than to ask for an extra couple hours and I won't beg her. I said I'd bring the kids back early the following Sunday when it would have been my turn anyhow. But oh no. We have to follow the plan.... I bet they weren't doing nothing anyhow.

I took my kids to the Fred Meyer store in Lynnwood every other Friday evening for a year and he never once showed up. They knew what we were doing there—I couldn't pretend we were shopping. It broke their hearts.

It's not worth the paper it's written on. My husband has authority issues and he's not going to follow anyone's rules. He brings our son back when he's ready and I sit there wondering if this time he won't be back.

Then there are everyday issues—worry about the way an ex's lifestyle will affect the children, logistics, costs of sticking to the plan. You may be dealing with problems in your marriage now; with a parenting plan you'll face new problems.

Don't get me wrong—she's a good mother. But I don't feel that she sets a good example. Every time I go over there, there's a different fellow there. Oh they're nice enough, don't get me wrong. And it's all very pleasant—she always introduces me, we chat. But a different one every week. I don't care who they are and what they're like, I don't think that's a good example for a young black girl to see.

I've got a house and a car, and it's a nice place for children. But he's still living like a college student—in an apartment with a bunch of guys. I know they have women there. It's just not a good place for children.

She moved. So now, every other Friday, I sit on the bridge in rush hour traffic. So sometimes I'm late. I can't help it—but she gets pissed. She keeps threatening not to wait for me. Of course, she drives on Sunday evening when the bridge is deserted.

We spend all our time together in the car, it seems like. Oh we talk and stuff. There are some good things about it. But it's not real. It's not living with your kids—driving around with them.

So what if the plan doesn't work out, or if one parent feels it's unfair? Well, nearly all the focus group participants had the fallback of mediation, but that was another imbroglio.

I don't know how it works—how do I start off the dispute resolution? I don't know who to call.

It takes two to mediate and she wasn't interested.

I sat in a room for three hours getting badgered. There was
no negotiation—they just kept telling me "do this." So I gave in.
I wish I would have gone to court.

Your life and your children's lives will be circumscribed by a judge's
ruling. Some focus group parents taped copies of the court-mandated schedule by the telephone or stuck them to the refrigerator, according to Dr. Lye.
"Several of these parents brought well-thumbed, heavily annotated copies
of their plans to the focus groups, and some asked how they could get extra
copies." After all, on these papers were the rules controlling their, and their
children's, lives.

Most people considering divorce want *freedom.* They look ahead to a
life liberated from a spouse who's boring, oppressive, hostile, or detached.
If your spouse exhibits these qualities before divorce, he's likely to continue
or even amplify them once rid of your criticism and influence. With your
divorce decree, the law makes him your partner implementing the parenting
plan. Rather than being freed from this person, you're now chained to him
and the big lead ball of the legal agreement you and he signed.

If that's not a good reason to work on your marriage and avoid divorce,
what is?

THE "TWO-PARENT PRIVILEGE"

Perhaps you've heard about campus protests against "white privilege"—
the economic and social advantages that white people supposedly enjoy
simply because they're white. The always incisive Dennis Prager puts the
controversy in perspective by pointing out that the most powerful "privilege" a person can be born with has nothing to do with race: "If you are
raised by a father and mother, you enter adulthood with more privileges
than anyone else in American society, irrespective of race, ethnicity or sex.
That's why the poverty rate among two-parent black families is only 7

percent" while it is 22 percent among whites in single-parent homes. He concludes, "Obviously the two-parent home is the decisive 'privilege.'"[52]

Having two parents who live together in marriage confers another potent advantage. In a biological (or adoptive) nuclear family, two people with a deep stake in the child's happiness and fulfillment are working with the child to decide the activities and interests he pursues. But when there's a divorce, parents no longer make those choices, nor do they retain the flexibility to change them. The courts take over. "Judges routinely decide where the children of divorced parents will attend school, worship and receive medical care," says Robert Emery, a divorce mediator and psychology professor at the University of Virginia.

When married, both parents together shape their children's values and experiences. For example, when our three children were younger, my husband and I decided on their educations based on our and each child's needs. At different times, that meant homeschooling, public schools, part-time tutors, or Jewish day-schools. We chose our family vacations and weekend hikes, we gave permission for our children's sleepovers, and, as the school year wound down, we'd discuss with our kids the range of summer day camps and play options, look at our finances, and craft schedules to keep them busy and entertained.

But if you get a divorce, no longer are these joint decisions. Nor are they made by one or the other parent. They're subject to the legal agreement made when the divorce documents were signed, under the judge's determination of "the best interest of the child," which may or may not be what you or your spouse would choose. Courts sometimes "split the difference" when the parents' desires conflict. If parents, rather than judges, could make binding agreements, Dr. Emery says, "parents could make a deal, for example, that a parenting coordinator could make decisions for them in the future if they fail to agree."[53]

To which I say: "Who wants *this*?" If you love your children, do you want a judge or a "parenting coordinator" deciding how your children are raised? Or, in a best-case scenario, do you want to hammer out with your estranged spouse and dual attorneys now, the details that will carry your child through to adulthood? And if you have more than one offspring, are you really comfortable signing on to a plan you're not allowed to adapt with time or with your children's individual personalities?

Chances are that relations between you and your former spouse will *not* stay harmonious enough to make joint decisions possible over the years. The study of parenting plans in Washington State found that "while 75 percent of parenting plans granted joint decision-making, most parents didn't get along well enough with their ex-spouse to carry it out." And more freedom in crafting schedules doesn't help, either. "About 20 percent of the parenting plans had no specific time-sharing schedule, leaving the details to be worked out by the parents, an approach the study called a recipe for conflict."[54]

Children with the "two-parent privilege" benefit throughout life from being raised by the couple that brought them into the world and has the greatest investment in and love for them. By staying together, you launch each of your children from a firm base. If you and your spouse pass through difficulties, even *heartache*, in your relationship, your choice to overcome those problems provides the security that lets children focus on their own futures.

But you and your mate also benefit from the "two-parent privilege." Remember the joy, the sense of the miraculous, that you felt upon the birth of each of your children? Giving life to a new soul that springs from their loving union fills parents with gratitude for the opportunity to nurture and protect that precious gift. Divorcing not only severs your connection with the one with whom you created your child but also ruptures your ability to determine and influence that child's development.

THE IMPORTANCE OF DADS

Are you a dad or an inseminator?

You don't need marriage to inseminate, or even, nowadays, to be a dad. But there's a big difference between the two. The continuum of involvement runs from full-time, stay-at-home caretaking fathers to those who completely abandon their children, perhaps unaware that a night's congress created someone new. Where do you fall on that continuum?

If you're living with your spouse and child, if you're available for the daily routine, the highlights and lowlights of life, if you're communicating naturally and teaching by example as well as instruction, you'll have one level of influence on your children. On the other hand, if you're not there, if you live separately and leave the child-raising to someone else, your kids can call you "Dad" and know you love them, but you've got a very different role.

Why should you stick with your difficult marriage when you can share fifty-fifty custody and the rest of the time use Facetime or Skype? Two looming and important reasons: for the benefit of your child, and for the benefit of *you*.

If we were living in the 1950s or even the 1960s, we'd assume that Dad's primary role was to earn a living for his family. He'd greet the kids as they got ready for school then disappear to his job. Mom would take care of the home front, perhaps making Jell-O mold while wearing a shirtwaist dress, high heels, and an apron.

Actually, my own mom was one of those ladies, minus the heels. She'd send us kids out walking to school with our metal lunchboxes, and at 3:30 she'd be waiting at home with two cookies and a glass of milk. She made dinner—in those days you needed "protein" which was usually some ground beef creation, a "starch" like spaghetti or potatoes, and a vegetable, often canned or frozen. And of course lots of whole milk.

Life was like the classic television sitcoms—until inflation drove the prices of everything up and the women's movement opened employment opportunities and eased the stigma of wives working. My World War II–vet dad was proud he could support his family (working for the state unemployment office), but rising property taxes eventually squeezed the family pocketbook. By then my mom could take a secretarial job without shame.

Women's income is now essential for most families to cover mounting recurrent expenses like health care, childcare, orthodontia, internet service, cloud-based computer back-up, and multiple cell phones. A galaxy of new businesses add their monthly fees to your domestic budget—the home security service, satellite TV, gym membership, the service you pay to get ratings of other services. In 1960, 70 percent of married couples with children under eighteen relied on only the father's income, while 25 percent had dual incomes. By 2012, however, 60 percent of such couples had two incomes, while only 31 percent lived on income from the husband alone.[55]

With Mom's job as important to family survival as Dad's, where do *his* kudos come from? What keeps him needed at home? The infatuation and excitement that led to the marriage ebbs as the children arrive,[56] and what's left are two undifferentiated equals. And the party winds down.

Too many couples decided in the post-feminist years that the husband *wasn't* especially needed, and the divorce rate climbed, from 2.5 per one thousand persons in 1965 to 5.4 per thousand in 1980.[57] This growth in divorce provided abundant evidence that a father's absence harms his children. It turned out that a dad provides much more than an extra hand to lug in the groceries—he is a joint shaper of the children's values and aspirations. Children learn from having him at home not only how to be a dad but how to be a husband.

We've already seen the problems children of divorce face in forming and sustaining their own marriages. But the combination of two particular married parents produces a unique climate in which their child can flourish. The father has a crucial double role—contributing to the task of parenting and providing a masculine role model.

In his beautifully written *Fatherless America*, David Blankenhorn describes the roles and expectations of fatherhood, including the "New Father," who boasts "new and improved masculinity," "unafraid of feelings…without sexism." "Fatherhood as fifty-fifty parenthood, undistorted by arbitrary gender divisions or stifling social roles."

Very nice. But Dr. Blankenhorn points out that "much of the New Father model depends upon denigrating or ignoring the historical meaning of fatherhood in America. Indeed, much of the New Father ideal is based explicitly upon belittling our own fathers," as well as on accepting feminist rhetoric about children's needs. "The essence of the New Father model is a repudiation of gendered social roles," Dr. Blankenhorn explains. "But fatherhood, by definition, is a gendered social role. To ungender fatherhood—to deny males any gender-based role in family life—is to deny fatherhood as a social activity. What remains may be New. But there is no more Father."[58]

So, dads, *you are needed* to complete the home that only a child's two parents can provide. Other living arrangements may approximate the two-parent home, but they cannot match the natural advantage of a direct blood connection. Adoptive homes, in which two loving, committed people raise a child, come as close as possible. And yet insider-outsider tensions sometimes surface when children don't physically resemble their parents or share genetic characteristics. The love of family members may be equally intense, but the original, intact nuclear family still offers children the best shot at health, academic success, career achievement, mental well-being, and their own happy marriages.

Staying married to the mother of your children is the ultimate gift you can give to your child. But it's also a reward to *yourself*. Living in the home with your children as they grow and develop gives you the opportunity to inculcate your values, to teach them your viewpoints and to give them the choice to become your legacy. You benefit in long term but also in the every-day joy of presence and connection—laughter, pride, insights about who they are, relating to your spouse, and just observing the clever, cute, and precocious things they do.

Being a hands-on dad changes you for the better. You may stay in your marriage as a gift to your children, but their being the magnet back to your spouse is a gift to you. By choosing to honor your commitment, you practice and ingrain commitment itself. By guarding your child from harm, you learn to think first of another rather than yourself. By giving up your own comfort and fun to be responsible and reliable for your child, you become the kind of mature, caring person who invests in selfless and altruistic goals.

Every parent acknowledges that parenting is an education—primarily in *patience*. Patience is the antidote to narcissism, because irritation and anger grow from the arrogance of believing your interests, right now, trump all else. When your baby needs a diaper change, when your toddler scrapes his knee, when your six-year-old is "starving!" because his stomach growled a few times, you have to subjugate your pleasure to his welfare. Which ends up adding to *your* welfare as you expand your kindness quotient and with each experience build toward even deeper love for your child and your family.

Perhaps the most important part of staying married to the mother of your children is simply *being there*. As Woody Allen says, "Showing up is 80 percent of success."[59] You can't parent from afar. WhatsApp can keep a soldier close to his family when he's on duty far away, but there's no substi-tute for the feeling of a hug or being the long arms that reach down and hoist a crying child toward your heart. When you remove yourself from your family home, you deprive yourself of that nurturing role and the memories of childhood that slip away so fast.

Paul Raeburn answers the title question of his book, *Do Fathers Matter?* with a resounding "yes." He tells of his younger years parenting in his first marriage, rising early, heading to his newspaper job, working until 6:30 p.m. "with just enough time to ask them about their day and read to them before they went to bed." In his current marriage, he and his wife "both work at home and I can adjust my schedule to spend much more time with my children." Mr. Raeburn acknowledges, "I'm glad to know my involvement is a good thing. But that's not why I spend time with my kids. I do it because I *like it*."[60]

With gender roles melting, the stigma of the stay-at-home dad gave way to an "I wish I could do it too" ideal. Rom-coms show a dad moved to tears as instant chick bait. While the extremes haven't become the norm, they've freed men to admit it: kids are fun. And not just for roughhousing, which, research has shown, makes kids "smart, emotionally intelligent, loveable and likeable, ethical, physically fit and joyful."[61]

Nowadays it's chic to take manly delight in such mundane tasks as making breakfast, shuttling kids to activities, and, yes, changing diapers. Take a look at all the parenting blogs for dads. My friend Bruce Sallan started his blog and then radio show, *A Dad's Point of View*, after his wife left him and he became the "primary residential parent." He enjoyed raising his two sons so much—and talking about it—that he dropped his day job as a Hollywood producer and became a full-time, professional dad.[62]

Unless your children's mom has bolted—and that's rare—you'll have your kids only half the time at most. No more uninterrupted routines and the spontaneous flow of life. And she'll be missing from all the experiences you share with your children—a phantom figure in every family snapshot.

David Blankenhorn writes about the inhabitants of the Trobriand Islands off New Guinea, whom ethnologists studied in the early twentieth century.[63] They believed a mother was impregnated by an external spirit, but her husband was crucial in shaping the child from the first awareness of pregnancy, touching the mother, infusing "growth and vitality" with frequent intercourse, catching the child at birth, choosing the child's name, bestowing special gifts of jewelry, and doting on the child tenderly. When weaned, the baby slept with the father. This enveloping care, the Trobrianders believed, molded the child spiritually and even physically to look like the father, cementing a permanent connection.[64] We too understand the power of our words and acts to form our children. And our children form us as well. We become better persons because of our relationships with them.

The role of today's married fathers is more willing, more connected, and deeper than ever. Fathers in intact families have nearly doubled their weekly childcare hours, from 2.7 in 1975 to seven in 2011. (Mothers' weekly hours with kids in that same period soared from 8.2 to fourteen.)[65] This suggests that children are more of a priority in family life—perhaps because after waiting longer to have them, parents have the financial wherewithal and career footing that make children a bonus rather than a burden, a delight rather than a distraction.

At the same time, however, more fathers don't live with their children. In 2010, 27 percent of fathers lived apart from their kids—up from 14 percent in 1970, when divorce rates started to climb. Some of these dads (22 percent) do see their offspring several times a week. More have personal contact one to four times per month (29 percent). A chunk of them drop their visits to "several times a year" (21 percent), and sadly, 27 percent of nonresidential fathers *never* see their children in the course of a year.[66]

But what about electronic communication? Nowadays, no one's without his cell phone. Surely these fathers drop their kids text messages, chat on FaceTime, or just give them a call? Forty-one percent of nonresidential dads do take advantage of these forms of easy communication at least several times a week. Still, 31 percent communicate "less than once a month." There was no survey category for less often than that.[67]

Fathers are far more involved in their children's lives when they live together—out of desire or simply because they're there. Ninety-four percent of fathers at home have a meal with their children "at least several times a week," compared with just 16 percent of fathers who live somewhere else. Sixty-three percent of married at-home fathers help with homework, compared with a mere 10 percent who are living apart. Ninety-three percent of resident dads say they talk to their kids about the events of the day "at least several times a week," compared with 31 percent of nonresident dads.

How can you pass up the total fatherhood opportunity? Imagine yourself at the end of your life looking back. Will you wish you'd made the extra effort to heal your marriage so you hadn't missed the fleeting and precious years of your progeny's childhood? Or is the division in your marriage so unbearable or impossible that those together-family years must be lost?

AN "UNHAPPY FAMILY" VS. AN "UNHAPPY MARRIAGE"

In *How to Know If It's Time to Go: A 10-Step Reality Test for Your Marriage*, Drs. Lawrence Birnbach and Beverly Hyman have you conclude your evaluation of your marriage with the question, "Have I exhausted every remedy to heal my marriage?"[68] In my view, that's the question that should come first. Especially when children are involved, it's crucial to do *everything* to avoid divorce before deciding that divorce is on the table.

Birnbach and Hyman also ask, "Is your unhappy family affecting [your children's] school performance, behavior and self-esteem?" Well, how could an "unhappy family" *not* affect the children? But the dynamic between the parents *alone* may affect them only minimally and need not impair them. Kids live in their own universe, and as long as everything's stable and their parents are reliably there *for them* when needed, they may develop along just fine even if the parents don't like each other. Lots of adults don't remember much if any affection between their parents but nevertheless recall their family as perfectly functional.

"Unhappy family" implies that everyone participates in the conflict. If Mom's screaming, of course everyone's on edge, but screaming because the kids aren't ready for the school bus is not the same as screaming at Dad because he spent the night with another woman. An "unhappy marriage" can coexist with a loving family. It's just not true that everything Mom and Dad say and do with each other determines the entire family's happiness.

Liane's mom was a fourth-grade teacher, her dad was an insurance adjuster with regular eight-to-five hours, and they both had their household jobs. She remembers her mother's frequent irritation with her father. He'd stay at work and not even call. He'd forget to run the errands he'd agreed to do on the way home. Likewise, her dad groused about her mom's messiness—piles of newspapers, laundry not folded or put away, knitting needles left on the floor. Liane barely heard the back-and-forth; it was the expected background noise. And with her three brothers adding to the chaos, well, that was their household.

It never occurred to her that her parents would split. But as soon as she got settled in her dorm at college, they did. Liane's world crumbled. All four of the children tried to convince them to work it out. Just get counseling. Just hire a housekeeper. Just realize what the family meant to all of them. The pleas didn't work. The family home was sold, the parents went their separate ways. Their dad remarried, and their mom continued ruing all the things he had done. Liane is still distressed about it.

Plenty of kids are flummoxed when their parents sit them down and announce they're getting a divorce. Adults like Liane are shocked that their parents could call it quits after enduring so much together. After all, most caring parents take great pains to keep their marital hostilities private. "No arguing in front of the kids" is a fairly common belief. And even in cases where the parents do express their marital dissatisfactions or even fight openly, kids might assume that's just normal. In such cases, there's really no reason to shred the family, but plenty of reason to face the unhealthy marital dynamic.

Unfortunately, popular wisdom and well-meaning friends and therapists encourage a phenomenon called "gray divorce." A couple raise a family together and then decide to end it. As in Liane's family, one partner usually enjoys his or her freedom, and one partner remains alone.

DOUBTING THE "BRIGHT SIDE" OF DIVORCE

Once divorce actually happens, everyone affected by the breakup needs to move on, eventually. Each person has to come to terms with the riven relationship and vent, heal, or find some way to recover from the blow. To that end, many authors offer a helpful hand.

Max Sindell published *The Bright Side: Surviving Your Parents' Divorce* in 2007, the year he graduated from Johns Hopkins University, offering older kids and teens the guidance of a peer.[69] A survivor of his parents' and other relatives' divorces, Sindell has compiled lists, "tips," and advice for surviving the jolt. Many of his pointers are about handling situations usually not thrust on kids, like finding your way alone in a strange airport, meeting a stranger who may become your stepmother, keeping the differences between parents' homes straight.

What intrigued me is that a book actually titled *The Bright Side*, like most divorce recovery books, is bursting with horrible experiences accompanied by suggestions for wading through them without becoming permanently debilitated. Sindell boils the "downside" of divorce down to six inescapable facts:

> You are never going to have one home again.
> Your parents are going to fight.

You may learn things about your parents you didn't *ever* want
to know.
You will probably move more often.
Your parents will lose friends. ("Remember you are the most
important person in the world to them, and.... you can comfort
them better than anyone else can.")
Your parents will have less money.

This gloomy list is followed by the "upside," the silver lining:

You will see more new places.
You will have more independence. ("Since they can't take care
of you all the time, you'll get to start taking care of yourself.")
You will learn how to fly (on a plane, alone).
You will meet a lot of new people (step-parents, step-cousins,
step-aunts, new neighbors—and so you'll learn a lot).
You can become a resource and a mentor for other kids.
You will gain insight into relationships between people (i.e., how
not to act).

It looks to me like the "downside" and the "bright side" could be the
same list. "You *get* to start taking care of yourself"? "Seeing more new
places" is an ominous threat—places like your step-sibling's dad's house,
the inside of a lawyer's office, a therapist's waiting room? Why not just
roll the bright side into a single point: "You 'get' to act like an adult and
lose your innocence." In our book *Saving Childhood: Protecting our
Children from the National Assault on Innocence*,[70] my husband, Michael,
and I argue that childhood is precious, and in our hook-up, sex-obsessed,
mini-me culture, schools, parents, and media cheat kids out of their special
time of imagination, exploration, lack of responsibility, and space to
develop. People ill-advisedly want their kids to be precocious, to be "prepared" for "the real world" that they'll inevitably face. But why rush it?
Why push them into early adolescence with lessons on sexuality when their
bodies are still immature? Why provide the life lesson that people who
once loved can stop loving?

Yes, children adapt to the circumstances in which they find themselves. They develop new skills and understandings, and in the long term the breakup may not interfere with success and achievement. But while they're still at home, divorce robs children of the triple birthright—security, wonder, and optimism—that equips them to venture forth into a challenging world. Parents whose relationships need repair can agree on the centrality of their children's welfare. Try on the notion that softening toward your spouse could save your children's lives. From this motivation you can rekindle the love and romance that brought you and your partner together to create them.

WHEN CHILDREN ARE THE PROBLEM

In some cases, though, the children themselves might be fueling the desire to divorce. When Christine's daughter, Amy, was a little kid, Asperger Syndrome was poorly understood. Amy bounced off the walls in social situations and was the bane of her teachers in school. Christine was frustrated dealing with the administration, who suggested Amy was immature and needed control and discipline.

Amy was diagnosed with Attention Deficit Disorder, the usual approach for kids who couldn't conform, and it was a constant battle for Christine to balance the school, the doctors' prescriptions, and Amy's behavior. The school finally said they couldn't keep Amy in a mainstreamed situation, and moved her to a Special Ed classroom.

Amy's husband, Graham, felt powerless. He loved Amy of course, but got much more reward from their two sons than from this awkward daughter, who didn't seem to return his attention or affection. As Christine became consumed trying to help Amy, Graham backed off. Amy's needs pulled Christine and Graham apart, and Graham finally felt unimportant to his wife.

Amy finally received the proper diagnosis when she was seventeen, but Graham and Christine lived through their distance. Realizing that they needed to reconnect, they attended a church-sponsored weekend marriage retreat, during which they talked about Graham's feeling excluded from Christine's efforts for Amy. He admitted putting up walls so he wouldn't feel hurt by Amy's—and therefore Christine's—rejection. You couldn't say

that Amy herself was the "problem" in Christine's and Graham's marriage—
she was a child whose situation simply required a big investment of time and
energy. But Graham's discomfort with Amy's condition kept him from joining with Christine to help their daughter together. At the same time, Christine accepted responsibility for Amy's education, and sensing Graham's
reaction, went on her own crusade for her.

Birnbach and Hyman, discussing "How Children Falter," describe ways
children act out when their parents aren't getting along, suggesting that parents' staying together in "an unhappy family" has dire consequences for their
children. It can indeed, and the authors discuss children who become
depressed, use bad behavior as a "lightning rod" to get parents' attention, or
become habitually fearful or "cry-babies." It's not pleasant or desirable to live
in a stressful environment, but imagine how much *more* cause these children
have for misbehavior when their parents actually go through with a *divorce*.

Certainly "high-conflict" families pose greater risk to children. But the
continuum of levels of conflict is long, and a degree of discord that might
affect one child could go unnoticed by another. Tzippy told me that her
family was constantly yelling. Her grandparents lived with her family, and
her grandmother would yell at her husband and both Tzippy's mother and
father. The response was always in kind. Anyone who observed Tzippy's
family would have thought her parents were bound for divorce court.[71] But
that was the family style. Calling each other names, raising their voices, and
throwing non-breakable items were their ordinary means of communication.
No one doubted that everyone loved everyone else.

Most families aim for *no* conflagration, but reality brings passions and
disagreements anyway, and even in the most tranquil settings, some children
will act out and others will have problems. As every parent knows, there are
no guarantees in raising children.

But when parental turmoil does become stressful for children, should
the couple divorce? Except in cases of untreated addiction or unrepentant
abuse, divorce might well make the child's problem even *worse*. The pro-
divorce logic is that battling parents cause problems for kids, so a divorce-
induced cease-fire will restore them. But then stopping the fighting by
mending the marriage and staying together should restore the children
better and faster, since they avoid the additional trauma of divorce followed
by the constant change-ups of joint custody or living with a single parent.

Naturally, when children get in trouble, the solution is more complex than parents changing residences, "kissing and making up," or hiding the problems. Parents typically need to improve communication and sort through the differences that lead to conflict, while relating more effectively with their children. Often the substance of their arguments isn't the real problem—it's the willingness of one or both spouses to give in or to show enough commitment to the relationship to work through feelings rather than withdraw.

When Birnbach and Hyman ask couples considering divorce to assess the effect of their chasm on the children, the assumption seems to be that the pair can't control, mitigate, or solve their problems. It's as if being an "unhappy family" were a permanent state. But if you talk to long-married couples, as I have, they tell you that they've gone through phases when their marriages felt distant, stressed, troubled, or even angry. They might even describe the relationship as "unhappy." But at the same time, they view "the family," *their* family, as distinct from their *marriage*.

A dad can get lots of joy from his kids and look forward to coming home to those innocent or mischievous faces while just coasting in his marital relationship. A mom might be overwhelmed with career demands for a time, seemingly putting her marriage on "hold," while she continues fulfilling promises to her kids. One partner might go through a personal challenge—such as an addiction or mental illness—that rips into the marriage, but that personal hurdle can then unite the couple. Or the marriage itself may teeter, with the spouses enduring a wrenching split (as with infidelity), but the solidity of the *family*—the children and parents as a larger unit—remains.

CHILDREN CAN BRING THE SOLUTION

Children often suffer from parents' problems. They can also cause problems for the family, the parents, and themselves. But there's a third possibility: children can directly and indirectly bring a solution to parental discord.

This can happen in several ways. First, the positive. When parents riven by interpersonal problems both derive joy from their children, they've got an important source of unity that improves the rest of their relationship. They might joke that little Joselyn makes the funniest drawings of her siblings or nod to each other with pride when Pablo curls up with another aerospace text. They might enjoy attending Patricia's soccer games, cheering along with the other parents whom they've befriended as a couple. None of this does away with the undercurrent of discord or solves financial or sexual problems, but children create worthwhile bonds with circles of people who view the parents as a couple. These "outside eyes" encourage spouses to live up to expectations that their family is stable and permanent—expectations that can be self-fulfilling.

Most powerfully, a man and a woman who together have brought into the world one or more unique human beings who are the very embodiment of their union have a stake in the family that is greater than either spouse. The narcissism and immediacy that snare angry, disagreeing couples in their right-now emotions undercut their opportunity to perpetrate the best aspects of their bond. Their children are a lasting connection, a legacy of their joining that can never be undone.

"Staying together for the sake of the children" is not masochistic. Parents who do that should be praised for placing their children's futures ahead of their own comfort. Even better, though, is "staying together for the sake of the *family*." The family is the precious, unique assemblage that the love of two parents has created. "The sake of the family" must include the marriage on which it is founded, of course. Parents who stay together "for the sake of the family" benefit from the continuation of their relationship as much as their children do. And that should be the goal: for *every* family member to flourish as an individual and as a valued and respected part of the family. If that's not happening, it's worth enlisting outside help.

Pride in their family and shared interests can draw parents together, but so can misfortune. For Carrie and Joel, it was the phone call from their son's high school informing them he fell and broke his arm while climbing a human pyramid. Though often snappy or arguing, when their son came out of surgery, they were both at the hospital, bonded in their love for him.

Children know their parents will rally around them. They'll sometimes fail academically to manipulate their parents into a combined effort to help. It may not be a conscious conniving, but kids also learn that when they're sick, their folks respond. In some cases, children malinger or develop psychosomatic symptoms to provoke parental collaboration.

On the other hand, children can *directly* influence their parents to overcome problems and strengthen their marriages. Adult children who have learned from their own therapies or who chose a profession in mental health could well apply those skills in helping their parents. One study found that children taught in school to become "change agents" could improve their mothers' bad eating habits. The mothers of change agent students lost more weight and racked up more physical activity than the control group during the experimental period—showing that adults can learn from children, not just the other way around.[72]

Of course, they have to be open to it. I've seen too many cases where adult children come to their parents suggesting a path to reconciliation or expressing anguish over their parents' plight and begging them to change. Adults have told me how their parents divorced as soon as the youngest went to college, leaving them feeling the happy family they remembered was only a sham. Some couples label their entire relationship a "difficult marriage" when in reality there are many warm and even joyous aspects. If the parents focused on those joys instead of bearing with clenched teeth what they've decided is an unhappy marriage they might realize that divorce won't solve their problems. In many cases, the problems are the attitudes of the parents, not the day-to-day reality of the family's life.

CHAPTER 10

The Ruinous Ripples
of Divorce

HURTING THE ONES YOU LOVE

Too many people go into marriage thinking "It's just us against the world!" As Tyler Connolly sang to his wife (at the time), Christine Danielle:

We've got our backs against the ocean
It's just us against the world
Looking at all or nothing
Babe, it's you and I.

Well, not quite. When you're contemplating divorce, you'd rather *think* your backs are against the ocean and it's just you two against…well, at this point, *each other*. But you've got a whole cast of characters to whom your marriage is important, even crucial. By taking the "us against the world" stance, you can ignore the pain and sorrow you're inflicting on these others. Truth is, you're abandoning them. And you're conveniently forgetting how *you* rely on *them*. Do you really want to alienate and harm people who are central to your life?

ONLINE SOCIAL NETWORKS: CHEERFUL CONNECTIONS OR DOORS TO DIVORCE?

Your mom and dad. Your aunts and uncles. Your sisters and brothers. Co-workers. Friends. They're all caught up in the web of caring that Facebook and Instagram are constantly spinning. Now you've got a stream of photos and comments and links and birthday notifications that keep you in touch at all times. When you update your status, you rock the consciousness of, what? Eight hundred "friends"? That tweet you send out in a moment of frustration echoes for days and weeks in retweets and replies, breeding sorrow and doubts throughout your social media world. The breakups of far-flung acquaintances boomerang in subtle encouragement for you to leave too.

Probably the most consequential technological development of recent years is the smartphone. It's always at hand with game apps, Facebook, and Twitter to fill minutes waiting in line or when you're feeling bored. People with necks bent run into posts and humans posting on the street. In a group of people, one "ding!" makes several grab their phones to see if the incoming text is theirs. Couples dining at fine restaurants sit silently, thumbs scrolling beneath the table. We give priority to our virtual social networks even during our visits with real people.

Most use social media to share something cute or happy, but when your marriage is crumbling, they can be an all-too-easy way to vent—which only increases your ire. In her classic *Anger: The Misunderstood Emotion*, Carol Tavris reported that rage builds on itself the more it's expressed.[1] People who stew in their anger only become angrier. Venting might feel good, but "[j]ust because something makes you feel better doesn't mean it's healthy," warns Dr. Brad Bushman, who researches the subject.[2]

"E-venting is particularly risky," cautions the *Wall Street Journal* reporter Elizabeth Bernstein. "We think it's private because we can do it in a secluded place, like our bed while we're in our pajamas. We have our phones with us all the time, so we often e-vent before we've had a chance to calm down. A rant put out via the internet is a click away from being shared. And shared. And shared."[3]

Slater and Gordon, a large British family law firm, noticing "an increase in the number of people citing social media use as a cause of divorce year on year," commissioned a poll of two thousand married respondents. The findings were shocking.

- Fourteen percent had contemplated divorce because of their spouse's activities on Facebook, Skype, Snapchat, Twitter or WhatsApp
- Nearly a quarter said social media use caused at least one argument a week, and 17 percent said they fought every day because of it
- The top causes of arguments were contact with an ex-partner, sending secret messages, and posting inappropriate photos
- Fifteen percent considered social media dangerous to their marriage, with Facebook the biggest threat, followed by WhatsApp, Twitter, and Instagram
- Ten percent admitted they hid images and posts from their partner; eight percent admitted having secret social media accounts
- A fifth of respondents said they felt uneasy about their relationship after discovering something on their partner's Facebook
- Fourteen percent checked their partner's accounts because they suspected infidelity
- A third said they kept their social media password a secret from their partners, though 58 percent said they knew their partner's password, even if their spouse wasn't aware of it[4]

A 2010 survey of members of the American Academy of Matrimonial Lawyers underscores that social media factor heavily in divorce. Overall, 81 percent of AAML members said they had culled more evidence for their divorce cases from social networking websites in the past five years than they did before. And 66 percent of polled attorneys said their primary source of evidence is—you guessed it—Facebook.[5]

A more scientific study in 2014 looked at how social networking sites endanger marriages, correlating social media use with higher divorce rates on both statewide and individual levels.[6] After controlling for a host of variables, they found, predictably, that as Facebook use went up in a state, so did the divorce rate. And their survey on a personal level "revealed a positive correlation between more frequent use of [social networking sites] and the variables that reflected lower marriage quality, marriage unhappiness, experiencing a troubled relationship, and thinking about separating."

Other research examines *why* social networking sites disrupt marriages. Social media can become so compelling that their overuse becomes a *psychological disorder.* A 2011 overview of research reports that 350 million people around the world suffer from "Facebook Addictive Disorder."[7] Ongoing Facebook connections with old lovers and friendships with people one's spouse doesn't know arouse *jealousy,* which can become a loop of increasing distrust and surveillance.

Facebook *facilitates cheating* by enabling users to find partners through its many search options (by name, location, job, college, common friends, email, and so on), suggesting "people you may know," and allowing multiple profiles. Facebook's many communication channels simplify making arrangements to cheat.

Social networking sites provide *support for leaving* a marriage. Messaging options (status updates, wall posts, inbox messages, chat) spur others to encourage you in your decision to break up. One study found that using Facebook several times a day provides half the emotional support of actually being married or cohabiting.[8]

Social networks can be used for good or ill. Aside from the problems they can cause in your marriage, they can also *broadcast* those problems to people you care about, lowering confidence in their own relationships.

FRENEMIES: ONLY TRYING TO HELP

Heather and Megan were best buds since elementary school in Bellevue, Washington. They lived only three blocks apart and did everything together—campouts with their Brownie troop, the summer swim team at the local pool, babysitting in middle school, cheer squad in high school. Heather was the brunette beauty and Megan her blonde counterpart; people laughed when the pair tried to pass themselves off as twins. Together at the University of Washington, they pledged the same sorority. Yep, BFFs.

It was hardly a surprise that with thirty-one fraternities and only sixteen sororities on campus, both of them got snapped up by attentive guys. Heather and Kyle were an odd pair—she was so bubbly and outgoing, and he was quiet and cerebral. But they seemed to complement each other, especially since both came from happy local families and accepted one another's idiosyncrasies. Their relationship fell into an easy rhythm, and having a reliable date for weekly social events made life so much easier. Megan went through several months-long liaisons before meeting Travis in her senior year. With plans to go to law school, he was exactly what Megan always wanted.

The two couples got along fabulously. Megan and Travis were the first to marry, and Heather planned the whole thing with Megan's mom. The day was beautiful, and as the bridal couple drove off amid confetti and noisemakers, Kyle took Heather aside and proposed. A year later, everyone returned to the same venue for the second wedding.

Travis started law school while also working for a financial planning firm. Megan starting working for an internet marketing firm, and they were off on a great millennial lifestyle, buying a condo and taking weekend jaunts with Heather and Kyle to Mount Adams or Victoria or the Walla Walla wineries.

Heather and Kyle bought a house, a little fixer-upper in West Seattle with a peek-a-boo view of Puget Sound. Teaching certificate in hand, Heather taught second grade a half hour from her home, and with an inheritance Kyle bought a bar and started to brew craft beers.

Heather had just returned home from school one Wednesday when she got the shock of her life—a hysterical call from Megan saying Travis had walked out. "I never thought he'd leave," Megan wept. "I told him I loved him; I told him whatever he wanted I'd do, but...." She dissolved in sobs. Heather rushed to Megan's place, where she found her friend lying on the sofa, smudged mascara making raccoon circles under eyes red from crying.

"He won't answer my calls...."

"What was this about?" Heather asked.

"He caught me. I have a boyfriend." She started to cry again.

Heather was stunned. She had had no clue her lifelong friend was cheating. Everything seemed fine; their easy banter was never strained.

"Well, what do you want to do?" Heather asked. "You can't keep seeing this guy. Who is he?"

"Brother of somebody I work with. He was helping set up for the party.... I didn't mean for it to get physical; I didn't mean for it to ruin my marriage...." More sobs.

Heather would never cheat on Kyle. How could Megan do it? But BFFs have a job, and that's to pick up the pieces when necessary. She grabbed a washcloth in the bathroom and ran the hot water, squeezed it out and brought it to her friend. "Here, clean up and take some deep breaths."

Two hours and some pretty interesting stories later, Heather understood the attraction Megan had felt for Dustin. She knew Travis was studying some nights and left Megan to her own devices, but didn't she care that she was playing with fire? And it wasn't a one-time encounter, either, but had been going on for a *month*.

"I was in denial," Megan said. "I knew I was attracted, but it just seemed like playing, like make-believe. After all, I'm being creative all day. Imagination is a tool of my job."

In her head Heather was thinking, "Yeah, that Dustin's a real tool, all right," but she said, "I know. You didn't mean to. I know you really love Travis."

Heather picked up some Chinese take-out, and as they ate it with chopsticks out of the cartons, Megan reassured her friend that she would never abandon her. Then they marathon-watched *How I Met Your Mother* and found themselves giggling as when they were teenagers. Megan fell asleep on the couch, and Heather said a quiet goodbye and drove home, disbelieving the evening she'd just experienced.

Kyle was waiting for her. He was upset, too. "I got a call from Travis an hour ago," he said, brow furrowed. "He told me what Megan did. Who *is* that woman? How could she do this?"

Not only had Megan's misdeeds spoiled her marriage, but now they'd placed Heather and Kyle on opposite sides. Heather was committed to helping Megan through this, and Kyle was as devastated and bereft as his male friend. It was a crisis for two couples.

Travis slept at his folks' for two weeks and wouldn't take Megan's hourly phone calls. He wouldn't respond to her texts or Facebook messages. He'd been completely above-board and trusting, and now his entire future was in question.

Kyle consoled him and ignored Heather's urging that Travis should give Megan another chance. Kyle put himself in Travis's shoes, knowing he'd turn away if ever Heather did something like this to him. If Megan could cheat, then anything was possible. Travis started showing up at the bar after work. Megan asked Heather to spend evenings with her, saying she didn't want to be alone in the condo. Megan's month-long fling was opening up chasms in *four* people's relationships.

Loyalty in friendship is precious. And when friends need us, we respond by supporting them whatever direction they want to go in, even if it's the wrong one. But that's doing a disservice to them and to ourselves. In a breakup we take our friend's part, sometimes unwisely, and we sympathize even if we should be doing some reality therapy. By trying not to be judgmental when a friend is suffering, you *endorse* what's happening, even if it's destructive, unfair, or cruel. And by standing back, you let the tectonic shift reverberate over time and space, damaging each relationship in the temblor's path.

IS DIVORCE CONTAGIOUS?

Social networks spread "social contagions." A young woman becoming pregnant, for example, influences her best friend to become pregnant as well,[9] though when it comes to getting married, the influence of the larger peer group is stronger than that of individual friends.[10] What about divorce, then? Is it "contagious"? The short answer is *yes*.

With divorce, the influence of friends is extreme. The conclusion of one large study, which interviewed subjects periodically over three decades, was that those "who have a friend who has previously gotten divorced are 270% more likely to get divorced themselves by the time they come to their next [interview]."[11] Looking at friendship *networks*, the same researchers found that persons in the same crowd were *75 percent more likely to divorce* if just one person in their group got divorced. And this influence moves outward to friends of friends—that's "two degrees of separation"—who are 33 percent more likely to divorce, even without knowing the busted couple personally.

Heather and Kyle, at just a single degree of separation from Megan and Travis, are in a precarious position. Torn by differing allegiances to their best friends and under the stress of propping them up emotionally, their relationship is already vulnerable to trouble, especially if Megan and Travis do eventually divorce. The story of these four friends is another sad example of how quickly everything can change.

A letter published in the syndicated column *Ask Amy* under the headline "Friends' messy split leaves everyone feeling the pain" might have been written by Heather:

> Dear Amy:
>
> A couple very close to my husband and me split up recently because of repeated infidelity on her part. The impact of this split has been heartbreaking to us and our other friends.
>
> The husband confides in us and lives nearby. The wife has moved out, maintained toxic relationships with grad-school friends and has not chosen to confide in us. She and I are childhood friends. Most recent encounters have been dishonest and painful.
>
> Things recently hit the fan when we hosted a gathering to celebrate the arrival of our second daughter. I invited the husband but not the wife—because of the general pain and awkwardness it causes.
>
> When the ex-wife found out about her exclusion, she responded angrily to me—wanting to meet, express her unmet expectations and dish out childhood baggage about how she's been wronged.
>
> I say I love her, and we are friends, but it is uncomfortable and extremely painful to have her in a situation where her ex is also there. We seem to get nowhere in understanding each other. I admit to her that I still feel angry about her infidelities and general lack of love in the last year or so. I'm not trying to shut her out, but at some point this is all very exhausting, confusing, and too much work.

How can I communicate a nonjudgmental presence while still protecting our family gatherings and friendships?
—Not-So-Fast-Friend

How would you answer her? I'd say Not-So-Fast is showing the mercy of Mother Teresa, and I wouldn't put up with even a childhood chum who was "dishonest and painful" to be around. And when I see that word "nonjudgmental," I want to shake that woman's shoulders and say, "Judgments are *good*!"

Columnist Amy's response is much more noncommittal:

> Dear Friend: You can't communicate a nonjudgmental presence when you're busy judging. I'm not saying your judgment is flawed—but more that you should cop to it and live with it. And so my basic advice could be summed up like this: Whoever causes the least trouble gets the brunch.... You two old friends should try harder to be patient with each other until things settle down.

Most problems in a friendship do call for patience and understanding. Most fall somewhere between right and wrong, where it's okay to withhold judgment because there are pros and cons to whatever one chooses. But not this one! Is it *wrong* to cheat on a spouse habitually (or at all)? Is it *wrong* to bitch and moan if you're left off a baby-welcoming brunch? Is it *wrong* to unload on your longtime friend when she was simply protecting her guests from awkwardness and pain? Come on.

Choosing to be nonjudgmental is in itself a judgment. When you take that stance, you leave your friends in a free-fall, letting their emotions dominate their decision-making. Remember, in romance, marriage, and divorce, *emotions trump logic*. By letting your friend succumb to passionate pitfalls, you're neglecting the duties of friendship. Instead of rescuing someone you care about from an unbalanced choice (that is, one based on emotions, no logic), you zip the lip and watch her fail.

If your friend insists on behaving atrociously, so be it. But if she tries to pull *you* into it, expecting you to abet that behavior even if it pains you, it's time for a judgment call. First, be forthright with your friend, as you'd like a true friend to be with you. Second, if divorce is contagious, you have to put on a mask, gulp tea with lemon, and *isolate yourself* from the virus of discontent. If Not-So-Fast-Friend's childhood buddy wants company in her misery, the advice-seeking pal can just opt out. *Don't knowingly expose yourself to the disease of divorce.*

The way to avoid exposure is to surround yourself with people you want to emulate, people who reinforce the values you want to cultivate in your marriage and in yourself. Above all, stick to your partner like glue! Resisting divorce starts with your own values and actions. "People with better social skills may select into better marriages and also have access to more supportive friendship networks," writes the social scientist Rose McDermott.[12] In turn, "Those supportive friendship networks may also make it easier for individuals to weather inevitable marital stresses without having to resort to marital rupture."[13]

Earlier work shows that couples whose social circle consists of solidly married couples are themselves less likely to divorce, no matter how long they have been married.[14] "Those with a good relationship also possess a strong, supportive friendship network, and vice versa," writes Dr. McDermott. Just as troubled couples can contaminate their friends' marriages, solid, happy couples can boost their friends' immunity.

FRIENDSHIP'S ULTERIOR MOTIVES

Friendships can be complex. Your friends will be there for you when you're a puddle of tears, but they'll also be there *for themselves*. And sometimes their needs may conflict with what's best for you.

Imagine you're Stephanie, whose husband of three years, Randy, just jumped ship. You have no explanation—he just "had to leave," and now you're a mess. You text five of your reliable confidantes, the crew you meet twice a year for some "girl time." Two of them went to high school with you, two were in your college dorm, and one you've known since you worked together at a summer camp when you were freshmen. These are your best buds, and right now they've dropped their plans for the evening to help you cope with your devastating news. They're sitting on pillows and poufs in your living room holding glasses of the merlot Brianna brought.

Becky, a never-married high school friend whose parents split when she was six: "Steph, this isn't the worst thing in the world. You're healthy. You're brilliant. You've got a great job. So many people get divorced, it's just the norm nowadays. You're lucky you don't have kids—that would be a disaster. But look, you're free as a bird and your marriage and divorce can just fade into the background. It's the start of the rest of your life!"

Brianna, who works at a winery and shares a rental house with Becky: "There's really no reason you have to even *tell* anyone about your marriage. You're beautiful, and you'll have your pick of guys. I'll teach you how to get dates on Bumble and Hinge, and there's really no risk, no creeps stalking you. Staying married is like wasting your talent! You're lucky you'll get to see the wider world out there!"

Rachel, Stephanie's college dorm-mate, has been living with Tim for four years and complains he doesn't want to commit: "Steph, you got married so young, you couldn't expect Randy to just settle down. He was only twenty-one at your wedding! I know he was ga-ga over you, and you had a great run, but boys will be boys. They've got a genetic predisposition against permanence. Tim says the days of marriage are over, and everybody in a relationship chooses every day to stay or go. And it's true—anybody can leave at any time, if you think about it."

Willow, the fellow camp counselor, married three years and due in October: "That's right; Randy just showed his true colors. He pretended to love you all these years, but then one day he turns around and does *this*? What kind of scumbag just abandons his wife? What kind of jerk plays along like everything's fine and slaps you in the face this way—you, the person who gave your whole *life* to him? Now you know you can never trust him. Even if he didn't fool around—and you don't know the whole story!—you'll never be sure you won't turn around one day and he'll do it again; he'll be gone!"

Finally Tara speaks up. She's a social worker in an adequate marriage, hoping to afford to buy a house: "Well, maybe we don't *know* what kind of jerk he is. I mean, maybe he was secretly unhappy for a long time but didn't want to bring *you* down, Stephanie. Maybe he just bolted when he finally had enough, running for his life. You *can* be a bit forceful, Steph. You know we love you for it, but...ya gotta put yourself in his place. He must have had a pretty good reason to leave."

Five friends, five sincere attempts to soothe and buck up their buddy. And not a one suggesting Stephanie's marriage should continue. Not a one saying maybe the relationship should be rekindled, that the problems that drove Randy out should be examined and the marriage repaired. Their perspectives left Stephanie with only the option of accepting Randy's exit and trudging forward, their supportive shoulders there to lean on.

But of course Becky is remembering what it was like to live through her own parents' divorce—the emotion, the dislocation, and finally the routine of changing houses every other weekend. Her world was populated with siblings enduring the same shuffle and friends at after-school day care, nearly all from divorced homes. She learned to accept it, to have self-confidence, and to make her way as an adult. She projects that divorce is simply a part of marriage, to be expected. Stephanie should just get used to it, as she did.

Brianna, eager to find a boyfriend, is caught up in the whirlwind of dating and meeting-people apps, pushing herself to make enough contacts so that eventually she'll find the right partner. She gets a lot of compliments and come-ons to bolster her ego and convince her that she's taking advantage of her youth. Now's the time to get dating out of her system, and yes, she enjoys many adventures. She has a stake in the lure—and the lie—of the singles' scene.

Rachel secretly wants what Stephanie had. She's been living with Tim because she loves him and can't understand why he won't marry her if he loves her as much as he says he does. Why won't he give her what she wants more than anything—the security of marriage and the confidence to have a family? Put a ring on it! But unable to convince Tim to budge, she'd rather *have* him than *lose* him. At least if they're together, there's the chance he could change his mind... so she accepts his argument that marriage isn't necessary and in fact isn't even natural.

Willow, her baby ever on her mind, is insecure. She doesn't have any real reason to doubt her solid marriage, but she's feeling vulnerable with this new life soon to become her responsibility. Her unspoken fear is that her husband will leave her—a fear based on underlying nervousness about becoming a mom and worry she'll be stranded and unable to care for her infant alone. An only child, she's had little experience with youngsters and suspects she's incompetent. So Stephanie is living the abandonment scenario that terrifies her.

Tara, whose job is to empathize with her social work clients, identifies with Randy because *she's* struggling with lack of fulfillment in her own marriage. She's fantasized many times about up-and-leaving, but she could never go through with it. She feels especially bad because, a therapist herself, she should *know* how to correct her situation; she should *know* to communicate rather than suffer in silence with her well-meaning and unsuspecting husband. She wishes she had the gumption to do what Randy did.

Listen to your friends' marriage-doubting advice with gratitude for their caring but clarity about their bias. Their response is *colored* by their individual situations and life experiences. In our marriage-discarding culture, most people have divorce in their families if not in their own histories. Articles and news stories talk about rebounding after divorce rather than the troubled-marriage or decision-making phases that precede the actual split. Think about how many posts and pieces you've seen about "getting along with your ex for the sake of the children" or "returning to the job market after divorce." Once you drop the D-word, all that backdrop informs your friends' responses.

In a culture that overwhelmingly accepts divorce, you'll have to seek out advocates for the tough job of rebuilding. Friends see their job as comforting and bolstering you *where they find you*. Friends know how to rally round if you get divorced; how to help you restore a troubled marriage isn't so clear. Beware well-meaning friends!

DIVORCING AN EXTENDED FAMILY

"I wanted grandchildren since my own kids went off to college, and I've had to wait till I'm fifty-five for my first one, so you darned better believe I'm going to spoil her!" Carmen insisted. "Now I've got Mia, ten, Camila, eight, and Mateo, five, and I wouldn't trade a day with them!" She showed me a string of selfies on her phone with each of the smiling kids—at the park, on the Venice boardwalk eating cotton candy, at the doll museum. "On my babysitting days I take them out together and one-on-one. Well, that is I *took* them. Ever since my son and daughter got a divorce, I hardly ever get them. They're traded back and forth like potatoes!"

She quietly put her phone back in her purse. "Sunday is our family day—we all go to the park and make a big lunch after church," Carmen explains. "The boys play catch, my sister and I bounce the girls on our knees...till they get too big, and then we braid their hair and do their nails, and somebody brings out a guitar." But now the extended family is missing her precious grandchildren; they're with their mom and her relatives.

"Divorce? Whoever expected that? I knew the kids didn't get along sometimes, but my husband would always say that they could work it out. God brought them together, and He could help them through their problems." Tears glistened in the corners of Carmen's eyes.

"I don't think they'll ever fix their problems now—it's been a year since the divorce and my son brought a nice woman last Sunday. She has two kids of her own. After college, my son went for his master's and started teaching history at a community college. I'm proud of him, but not for the divorce. I tell him how much I miss the kids, how much I miss Sara, his wife. She was my daughter. I let her into my heart, and now I can't even call her. I feel like now I've lost her and my own grandchildren."

When couples split, their parents become a resource. A place to head with a packed suitcase. Somebody to watch the kids during appointments. Unconditional love and support no matter the hurt or complaint. Adults whose parents are healthy assume Mom and Dad keep their protective roles until they die.

But as elders whose children divorce relate, their role as *grandparents* is by allocation and permission only, out of their control. They see their grandchildren if and when the custodial parent chooses. Grandparents, like children, become collateral damage to divorce. Sometimes they don't accept it so easily.

Divorcesource.com reports: "A large percentage of grandparents have petitioned the court in the hopes of obtaining a regular visitation schedule with the grandchild(ren). Quite naturally, as a by-product of these factors, the individual states have had to address the issues of non-parental custody and the visitation rights of grandparents. As is the case with other divorce-related issues, the laws with regards to grandparent custody and visitation differ from state to state."[15] Grandparents' rights include custody (when parents can't or won't take over) and visitation, which sets a schedule. If a vindictive wife won't relinquish kids to visit their paternal grandparents, sometimes the only alternative is to sue.

Divorcesource.com continues:

> In any situation where a grandparent goes to court in an attempt
> to secure visitation rights, it is naturally assumed that there must

be animosity amongst the respective family members. The rationale is that if such animosity did not exist, there would be no need for the intervention of the court. Case histories have amply demonstrated that even when the grandparents are awarded a visitation schedule, the parents who oppose are not likely to comply with the court order. While grandparents do have outlets to enforce court orders, such as contempt and incarceration, it is generally recognized that the existing animosity will only increase. Often, the court takes this into consideration as they feel that such situations only serve to increase the stress placed upon the child(ren) and therefore work against the "best interests" theory.[16]

In other words, estranged Granny, even the court might be against you. Just demanding a chance to *see* your grandchildren can be viewed as detrimental to their welfare.

The expectation seems to be that grandparents, whose hearts are breaking over both their children's divorce and the loss of contact with grandchildren, should just shut up and be supportive. As the saying goes, "blood is thicker than water," and even if their child has been a betrayer or an abuser, parents usually back their offspring (and thereby alienate the victim).

The following true story rocked these couples' small community. Ruth and Joel lived just a mile from Sylvia and Christopher. They often went on outings together, bringing their children, who were the same age, and the two couples had a weekly rhythm of trying new restaurants then catching the opera, a jazz club, or a movie. They enjoyed simpatico closeness—until Joel and Sylvia started flirting. They were subtle at first and over time came to meet midday. Christopher was the one who first noticed—a giggling phone call when Sylvia was supposedly setting up their son's birthday party. He knew her affect well enough to tell something was going on, and he confronted her. His tolerance for her deception with his good friend was zero.

Sylvia's and Joel's stunning audacity caused the destruction of two families, affecting six children. Innocent, naïve Ruth couldn't believe her husband would do such a thing. Christopher got it immediately and hired a private detective to uncover as much as he could. When he presented the evidence to Ruth, Joel's lies crushed her.

When the couples broke up, Joel took his suitcases to his parents' house. Still living on the property where he grew up, they had a separate-entrance guesthouse that Joel took over, (as well as two extra bedrooms, including the one frozen in time since Joel graduated high school). They were shocked by their son's disgraceful behavior but felt an obligation to support him. In so doing, they were forced to ignore the fifteen years Ruth and Joel had been together. They loved Ruth, they loved their grandkids. But they wouldn't refuse their son a place of refuge, and losing the rest of his family was the regrettable fallout.

Joel lived in his folks' guesthouse rent-free for three years. Seven years after the two divorces, Sylvia and Joel finally did get married. Christopher carried a hatred for both his ex-wife and former friend. It was a mess. But the grandparents suffered too. They knew Ruth was in deep depression, that their son had flattened her kind heart and childlike trust. But they couldn't reach out to her because of loyalty to their son and their own embarrassment for sheltering him.

Steve Salerno, a grandfather, shared his own story in the *New York Times* magazine. He recalled the day his twenty-six-year-old son, Graig, had come over and admired a photo of his daughter, Sophia, snapped by the writer's wife, Kathy. The child is alone in a park gazing at the camera. "At 18 months, she stands with her chubby arms at her sides, in the shade of a large oak, amid ankle-high green grass...."

The melancholy triggered by that photo, one "I could not bring myself to box up," illustrates a grandparent's loss:

> We didn't know it that day, but it would be the last time we would see Sophia—the last time before her mother scooped the baby up one afternoon and ran out on Graig. Then, when he reported her for abducting his daughter, she played her trump card, admitting for the first time that my son might not be Sophia's biological father. Within a month, mismatched DNA settled the matter. At that point, Graig's ex decided that since Sophia had been the only thing binding her to Graig, she now wanted nothing more to do with any of us. Her relationship with my son, not unlike my own, had been an endless succession of quarrels. And though Kathy and I always got along well with

her, she now blamed us for showing partiality during the legal wrangling. Just like that it was over. Legally, none of us had any further right to see Sophia if her mother didn't want us to. And she didn't want us to.[17]

SIBLINGS, STEPS, SOCIALIZING

The marital status of your brothers and sisters affects your own marriage and vice versa. You're 22 percent more likely to divorce if you have a divorced sister or brother.[18] But siblings—if you have enough of them—can also provide a defense against divorce. A 2013 study of a huge national sample found that siblings in larger families (four to seven kids) have lower divorce rates than those from families with one to three children, even controlling for a range of factors like education, race, age, religion, and being raised by a single mom or intact family. The authors speculate that the give-and-take between a large number of people provides conflict-resolution practice.[19]

Divorce makes families complicated. So family members must practice their conflict-resolution among an increasing assortment of in-laws and, well, "outlaws." Consider the complex permutations of relationships brought about by gay and straight couplings, living together, babies out of wedlock, and serial monogamy.

My daughter was best friends with Olivia, the daughter of an excellent teacher at their high school, Mrs. Bright. Olivia was one of six siblings, and their family welcomed all the friends of each outgoing child to their home. We included Olivia on one of our family vacations, and viewed her family as strong and happy. The girls graduated high school, and Olivia started off a gap year building homes in Honduras with Habitat for Humanity. Always civic-minded, she planned to earn a degree in social work.

Shortly thereafter, Mrs. Bright came out as gay and announced she wanted a divorce. The kids, completely flummoxed, coped as well as they could. Their dad had known it was coming but had wanted to maintain their family life as long as possible. The house was sold and the proceeds split. The two oldest children were already on their own, but when the teacher mom married her lover (who had five children of her own) and took another teaching job, she moved with the three youngest kids to another state.

Suddenly Olivia had double her already large family. When Mrs. Bright and her wife invited all the kids together one Easter, Olivia said, "Her house felt like a hotel, not a home. We were used to a level of chaos before—we had a pile of white socks and all just took a pair every morning, stuff like that—but this was different because I only knew half the people there, and I was supposed to treat everyone like family, all the same. It was really awkward."

Wouldn't you want to keep your life *simple*?

It's true that people aren't inspired to mend their marriages just to avoid a chaotic conglomeration of relations. These hodge-podge families are more often imposed by others' decisions. But it's worth considering how frequent shuffles of spouses and live-ins break and complicate the love-links we forge. If you're uncomfortably exposed to exes and steps and a far-flung list of others because relationships are unpredictable, are you more or less likely to get close to that transitory tribe? Do you invest your emotion in your father's new wife and her daughters and their kids? Or do you hold back lest the investment be in vain? Not knowing who will be long-term and who won't inhibits you from becoming loyal and vulnerable to *anyone*, fostering superficiality in the family and community.

In a column for the *New York Times*, the novelist Ann Patchett described an annual Christmas Eve party that she and her husband hosted so that different family factions could come together in a relatively conflict-free zone. "Because my parents divorced when I was very young and my father was never friendly about being in the same room with my mother, I thought I was creating the holiday equivalent of Switzerland," she explained. "You could see your mother and your father and your stepparents and grandparents and step-grandparents in the same room and wish them a Merry Christmas instead of driving all over town like a crazy person trying to fit everyone in."

You can understand her dilemma: "Of course, this was easy for me because I lived in Nashville and my father and step-mother lived in California, and the person I thought of as my stepfather, who was my mother's second husband, lived in Texas, and his four children, two of whom I am still very close to, lived far away, which is to say the real complexity in my own family was someplace else on Christmas Eve."

Without knowing anything else about this family, one might conclude the problem is less location and more the propensity to divorce.

After her mother's third husband protested that he could not take the hated party one more year, the project fell apart. "It turned out our holiday bash was almost universally despised and the people who attended did so mainly because they thought it was The Right Thing to Do," Ms. Patchett admitted. "The modern family is a dark and twisted river. All I can say is I was trying to navigate as best I knew how."[20]

Somebody's got to say no, like Ms. Patchett's mother's third husband (who has three children) and Ms. Patchett's husband (with children in their teens when she met him). But instead of resisting pressure to socialize in a meaningless sphere of barely-known relations, why doesn't each of us, personally and publicly, say no to prejudice against the family-making marriages we already have? It's bad enough to say bye-bye to one you once loved; it's eternally consequential to end a marriage that produced offspring. The more confusing and less connected the mélange of relationships gets, the less we will care about each other. This is the legacy of the new norm, serial monogamy.

Your divorce makes a difference even to mere onlookers. The researcher M. Christian Green has written about the "bystander response" to divorce. It's the term coined in response to the 1964 murder of Kitty Genovese in New York City, supposedly witnessed by thirty-eight bystanders who ignored her screams. Relatives and friends who don't want to get involved in your marriage may just step back and do nothing instead of intervening. Siblings, friends, and families of a divorcing couple offer the excuse that a marriage is *private*. "Yet putatively private relationships have increasingly been shown to have wider effects...on the views, decisions, and choices of a range of bystanders," Ms. Green writes.[21] Even watching a couple's breakup from the sidelines or family fringes affects your values and your relationship as well as theirs.

WORKPLACE WOES: CO-WORKERS AND DIVORCE

The ruinous ripples of divorce lap outward to your colleagues at work, even as your colleagues' toxic attitudes about marriage affect you. Sue Shellenbarger, the *Wall Street Journal*'s "Work and Family" columnist, reported on a 2001 Swedish study of thirty-seven thousand employees, the first to explore the effect of co-workers on employees' marriages. The researchers found that "working with co-workers who are all of the opposite sex increases the divorce rate by a startling 70%, compared with an office filled with co-workers of the same sex. Whether the co-workers were single or married had no impact."

Even working with people who are of the same sex as yourself can be dangerous to marriage. "The risk of divorce rises 60% if all co-workers of the same sex are single, rather than married—perhaps because the co-workers provide role models for the single life," writes Shellenbarger.

And as it is among friends, divorce at the workplace is contagious. "A married person is 43% more likely to get divorced if one-third of his or her co-workers are recently divorced people of the opposite sex, than if none of the co-workers were recently divorced." So your divorce hurts many more than just you and your family and friends.

Shellenbarger quotes a man who lost his "trusted wife" of twenty years after she started working at a clinic: "I believe a sort of euphoria and infatuation takes place between some people who work closely together." A New Jersey production supervisor used willpower to resist a handsome flirting co-worker, "Quite honestly, there was a thrill to it. It's something to look forward to when you come to work—the little innuendoes, the sly looks." Apparently the antidote is to work alongside your spouse—which reduces the risk of divorce by 50 percent.[22]

And that's the important message: bond to your mate. The more contact, the more interchange, the more affirmation of your value to each other, the stronger the relationship.

All the (Wrong) Reasons: Answering the Arguments for Divorce

CHAPTER 11

When Divorce Is Necessary: How to Know When to Quit

ADDICTION

C ertain circumstances demand immediate disengagement—specifically, any physical abuse, persistent emotional abuse, and untreated addiction. I mentioned before the urgency of calling an abuse hotline if you're ever subject to physical lashing-out. If your safety is in question, better to err on the side of caution. And counsel from a professional on the details of leaving could save you from the dangerous fit of anger that a wife's exit sometimes sparks.

A partner's refusal to acknowledge or treat an addiction is another justification for divorce. In a survey of four thousand divorced persons conducted for the Austin Institute in 2014, 23 percent cited alcohol or drug abuse as the reason for their divorce.[1] There is a genetic predisposition to addiction, and many who succumb require medical intervention and ongoing vigilance to avoid relapse (which is common in any case). The powerful physical pull of the addiction causes desperate addicts to commit irrational, deceptive, and reckless acts that override any love or consideration for the spouse.

One of the best motivators for an addict to stay strong is the support of a loyal and loving mate, but it's not always enough to save a marriage. Lance, a nephrologist, became addicted to painkillers after a back injury. He resorted to writing prescriptions for his wife and children, and later used the names of his mother-in-law and siblings and anyone else he thought wouldn't check. Eventually, of course, he was found out, and his medical license suspended. Marcy and their three boys—aged fourteen, sixteen, and seventeen—were shocked, but they realized Lance had a disease. He checked into a residential rehab center about 150 miles from home, where he underwent drug withdrawal and intensive therapy, including several hours daily of group therapy with other medical professionals.

After two months, Lance was welcomed home by Marcy and the boys, and he started the rounds at Alcoholics Anonymous, while his ever-supportive wife began attending daily meetings of Al-Anon, the national support group for families and friends of addicts. Each day, while she was at her job managing a women's clothing store, Lance spent hours watching TV on their sixty-inch screen. He didn't talk about his time in rehab, but the two months there had left him distant and lethargic, frustrated by the loss of his hospital job.

That wasn't going to stop Marcy from reading everything she could on addiction, trying to be the most supportive partner she could be. After she learned that people are genetically predisposed to addiction, she came to some insights about Lance's family background, and urged him to get therapy, alone and with her as a couple, despite their quickly-draining savings.

One Saturday evening about four months after Lance had returned from rehab, with the boys all at friends', she asked Lance if he'd like to go to a movie. "Are you more in the mood for a thriller or a comedy?" she asked.

"Actually, I don't want to go with you to a movie or anywhere. I've been wanting to tell you, I realized that my needs aren't being met in this marriage, and I want out."

Marcy couldn't believe her ears. Aside from her hours at work, her whole life was immersed in her husband's recovery. Didn't her unwavering support while he was in rehab, dutiful strength maintaining their home, and reassurance to the kids that Dad would pull through prove her devotion? She went to Al-Anon meetings every day; they helped her cope but were centered on him.

"What can we do to fix this?" Marcy pleaded.

"Nothing."

"What was wrong with our marriage?" she begged, though she knew their sex life had been nil for two years. She attributed that to the drugs and dealing with rehab. She suspected he was impotent, though he rebuffed her suggestions to see a doctor.

"Nothing. I respect you, but I'm no longer in love with you."

He packed a single suitcase and said he'd be in touch. "Where are you going?" she pleaded.

"A hotel. You can tell the boys."

She had the presence of mind to respond, "No, *you* tell them. I don't understand why you're doing this."

No reply. That was it, the "chop-and-run" that completely changed Marcy's life. Lance gave her little information except that rehab had empowered him to finally do something about his discontent. He'd been shifting their finances and preparing for this moment since he got out. Marcy came to refer to rehab as the "Greek chorus" of men who urged Lance to leave.

This was a case of no recourse. Soon after leaving, Lance spoke to their minister, a preemptive tactic, it turned out, because when Marcy came to ask him how to restore the marriage, the clergyman responded, "You're lucky to be rid of him."

And the counselor they'd been seeing was equally primed. "There's no hope of his returning," she told Marcy, though the therapist could not divulge more than that.

Marcy's and Lance's case is complicated because it revolves around two factors, drug abuse and the desire to chop and run to a completely different life. He left behind everything except half his clothes, telling Marcy to give them to Goodwill. Their sons were devastated, and Marcy could barely function. The oldest boy had to make meals and care for his brothers while facing his own distress.

If you are married to an addict, you have a lot of company. Marital conflicts plague the twelve to thirteen million alcoholics in the United States, as well as drug addicts. "According to results from the 2010 National Survey on Drug Use and Health, an estimated 2.4 million Americans used prescription drugs non-medically for the first time within the past year, which averages to approximately 6,600 initiates per day," the National Institute on Drug Abuse reports.[2] There were 8.76 million prescription drug abusers in the United States in 2010.[3]

When substance abuse threatens in your marriage, much depends on the behavior of the addict himself. An addict may sincerely wish to reform, and yet his compulsion may control him. In such a case, you must weigh experience against potential. A spouse unable to stick with a program to address his addiction, acting primarily for his own gratification, may also be incapable of providing the respect and affection you deserve. The family message board on Al-Anon's website is filled with poignant testimonies about "how divorce fits into our recovery process":

> The process of divorce is heart-wrenching, even when you *know* it is the right thing for everyone (which I knew). It truly is like a death, and if you decide to divorce, there will be some very dark days.... I also tell people that if they choose not to divorce, working on themselves (instead of trying to fix their spouses) will also almost surely lead to a happier existence.

> I've thought about things like what would sleeping alone be like, where would I live, would I get an apartment or could I afford a house, how could I ever live without him, how could I ever be with another man, what will his family think, will they hate me, and most of all, I think: how could I ever possibly say goodbye to the unbelievably amazing man I fell head of [sic] heels in love with. The man who used to make me laugh, who laughed with me, who supported me, loved me, encouraged me, surprised me with flowers.... I just cannot yet imagine not being with him.

> But, he has this alternate (drunk) personality now that I cannot live with for much longer. I miss the man I fell in love with. But, I also miss the old me, and I'm trying to get her back, get my life back, get my confidence back...so, who knows how I'll feel when that truly happens.

A simple suggestion would be another "D" word...Work on Deeeeetachment before thinking about using Deeeeevorce. It is a form of divorce but not permanent, works best one day at a time and has much better wholistic [sic] consequences.[4]

As these posts reveal, alcohol and drug abuse often changes an addict's personality for the worse, transforming him into an unrecognizable and unreasonable partner. They underscore that divorce, even in extreme situations, entails deep feelings of loss. They remind us that no one has real control over another—influence, perhaps, but not control. Sometimes efforts and good intentions fail, and sometimes it's misguided even to try to change another person (though that can be a rationalization for withdrawing). The last post I quoted suggests an important alternative to divorce—detaching from the other emotionally as a step toward eventually resetting the marriage. Choosing to detach while at the same time remaining in the marriage may be a wise intermediate step that severs a co-dependence and allows both parties their own recovery paths. When the addicted spouse regains strength and sobriety, the door to reconciliation remains open.

In some cases, no matter what you do, you cannot convince, cajole, manipulate, lead, plead, or otherwise change the mind of a spouse who is determined to leave. But in other cases one or more methods *work*. Do not be afraid to try every possibility that might strike the right chord with your partner's particular outlook and experience. This is *your marriage*.

By the way, "manipulation" has acquired the nefarious connotation of underhandedness. We think of someone who's "manipulative" as selfishly and perhaps deceptively influencing others. But we can also manipulate people and events in a beneficial direction. Everyone manipulates his or her environment and others every day—that's our power "to win friends and influence people," to shape events. That's the core of creativity and innovation—manipulating something or someone into something better.

When it comes to your marriage, others might shrink from judging, but *you* don't have that option. In fact, you are *the one person* who will decide what happens in your marriage next. You are entitled to judge. You are entitled to believe in your marriage even if you receive little or no validation.

Expect other people to nod their heads in approval no matter what you say. Then explicitly seek out support for your goal to rebuild your marriage.

Susan Pease Gadoua, a social worker writing in *Psychology Today*, expresses the devastating effect of addiction on marriage:

> Because all addictive illnesses are progressive, the only path for the addict and his or her spouse is a downward spiral—if they don't get help. While this decline seems preventable—and there is no shortage of rehabs, 12-step programs and other types of supports—an addict has to want help in order to stop acting self-destructively.
>
> But addiction is a disease that tells the addict s/he doesn't have a disease. Unlike other diseases, such as cancer that may invoke a patient's survival instincts, addiction wants its victims dead (but, as the saying goes, it's content to just make the person miserable).[5]

So divorce may be inevitable if the addicted person:

- Refuses to admit he has a serious substance abuse problem, and resists counseling or treatment
- Admits the problem, but won't involve you in doing anything about it, and
- Frequently relapses or doesn't follow through with treatment or sobriety. This may occur over a period of years, with cycles of compliance and recidivism. Many times, the addict lives a self-fulfilling prophecy of failure

EMOTIONAL ABUSE

Physical abuse is relatively easy to identify. Early in this book, I urged anyone who fears for her safety to speak immediately to a domestic abuse counselor to determine the most prudent way to remove herself and her children from danger. Emotional abuse may be equally damaging and more pervasive, but it may be more difficult to detect. It is not always accompanied by the rage that precedes physical abuse. Anger may be the motivation for cruelty, but a range of other emotions and causes may be present.

Gregory Jantz, in *Healing the Scars of Emotional Abuse*, defines it as "an intentional assault by one person on another to so distort the victim's view of self that the victim allows the abuser to control him or her."[6]

"An abusive relationship is more of an attitude toward you than a rare moment of anger or irritation over a difference of opinion," writes Patricia Evans in *The Verbally Abusive Relationship*. She describes "Power Over" tactics used to dominate and control. Though women sometimes blame themselves for selecting this type of husband, she observes, the abuse is not always predictable. A woman might choose an affectionate and attentive man who courts her, but

> if he believes that "now" he has certain entitlements and pre-rogatives, is somehow superior, is inferior if he shows vulnerability and warmth, is weak if he reveals his own feelings, is born to be in charge of a woman, has no responsibility to build and maintain the relationship, should be the center of her attention and she should do his bidding, his attitude toward her and his treatment of her will change.[7]

Sadly, women often believe that if they're compliant enough or pleasing enough the anger and insults will stop, but the root of abusive behavior is often in inner problems so entrenched that wives can't touch them.

What are the signs of emotional abuse?

- You start to question your own self-worth, even doubting that you deserve better than the treatment you're receiving
- You start to think that your spouse's insults might be correct and find it difficult to stand up to him
- Your feelings of powerlessness express themselves with physical symptoms—pain in various parts of the body, headaches, fatigue
- You notice yourself changing your behavior to prevent an outburst—walking on eggshells, avoiding topics or people he dislikes
- You hide things or information from your spouse out of fear of reprisal. Living with fear becomes the norm in your marriage over a period of weeks or months

This is not an acceptable way to live. Call a local anti-abuse hotline; they await your call in every major city and can advise you about the next steps to take. Line up support, such as a friend's place where you can stay and family members to help with children. Get a separate email account. Disentangle as much money as possible. Once you make the decision to leave, stay resolute. You're protecting your children and your own sanity.

WHEN IT'S TIME TO GIVE UP

Occasionally life with another becomes so depressing and punishing that after years of wear and disintegration, the marriage has to end. It happens, but too many people *make* it happen.

Partners' impatience, unrealistic expectations, intolerance, and our divorce culture conspire to make potentially functional relations seem oppressive and unbearable.

A few years ago the *New York Times* began running a column called "Unhitched," in which couples describe how their marriages began and unraveled. Why would a newspaper want to publish a column about failures? Perhaps because it's interesting reading, and couples in "meh" marriages may feel comforted about their own situations. In any case, the stories, each revealing some idiosyncratic flaw that led to divorce, seem to confirm Tolstoy's observation in the opening sentence of *Anna Karenina*: "Happy families are all alike; every unhappy family is unhappy in its own way."

But if you read their stories, you wonder why the flaw had to be fatal.

Ram and Barbara Samuel married when he was thirty-five and she twenty-three. Their twenty-year marriage began shortly after Ram had lost his first wife; Barbara's past included a short-lived marriage with no children.

Meeting at a party, where she was entranced by his "Southern accent beautiful voice," they "talked about music, politics and race relations (he is African-American, she is white)."

"She was cute, but her beauty really was from within," Ram, a carpenter, recalled.

"He was handsome and tall, and I loved his hands," Barbara said. "His skin was beautiful, the color of mahogany."

They talked about marriage "a long time" and after three years together, when Barbara became pregnant, they married. Their families were initially "hesitant," and "worried" about the interracial combination, but the couple won them over.

Seven years and two sons into the marriage, they faced a tough time. Close family members of Ram's died of Hepatitis C, which Ram contracted. Barbara, a writer, was expanding her career and traveling. It was while she was away that Ram had an affair.

He claims the divorce was "100 percent" his fault because of the lapse. Barbara demurs, "He needed me and I wasn't there. People go astray when they are lost."

They tried therapy for a few months, but instead of repairing the lack of trust, "it clarified the end. She loved him, but they were headed in different directions, she thought." Ram understood his wife's hurt: "You don't realize how much trust matters until it's not there. It's hard to repair." External events triggered the marriage's demise. An argument on the morning of 9/11 as the World Trade Center towers fell led Barbara to ask for a divorce. "I saw what people were going through in New York. I knew I could go through whatever I needed to."

They recall their reactions to the split. She felt "as if her life were over." He was "Guilty. Scared." He didn't want to lose the family; their sons wanted their parents to stay together. A few months after the divorce came through, Ram, in his native St. Louis for a funeral, reconnected with an old flame and they married. Shortly thereafter, Barbara began to date.

Interviewed ten years after the divorce and asked what they would have done differently, Ram says "Undo the affair, it was so not worth it." He says "it's still hard;" he still misses her. Barbara would have cut short the separation period, but acknowledges, "My life is so much richer and deeper and broader because we met and we had children and shared all those days and nights and a billion conversations."

Ram's advice for others is "Stick with it. Don't tear the sheets too easily. Compromise when you can. Don't break your vows." Barbara says, "Don't marry young. Be honest. The first time you tell a lie, everything starts to fall apart."

Naturally, as healthy people do, they've moved on from the divorce, and at this point, seriously involved with others, both seem content. Outsiders can never fully know the interior of anyone else's marriage, but were their problems so serious that they needed to tear apart their family? They "still

talk several times a month, and are in contact with each other's families."
Do I detect a bittersweet undertone to their story?[8]

As I read about these breakups, it seemed obvious to me that with
determination, the ills afflicting these "Unhitched" marriages might have
been cured. Take the story of Alec, a rock musician, who met Cynthia, a
neurologist and keyboardist, when she auditioned for his band. "She worked
her day job at a hospital; they gigged at night and always had music playing
at home." Five years after meeting, they married, and five years later had
their daughter, Julia, "our hit record," Alec boasts.

They never co-mingled funds, and they "divvied up their bills," but
"Alec said he was embarrassed that his income never came close to his
wife's." When Alec secretly racked up big debts and Cynthia had to bail him
out, they began arguing. Trying therapy on and off, they separated, then
reunited, to the delight of their then-five-year-old daughter. But a year later,
they split again. Cynthia, whose demanding career required travel, was
troubled by Alec's "habits about money, food and messiness." The second
move-out spurred Alec to "face my issues myself." He "cleaned up his debts.
They shared child care."

The article doesn't say why they went ahead to formalize the divorce,
but a mediator was involved. "After they signed the divorce papers," we
learn, "they went to lunch." According to Cynthia, "We still loved each
other."

She said she missed being married. "People say 'now you can find the
love of your life,' but I think I already had found him." Asked if they should
have divorced sooner, Alec said, "only if it was before having a child." "We
did the best we could, but love blinds you to behaviors that might put the
marriage at risk," added Cynthia.[9]

Blinded—and divorced—by *love*. Reading through their stories, I notice
that many of the "Unhitched" couples went to therapy, usually for a period
of months, but they tended not to apply its lessons afterward. I'd venture
that couples who go to therapy and take its insights *seriously* seldom turn
up in the "Unhitched" column.

When is it time to give up?

- When you're abandoned by a chop-and-run character who
  won't return your phone calls week after week or who has

unilaterally moved toward divorce with such steps as separating financially and making arrangements for future domiciles

- When you've tried earnestly and repeatedly to sit down and discuss the issues that divide you but receive only resistance or indifference. Productive conversation usually requires sincere listening, clarifying what your partner thinks and feels, compromise, and willingness to change
- When you've written letters and emails to express those thoughts and offers (sometimes indirect communication works best) with hostile or no response
- When your partner refuses your request for marriage counseling or clearly considers therapy a box to check off before exiting, with no intention to resolve problems
- When you have gone to counseling yourself and begun to change your own habits, especially those that might have contributed to your marital schism—the most effective proof you're serious about revitalizing your marriage. If you have given time and emotional dedication to those changes but your partner disengages further, it might be time to leave

If your marriage meets one or more of these criteria, you may have no choice but to divorce, because likely you're alone in that relationship. Still, getting to that point takes at least several months, perhaps years. If it's your partner seeking divorce, ask for a hiatus pursuing it. If you're the initiator, realize that you take your experience with you into the next relationship. If you never resolve the problems of your marriage, you may find them repeating like a bad bowl of beans.

A CONSIDERABLE DECISION

Bruce Derman, a psychologist who specializes in "assisting couples move through the divorce process in a way that is constructive for the entire family," and the family therapist Wendy Gregson, propose eight questions to help you decide if you are "ready for divorce."[10] Here are their questions, each followed by my response:

(1) *Do you have feelings for your partner?.... If [you do], it is best that you work on your relationship prior to deciding to divorce, otherwise your feelings of loss will overwhelm you and you may find yourself worse off after the divorce than you are now.*

I agree with Derman and Gregson that any warm or sentimental feelings for your partner can be the springboard to solving your problems and bettering the marriage. And they're right—better to exhaust every possibility for reconciliation than suffer from regret the rest of your life.

I'll never forget the sad case of a controlling husband whose wife finally found her voice and insisted they go to counseling. Like many husbands of this ilk, he insisted he had no problem; it was all his wife's issue. After years of pleading, she finally left him. A sweet, loving woman, she'd had admirers from afar, one of whom approached her with kindness and sympathy after her acrimonious divorce from the controller (who felt victimized). Appreciation and respect were such a welcome pleasure that she fell in love, and the two married a year after the divorce.

The controller, not to be outdone, met someone online and in short order married her. When that marriage ended in less than a year, he realized that his selfishness and pride had cost him a quality woman and the animosity of his own children.

The most combative divorces occur because spouses *do* have feelings for their partners—often of hate. I've found it takes at least half as long as the relationship lasted for emotions about the marriage to subside. So even if you feel liberated, you'll still revisit the relationship long after it's over.

(2) *Were you ever really married?.... If you have not developed a genuine "we" in your relationship this would be the time to either commit to learning how to do that or to admit that you have never really had a marriage.*

Shouldn't the *first* task be to commit and get that "we" together, since you're already married? Saying "we were never really married" is a classic cop-out used by people rationalizing their divorces. Don't fall for it.

(3) *Are you truly ready for divorce, or are you just threatening?*

Spouses often threaten divorce, write Derman and Gregson, in the heat of an argument, out of frustration, to manipulate the other spouse, or to be taken seriously. If you're ready to divorce, you can honestly say, "I wish to close a chapter of my life, and I am at peace with the fact that there is no more that I can do or give to this relationship."

With insincere threats of divorce, people can unintentionally start the ball rolling downhill, and it quickly picks up momentum. Being able to say, "I wish to close a chapter of my life" is an excellent barometer of your underlying feelings. When you say that, if you detect feelings of protest or regret, say out loud that you're *not* ready to close this chapter; that there's *always* something else you can do or give to the relationship as long as your partner's around.

(4) *Is this a sincere decision based on self-awareness, or is it an emotionally reactive decision?.... Emotionally charged decisions do not last and if acted on do not resolve the underlying problem. People who divorce out of anger stay angry even after the divorce is over.*

I'll say it again—in romance, marriage, and divorce, *emotions trump logic.* Logically, people should be able to solve their problems. Given your long-term investment in your marriage and the harm divorce does to your health, your finances, and especially your children, logic dictates that you stay together. If only you were Mr. Spock, you'd never face divorce. Or marriage, perhaps. Try this exercise: pretend you're a thoroughly objective observer with no emotional connection to your family. How would you view this marriage and what solutions might you suggest?

Derman and Gregson ask if you're making an emotionally *reactive* decision. "Reactive" suggests the decision is a response to the other person, (and most divorcees *do* cite uncorrectable traits in their partners as the cause of marital dissolve). Yet marriage itself is *all about* "reaction." Constant adaptation to each other's moods and needs is the warp and woof of the marital fabric. Perhaps your incompatibility is due to a lack of flexibility and accommodation by *you.* Could you find a way to compromise about what's bothering you or, with generosity of spirit, let it go? Respect for differences is key in *any* relationship.

Is your "emotionally reactive" decision driven by anger or, worse, your desire for retribution? Your partner did something horrible; she can't get away with it. You won't stand for it and want out. Revenge is always a lose-lose proposition. Are you really the kind of person who'd base an enormously consequential life decision on the immature desire to retaliate?

(5) *What is your intent in wanting a divorce?.... Divorce has no power to right wrongs [or] change people's hearts and minds. Divorce can only do one thing, end a marriage, and in so doing free each person to make new attachments to new people.*

Some people think a divorce will cause a neglectful ex to miss them or that a detached dad will suddenly care for a child he might lose. What a twisted way to re-engage an apathetic partner!

(6) *Have you resolved your internal conflict over the divorce? Everyone who goes through a divorce is conflicted.... Recognizing the conflict and owning that different parts of you will be struggling with the impact of divorce, at different times, is part of the process of getting ready for divorce.*

Yes, every divorce entails a mixture of feelings, and every divorcee, at some level, questions the move. An internal conflict is an opportunity to explore the issues and tease apart the divisions between you and your mate. Internal conflict is human and never disappears completely. Before going anywhere near divorce, realize that your conflicting feelings *in themselves* reveal some desire to stay. That desire is worth cultivating first.

(7) *Can you handle the unpleasant consequences of divorce?*

You are not ready for divorce, Derman and Gregson say, if you are not prepared for *changes to your finances, lifestyle, or traditions*; if *you cannot accept your children's sadness and anger*; if *you cannot accept times of insecurity, fear, and the unknown*; or if *you are not willing to let go of your spouse mentally, emotionally, and spiritually.*

All true. Indeed, I wrote this book to make the case that the unpleasant consequences of divorce are so severe that divorce is often a cure much worse than the disease. On the other hand, if you're so dependent on your mate that you can't act independently or adapt to change, well, that's a problem to solve as well—ideally, while you stay together.

(8) *Are you willing to take control of your life in a responsible and mature way?.... The attitude you choose will determine the type of divorce you have.*

Divorces happen when one party or both are *not* mature and responsible. That's often a problem within the marriage and why breakups tend to be messy and emotional. Divorce makes people "man up" (or "woman up") and take responsibility for themselves, often unwillingly. That's one way to grow. But it's not the only way. You can develop skills and stretch yourself by understanding and resolving the problems while staying in your marriage. You'll have to make an effort in any case. Better to expend your energy on mending your marriage than on moving, dealing with attorneys, soothing your children's anxieties, and venting in a divorce support group.

CHAPTER 12

It's About *You*

R easons for decamping come in three categories: "It's all about *you*," "It's all about *me*," and "It's nobody's fault." In the next three chapters, I'm going to refute each of these excuses. Let's start with the most common—pointing your finger at your spouse, who has some unbearable flaw—which comes in several varieties.

I CAN'T TAKE YOUR EXCRUCIATINGLY BAD HABIT ANYMORE.

Lily and Blake faced a relatively mild problem, but it grew into the cause of their divorce because of stubbornness. At first it seemed cute. Lily loved clothes and always looked great. She could put together the cleverest combos—black t-shirt under turquoise denim jacket, topped by black-and-white large-plaid fuzzy poncho. Twelve thousand Instagram followers awaited her morning post each day. When she made *Harper's Bazaar*'s list of top fashion Instagrammers, she was over the moon. She was offered free clothes from stores and friends.

Blake, an IT manager for a hospital chain, was proud to be with someone so good-looking, even though she didn't have much real income from her job at a high-end cosmetics store. They'd go to hospital-related charity events, and the next day her poses appeared all over their friends' feeds. Setting up her Instagram shots was her real passion.

But Lily was a slob. Her closet was only half-full because most of her wardrobe was piled all over their house. After she'd wear something, she'd peel it off and leave it on the floor, or a chair, or the couch. Seldom would she go through her piles, and many items needed washing. She hated doing laundry, too, so every week or so took a big load to the cleaners.

Blake would occasionally undertake the job of sorting the stinky duds from the wearables. Many were wrinkled, and if she got an idea for a new combo, sometimes she'd tear apart the house to find the piece she wanted and quickly get out the iron. But the rest stayed put.

Blake had his den, his man-cave, where everything had a place. Only his laptop stayed out on his desk. For two years, he talked to Lily about organization. "I knew I couldn't expect her to just switch from a slob into a neat-freak," he says from the vantage point of five years out. "I worked with her. I got a home-organizer in there to teach her. She got rid of half her things. For about a week she was folding her socks into neat little packages, standing them on end in her drawer, and we got along fine."

Unfortunately, she quickly reverted. "I hired a housekeeper to come in every week. But Lily would scream at her because she didn't know where to put things, and Lily would tell her not to touch anything."

On the other hand, when *they* touched, the result was magic. "I stayed with her for the sex," Blake confesses. "She was fabulous to touch, so smooth, so taut. She should have been; I was paying five hundred dollars a month for her personal trainer."

After three years, Blake was getting frustrated. "Here I had this gorgeous celebrity, but I felt like I was just feeding her habit. She was all about her blog, and while the sex was still great, she didn't care about my interests or aspirations."

When Blake threatened divorce, Lily gave him a puppy-dog face but didn't say much. "She actually thought that being adorable would keep me happy. I'm in a high-powered job in a complex field. I see smart people all the time, and she was brilliant at marketing herself, knew a lot about creating the Lily brand, but not about staying married."

What would he say was the final straw? "When her pile of clothes started covering our bed. To me, that was symbolic that her look, her exterior, was more important than our relationship," Blake answered. "I wanted marriage counseling and asked her to make an appointment, but she said she was so busy she couldn't do it. After thinking of all the housekeepers and organizers and unfulfilled promises she made to at least confine her mess to one room, I realized I'd been pretty patient. And not caring enough to even make a counseling appointment after I said I wanted a divorce sealed the deal."

An irritating habit is one thing; ignoring a partner's response to it is another. As with many of these cases, unwillingness to work through the clothes-piling issue bespoke a deeper selfishness that was stronger than Lily's commitment to the marriage. Blake made the divorce easy for her, agreeing to alimony for five years or until she remarried or earned as much as he did. With no children, they could end the marriage without long-term consequences. "She got snapped up right away," Blake smirked. "A guy twenty years older than her. She sure doesn't need my alimony any more. Plus, he's moving to L.A. Who knows, she might be the next Heidi Klum."

Frustration with a spouse's unbearable habits is often the result of *unmet expectations*, and in Blake's and Lily's marriage there were several. He expected that someone so concerned with clothes would take care of them, that she would work with him to find a solution to her sloppiness when she realized what it meant to him, that she would care enough about their five-year investment to make counseling the highest priority, that she genuinely cared about every aspect of him as much as their robust sex life suggested. Those sound pretty reasonable.

Lily *was* consumed with building her fashion career, and it's true she gave only secondary attention to her marriage. Her failure to participate in counseling reinforced the message she sent to Blake about her priorities. But Lily had expectations of her own. She expected Blake to give her a pass on her clothes, especially since he usually said nothing about them. Her expectation seemed reasonable, too, since he enjoyed the results of her fashion passion and always responded to seeing her dressed up. He could afford someone to clean up.

Was this a marriage that needed to end? Was Blake justified in leaving? *Both parties* might have put more effort into saving the union. Blake was testing Lily when he asked her to make the counseling appointment, a test she deliberately failed, wondering why he wouldn't *drag* her to therapy if it might help. Just as Blake wanted Lily to care for him, Lily wanted the same, but their mutual stubbornness meant the end.

When she made that puppy-dog face at Blake's announcement about divorce, he perceived correctly that she wanted him to melt and relent, but it backfired, and instead he was angered. Lily always felt less intelligent than Blake. She responded to his divorce declaration with a pleading look because *that's how she pleaded*. He wanted her to protest, but she believed her only power with him was looks, not language.

Lesson: don't play games with your communication. Say (or write down) exactly what you feel, and especially what you *want*. Lily and Blake weren't unhappy together, and each craved the other's affection and attention. For the most part Blake ignored Lily's mess, so Lily thought it wasn't important. And yet, if you asked what drove him to divorce, he'd say the piles of clothes. He let his irritation about them fester (instead of telling her they were an unavoidable symbol of apathy), and when it finally erupted, he set the phone-the-counselor test that she failed—because she turned it around to test *him*. Each would say the other caused the divorce.

Blake's and Lily's divorce was not inevitable, and neither—if your spouse is doing something to drive you crazy—is yours. Here are eight suggestions I've compiled from my research and practice for keeping a disagreeable habit from becoming a divorceable one.

(1) *Define the problem.* Complaints usually have a root in reality. Disgust with a mate's personal habit highlights that the habit exists. Lily's piles *were* smelly and hard to ignore. Sometimes an objective observer—or just imagining some objective observer evaluating the situation—can clarify what behavior needs revision. Define what's really going on so that both of you accurately understand the boundaries of the problem.

(2) *There may be a neutral solution.* If it bothers you that your spouse squeezes the toothpaste in the middle, solve the problem with separate tubes. For a more serious problem, like habitually falling into debt, you might need a deeper conversation and professional advice. In some cases, removing the opportunity to falter or the triggers for bad habits can reduce or eliminate

the problem. If you can come up with an innovative way for both of you to get what you want, it's a win-win.

(3) *Your spouse knows his bad habits but needs a strong reason to change them.* And he probably understands he should reform, but when you confront your partner, the issue changes to a turf war or a matter of respect. Most bad habits weren't developed to spite anyone; they usually produce some sort of reward or arise out of laziness. Racing to the airport to catch a plane brings the chronically late person an adrenaline thrill. Staying out beyond the time you said you'd be home recalls that exhilarating defiance of your teen years. Lily's problem was simple: she was lazy, and she wouldn't make an effort.

Yes, there's even reward in arguing—you command your spouse's attention. Still, there's damage with each affront, and on small issues, you should ask, "How important *is* this? Can I let it go for the harmony of our marriage?" As an adult, you learn that peace in your marriage outweighs short-term kicks or other minor rewards.

(4) *Come on, say you're sorry.* If your spouse is upset over something you do, that alone is something to apologize for. Practice solo if you must, but even if you disagree with your partner's position, you can always say "I'm sorry [name the issue] is causing a problem between us." Lily might have said, "I'm sorry, my clothes piles are just my 'thing.' I don't mean them to bother you." Apology doesn't mean you cave or that you've solved the problem—just that you recognize that your spouse's feelings are important.

(5) *Willingness to change goes a long way.* Just *offering* to change may in itself soften your partner's stance. After that, you might discuss compromise: "Is there any way we can work together so that we both get at least part of what we want?" Lily might pledge to keep her mess in a specific area or to sort through her clothes once a week. Of course, if you don't follow through on your agreement, you worsen the problem.

(6) *Keep it in perspective.* If you value your relationship, go out of your way to please your partner. Realize the priority of your marriage in your life. Go back to "the tombstone question"—what do you want on your tombstone, "Valued Employee," "Most Popular Person," "Beloved Husband and Father," or... "*She Was Right*"? Americans place marriage and family above job success—84 percent in one survey rated it as "one of the most

important" or "very important" things in life, while half said the same about attaining a high-powered career.[1]

(7) *What did you expect?* Both you and your spouse should ask yourselves what you expected from each other so you can pinpoint the source of your irritation. Lily was always a slob, and Blake knew it, but he expected her to hang up her clothes. He expected her to *change* because she shared his home. Lily never thought she'd have to change her habits—she didn't care about neatness. When Blake complained and asked her to put away her clothes, she did it once and then just reverted to her old self.

That's no excuse for her disorganization, but it's an explanation. Blake thought he was magnanimous in hiring an organizer to teach Lily tidiness, but without her personal commitment, the new regimen couldn't stick. Blake needed to express his expectation of a tidy home. From there they might have brainstormed resolutions acceptable to both. How about a few large wicker baskets as clothes-drops? How about making a schedule for picking up the place together? They might have hired a daily housekeeper to straighten, launder, and put away all the clothes. It was a joint problem calling for a shared solution.

(8) *Use the power of the preface.* You can say nearly anything and receive a positive response if you frame it right. Before you express your dissatisfaction, think of a preface that lets your partner know where you're coming from—which ought to be a place of honest, mutual problem solving. A preface isn't complicated—just explain how you noticed there was a problem or that you've been thinking about how to convey this in a loving way. Before you get to your gripe, you might say outright that you're composing a preface because you respect, love, and care about your partner and want her to respond in the spirit in which it's offered. At the least, start off with "I love you, and...." The "and" is important; you *know* what you'll hear if you say "I love you *but...."*

These anti-divorce tactics work in any situation in which you're tempted to blame the other person for the problem. Keep them in mind especially as we continue through the other divorce excuses in the next chapter ("It's about *me*").

I CAN'T HANDLE YOUR BAGGAGE.

Baggage is a biggie. Especially the three marriage-crushers: *children, in-laws, and friends.*

(1) *Your children are ruining our marriage.* You'll find "data" suggesting that second marriages start off with a poor prognosis; some media sources say 60 to 67 percent of second marriages end in divorce.[2] But those debatable numbers serve only to undermine hopes and discourage couples about their futures. Dr. Kalman Heller suggests, "While data for second marriages is currently very limited, the early indication is that the frequently-stated 60 percent divorce rate is also a gross exaggeration, and that divorce rates for second marriages may not be any higher than for first marriages."[3] First marriages in Britain are even more likely than second marriages to crumble—as I've already noted, 45 percent of first unions there succumb, but only 31 percent of second marriages do.[4]

Nevertheless, when you marry someone with younger children, you take on a *family*, not just a new spouse. Each child becomes an important person to integrate into your life and soul. That child also must accept *you* and your new role of authority. And she needs to adapt to your usurping attention from Mom that formerly went to her.

I can just hear you. You've got so many reasons why your spouse's children are "too much baggage."

"My spouse puts her children ahead of me." Well, yeah. Your partner has known her children longer than she has known you. And the parental bond is unshakeable and unbreakable—so in conflict, she sides with them. Look at their history: your partner saw her kids through a previous relationship, and together they adjusted and cried and shared their stress; no wonder your spouse puts them first. Acknowledge that history, and *appreciate* your partner as the parent she is, but at the same time forge with her a *different* kind of relationship—a romance.

"I didn't really know what I was getting into with her kids." That's a cop-out. You *never* know what kinds of problems you'll be facing, even with your own biological kids in a two-parent marriage. Remember "if life hands you lemons, make lemonade"? When stopped by a roadblock, you deal with it—either wait out the parade or go around it. *Being married is a lifelong, daily re-acquaintance process*, with both your mate and with the children in your home, who develop and change every day. You thought your perfect love would transcend all the other issues in her life and yours? Get real— each person is constantly learning, testing, adjusting; each interaction shapes the relationship a little further.

What if, God forbid, your house burned down? You'd contact the insurance company and decide whether to sell or rebuild, but you wouldn't say, "Oh look, now I've got a burned-down house. I think I'll just walk away." Why can you face all sorts of challenges but not in your marriage?

"I was blinded by love." In other words, you didn't vet the person you decided to marry? And now that you're actually united, you don't love that person or respect your commitment enough to try everything until the final gasp? Realize that as you contemplate divorce, you're inclined to disparage your marriage retrospectively, saying things like "I was so desperate to get married," or "We were so physically attracted." Even if you *were* eager to wed, and even if you *were* so hot your brain melted (both enthusiasm and sexual compatibility are actually superb ingredients in a decision to marry), you *knew* he or she would always have a primary and primal love for his or her offspring. That was a given. The question then became how to integrate that relationship into the new duo you were forming.

Did you think that would be easy? Then your expectation was off. But break down the problems. Some child-related conflicts solve themselves in time: eventually children turn eighteen and leave. And some are confined to one child or one type of issue. Isolate the sources of conflict; be specific. When you use generalizations like "I couldn't get along with her kids" or "her kids didn't like me" or "we had different family priorities," you're sweeping away your whole marriage with one wave. But is that what you *want*?

"We couldn't blend our families." You're right that blending families is extremely difficult. You've got a bunch of people placed in a set of relationships they didn't choose. Each one brings a unique history, personality, and mindset that is, as we noted before, constantly evolving. Each one needs to form a relationship with every other one in the household. That means a lot is going on, and there's huge potential for misunderstandings, conflicting desires, resentments, and possessiveness.

Your spouse's kids want their parent's attention, which now is deflected to your marriage. Of *course* they'll react.

Each spouse expects certain behaviors, beginning with mutual respect, but you can't expect kids to conform without firm rules and ironclad consequences. That's a lot for any couple to set up and enforce, an immediate stress to the marriage. The National Stepfamily Resource Center website lists support groups in every state, and local jurisdictions almost always have resources. Divorcing brings further displacement for the children, worse for them and worse for their parents.

A post on the online support group MD Junction offers some good advice:

> Each parent has a stronger relationship with their own child than their spouse. If you don't have a battle plan for handling your children...you lose. Decide right now that your spouse is a permanent resident in your home and the kids are temporary. The kids do not have a say in the rules of the house. You and your spouse privately set the rules the same for all kids...bedtime, telephone, eating, chores, allowances, toys, cleaning, dating, homework...all of it.
>
> You and your spouse privately agree that you will never contradict each other in front of any of the kids. If you have to work out an adjustment or exception to the rules, do it in private and have a darn good reason. Children are very good at looking at parents' relationships and finding any weak link. The key is coming to an agreement and unity.[5]

You're skeptical, and that's justified. Blended families are notoriously difficult but not as impossible as media-reported divorce rates would suggest. Johns Hopkins University sociologist Andrew Cherlin says, "The fact that the divorce rate isn't higher for remarriages [than first marriages] shows that a lot of people are trying very hard and with great success to make their second marriages work."[6]

(2) *My in-laws are driving us apart.* Your spouse may have come with baggage other than children—his whole family, for example. Fifteen percent of divorced people cited "problems with spouse's family" in an Austin Institute study of reasons for divorce.[7] Googling "meddling in-laws" yields 506,000 results, and the topic is favorite fodder for advice columnists, who universally reply that the real issue is the jealous daughter-in-law or son-in-law, and resolution has to come from the meddler's child.

An unintentionally humorous online article by a "Newlyweds Expert" identifies "The Top 10 Signs of a Meddling Mother-in-Law." Of course, all of the faux pas are her doing. She: tries to take over your wedding, thinks she's your BFF, wants to come on the honeymoon, starts arguments between you and your husband, cleans your house and does your laundry, negotiates with you for her son's time, lays on the guilt, treats her son like he's still a baby, and wants to move in with you.[8]

The truth is that a mother-in-law–daughter-in-law relationship consists of two people. When you, the new wife, came on the scene, Mom already had a relationship with her son. Expanding that to include another party is a slow process, especially if her world has contracted because of retirement or widowhood.

I remember when I first got to know my husband's mom. His relationship with her had been amicable though slightly uncomfortable, but I saw her as a lonely, bright, and insightful woman who'd had an impressive career as a biochemist and then a teacher. I really don't believe I did anything exceptional, though I telephoned her every day. Aside from sympathizing with her perspective, I took the initiative to befriend her. As a happy byproduct, Michael and the other siblings grew closer to her and to each other. Most mothers-in-law really aren't shrews or threats to the marriage. They're just trying to navigate their own feelings of loss (of child to another woman) and uncertainty about the future.

A letter to *Washington Post* advice columnist Carolyn Hax from a well-intentioned but insensitive mother-in-law shows what can go wrong:

> I've upset my daughter-in-law deeply, but am not sure exactly how. She is a stay-at-home mom. When my son and husband wanted to go on a special father-son hike for my husband's birthday, she kindly offered to watch the baby alone. I thought this would be a wonderful opportunity for just us girls to spend time together.
>
> I suggested that I drive up... and help her out. She said that would "not be the best thing" and gave a few reasons it probably wouldn't work out. I considered them and thought I could deal with some of the things she pointed out.
>
> Well, I surprised my son and daughter-in-law by coming anyway. Much to my dismay, when my daughter-in-law saw me, she burst into tears and ran out of the room.... [She] ended up

pulling it together and was cordial, but distant. I enjoyed seeing my grandson, but I left feeling very unwanted and unloved.

What did I do that was so bad? How do I remedy a situation when I don't know what the issue is? I don't want to be "that mother-in-law."—How to Be Close?[9]

Ms. Hax, who's not a therapist, began her reply, "The issue is that you showed complete disregard for your daughter-in-law's wishes because you wanted to visit." Yes. The rest of the reply urged a full, unconditional apology and a tangible "I'm sorry" gift. The 1,800 comments this particular column drew from readers reveal the strong emotions this issue provokes. The most common term used by commenters was "boundaries." Adults set them, and other adults keep them or negotiate them and, once agreed to, respect them.

(3) *Your friends are driving us apart.* If your "too much baggage" exit line refers to your partner's long-term *friends*, you might want to consider whether your own jealousy contributes to the problem. If your partner's allegiances to his buddies are the issue, after fully disclosing your concerns, a "winning by letting go" approach might work best, leaving changes in the relationships up to him.

You'll need a more proactive solution if friends insert themselves in the middle of your marriage life.

Robert and Crystal and their three teenagers had lived in a condominium complex in Mountain View six years when a family with teens moved into the next building. The kids met at school, and soon thereafter the parents, Carl and Stella, invited them over.

"I thought it was nice to get the invitation," Crystal remembers, "but when I got there I was uncomfortable. They served martinis, and Robert got tipsy. I'm not much of a drinker, but it was clear these folks considered it a lifestyle."

Robert and Crystal normally sat down to a family dinner, but Carl's and Stella's frequent invitations for cocktails left the kids foraging for themselves. "After a few weeks of after-work drinks, oh, three times a week, I was starting to feel pressure," Crystal recalls. "I didn't like seeing Robert nearly-drunk that often. These people would seem hurt if we couldn't make it." So under this subtle pressure, Robert and Crystal attended this obligatory not-so-happy hour.

"I began to realize Carl and Stella weren't such a good influence on our family," Crystal says. "I'd suggest we say we're busy, but by then Robert looked forward to his little weeknight binges. I stayed home after that, but Robert wouldn't give up his friendship with this couple."

Crystal's sister suggested she explain to Stella why she stopped coming, and what the drinking was doing to their family. "It took all my courage, because Stella and Carl were always together, but I phoned her and asked to speak to her separately. She said, 'why not just come over with Robert and they could talk later?' So I spilled the beans. I told her how their little evenings of drinking were turning my husband into an alcoholic. Saying it that way was a big mistake," Crystal realizes. "Stella got angry and said Robert was a big boy, and they enjoyed his company, and why didn't I mind my own business!"

Crystal got depressed. "I had nowhere to turn, so I decided to pray to the Virgin that something would happen to stop the situation."

Apparently her prayers were answered. "Miraculously, Robert and Carl got in a big blowup. Then after that Carl and Stella were off for her niece's wedding for two weeks." That hiatus—and a grudge over the fight—ended the friendship. "Those were the worst three years of our life," Crystal admits. "These 'friends' nearly ruined our marriage."

Crystal's reticence let a deleterious friendship damage her marriage too long. An earlier, more forceful intervention might have minimized the pain and strengthened the marriage. Don't hold back when outsiders wedge between you and your spouse—keep your marital closeness the first priority.

I'M NOT ATTRACTED TO YOU ANYMORE.

The next item in the list of "it's about you" excuses for divorce gets personal. At one time she was cute. She had a nice figure, a sweet face. She wore that goofy smile. It's interesting that most complaints about physical attractiveness come from men, but occasionally women too find their partner so different from the person they met that they pull away.

Deidra was a busy stay-at-home mom of two sons and two daughters. All four kids were active in soccer, and she was a volunteer coach, but over the fifteen years since her marriage, her weight had crept up, and now she only took a quick look at her face in the mirror before heading out, unhappy with the view of her body.

Deidra was one of eight women in a session of the workshop I developed to free clients from dieting tyranny. The first checklist helped group members identify their problem: "Do you eat when you're nervous, bored or sad? Are you ashamed of your overeating and hide it?" As the other participants filled out their forms, Deidra began to sob softly. After the meeting, we spoke privately. "I'm sorry I broke down," she began, "but my husband just told me that if I have so little respect for myself that I can't take care of my body, he'll get a divorce. We have four kids—they're everything to both of us! But he'd ruin their lives because I'm heavier than I used to be. I'm still the same person. Why won't he see that? He's staying with his brother!"

Her husband, Len, had nudged her for years to slim down. And she'd tried every diet in the book, but nothing lasted. "I can't help myself," Deidra moaned, "I just have the urge to snack. Especially when I'm under pressure. But then I hate myself. You're my last hope."

At the same time, she was scared. She was more pudgy than fat, but Len hadn't approached her for sex in nearly a year. She didn't mind, because she dreaded his touch on her skin. She knew their lack of sex was a big part of his ultimatum.

I've worked over the years with thousands of people who've failed on diets. Their metabolism makes up for starvation by requiring less fuel, and so staying thin becomes even more difficult. Deidra knew the problem personally. My estimate is that about 70 percent of women and half of men suffer from what I call the "fat mentality," even if they look fine. But the guilt and worry about everything they eat oppresses their daily existence. Knowing that Len didn't find her attractive was a much heavier weight for Deidra than the pounds on her frame.

An appearance or eating problem begins with Mom, or the culture, or a well-meaning doctor, or a magazine article, or a number on the bathroom scale at age thirteen. We absorb all sorts of "authoritative" pronouncements about what we should look like and what we should eat, and rather than do what children achieve naturally—eat when hungry, stop when full—we overlay food's pleasant taste with all sorts of associations. "Clean your plate. There are starving children in China!" "Carbs are bad for you." "Always eat breakfast; never eat after eight p.m." "Raw veggies don't count." "Your mom worked so hard to make that, you have to eat it." "You gained two pounds today; skip dinner." "Kale smoothies with protein powder will clean you out."

With all that swirling around in your head, it's time for a pint of ice cream. And it was, for Deidra. "One time not long ago, on the way home from the market, I pulled into the lot at the park and scarfed a pint of Chunky Monkey. Lucky I keep a spoon in the glove compartment," she chuckled.

But now she was agonizing in the end stages of a common cycle. A wife has children and puts on pounds. She tries to diet and ends up on the success-failure-restart treadmill. Her husband gets impatient. He tries to be supportive, but her repeated failures confound him. Meanwhile, he might put on a few pounds too, but that's seldom an issue. The more anxious the wife becomes, the more she's driven to eat. And the greater the guilt. She pulls away, just as Deidra did, and after a while, her husband gets the message that she doesn't want to be touched. So he backs off and shuts up. They both try to ignore the problem, but the marriage becomes more platonic; the passion drains. Len told her he didn't need marriage counseling—he needed a wife who came onto him rather than pushing him away. But he *did* need to understand that their lack of physicality was a *joint problem* that they should approach *together*. Sadly, Len's admiration for Deidra shrank as his blame for her size increased.

Though we like to think marriage is about mutual support and compatibility, as unfair and sexist as it may be, men care a lot about women's physical attractiveness. A Chapman University study revealed that 92 percent of men and 84 percent of women said it was "desirable/essential" that their potential partner was good-looking. Eighty percent of men and just 58 percent of women said a slender body was "desirable/essential."[10] What guy would choose a woman from a dating site who didn't post a photo?

It's important to realize that both attraction and obsession with food or shape are as much psychological as physical. And since you *were* attracted once, there's hope that with understanding, respect, and tenderness you can not only regain appreciation for sexuality but also expand the definition of attractiveness.

We're all aging and changing. After you've shared more than a decade and created four children, your relationship includes a depth of history, a time-bound richness. By then, there's more to the relationship than mere physicality. That bond can hold you together while you look at the *internal* problems that divide you. For example, Deidra's self-hatred compelled her toward a "fix" of food. Coming to my workshops, Deidra began separating her worth from her girth. She learned that food was not a neck-up tranquilizer or the enemy causing her downfall, that food isn't imbued with a "good" or "bad" nature. She saw how her obsession with losing weight was keeping her from accomplishing other goals. She always wanted to finish her master's, learn French, and volunteer in her kids' language lab, but the fear and low self-esteem that made food her secret friend held her back.

Slowly, Deidra learned to relax with food. She stopped weighing herself and savored the taste and texture of what she ate. Len lasted only a week at his brother's; he came home because he missed his kids and hated the pitying looks of his brother's wife. But with Deidra loosening up, he liked her better, too.

Loss of desire is often about more than the way your partner looks. Rather than discarding the marriage because physical attraction is lost, focus on the desirable and admirable characteristics of your spouse, and from there probe your own psyche. Perhaps the problem is rooted in your feelings about aging and decline. You might harbor resentments or anger that spur you to push away your spouse. If you find sex with your spouse boring or unfulfilling, look for playful ways to bring variety into your sexual experiences.

If your mate desires you, responding with "I'm not attracted to you anymore" is not only a turn-off but an insult. It's one of the most frequent "chop and run" excuses because the offended spouse can offer no solution in return. Honor your marriage vows enough to thoroughly explore why you're using this exit line and possible solutions.

Desire can be kindled by appreciation. I'll never forget the elderly man who approached me after a speech. Beaming as he stroked the shoulder of his wizened wife of fifty years, he exclaimed, "Isn't she the most beautiful woman in the world?" Cultivate in yourself the clarity of that man's vision.

I RESPECT YOU, BUT I NEED A DIFFERENT KIND OF PERSON.

Whom did you think you were marrying in the first place? You loved your spouse enough to publicly proclaim him or her your soul mate. To support throughout changing phases and evolving interests. The line "I need a different kind of person" suggests that you misidentified the person you chose or that *you're* the chameleon who changed, and the personality of your spouse is no longer good enough for your new direction. It might mean that you expected the one you married to stand still, never bending or reaching, and now that he or she is exploring a new direction, you won't put up with it.

This is the ultimate expression of narcissism—thinking you can discard another human being because right now he or she doesn't conform exactly to the profile you prefer.

And you'd never act that way in other situations—only in your marriage, the relationship that counts most. For example, what if you love your job, but one day your boss is gone, replaced by somebody completely new. Do you say, "I've got to leave, because the new boss has a different leadership style"? Do you say, "I'll resign unless I can get the new boss to act like the old one"? Would you say, "I respect the new boss, but I need this work environment to suit me"? Of course not—you'd adapt to the new boss's style, you'd be flexible enough to accommodate a new direction that might help the company. And yet, you'd have zero tolerance for change in your marriage?

Or maybe that's not the real issue. Maybe this is an excuse so you can find somebody new—"Just slip out the back, Jack"—without recriminations. It's been done before by other snakes.

YOU DON'T APPRECIATE ME.

You've heard the bromide: What do men want? Sex. What do women want? Talk.

From my clinical experience counseling hundreds of couples in trouble, I can report that the talk most women want is about two things: connection and affection. Women want to know what's going on with their spouses, what happened during their day, what they think about the book they're reading, a news event, or even the sports they're following. The content doesn't really matter as long as a wife feels she knows what's important to her partner. For her, that's intimacy.

If you want to put into practice the maxim "happy wife, happy life," show appreciation. I've included in this book an experiment to test whether you and your partner can experience a relationship flavored with favor. Central to such a relationship is an effort to verbally (and otherwise) appreciate each other. That's a prime benefit of marriage—you gain a reliable source of recognition and appreciation. Or at least you *should*.

Without it, well, you can function. I've heard many women tell me, "My husband isn't very verbal." "My husband is uncomfortable expressing emotions." "My husband didn't hear 'I love you' growing up." These excuses remind me of the song from *Fiddler on the Roof* in which Tevya prods his wife to acknowledge that she loves him. She has difficulty admitting it, but after recalling

> For twenty-five years I've lived with him,
> Fought with him, starved with him.
> Twenty-five years my bed is his.
> If that's not love, what is?

She admits, "I suppose I do." And having heard the declaration he craved, Tevya responds contentedly, "And I suppose I love you too."

Unlike Tevya's, your marriage was not arranged. You married *because* you loved your intended. To be "in love" implies a blindness to foibles, an admiration tinged with lust. Love spurs "mating rituals" like attentiveness and uncharacteristic expressions of appreciation for the beloved. If infatuation, that atypical part of the relationship in which bad habits are excused and superlatives flourish, culminates in marriage, you declare your intent to maintain those feelings. But once a marriage occurs, too many spouses relax their efforts, causing disappointment to a now permanently-joined mate used to being admired and pursued.

If you're muttering the exit line "He doesn't appreciate me" as you're walking out the door, you may be sending up a flare. This is often a ploy, a phony threat from a wife who loves her husband and wants him to reciprocate. It's frequently a last resort when a partner has pulled away or withdrawn, sometimes in reaction to a suspected affair.

If you want appreciation, you don't have to manipulate by threatening divorce—you simply need to be clear about what you'd like and, most importantly, *model* appreciative behavior yourself. The primary reason you *want* your spouse's regard is because you're insecure about his feelings; you likely crave reassurance of his love. You might have let your anger at a perceived lack of affection simmer and then build on itself, until now *you're* the distant one.

If you're using this exit line, you don't want a divorce. You want your life's partner to acknowledge that you and your marriage are the central priority of his life—just as they are to yours.

CHAPTER 13

"It's All About *Me*"

In this relativistic, non-judgmental culture, we hesitate to express even well-meaning opinions lest they be deemed "micro-aggressions," or bullying, so we've lost a potent tool that could spare couples from divorce. I'm not arguing for stigmatizing divorce again but the opposite: the elevation of marriage. Truth is, marriage is good for people—it improves health, spurs wealth creation, provides children security, and cures loneliness.

The exit clichés we're about to evaluate, however, suggest that marriage has no firmer foundation than the flaccid, wispy emotions displayed at the ceremony, which each spouse will re-evaluate the next and every subsequent day. If one day one partner's original feelings flag, then the whole enterprise may be treated as a mistake worthy of demolishing. It's easier to cut protest and pain when the detaching spouse explains, "You're wonderful, but it's about *me*." Yes, you're wonderful, but our marital demise is only about me. You just stay right there and don't change a bit while I go off and meet my needs. Let's consider some common versions of this cop-out.

I'VE FOUND THE LOVE OF MY LIFE.

Infidelity doesn't have to mean the end of a marriage—unless one part-ner dumps his spouse to pursue a lover. Thirty-seven percent of the divorcees in the Austin Institute study cited infidelity by either party as a cause of their split. Twenty-eight percent specifically cited infidelity by their spouse, while only 12 percent said a reason for divorce was their own infidelity.[1]

If you're leaving your spouse for a lover, stop for a minute to consider what you've learned along the way. You've learned that your lover has no compunction about stealing another woman's husband. (I'll use the illustra-tion of a man leaving his wife; of course it could be the other way around). She has little compassion for the family she's wrecking; she can't put herself in your wife's or your children's place.

You've learned that you take your own vows lightly. Your new lover knows this about you and doesn't mind taking the risk that your morals will remain the same, and you'll dump her as well.

You've learned that you can't control your sexual attraction. Even though you devastate your wife and harm each of your children perma-nently, your electromagnetic sexual urge overpowers you. You do *not* know, however, if and when this weakness will strike again, leading you to cheat on your new lover.

You've learned that you can discard the investment of a huge chunk of your life, leaving the stain of your infidelity on all those years of your mar-riage. You've learned that you have the capacity to hurt your children. You may claim they're the most precious part of your life, but your actions show a willingness to turn their world akimbo, rob them of a stable home, and force them to navigate two conflicting worlds.

You've learned that excitement and novelty are alluring to you and to your lover. The titillation of an affair is its furtive fun, the thrill of an emotion-ally and physically gratifying secret. Once the excitement is replaced with the realities of above-board life, complicated by custody arrangements, alimony, and an ex in the background, the affair fades into a mere relationship.

You've learned how to lie. Maybe you knew how before, which wouldn't say much about you, but now you've had lots of practice, and skills of decep-tion integrate into your values.

If, on the other hand, you choose to return to your marriage, you will of necessity learn humility and contrition. You will remember the sacred nature of your vows, and you will practice honesty and transparency. Which direction leads to the type of person you'd like to be?

I'M NOT CUT OUT FOR MARRIAGE.

Could there be something to the argument that certain personality types, moral values, or experiences predispose people to marital failure? Many think so. But if something in a person's psychological and moral constitution really precludes marriage, he's got more than the benign "allergy" to partnering that the phrase "not cut out for marriage" suggests. He's got a serious *disorder*.

It's true that some disorders produce such awful behavior that they can doom a union. Mark D. White of the College of Staten Island/CUNY suggests, for example, that serial adulterers—spouses who cheat repeatedly and, despite the consequences, keep going back for more—have a personality flaw. "I would say that serial adultery *is* an issue of character, that it reflects something inherent in the person's decision-making process that drives him (or her) to cheat repeatedly." Dr. White distinguishes repeat offenders from one-timers. "Cheating once also reflects on a person's character, and not well," he writes. "But if it happens just once and never again, his return to fidelity does speak well of his character, and indicates that it was a momentary transgression, a chance temptation.... "[2] If your partner cheats and repeats, restoring trust will require vigilance, dedication, and therapy.

Narcissistic disorder is a frightening problem that also predisposes someone to marital dysfunction. Family therapist Karyl McBride, author of a book on divorcing a narcissist, warns that "They come into the relationship with this charming and very seductive beginning. But that turns into emotional warfare. Narcissists are people who lack empathy, who are not accountable for their behavior." Divorcing such a person is especially hellish. "If you leave the narcissist, they never get over it. They seek revenge, and the court system is an incredibly great platform."

"You have to think of narcissism as a spectrum disorder," says Dr. McBride, and some in the middle of the spectrum might manage a marriage with help. But "[p]eople with full-blown narcissistic personality disorder don't seek help. They're not introspective or in touch with their own feelings, and they blame everyone else. They are difficult to treat, and they don't seek treatment. If they do, it's only to tell you how often everyone else is wrong."[3] You can see why such a person may not be the "marrying kind."

The psychologist Susan Krauss Whitbourne offers an ominous overview of spouses with personality disorders: "If they are able to get into close relationships with others, their distorted sense of self, unstable emotions, or out-of-control behavior mean[s] that any long-term partners must be willing and able to put up with a great deal of turmoil, especially when life circumstances aggravate their already precarious hold on their feelings and behavior."[4] A professional association that educates about Borderline Personality Disorder, a condition that causes poor management of emotions, says 5.9 percent of Americans will suffer from it at some point in their lives.[5]

Researchers have found two major classifications of personality disorders that correlate highly with divorce, writes Dr. Whitbourne. The first, "histrionic personality disorder," is a lot like narcissism, with the addition of behaviors that are "sexually seductive in an indiscriminate manner, overly theatrical, capable only of superficial feelings and relations with others, and unhappy when they are not the center of attention." Then there are the paranoid personalities. "They are suspicious to an extreme, meaning that they readily become jealous for no reason at all," she explains. "Very sensitive to real or imagined insults, they are quick to conclude that other people want to harm them. Their two main characteristics, suspiciousness and hostility, mean that it's difficult for them to get close to and trust others."[6]

If you're already married to someone with a personality disorder, keep in mind that at one point he or she was capable of a commitment with you. If there was a deceptive courtship, and narcissism or another disorder manifested after the ceremony, the first response should be diagnosis and proper treatment. If your partner is in denial or refuses help, consult your doctor about options. And don't give up without talking to family members, friends, clergy, or anyone else who might support you in helping your partner. But if the disorder is serious enough, perhaps you are one of the exceptions, and a divorce is necessary.

Everyone is idiosyncratic, and even highly successful, emotionally healthy people have their quirks, their ups and downs. Even those actually diagnosed with a personality disorder may not evince problems until later in life, or they may endure a bout and then recover. Many can manage a disorder with therapy or medication, so don't give up on a sufferer—keep in mind the person underneath the problem. If you were struck by a mental illness, wouldn't you want your spouse to help you through?

But people with actual disorders aren't the ones using the "I'm not cut out for marriage" exit line. This is a classic for men (and women) in a mid-life crisis who want to recapture their youth. With a shrug, they offer the generality so they can avoid mentioning their *real* reasons for ditching their partners, like wanting to play around or to replace a perfectly fine spouse with somebody more alluring. This line allows a jerk to slink away with the wave of a phrase. If your partner hands you this line, call him on it—probe under the surface and you'll probably find a selfish core. If *you're* the one proffering this phrase, may I suggest you come up with something more honest?

I NEED MY OWN IDENTITY.

First off, let me say that co-dependence is a good thing in marriage. At least "co-dependence lite": knowing you and your spouse can—and do—depend on each other. In other contexts—substance abuse, for example—"co-dependence" means something quite different, suggesting mutual needs, met and perpetuated in harmful symbiosis. Perhaps a better term for healthy, normal spouses is "interdependence," because it's the essence of marriage for "opposites" to complement each other, providing for one another a contrasting perspective. Sharing the same goal but bringing different viewpoints, the couple enjoys a broader vantage and wider range of possibilities. In a good marriage, you retain your own identity and benefit from your partner's *difference*.

Actually, there's a biblical basis for this idea, and it starts, as everything did, in the Garden of Eden. You may recall that at first Adam was there by himself. He named each animal, according to its most salient characteristic. (For example, Adam named the dog "kal lev" in Hebrew, which means "all heart.") But none of the creatures fulfilled his need for a partner. So God put Adam to sleep and divided his two "sides" (the Hebrew word for "rib" also means "side"), separating the feminine from the masculine. When he woke up, there was the womb-man (woman), ready to provide her creativity for the next generation and her differing perspective to her man. Actually, the Hebrew for man, "Adam," means "earth," while "Chava" (Eve) means "life."

The Torah makes it clear, then, that God set it up so Adam would understand the benefit of a "helper opposite him" (in Hebrew, "eizer kenegdo"), someone to offer an opposing view so that together they could come to the most well-informed and considered decisions throughout life. Together, by integrating "opposing" perspectives, they form an encompassing whole. The person who divorces so he can develop his separate identity deprives himself and his spouse of that advantage. And most spouses feel that their individual identities are *enhanced* by having a consistent source of love and support behind them.

In a solid marriage, there's no need to split just so the partners can individually achieve. That's why this exit cliché implies that there's *a lot more going on* in the relationship—most often that a husband is stifling and controlling his wife, preventing her from exploring or fulfilling her aspirations.

A "controlling spouse" does pose a serious problem. The controller uses an array of unsavory tactics to dominate and subjugate the other. It can be either partner, but more often than not it's the husband, as it was in the case of Abby and Dennis. A physician, Dennis seemed perfectly pleasant, but Abby confided to me that he forbade her from pursuing a career and limited the occasions she could see her sisters. She was allowed to oversee their home and plan social events (and they hosted many), but if she failed to do as instructed—committing even the smallest oversight—Dennis would say "go sew," which meant she was confined to her sewing room until he felt her punishment was sufficient. As a result of this oppression, Abby ate. Secretly. Whole boxes of crackers and cans of nuts. Abby felt guilty because sometimes Dennis was loving, and she appreciated those close moments. But at times she hated Dennis. And she hated that she made everything worse by getting heavy. Food was both her comfort and her revenge.

Psychologist Andrea Bonior identifies twenty hallmarks of a controlling spouse, including isolating, chronic criticism, threats, grudges, conditional acceptance, imposing guilt, close surveillance, jealousy, requirements to "earn" good treatment, belittling the spouse's beliefs, ridicule, intimidating forms of sexuality, and pressure to do unhealthy activities. Many of these behaviors constitute emotional abuse, which 35 percent of the women in the Austin Institute survey cited as a reason for their divorce.[7]

In most cases, a controlling husband provides enough love and support that his wife puts up with the one, two, or three restrictions he imposes.

Wives of controlling husbands often find that friendships and their children can keep their self-esteem intact. Many times, they're well aware of their husband's patterns and manipulate their home lives to minimize his influence and maximize their freedoms.

Those strategies allow a functional, somewhat rewarding existence, but they don't solve the problem. Controlling spouses usually believe any relationship problem is the fault of the other partner and deflect any suggestions to modify their own behavior. An experienced therapist knows tactics to influence a domineering spouse, and having to pay for professional services tends to augment the spouse's respect for the therapist's authority.

Everyone deserves to establish and express his or her own identity. Perhaps the biggest benefit of marriage is that the success of one person enlarges the other. The struggles of one can be shared by both, and when the hopes of one are fulfilled, the other feels a special pride. In a touching scene at my son's university graduation ceremony, a beautiful African-American woman beamed as she strode across the platform to receive her diploma. Before the official photographer went to work, she was joined by her grinning husband and their three small children. Each child gave Mom a big hug and kiss; I'm sure those were the photos they treasure most.

I'M NO LONGER IN LOVE WITH YOU.

The most succinct response to this, the most popular "it's about me" exit cliché, might be "So what?"

"I don't love you" seems unassailable, but it is based on eight quite ridiculous assumptions.

- It assumes that being "in love" is necessary for marriage
- It assumes that being "in love" is a static feeling that ought to be the same as it was when you married
- It assumes that divorce is the solution to the problem of no longer being in love
- It assumes that love comes in only two varieties: the old reliable, unadorned "love" and the super-necessary-for-marriage "*in* love." A continuum of affectionate feelings that change over time is excluded

- It assumes that a person has no control over his feelings. Once, the magical "in love" was present, but as the song says, "now it's gone, gone, gone"—for no apparent reason
- It anthropomorphizes love, giving it a mind of its own. It can cozy up to a spouse, inhabit one's brain like a demon, then notice it's getting late and head out
- It assumes that once being "in love" is gone, it can never return
- Above all, it assumes that no one's at fault or to blame. That's why it's so useful; it sounds like merely a fact. I'm no longer in love with you. The end. Period

If your partner pulls this one on you, you might explain how normal, happy marriages function. Two people make a commitment to weather continually changing emotions together. They form a *family*, sharing happy and sad times while feelings shift and ebb. And not just the "*in* love" feeling (which may take many forms) but all sorts of emotions. One day there may be an argument, and a partner will be "in hate," but then they work through it, make up, and "in love" returns. Sometimes a partner endures a challenge, and at that time, "in love" recedes, and "reliable" comes forward.

In a normal, happy marriage, many emotions can co-exist. Against a backdrop of deep love, irritation might pass through. There might be a period when attention must go to a child or an ailing parent or a project with a deadline (like writing this book—thank you for your patience, honey), and "in love" takes a back seat to support. When the task is completed, support gives way to admiration and pride.

In normal, happy marriages, the two spouses' emotions play off each other. When my husband feels anxious about something, I become concerned. When I'm ecstatic, he's grinning too. When a romantic moment arrives, "in love" comes forward again.

It puzzles me to read of divorced couples who claim they retain strong bonds of love but break up anyway. Like Lara Bazelon, a San Francisco lawyer who wrote in the *New York Times*' "Modern Love" column about divorcing the father of her two children and then finding out they could have a happy vacation together. She does admit, "[M]y husband and I did not treat each other well during our short marriage," but she adds, "and yet, we had been in love with each other once, fiercely and absolutely."

She worried about honesty with her children and "practiced saying the words 'Mommy and Daddy don't love each other anymore.'

"Then I woke up one day and realized it wasn't true. There was love, an abundance of it; we just had to respect and accept that it was not the love of happily ever after."

Here comes the caveat that I can't evaluate others' marriages—but theirs didn't *seem* like a union with insurmountable problems, given that they then took a Fourth of July vacation together as a family that "went so well (I am not kidding) that my ex-husband suggested that we stay an extra day. And we did."[8]

And I'm thinking, forgive my unkindness, "If you can make it work now, why did you have to tear apart your family then?" Sometimes arguing and clashing does make life miserable, but maybe that means a little time in separate corners to recoup and invent a fresh approach, especially if you have children. By the time Ms. Bazelon realized "an abundance of love" remained, it may have been too late. You, dear reader, may be in a position to recover the love that is merely hidden in the darkness.

CHAPTER 14

"It's *Nobody's* Fault"

I n our non-judgmental culture, the easiest explanation for marital demise is "It's *nobody's* fault." This is the answer that clears the path out the back without inviting questions. There's no bad guy, just circumstances. Who can argue with that? Anyone who cares about marriage, and in this chapter I'll take on four common versions of the exit cliché "It's nobody's fault."

WE'VE GROWN APART.

If you live in one of the six states that still haven't adopted no-fault divorce, "We've grown apart" won't cut it. These states do have neutral grounds, like "irretrievable breakdown of the marriage," "irreconcilable differences," and "incompatibility." But "we've grown apart" isn't serious enough to fit into even one of those capacious categories.

"We've grown apart" should elicit a yawn. Every happy couple spends a lifetime growing apart and coming back together. Their interests diverge and converge. In the years when children are small, parents' attention turns to their needs; even in egalitarian marriages, one parent at a time focuses on childcare. True, surveys often find that the demanding phase when young children require extensive tending is the least romantic stage of most marriages. But does that "apart" period undermine the foundation of the family project?

Most young adults aspire to complete their education, establish themselves in a career, get married, and have children. They understand that each of these endeavors will require sacrifices and dedication that bring bounteous rewards, mostly after their enormous investment. They anticipate that caring for little kids will be a different experience from the honeymoon. But older parents look back on the chaotic time when their kids were small with great sentimentality and fondness. The marriage in that phase can be strong, even if it's not close.

An implicit assumption in this exit excuse is that the "we" who've "grown apart" are a single, identifiable entity. Every relationship is infinitely complex and never unidimensional. The "we" in my own marriage includes activities we share and many—the majority, actually—that we don't. The waking hours spent in each other's company during the work week are far outnumbered by those in which we're engaged in separate pursuits. He's preparing for his radio show; I'm taking (or teaching) a class. At home we may sit down to share dinner (even if only one of us is eating) and then retreat to our separate computers to write. We create touchstone moments through several daily phone calls, forwarding and writing emails, and making a point to send off and greet at every departure and arrival. We also enjoy some true together-time, most importantly the Jewish Sabbath.

When you're part of a "we," you share the travails and triumphs of your "other half." You vicariously experience everything he or she chooses to share.

That sense of "we" weakens if partners don't choose to share. And it fades if one partner doesn't show interest in the other's pursuits, even if the listener has little comprehension of details. For example, two marriages I know: In the first, the wife of a banker hated numbers and knew little about investments but listened avidly when her husband discussed the transactions of his day. In the second, the wife told her husband, a dentist, that she didn't want to hear about "all that gross stuff," so he didn't mention what happened at work. Which of the two couples do you suppose "grew apart" later?

Closeness can't be defined by the number of hours a couple spends together, or even physical proximity. Some of the most intense relationships occur when two people are thousands of miles apart, Skyping or chatting online. Soldiers stationed in Asia share intimate webcam conversations with their wives. The heart of the mom at work melts in the five minutes she watches her preschooler on "mommycam" building blocks at home with the babysitter.

"We've grown apart" is a lame reason to divorce because it's so impersonal, absolving partners of any responsibility for their drift. "We have grown apart" should be rephrased to "we chose to disengage." In other words, "we did this to ourselves."

"Growing apart" isn't the work of a moment; it takes months, or more likely years, of minor separations, the most destructive being neglect. Every relationship needs maintenance. You'll lose touch with a friend if nobody bothers to call or email or remember a birthday. Likewise, you and your mate will lose touch if you immerse yourselves in separate interests and then fall into bed exhausted without taking the time to talk.

A sweetly accommodating partner can unwittingly foster divergence. Ashley knew her husband, Christian, the head of a high school math department, was under stress as he completed his master's in school administration part-time. Most evenings he either had class or studied in the library, in part to escape the hubbub of their two teen boys and their friends. Ashley's reaction was to roll with it. She worked at a florist's shop thirty hours a week and took horticulture classes at the community college, so her own plate was full.

"Rolling with it" was a mistake. Christian was asked by his professor to help with a project on math curricula, requiring extra hours. At the completion of the four-month-long project, he was part of the writing team. Ashley planned around him. Christian was involved in his sons' high school cross-country meets and spring baseball league, and he played basketball with them at the nearby park on the weekends, but Ashley was left out. By the time Christian declared "we've grown apart," it had been almost two years since they'd had significant time alone.

But if you can slide apart, you can turn around and willfully stride toward one another. In Christian's and Ashley's case, it didn't take too much. Christian hadn't asked for a divorce—he was really pleading to reconnect. To say "we've grown apart" is not to say "we're through." One method I've found effective in counseling revives loving memories. I ask the pair to bring their wedding photo album or their flash drive and an iPad, and to sit together, describing their recollections of each scene. For most couples, their wedding day was the happiest of their lives, and reliving that special occasion motivates commitment. If the process works, I suggest they enlarge and frame a copy of their favorite picture or use it as their desktop background as a reminder.

The response to "we've grown apart" is "then why can't we grow back together?" Anyone using this line won't be expecting a reply, but he or she may need it.

WE'RE NOT WELL MATCHED.

To debunk this exit cliché we turn to arranged marriages, of all things. Yes, marriages between a man and a woman who never met, or experienced only limited and supervised meetings, before they were bound together for the rest of their lives. Personal characteristics or desires other than, say, their religion or their clan or their village didn't figure at all in their "match." In many of these cases, the main commonality between the prospective couple was a familial acquaintance with the deal-maker who brokered the arrangement. Sometimes the betrothal requires approval from a consortium of relatives who select from a matchmaker's list of candidates. Would you assume these couples are well matched? As a matter of fact, they usually make it to the end. Now, they tend to live in cultures with little divorce. They're not exposed to popular media that exaggerate the divorce rate, warning them that when they tie the knot—who knows, that could be literally—they have as much chance of splitting up as staying together. But they're not just gutting it out for fifty years because divorce is not an option. When the end nears, spouses in arranged marriages tend to be more in love with each other than couples who made their commitments after studiously weighing compatibility.

Dr. Robert Epstein, a former editor of *Psychology Today*, interviewed seventy arranged-marriage partners from a variety of cultures and found that "feelings of love in arranged marriages tend to gradually increase as time goes on in the relationship, whereas in so called 'love marriages,' where attraction is based on passionate emotions, a couple's feelings for each other

typically diminish by as much as fifty percent after only eighteen to twenty-four months of marriage."[1]

Indian arranged marriages are particularly successful, with a divorce rate of an astoundingly-low 1 percent. Rice University marketing professor Utpal M. Dholakia, who left his native India two decades ago, writes, "Even today, a vast majority of Indians and Indian Americans that I know, including family members, friends, acquaintances, and my students, many of them among the highest educated and westernized strata, choose an arranged marriage over a free-choice one."[2]

He explains that family members ask around, or perhaps use matrimonial websites, and screen prospective mates. When they've winnowed out all but one, the prospective couple meets in a family setting and have a few chaperoned dates. If neither objects, the duo can "spend time" alone, but then must say yes or no. A 2013 survey by the Indian research organization IPSOS found that 74 percent of Northern Indians between eighteen and thirty-four preferred arranged marriages.[3]

Dr. Dholakia says three benefits of Indian arranged marriages explain their success. First, prospective brides and grooms leave the difficult work of finding suitable candidates to people they admire and trust, usually their parents and elders, who are unlikely to be distracted by superficial factors like looks. The pre-vetted prospects "share many characteristics such as social class, religion, caste (yes, even today, for Hindus), and educational attainment that signal similarity and may be important predictors of longer-term marriage success."

The second reason arranged marriages work is that the constrained courting period leaves little room for rumination. Dr. Dholakia says the structured dating format requires gut-feeling decisions, "which in turn may lead to more satisfying outcomes. In free choice marriages, on the other hand, the long and elaborate dating process provides lots of time and opportunity to judge potential partners critically and deliberately, and long for the ones that got away."

Finally, with so little information about one's partner, Indians enter their marriages with low expectations, so they're seldom disappointed. "In a free-choice marriage, in contrast, high expectations often develop during an elaborate dating period, with the culture placing great weight on the romantic love ideal."[4]

Naturally, some arranged marriages are unhappy, and in a culture with strong divorce stigma, the partners may be forced to live in misery or even endure abuse. The percentage of arranged marriages that are disasters is unknown, but that risk—however low it may be—is obviously too high for Americans. But we can learn an important lesson nevertheless. "According to Dr. Epstein, relationships are organic and can be infused at will with deep commitment and lasting love, an empowering thought that he thinks will solve many marriage crises."[5]

After many years running workshops to help couples solidify a marriage decision, I've found that both aligned and greatly differing brides and grooms create great marriages. Initially, it's probably easier for couples with many similarities to form an "on-the-same-page" bond than it is for "opposites attract" duos. But remember Adam and Eve. God gave Adam a "helpmate opposite him" rather than forming a matched pair. Who wants to be married to a mini-me? How boring.

Certainly deal-breakers arise. A couple who originally anticipated having a family may hit an impasse if one of them changes his mind and refuses to have children, or if a spouse gets hooked into a demanding religion or cult. But most differences can be bridged or abided.

"Well-matched" doesn't mean "identical" or even necessarily close. Couples with sharply conflicting views on certain matters can agree to disagree on those and let other aspects of life meld them together. As the arranged marriages demonstrate, it's all a matter of commitment.

WE GOT MARRIED FOR THE WRONG REASONS.

Related to the "not well matched" exit line is this wimpy excuse. Would you say the slightly-acquainted Indian couples who bowed to tradition rather than passion married for the "wrong reasons"? Do you think eliminating physical attractiveness as a criterion dooms them to a bad sex life? Do you believe reaching a certain age is an insufficient reason to wed? What are the right reasons?

Answering a reader's question "Why get married?" Rabbi Aron Moss of Sydney, Australia, identifies four "classic reasons to get married" that are no longer relevant for many people:

So we can live together.... [T]his reason no longer applies to the many couples who live happily together without getting married.

So we can have children. Again, it is possible to have children and be wonderful parents without getting married.

To make a solid commitment. That's a charming one. We are getting married to make it harder to walk away from each other. How romantic.

To make our relationship official. You could achieve that by placing an announcement in the newspaper saying, "We are now official." You don't need a caterer to serve gazpacho soup in a ballroom just to make it official.

Today, says Rabbi Moss, "we are left with only one true reason" to get married: "Until they are married, a couple's commitment to each other is a human commitment, with all the limitations of being human. We can't see the future, we can't know what may change and what may eventuate, and we make mistakes. [Marriage] elevates the commitment beyond human limitations." The element that marriage adds is the *divine.*[6]

If you're Christian, Jewish, Muslim, or any other religious tradition, you've probably felt it, at your own wedding or that of someone you care about. A clergyman uniting a couple with the rituals of faith invests the marital compact with a spiritual dimension. Even people with a weak religious affiliation or none at all understand that standing before others and making a solemn promise elevates the relationship, infusing it with a deeper meaning and beyond-us breadth.

Ever cry at a wedding? What's that about? The occasion isn't sad, so why the tears? As a three-Kleenex guest, I'd venture that it's because the couple's love has become momentous. It has expanded in significance. With the intensity and intent of the moment, even if God is never mentioned, the relationship takes on a more universal, emotional sanctity. The unidentifiable quality that induces tears places the relationship outside our limited sphere.

The exit cliché "We married for the wrong reasons" really refers not to the wrong *reasons* for marriage but the wrong *intent.* If, like the Indian couples whose divorce rate is 1 percent, you enter into the relationship with the commitment to make a lifelong pact, the reasons that led you to the altar become a quaint backstory. It doesn't really matter what brought you there;

all that matters is that you'll do whatever it takes to stay there. It's the unshakeable determination to deal with the inevitable differences and problems that impose on tranquility, allowing anger to pass and solutions to arise.

Our sex- and passion-driven culture encourages some questionable reasons for matrimony—chemistry, sexual compatibility, timing after schooling and career launch, "next step" after cohabiting, and pregnancy (or a ticking clock). Are these reasons so much better than those of Indians who enter arranged marriages? Divorce rates would certainly suggest *not*.

WE ARGUE TOO MUCH.

How much arguing is "too much" is a question that requires constant reevaluation, because the frequency and subject matter of disagreements change as a relationship passes through different phases. The renowned literary scholar and polemicist Stanley Fish, author of *Winning Arguments*: *What Works and Doesn't Work in Politics, the Bedroom, the Courtroom, and the Classroom,* was raised in a squabble-zone. "A friend who lived next door said that he didn't need to turn on the TV to be entertained; all he had to do was open the window and listen to our family." He married an only child with "the opposite experience. In her childhood house, she never heard an argument or even a raised voice. The universe she lived in was without conflict (as far as she could tell) which made it difficult for her when, later on, conflict entered her life, as it always will."[7]

It seems Professor Fish believes argument is the spice of life, and indeed, anyone trying to persuade anyone of anything might be said to "argue" a point. But the kind of arguing that plagues and may destroy a marriage isn't about persuasion or even logic. It's about our old friend *emotion*. Fish offers four "truths" about arguing, which I enumerate here with my comments.[8]

1. It's easy to fall into a quarrel but almost impossible to get out of one.

I'd say it's easy for *some* people to fall into a quarrel. Professor Fish's wife is an unlikely candidate, but he himself admits "a good shouting match seems to me like a clearing of the throat." May I submit that the more a partner trusts the other and becomes comfortable in his communication, the more accurately he can predict reactions and thus avoid dangerous ones? The more practiced a couple is in communicating and the more life issues they surmount, the less need there is for disagreement—unless it's recreational.

Some couples' style is argumentative, but it's understood that squabbles never threaten love. Marriage researcher John Gottman calls them "volatile couples": "There is a lot of negative affect expressed, including anger and feelings of insecurity, but no contempt. They have no clear boundaries around their individual worlds, and there is enormous overlap. While they have to argue a great deal about their roles, they emphasize connection and honesty in their communication."[9]

To say these couples "argue too much" given their perfectly secure and comfortable relationships would be to judge them using the observer's values. If you asked *them*, they'd probably admit to their feisty format but regard their marriages as strong.

In contrast, some folks' style is copacetic. Arguments are rare (and therefore more upsetting because of their contrast to the tranquil norm). This kind of environment can be cultivated—I know a beautiful, slender, youthful mom of eighteen children, including two sets of twins and one set of triplets, who is famous for never, ever raising her voice. She speaks in a soft, melodic lilt, and her sweet, endearing demeanor conveys the expectation that all in her presence will act similarly. And they do; she has the most soft-spoken, considerate children you'll ever meet. Coincidentally, her name is Aidel, which is Yiddish for "cultured and refined." In her home a single fray would be "arguing too much."

As for the difficulty of ending a quarrel, well, there's *always* an end (even if grudges carry on and resentment simmers to boil another day). The maxim "never go to bed angry" might time-limit some tiffs, but actually *going* to bed angry can resolve others. In the morning light, as they say, everything looks brighter. What seemed offensive as bedtime approached can be broached with fresh perspective once you "sleep on it."

2. Arguments are seldom about their surface content. They are about needs that each party is intent on satisfying in ways that trigger negative feelings for the other.

Recreational fighters love sparring; the combat makes them feel alive. But when other couples really go at it, this principle about deeper needs holds. I'd disagree (politely) only with the idea that partners are "intent on" meeting their needs in an abrasive way. What I observe is that partners seldom realize what their underlying needs *are*, so they harp on some sticking point and never really resolve the issue. Here's my short, three-point list of typical base needs that superficial arguments are trying—usually unsuccessfully—to tap:

- A need for recognition and respect
- A need for affection and tenderness
- A need to feel connected to the partner

So many arguments totally backfire—a wife wanting affection ends up pushing her husband away. A husband desiring respect ends up belittled. A wife wanting connection to her husband makes him clam up and withdraw. This is the dance of marital contretemps: one steps forward, the other backs up; he advances, she retreats. Meanwhile, frustration grows, voices amplify, and anger escalates.

A suggestion: write down the three underlying needs, and as you feel yourself growing angry, go pick up the list. That action alone will put a brake on your accelerating ire. Ask "what do I really want here?" and read the list aloud. Truly, it's not that tough, when prompted, to choose one. What's tough is breaking away from the mounting fight because the competitive need to be right draws you in. But most arguments aren't about who's right; they're about whose rightful need can be met.

3. Trying to walk back words that have precipitated a quarrel doesn't work.

Since arguments build on themselves, early accusations and blame become the framework for subsequent charges. So, yes, you can never "walk back" words (especially attacks and confessions) that escape your lips.

The best you can do to cut short your row is capitulate. And what's wrong with that? The first person to say "I'm sorry, you're right" stops the argument cold. I've seen a smart spouse use that method, suddenly interjecting those magic words, and the befuddled arguer, already in the throes of escalating, ignores the apology and just keeps going where he left off. It took the peacemaker three repetitions before the arguer understood there was no need to continue.

It's hard to "walk back" what you've said because words have consequences and because anger disarms your inner censor. You've heard the expression "hold your tongue," but the tongue is so slippery that harsher words "slip" out even when you know they'll just intensify the argument. Anything you say will be used against you.

The repercussions are even worse if others overhear your spat. Remember that children learn conflict resolution from the way their parents handle their own disagreements. You increase the damage to your marriage with each complaint about your spouse you make to someone else. There's a Chasidic Yiddish story about the harm caused by hurtful words ("lushon hara," in Hebrew), which I'll condense from my friend Rabbi Joseph Telushkin's *Code of Jewish Ethics*:

In a small town, a man spread malicious rumors about the rabbi. Some were true, others not. At one point he realized the damage he'd done to the rabbi's reputation and came asking for forgiveness, filled with remorse. The rabbi was shocked and told him, "Go home, get a feather pillow, and go outside. Cut it open, and scatter its feathers to the winds. Then come back to me." The man thought the request bizarre, but relieved that this act would gain the rabbi's forgiveness, he followed the instructions precisely.

"Now am I forgiven?" he asked upon returning.

"One more thing," the rabbi replied. "Now go and gather up all the feathers."

"But that's impossible," the man said.

"Precisely," the rabbi answered. "And just as you can never gather all the feathers, so too you can never fully undo the damage you have caused me."[10]

This is the way accusations and hostility affect a marriage. Even after apologizing, you can't stuff them back in the pillowcase. Your spouse remembers those words, ruminating on them and stockpiling an arsenal of retorts ready to use in the next battle.

4. Deep knowledge of the ways of domestic argument doesn't insulate you from falling into the innumerable traps awaiting anyone who enters that arena.

Professor Fish says he studied self-help books on avoiding arguments but emerged no better: "my behavior isn't much different from the behavior of the bumbling, terminally defensive and self-regarding boob I was before I read a word of these books." He concludes, "If you perform any better the next time you stumble into a crisis (as I hope to do), it is likely because you've been around the track a few times and are finally beginning to get the hang of it."

Fish is right that jogging "around the track a few times" makes you familiar with its potholes. Taking these laps *teaches* "deep knowledge of the ways of domestic argument." (And self-help books help, too.) The more you learn about your own and your partner's trigger words, sensitivities, and patterns in arguing, the better you become at avoiding them. Practice makes perfect—either in handling disagreements before they ignite or in resolving full-out fights.

My years as a therapist have taught me that you can—and usually will—improve the way you handle differences with time and attention. If arguing is torture, you can get a divorce and walk away from this opponent with exactly the same skills and approach to arguing you found unproductive, or you can join with your partner (and family) to reduce disagreement.

Even if the "arena of domestic argument" contains many, in fact *innumerable*, traps, you need not *enter* that perilous territory. If money is your bugaboo, the "arena" you can't seem to escape, reserve your financial discussions for the company of your accountant. Prime your spouse with a warning that this is a sensitive topic for you so you'd like a referee who can provide guidance in solving your problem. If your problem is sex, a therapist might be the right person to intervene. If it's childrearing, involve another parent (even a friend or sibling) in the discussion, making sure your third party understands the mission and is willing to listen and opine.

And what if none of these helpful outsiders is on the scene when you feel those argumentative juices flowing? Take out the list of three underlying needs and ask, "What do I really want?" Once you get that out in the open, the practicalities of the issue are usually details.

One more strategy—the written word. Write out your perspective. Ask your partner to do the same (email is great for this), and then read each other's viewpoint and respond in writing. Putting your perspective in writing forces you to think about it. Try it—the written word is a step beyond the ephemeral spoken words of quarrels (which are the step beyond unspoken thoughts).

"Too much arguing" was number two on an MSN survey of the "8 Most Common Reasons for Divorce,"[11] but arguing is a symptom, not the malady itself. Your style of arguing, and the feelings you take away from the altercation, are more telling than the frequency of confrontations. If like Professor Fish you emerge feeling as if you've "cleared your throat," arguing is harmless to your marriage. If like his wife, you feel like you've suffered "an assault," you should aim to avoid disputes. Arguing is draining, discouraging, and damaging in most cases, but reducing the amount of arguing is one of the more easily accomplished marital repairs.

It's my observation that most battles begin by assigning fault. Someone is blamed for a slip-up, and that forces him into a defensive position. The accuser has to stick by his assertion, and you're off on a tangle. Blame kills relationships. It's that simple. It's the root of all grudges. Ban blame. This alone will prevent and diffuse nearly every argument.

A husband and wife are partners in a joint project—their marriage—and even more importantly, their *family*. The assumption (which should be spoken, and repeated!) is that everyone is on the same team with the same goals and the desire for harmony and well-being. If someone makes a mistake or does something stupid, *that is irrelevant*. Acknowledge that it happened and go from there. Don't look back to assign blame. The blame game may be a habit, but it's poison. Let your mantra be: "Everyone's trying his best. Everyone's trying to make ours a happy family."

CHAPTER 15

There's No Such Thing
as a Good Divorce

When Constance Ahrons was writing *The Good Divorce*[1] in the
early 1990s, she received one of two responses from people who
heard the title of her then–work in progress. Most often she'd
hear, "Isn't 'good divorce' a contradiction in terms, like saying 'sweet sorrow?'" But others would express approval for presenting the positive side of
what the media at that time portrayed as universally negative.

"A good divorce is not an oxymoron," Dr. Ahrons protests. "A good
divorce is one in which both the adults and children emerge at least as emotionally well as they were before the divorce."[2] That's setting the bar pretty
low. But okay, if she'd like to use that definition, it's true that some people
"emerge," often many years later, in the same emotional health that they
had prior to the divorce. That doesn't convince me that anything about
divorce is "good." It just says that people who enter a divorce "emotionally
well" (whatever that might mean, given that anyone going through a divorce
must be a wreck emotionally) later return to that same level of emotional
health.

A baseline state of emotional health is often a wonderful gift of birth. Most people from loving homes tend to function well, learning social and interpersonal skills that get them through life's tasks just fine. Emotional health is what allows people whose marriage is ripped out of their control to take those lemons and open a stand on the roadside, complete with paper cups and a sign that says "50 cents."

Some people, however, are not as generously blessed with mental health. Chemical or genetic tendencies can get in their way. They may be depressive. They may have an addictive personality. They may lack anger control. They may have been raised in a home where the wife was abused or disrespected or the husband verbally trashed behind his back to the kids. Children learn what they see, and unfortunately, not everyone sees good role models or experts at conflict resolution or expressive communication.

These people may unfortunately carry their "pre-existing conditions" into their marriages, finding it difficult to join with their partners in a happily functioning union. Each individual spouse going into a marriage brings his or her own history and personality and idiosyncrasies. The combination of those two packages often produces surprises. A woman can be pleasant and attractive when living in her own apartment, striving in her career, and forging friendships. That same woman, once married, reasonably might expect to have her own space and to continue activities like daily workouts. She might bring her decorating preferences to the newly created joint home. She might want to retain control over her credit cards and bank accounts. But if her new husband expects that their time together will take priority, that their living room will feature his recliner facing the TV, and that their finances will co-mingle, they'll have to figure it out. The entity they form together—their marriage—will be an amalgam of the two spouses. The differences they bring to the marriage can be retained, forfeited, or compromised, and these adjustments can cause problems. Even exquisitely functional individuals can make dysfunctional spouses.

So if the criterion for a "good divorce" is that you emerge after the breakup in the same emotional condition you started with, well, is that really "good"?

Dr. Ahrons, citing her study of ninety-eight randomly-selected families divorced in 1978 in Dane County, Wisconsin, passionately makes the case that divorce has been unfairly maligned, that it's "normal," and that its effects are not nearly as bad as pundits, media, and religious scolds suggest.

But the rest of the book describes how bad—or at least difficult and complex—divorce really is. We read about all the trials of "binuclear" families,
the difficulty of re-partnering and blending, and the four categories of post-
divorce parenting, with Venn diagrams of parted partners' intersecting
interests. "Almost 50% of the ex-spouse couples we interviewed had relationships that defied our stereotypes," Dr. Ahrons reports. "They weren't
filled with anger and bitterness, but rather their feelings toward one another
(not about the divorce itself, however) were more ambivalent. For the most
part, they acted civil, even amicable, and sometimes downright friendly."[3]
So "almost half" were "for the most part" civil, even amicable. These constitute Dr. Ahrons's "good divorces."

I understand that at the time when divorce rates were ascending and it
appeared that soon only a small minority of marriages would survive for a
lifetime, it was important to downplay the negatives and redefine divorce
as normal. This task has been largely accomplished. I'm glad to see the
demise of stigma and condemnation, especially because the parties hurt by
family dissolution deserve only sympathy and support. But now it's important that those victims of divorce—the partners who were dumped, the
children whose parents disregarded their needs in favor of their own selfish
pleasures—stand up and shout "Unfair!" Narcissism and injustice should
be condemned rather than accepted with a nonjudgmental shrug.

Divorce is "good" only as a last resort to stop abuse and rescue children
from addictive or high-conflict parents. But the conflict, cruelty, and toxic
emotions that lead to divorce are never good. Dr. Ahrons's main contribution
is in describing how healthy people recover, regain equilibrium, and ultimately thrive after a divorce.

Hooray for those who can move on after divorce forces a reconfiguration of their plans and expectations! Hooray for the healthy people who,
after suffering the repercussions of this disruption, re-shape the pieces of
their lives into something beautiful! Does the human capacity to make the
long-term aftermath of divorce civil, if not comfortable, suggest that divorce
is "good"? Even though some people are able, with time and dedication, to
function smoothly and overcome the pain and dislocation of divorce, it's
tough to label the source of that pain and dislocation "good."

"Divorce is not an event that ends with legalities," Dr. Ahrons writes,
"it is a process that lasts for the rest of your life." This should give anyone

considering divorce pause. It lasts for the rest of your life? You can never be finished with divorce?[4]

For her second book, *We're Still Family* (2004), Dr. Ahrons followed up with almost all of her original couples' now grown children. Their average age was thirty-one, so they were viewing their parents' 1978 divorces through the lens of maturity. She found that these adults described their parents' pre-divorce marriages in one of three ways.

First, children described what Dr. Ahrons calls "good enough" marriages. Keep in mind that these characterizations of *parents'* marriages were based only on the adult *children's* hindsight. When "good enough" marriages break up, "most kids...express real surprise, shock and confusion," Dr. Ahrons says. These are relationships that, from children's and outsiders' viewpoints, appear happy and stable. Matt, ten when his parents split, recalled, "I never had any idea there were any problems. I thought we were just a normal family." Cathy, thirteen at the divorce: "After they split I kept thinking that they were going to get over it and get back together, and then I got angry when they didn't." "Stephen's sister," twelve at the breakup: "It just fell out of the clear blue sky. I remember feeling ashamed and embarrassed. I was really sad about it for years." Dana, an adult of twenty-four when her parents parted: "And my initial reaction was that our childhood— which I considered at the time a pretty happy childhood!—was a sham!"

It's true that "you never know what's happening in another person's marriage," but that cautionary principle is invoked too often to justify an unquestioning, hands-off reaction to someone's divorce. Without knowing the back-stories, one still wonders if these couples could have repaired their relationships. Did those years of popularized divorce create a climate that encouraged splitting as a solution, in contrast to more recent attitudes empowering spouses (especially wives) to pursue therapy toward a more satisfying marriage?

Dr. Ahrons calls the second classification of pre-divorce marriages "devitalized." According to the adult children, these were distant, often estranged relationships without blatant discord. Jill, a teen at the time of her parents' divorce, remembers, "It wasn't until I was 25 and engaged my mother told me she felt no love for my dad. I was really surprised when she said that she had been thinking about leaving him for almost ten years." Emily, fourteen at the breakup: "I don't remember any talk about divorce and so it really shocked me. I couldn't understand back then why they just couldn't stay together." Aaron (age not given): "At the time it was all I knew. I thought I lived in a happy home."

Again, with the qualification that an outsider can't understand the dynamics inside a marriage, the children's points of view suggest that their lives blew up by surprise. This category, too, leaves open the question of whether the marriages might have been saved given the right attitudes and intervention.

The third group of marriages was "high conflict," in which children "suffer serious distress" because of their parents' fighting and may include physical abuse and substance addiction. Dr. Ahrons described this group as "nearly one-third" of the divorces she studied. In these families, children lived in fear of outbursts, threats of violence, or worse, and divorce was for them a relief from a tortured existence. These are the marriages for which divorce is appropriate, and even life-saving. For this relatively small group, the divorce itself might be seen as "good." But that's not really what Dr. Ahrons is saying. "Good divorces are those in which the divorce does not destroy meaningful family relationships," she writes in *We're Still Family*. "Parents maintain a sufficiently cooperative and supportive relationship that allows them to focus on the needs of the children. In good divorces children continue to have ties to both their mothers and their fathers, and each of their extended families, including those acquired when either parent remarries."

For Dr. Ahrons, it boils down to how well the parents get along after their split. How well do the two or three or four families that have sprung from the children's original home balance relationships so the children don't lose any of the connections? Seldom do these configurations fall neatly in place.

I know one family that appears to have a good divorce going for it. The dad, Rudy, and mom, Nora, married in New York when they were twenty-one and twenty-three, respectively, right after Rudy got out of the Navy in 1946. Though both were in school—Rudy on the GI Bill—they soon had little Davy. Nora's mom took care of him as the couple pursued their degrees, he in engineering and she in chemistry, an unusual choice for a woman at that time.

Over the years the family followed Rudy's career, moving to California with the aerospace industry, while having three more children. Relations between Rudy and Nora were often contentious, but with three boys and a girl, their home bustled with laughter and activity. Nora had put her career on hold to raise the kids, and she could be difficult. She found out about affairs Rudy was having, and felt betrayed, but as Rudy's outside interests usually fizzled after a few months, and she couldn't leave the kids to take a job, she'd wait them out, holding in her resentment.

Or not. Occasionally she'd release her anger and hurt to Rudy in a rage. He accepted it stoically and funneled his attention to the children, who adored him. He'd take the kids to sneak into a hotel swimming pool, frolicking until they were kicked out. He'd lead them hiking in the mountain wildflowers, or they'd jump in the car and go to a drive-in movie. There were enough happy times that the children didn't realize how serious their parents' problems were.

After Rudy didn't come home two nights in a row, Nora finally had it out with him, and they separated. By then, two children were away at college, and two were in high school. The older three, already aware through Nora of their dad's philandering, were nonetheless shocked it had come to this. But the youngest, Grayson, felt relieved. A sensitive, peace-making kid, he'd suffered from the tension in the home and was sympathetic and attentive to Nora when she went into crying jags in her room. The separation continued, and Rudy got an apartment and moved out his books and records.

Fast-forward two decades. The family is gathering for Thanksgiving dinner at Nora's house, Rudy in the kitchen dishing gravy into the bowl. Davy is there with his second wife and their two kids. The second son, Arnie, has a wife and baby. The only child yet to marry is Grayson, who seems to break up with each suitable woman before it can get serious. The daughter, Amy, there with her four-year-old, is divorcing.

Rudy and Nora, each unattached, preside over her golden-baked turkey with cornbread stuffing, with potatoes from Davy's wife and rolls, green beans, and pumpkin pie furnished by the other siblings. Rudy solicitously pulls out Nora's chair. The conversation moves smoothly from politics, to everybody's job, to their vacation plans, and where they'll all get together for Christmas. They look like a Norman Rockwell painting of a happy family enjoying each other's company.

That's the way it has worked out. Nora and Rudy kept in close touch with each of the kids, who in turn kept tabs on each other. Living in the same town let them get together for a birthday or holiday about once a month. No yelling, no teasing, no resentment to mar the occasions.

A good divorce in action. Rudy's upbeat attitude, which carried him through an unsuccessful second marriage to a sour woman, let him enjoy Thanksgiving dinner with only feelings of fondness for those around the table. But the divorce was still reverberating through the rest of their lives. Grayson was afraid to commit. Davy was lucky his first divorce involved no children. Arnie and his wife were living in a three-way relationship, and the other woman was now pregnant.

Perhaps worst off was Nora, who, after Rudy left, fell into depression. She lived alone in her own house, purchased after the sale of the lovely home she and Rudy had built, on income from her testing lab job and the yield from investing Rudy's settlement. But every day she ruminated on the divorce. Though she took medication for her depression so she could function, she couldn't forget about the affairs Rudy had. She couldn't get over the loss of their life together. Seeing Rudy—about once a month—always triggered the same thoughts. What if? Why? What could I have done? Look how we hurt our children!

This is a real family. I have spoken to each of its members several times over the many years their "good divorce" has kept them connected. Not every family has the number of challenges this one experienced. Yet each person in Rudy's and Nora's brood, while not in the conventional mold, has become a self-supporting adult with the desire, if not the ability, to form bonds and marry.

Dr. Ahrons says that "a full 20 percent" of her study respondents "felt that their parents' marriage, the divorce, and the postdivorce family combined to have a devastating impact, leaving emotional scars that didn't heal. They blamed their parents for their own difficulties and failures in intimate relationships as well as for other failures and disappointments in their lives."[5]

Still, that's only one-fifth of the study population, which leaves the remaining 80 percent to fill out the other points on the continuum of reactions, as Rudy's and Nora's family did. Dr. Ahrons's main message for parents is that their relationship with their "ex" will greatly influence how their kids turn out. By cooperating with one another, they can allow their children to feel they still have "family." Just as the "persistence of interparental conflict has negative consequences for children,"[6] its replacement with efforts to "[k]eep your family a family, minimize the negative effects on your children, and integrate your divorce in your life in a healthy way"[7] can make divorce less problematic. That's not saying it's "good."

RESEARCH: CHILDREN OF "GOOD DIVORCES" FARE WORSE

It seems counterintuitive, and it doesn't help Constance Ahrons's argument, but research led by the sociologist Norval Glenn of the University of Texas at Austin, published just before his death in 2011, found that children of "good divorces" end up with the same lower educational outcomes, and worse marriages, than those who escape from combative homes.[8]

This was "one of the first large scale studies, and included a comparison group of persons whose parents did not divorce." Glenn's team assessed the care with which divorcing parents avoided "destructive behaviors, and...estimated the degree to which this avoidance can make the children's lives as good as those of children whose parents have various kinds of intact marriages."

The study's findings were the opposite of Glenn's predictions. "We suspected that bad divorces would be associated with poor marital outcomes because they model poor relationship and conflict resolution skills for children and adolescents, and may give the impression that good male-female relationships are almost impossible to attain," he wrote. "However, the evidence concerning the effects of bad divorces on the marital outcomes of offspring are the least expected and most counter-intuitive of the findings from this study." It turns out that a bad divorce does no harm to men's marriages and produces a statistically significant *positive* result for women— meaning "women whose parents had a bad divorce were more likely to report they were in a good quality, lasting first marriage."

As strange as this seems at first, it is consistent with findings that children are more harmed emotionally when a low-conflict marriage ends than when a high-conflict situation is resolved through divorce. In a contentious marriage, Glenn explained, children can blame the divorce "on the parents themselves rather than the institution of marriage." He elaborated: "if good persons with good relationship skills cannot make a marriage work, then there is little reason to be optimistic about having a good marriage."

Two-thirds of divorces occur in low-conflict marriages,[9] and the children that come out of them are likely to be skeptical of their own chances to succeed.

In their 2011 article "Reconsidering the 'Good Divorce,'" Paul Amato, Jennifer Kane, and Spencer James compare the well-being of 944 parent-child pairs across three administrations of the National Survey of Families and Households, from 1988 through 2003. First, they applied criteria to designate families with "good" divorces, with the goal of testing whether good divorces actually bring better outcomes for children. Ten criteria defined children's well-being, including school grades, feelings about school, behavior problems, life satisfaction, self-esteem, and substance use.

The third data collection, in 2001–2003, let the researchers assess outcomes after the children reached early adulthood, the criteria being substance use, early sexual activity, number of sexual partners, early union formation, and emotional closeness to mothers and fathers.

"Good divorce" children and teens did exhibit "fewer behavior problems (as reported by resident parents) and rated their relationships with fathers more positively" than did youth whose parents cared for them "in parallel" or alone as "singles" rather than cooperatively. But the kicker is that "[a]dolescents in the good divorce cluster...were no better off with respect to self-esteem, school grades, liking school, substance use, or life satisfaction" than the children with only one active parent. The researchers continue, "Correspondingly, young adults in the good divorce cluster were no better off...with respect to substance use, early sexual activity, number of sexual partners, cohabiting or marrying as a teenager, and closeness to mothers." Bottom line? "Good divorce" isn't all it's cracked up to be.

CHOOSE A "GOOD MARRIAGE" OVER A "GOOD DIVORCE"

Dr. Ahrons and "good divorce" advocates do laudable and important work helping people who are already divorced to move on, bounce back, and, ideally, flourish. If your parents divorced, you deserve to feel you're still normal, that you're the same person you were before, worthy of the same respect. If others see you as pitiable or pathetic, that adds to the fallout from which you must recover. If you're a spouse thrust into a divorce, better you should have the undefeatable attitude that you'll provide the secure family your children need, even if that takes restraining your emotions and accepting duties and circumstances you'd rather avoid. If you're already divorced, better you and your former spouse work together to make it "good" than let relationships disintegrate or disappear.

But that's not you. You're not looking backward but still deciding the direction of a marriage in trouble. Reassurance that you can have a "good divorce" encourages you to try it. If you think that once you get past the initial unpleasantness your relationship with your ex-partner will work itself out, you're probably overlooking some less welcome facts. Most of the couples in Dr. Ahrons's books who forged a "good divorce" reached some level of civility only after painful discord surrounding the divorce. Couples who enjoy a "good divorce" right off the bat probably have enough good will left that they could reclaim their marriage. If you envision that kind of cooperation into the future, why not try to achieve it now? Much better to work on regaining a "good marriage" than a "good divorce."

Since that term made its way into relationship parlance, its lure has sapped honor away from marriage. We know marriage is a good and desirable state—after all, by age sixty-four, 93 percent of Americans have chosen it.[10] But now it's got competition from the "good divorce." If they can both be "good," when the going gets tough in marriage, why stick with it? It's a pain to have to work through problems with someone when you can cast her off and get someone new. It'll be so *good.*

True, if you have children, "casting off" their mother (or father) isn't so easy. Nor is it kind. But if you offer a "good divorce," one you promise will minimize acrimony (and you'll toss in a few bucks, too), you might more easily weasel out to start a thrilling new life.

No, you're not that callous. But please realize that even in the cases where couples *are* civil, and *do* get together without rancor, *some* family members will harbor resentments, feel awful at the sight of a replacement love, or have that awkward "wish I weren't here" moment (or years). Good divorces are good for some of the people affected but rarely for all of them. Kinship networks include a broad range of relations, and you can bet they'll take sides. Some of them won't like the person who initiated the split. Some will gravitate toward the spouse they knew since childhood, in a natural "blood is thicker than water" choice. Some of them will just be sad.

That's what happened with the Rose family. Elly, the mother of four daughters, for years had begged her pig-headed husband, Skater, to stop controlling her so tightly. If she didn't keep the house just so, or if the laundry wasn't done when he wanted and as he wanted, he'd explode. It got so that she avoided him, even as she tried to fulfill all his demands and not anger him. She felt more and more oppressed as the girls grew older and he started imposing his requirements on them as well. No outside activities on Sunday; it's the day for church and schoolwork only. No boys can come over, even to play with the six-year-old. Homework must be done by eight o'clock bedtime. You must finish all the food on your plate.

When Elly, encouraged by her girlfriends, repeatedly insisted that Skater come to counseling with her, he refused. "I tried several times to get him to come with me, but he absolutely wouldn't, and he wouldn't change, either, because he was 'right.'"

The marriage ended, and Elly had a tough fight to keep the house for herself and the two daughters still at home. Skater was angry—he thought Elly had no right to leave him; she'd walked out, so why should he hand over the house he'd worked to pay for?

She finally succeeded in court, and a year after the divorce, Elly met Frank, as sweet and gentle as Skater was forceful. Not to be outdone, Skater went on a dating website and met a lady with grown kids eager to marry. After a six-week courtship, Skater proposed and hurriedly planned a wedding. The nuptials took place in the church, and as Skater was one of ten siblings, the pews filled with sixty people. But for Skater's daughters and sisters, who loved Elly, the occasion was one of sorrow. His daughter described quiet sobbing in the sanctuary, as the overcome women consoled each other during the ceremony.

There's no such thing as a "good divorce" because even if the post-marriage "family" gets along—as Skater's daughters, siblings, and extended family did—there will be memories of hopes dashed and happy times now tainted by new divisions. Even a so-so marriage is better than a "good divorce" because there's the possibility of a rejuvenated future rather than merely a functioning remnant from a marriage past.

As "good divorces" abound, expectations for what constitutes a "good marriage" rise, becoming ever more unrealistic. A good marriage now must meet both spouses' emotional needs—almost all the time. When those needs (for affection, patience, consideration, clear communication, sexual satisfaction, time, and closeness—all the super-human characteristics we expect from our mates) aren't fulfilled, we're too quick to label the relationship "not working." With that idea planted, we start generalizing to the marriage as a whole. "It's not working."

At some tipping point, it becomes enticing to transform a bad marriage into a "good divorce." But the divorce itself is seldom "good." In *Splitopia*, Wendy Paris admits that divorcing "is the part to get through so you can build a better life on the other side. It's a *transition*, not a permanent state."[11] That may be true for marriages without children. But families with children—well, they've got an investment in the future. They've got tentacles clutching each child and both parents, and as time goes on, stepparents and stepsiblings and all their children, attaching them back to that original, now defunct, pairing. If those connecting arms break completely, it's not calamari, it's calamity.

But as Dr. Ahrons said before, "Divorce is a process that lasts the rest of your life." Wendy Paris may call it a transition, which it is—but what about the possibility of "transitioning" from a trouble-filled marriage to stability, to affection, and then to solid, loving connection? The transition of divorce is far more adversarial, encompassing, and harmful. Wendy Paris recalls her own divorce from someone who, in her book, seems caring and considerate. "We each wanted to be in a loving, comforting, exhilarating relationship—with someone else." Without knowing then who that would be, they were ditching a sure-thing—the once mutually loving relationship that led to their marriage—for an idealized fantasy with someone who may or may not exist. Snow White sang, "Someday my prince will come.... And how thrilling that moment will be.... When the prince of my dreams comes to me!"

The trouble is that you may discover halitosis with that thrilling first kiss. You may find that he leaves his princely knickers on the floor and the gel for that pompadour leaking on the counter. If there's a chance to improve the big issues in your marriage, better to uphold your vows and get through "for worse" in a commitment with someone whose quirks you know than to throw away your whole nuclear family for something that may turn out worse.

Section Four

Fixing a Hole—Why You Should Stay Married

CHAPTER 16

"Do Your Duty" or "Follow Your Heart"?

A re your aspirations so different from your parents' or grandparents'? When they got married, they too planned to spend a lifetime together. They hoped to form a partnership and together raise a family. They too learned each other's idiosyncrasies and foibles, overcame financial and career problems, tried their best as parents.

But underlying their aspirations to romance and family was a concept that has ebbed out of expectations nowadays: *duty*, to the marriage, community, job, and country. That additional bond made their marriage stronger.

The sense of duty to others has diminished with the elevation of *self*. During World War II, duty reigned, as men and women volunteered to serve and those left behind coped with a national tension of shortages, fathers at war, Rosie the Riveters at home, and newly-erected monuments to the local fallen in every small town. The ones who survived turned toward the future, determined to provide their children, the Baby Boomers, with an unburdened life, in contrast to the rigors of wartime. Though the Cold War

brought the specter of nuclear threat, the new medium of television featured
wholesome, loving families whose problems ended happily.

"Do your duty" faded in this glowing postwar light, replaced with the
Boomers' egocentric mantra, "Follow your heart." You could say a spoiled
generation undermined the objective, *logic-based* ideal of the family and
replaced it with subjective, here-and-now *feelings*.

Our glorification of emotion is the primary mover toward divorce.
Robert Ringer—remember him?—set the tone for the "Me Decade" (as Tom
Wolfe dubbed it) with the 1977 bestseller *Looking Out for #1*, at the time
a shockingly narcissistic concept. The Me Decade became the Me *Decades*,
which are still with us. Every product or service seems to start with "my"—
My Yahoo, My Verizon, My Apple...my goodness.

Which is the issue at hand—your goodness. When you're convinced you
deserve everything wonderful, you won't put up with less—not in your
children, your friends, or your spouse. If you're feeling unsettled, if you're
feeling unhappy, okay, you're mature, you can take it...for a few hours.
Maybe even for a day or possibly a week. But if you've got a problem in your
marriage that lasts much longer—well, no. This has got to go. Attaining
what you presently believe is self-fulfillment becomes so important that,
perhaps with some regret, you may break the heart of your soul mate, rip
apart your children's home and, should you desire another, pursue that
person regardless of her marital status.

"Monogamy used to be one person for life," the therapist Esther Perel
asserts in a TED talk. "Today, monogamy is one person at a time." Titters
in the audience. She continues, "We used to marry and have sex for the first
time, and now we marry and stop having sex with others." Chuckles.

She's talking about infidelity. "It's harder to stay faithful because we
live in an era where we feel we are entitled to pursue our desires." Yes,
indeed. "This is the culture where I deserve to be happy. If we used to divorce
because we were unhappy, today we divorce because we could be *happier*."[1]

Exactly. We require the most happiness possible. Not just adequate
happiness. In other words, we titter at the change to serial monogamy from
lifelong marriage. We chuckle about our "swipe right" hookups. We feel
we're entitled to only positive feelings in a relationship. But what does all
this bring us? We divorce because we *think* we could be happier. But are
we?

MARRIAGE IS A COMMITMENT

I submit that overall, serial monogamists are not happier than lifelong married couples. To see if I'm right, let's listen to what the couples who stay together for the long haul say.

In the minute-long video "Eugenio: Till Death Do You Part," a weathered but bright-eyed Hispanic American speaks to the camera: "Marriage is a commitment between two people." Clasping his hands together: "Solidly together till death do you part. And people don't understand the beauty of those words." He explains what that means:

> I stayed with my wife. I hugged her, gave her a nice little kiss. She rose her hand and said, "I'll see you in heaven, Gene." Her hand dropped, the pressure of her holding my hand released, she stopped breathing, and I just—that was the end of my wife. She died in my arms.

I shed a tear watching that.

Eugenio's story is one of 1,500 collected by the gerontologist Karl Pillemer and the staff of the Legacy Project at Cornell University, documenting the wisdom of older Americans. Dr. Pillemer sums up their lessons in seven points:

1. *Marriage is hard.* [It's] a discipline, like becoming an athlete or a musician—you never reach perfection, you are constantly learning, and you sacrifice short-term gain for something more rewarding later on.
2. *But marriage for a lifetime is worth it.* Being with someone for a half-century or more...is a sublime experience, a connection to another person unlike any other relationship.... [I]t even beats the heart-pounding passion of falling in love for the first time....
3. *Marry someone a lot like you.* Marriage is difficult for anyone, but it's much easier with someone who shares your interests, background, and orientation.
4. *Think small.* [M]ake a habit of doing small, positive things, [like doing] your partner's chore. Say it's 6 AM on a cold, rainy morning, the dog is scratching on the bedroom door,

and it's your partner's turn to walk him—but you get up and do it. That's money in the bank for the relationship.

5. *Talk, talk. talk.* One man put it colorfully: "keep yapping at one another."…. As one 80-something told me: "If you can't communicate, you're just two dead ducks."

6. *Stop trying to change your partner.* When you are getting serious about someone, the elders say you must accept your partner as is, *or don't get married.*… [A]t any point in a relationship, making your partner a do-it-yourself project only leads to anger and disappointment.

7. *Are we hungry?* Offer your partner something to eat when he or she is about to fly off the handle. According to the elders, rather than a therapist you may sometimes need a pastrami sandwich or a piece of pie. It's cheaper and more fun![2]

You will never know the kind of deep love these elders have experienced unless you stop your divorce deliberations and turn toward your marriage. I'd like to elaborate just a little on each of the elders' points, relating them to your situation.

"Marriage is hard." The difference between you and the elders is that they expected it, while you probably didn't. Surrounded by ubiquitous hype about stars' divorces and singles' opportunities, you probably thought that if you're unhappy you'll just get divorced. I would like to emphasize, however, that marriage is hard only in certain phases. It takes discipline to persevere during those times, but most of the time, even when family problems are difficult, marriage *itself* isn't "hard." In fact, it provides the comfort and support that get you through those challenges. Even if a lifeless or disrespectful marriage does require some hard work to persevere, *divorce is harder*, particularly if you have children.

In another Legacy Project video, Diane, an attractive African-American woman, says,

> Go into it thinking you're going to make it, be the best marriage ever. I listen to my grandchildren, their friends—they talk about marriage like it's not supposed to last, but I feel they have to look

at it as something they're going to *make* last. They're going to
communicate with their spouse; they're going to put a lot of
effort into it. Because it's not just something that happens by
itself.

I remember when I got married. Actually, my husband
wanted to get married more than I did, because I was afraid
(chuckle). But at the same time, I believed that if I got married,
I wanted it to be a life-long situation, and I was going to do
whatever I could to make it such.

Commitment meant something to that generation, but we were raised
in circumstances that didn't foster such virtues. Military service is now a
choice; earlier generations accepted that as duty. We seldom delay gratification, for there's little need to in our daily lives. Sacrificing for another person
is martyrdom, quite unenticing. So when the wisest Americans advise us to
expect difficulties in marriage and then to push ourselves with discipline to
overcome them by giving up comfort—well, no thank you.

But what if their second point is correct—what if lifetime marriage is
worth it? What if breaking off this family project means you'll never find
that elusive perfect love? At least you *know* the person you've already married. You know his despicable habits, what makes him laugh, and how to
steer clear of confrontations. You've already completed the learning curve.
Any other relationship requires you to start from scratch.

If you've got children, making it to the end together is worth it not only
to you but to them. They'll internalize the security of love that lasts and the
lesson that people with problems can surmount them. To be sure, if your
differences are severe, you'll have to address them; accepting an ambiance
of tension, while one option, isn't a rewarding way to live—though even
that can be finessed (keep reading).

On the third point, marrying someone like you: choosing a partner
because you fit well eliminates a lot of problems, but if you're caught in a
grand mismatch, divorce is not your only option. Chances are you still have
some important things in common, the ones that drew you together and,
significantly, your children. Consider it a starting point to center your
together-time around the interests you share, like kids' sports or field trips
with the family. Connect using simple proximity by working on your

separate projects in the same room. And you have to eat. Remember the elders' suggestion that a sandwich can conquer all? Making dinner and sitting down together provides a structure for discussion and an easy "discipline" for acting courteously. All this provides a framework for a pleasant existence, even with someone vastly different, while you put in the effort to rebuild.

And *vive la différence*! Instead of ruing activities that pull your partner away, appreciate the pleasure he gets from them and the individuality you bring to your marriage. Some make the desire for a separate identity their excuse to divorce when it instead speaks to one partner's too-tight control or resistance to change. Many of the elders married at a time when women's and men's roles were pretty much pre-determined and very separate. Working women chose then from a handful of professions, and men were expected to support the family even if their jobs felt like a burden. But now you can negotiate the tasks of marriage and the priority of each parent's career. You can establish your own identity *within* marriage, as long as you and your partner support what each other wishes to pursue.

The elders' next suggestion, to "think small," is simple yet crucial, because affection is the first casualty of marital decline. During this rough patch, small gestures express an intent to heal. Even if you can't fully confront major differences like an affair or serious money worries, you can do a spouse's chore or write a short note about a single, specific positive ("Loved the spaghetti," "Thanks for getting Charlie ready for school today," "I'll pick up your dress at the cleaner's"). You may feel an icy wall of low-grade anger between you, but a single gesture like this, *three days in a row*, will melt just about any frozen barrier.

"Talk, talk, talk," the elders' fifth suggestion, probably isn't your inclination as you struggle on the precipice of divorce. At this point, you've probably been disengaged for a long time. There may be perfunctory exchanges of necessity—logistics, immediate decisions, superficialities. But as you resign yourself to disenchantment, you don't want to invest any more of your inner being in your partner. Perhaps you're like two "dead ducks," eating in silence, striving to stay apart, confiding your frustrations to a friend or to no one at all. But if you commit to reviving your marriage, communication is your handiest and simplest tool.

Dr. John Gottman's University of Washington team can predict marital success based on some easy-to-practice acts of communication that you can adopt immediately. For example, *your response* to what your partner says, whether his or her utterance is positive or negative, determines the flavor of your relationship. Anything he or she says to you, anything at all, is a "bid" (request) for interaction. Spouses who fully turn their attention toward their partners, acknowledge the bid, and respond enthusiastically (or disagree respectfully) build the strongest marriages. Emulate that, even if you don't feel like it. After a few times you'll see results. The researchers, who video-taped thousands of interchanges, found this especially potent when the first spouse is conveying good news. An interested and ebullient affect from the responding spouse imbues the whole relationship with good feelings.[3] A much better union than two dead ducks.

The elders' sixth suggestion, "don't try to change your partner," is about the acceptance of "who you are" that forms respect. You respect your part-ner in full, including annoying habits and different ways of doing things. *Different* may not be as efficient as your way. It may not be as organized or inexpensive or attractive as your way, but there's more to your partner than these irksome incompatibilities. Don't enlarge the problem by generalizing a spouse's irksome habit into an immutable trait.

Accepting your partner as he is inspires devotion. A useful phrase when you're tempted to correct your partner's lunkheadedness is "we're on the same team." When he makes a ham-handed comment or a stupid mistake, remind yourself, "He didn't *mean* for that to happen; he was trying his best to do it right." And don't forget, blaming is one of the meanest ways to change someone.

Finally, the elders' seventh suggestion for a happy marriage is preventing disagreements from escalating with…a sandwich. You might say that when these seniors recognize they're at a stalemate, they "stuff their mouths" with the distraction of a snack rather than increasingly harsh epithets. It's a clever way to put the dispute on hold and unite in something neutral—refreshments in the best sense. While sipping lemonade or chomping pastrami, the couple's anger recedes enough for each one to think about the other's point of view. And yet they don't go their separate ways; they resume solving the problem without the venom that was there before. And they're right—*hunger makes people grumpy*. Ever hear the maxim, "The way to a man's heart is through his stomach"?

WHY "DO YOUR DUTY" RATHER THAN "FOLLOW YOUR HEART"?

If "doing your duty" means behaving according to reason, time-tested rules for living, and the conclusions of reliable research, and if "following your heart" means behaving according to mercurial emotion, ephemeral whim, untested speculation, and unconstrained physical pleasure, which is more likely to produce desirable results?

That's a trick question. It depends on what you mean by "desirable."

For some, "desirable" means maintaining the giddy, infatuated magic of being "in love," without which, they believe, a marriage loses its value. But mature people realize that marriage is a lot more than ecstasy. For them, it's a context, a secure source of reinforcement, companionship, sex, and shared goals. It's the basis for a flourishing family.

You already declared, in a witnessed ceremony, *your* desires in marrying your spouse. Whatever form of religious or secular wedding you chose, you made a permanent, legally recognized commitment to stay true to your partner for the grand adventure of married life. You may not have included the "for better or worse, in sickness and health" clause in your vows, but your intent was to weather the stresses and challenges of life as well as the gratifying milestones—the births of children, graduations, religious celebrations, holidays that mark advancing seasons and encroaching years.

This was your vow: to accept your partner into your heart, to create a family and nurture the offspring you bear into competent and confident adults who someday become your most important legacy on earth. Why take your commitment seriously? Because honoring commitments and contracts allows trust to form and futures to be planned in security rather than worry. That's your duty—to come through on your promises, to make good on your word.

If a couple has made up wedding vows that reflect the emotions of the moment and little else—"Do you, Caitlyn, promise to love Max for as long as you can? To care for him and love him until one of you loses that spark?"—what's going to hold them together? But many couples nowadays come up with vows that are binding, explicit, confining, and definitive. You can find hundreds of examples online, monuments to the composers' creativity if not to their poetical gifts, usually preceded by some sweet summary of their relationship, like "we rented an apartment, we adopted three cats, and we went to Costa Rica…":

- I promise to love you, unconditionally, without hesitation, on your best day. And I promise to love you even more on your worst day
- I promise to laugh and dance with you in times of joy and comfort you in times of sorrow
- I promise to treat you as an equal partner. I will share in your dreams and challenge you to reach your greatest potential
- I promise to love, respect, and trust you, and give you the best of myself
- I will fight for our relationship when I need to, and I will never try to hurt you just because I'm angry or tired. I will always work to be worthy of your love, and accept that neither of us is perfect
- I promise wherever you go, we will go together, where we will build a life far greater than we could ever imagine on our own
- I will trust you, even when we veer from GPS directions, schedules, itineraries, and to-do lists
- I promise you will always be my family, and we will always be a team
- I will stand by you for better and worse, in sickness and health, in sunny days and hurricanes

Nearly all of these conclude with some version of the promise traditionally formulated as "till death us do part"—a pledge to surmount every sort of challenge, to love and support each other for life. It's puzzling why someone who would never welch on a business contract would blithely cast aside a more personal and consequential guarantee.

But marriage, while a voluntary contract, is also a special kind of duty, which you were led to commit to by your emotions. It was your heart, in defiance of cold logic, that moved you to jump into such a momentous legal bargain in the first place, hoping that the emotions of today could carry you through.

So your marriage vows *combined* the commitment of duty with heart-felt emotion. But for those vows to remain strong, you must be determined to give *duty priority over feelings*. When your spouse has the flu and is vomiting and looking anything but appealing, you do your duty and help her to the bathroom, clean up her mess, and bring hot tea with lemon to her bedside. You do so out of duty, not desire. And yet that dutiful nursing is *inspired* by the heart, by an underlying compassion for the person closest to you, who without doubt would do the same for you if positions were reversed.

Duty first, infused second with heart. That's the driver of a solid marriage, as a story I heard from an oncology nurse illustrates. There was a man whose cancer was, with help of excellent medical care and God, treatable. He had surgery. He underwent chemotherapy and lost all his hair. He withstood radiation with debilitating side-effects. Every day, his hospital room was filled with family, most never leaving his side. His wife, taking leave from her job, slept there on a cot. His two sons and two daughters stayed in shifts, supporting their mother, reading to their Papa. They took turns, playing his favorite music, massaging his feet then replacing his warm socks, leafing through the album of their family vacation photos.

Papa barely survived the treatment, but every day his family was there celebrating, bolstering him, filling the small room with activity. And Papa began to recover. Finally, on the day of his discharge, Mama helped him into the wheelchair. He looked skeletal, with only a few stray wispy hairs. He could barely sit upright. But Mama was beaming. The boys tied balloons to the wheelchair handles. The girls carried the bouquets they'd brought. The family looked like a happy parade as they slowly pushed Papa to the elevator to go home.

In sickness and in health. That was what Mama and Papa taught the children, because that was what they lived. What kind of dissatisfaction would it take for divorce to cross their minds? What kind of dissatisfaction is enough for you to discard *your* vow, to refuse to do your duty—or even follow your heart?

In this milieu of only right-now feelings, we harm ourselves and our long-term happiness if we go with the cultural flow. Instead, some values transcend our momentary comfort and pleasure. No longer do we have stigma and shame to force us to conform. Now our noble acts must come from a voluntary acceptance of principles; they have to come from our aspirations to uplift our relationships toward a greater purpose.

CHAPTER 17

Divorce Won't Make
You Happier

E sther Perel, you'll recall, noted that we divorce not because we're
unhappy, but because we believe we could be *happier*. But people
who believe divorce will make them happier are plain wrong.

A team of family scholars led by Linda J. Waite of the University of
Chicago issued a research report called *Does Divorce Make People Happy?*
which answers that question with a resounding *no*. Take a look at these
selected major findings from their analysis of the National Survey of Families and Households, a nationally representative survey that assessed couples'
happiness and marital states over a period of five years, and focus group
interviews. You'll be amazed.

- Unhappily married adults who divorced or separated were
  no happier, on average, than unhappily married adults who
  stayed married....
- Divorce did not reduce symptoms of depression for unhappily married adults, or raise their self-esteem, or increase

their sense of mastery, on average, compared to unhappy
spouses who stayed married....

- The vast majority of divorces (74 percent) happened to adults
who had been happily married five years previously....
- Unhappy marriages were less common than unhappy
spouses....
- Two out of three unhappily married adults who avoided
divorce or separation ended up happily married five years
later....[1]

You may be skeptical. People who seek divorce are invested in the idea
that it will improve their lives, that it will liberate them from an uncomfortable or downright miserable relationship and allow happiness to
return. You may assume flaws in the analysis, or qualifiers that exempt
your particular circumstances from the statistics. But it's not so easy to
weasel out of the truth.

"Demographically, unhappy and happy spouses were more similar than
different," the researchers conclude, having measured several indicators of
well-being over five years. "Divorce was never associated with an increase
in the emotional well-being of unhappily married spouses. Divorce did not
make unhappily married spouses personally happier, or reduce depression,
or increase personal mastery, or self-esteem, even after controlling for race,
income, education, age, gender, employment status and the presence of
children in the home."

The report goes on, "Next we looked at subgroups of unhappy spouses
who divorced. Perhaps those who had remarried were happier than those
who stayed in unhappy marriages? No. Whether unhappy spouses who left
their marriages were separated, divorced but not remarried, or divorced and
remarried made no statistically significant difference in their happiness or
psychological well-being."

So if you're dumping your mate and running out to marry "the love of
your life," beware. You're not likely to be happier than you were before.

The partners who, in the five years between data collections, went from
happily married to divorced actually caused themselves harm. "Divorce also
appeared to reduce adult happiness and increase adult depression in the

majority of divorces which took place among spouses who had been (five years earlier) happily married."

But note: "By contrast, most unhappy spouses who stayed married ended up happier five years down the road." So if you're suffering now, perhaps the "tincture of time" will bring improvement to you, too. A final takeaway from Waite's study:

> If only the worst marriages end in divorce, one would expect greater psychological benefits from divorce. Instead, looking only at changes in emotional and psychological well-being, we found that unhappily married adults who divorced were no more likely to report emotional and psychological improvement than those who stayed married. In addition, the most unhappy marriages reported the most dramatic turnarounds: Among those who rated their marriages as very unhappy, almost eight out of 10 who avoided divorce were happily married five years later.

In a publicity stunt for *The Love Punch* (2013), a British romantic comedy about a divorced couple who reunite while pursuing the thief of their retirement funds, the producers commissioned a study of divorce, surveying two thousand residents of the United Kingdom who divorced or ended a relationship of more than five years. The results revealed that 54 percent regretted their choice, and 42 percent had considered reconciliation at least briefly. Twenty-one percent of those surveyed actually returned to their marriages.

The *Love Punch* survey also found that separation or divorce made 56 percent of respondents realize how much they actually valued their marriage and caused 46 percent to appreciate their former partner more than they did beforehand.[2] The *Daily Mail* quotes Jane Gordon, divorced eleven years since her twenty-five-year marriage: "When my husband and I parted, my view of divorce was simplistic. I believed in divorce as a clean break and imagined a 'fresh start' would solve all my problems," a common misconception. Only after her decree did she "realize the gravity of what I have done.... I had no idea of the true complexity in unraveling a life led in tandem with someone else for more than 20 years."[3]

NOT A FRESH START

Jane Gordon fell for a false hope—a clean slate, fresh start, new life—as if a divorce can close the door on your black-and-white past and set you on the Yellow Brick Road to Oz.

"Being independent is being autonomous," said Dawn Hobart, thirty-three, who separated from Edward after a six-year marriage that produced a daughter, now four. I was having coffee with Dawn, and Edward joined us via FaceTime. "Edward, you know you were overly clingy. At first I thought it was cute, but then it felt intrusive. We've been over this before." Dawn turned from my phone to explain, "We each lived alone before dating. Our views are really aligned, and we enjoyed biking together, but after we had Kerry, I started to feel smothered."

Edward just wanted to be with his wife. "I missed her when we were apart," he answered. "I still don't understand why Dawn left, especially since we have a child. I'm nice, I do the dishes. I'm not abusive or yell. But now we're supposed to go to a mediator and divide everything."

"I was home with the baby; he was making progress with his career. Couldn't he just trust me? But instead he insisted on knowing where I was at all times, constantly checking his Find My Friends app. And then he was hurt when I blocked him."

"Marriage is caring about the other person," Edward replied. "I cared about you. I still care. This divorce was a unilateral decision, and Kerry is suffering for it."

I looked down at the beautiful green-eyed little girl, seated so primly, nursing her hot chocolate and playing a game on her mom's cell phone. "Let's not go into that now," Dawn interjected. "I'm here to discuss the importance of feeling unencumbered. I don't want to be beholden to any-one."

"You'll always be beholden to me for jointly creating our daughter." With that, Edward hung up.

"Kerry is a joy, and now that I'm finally back at work, I enjoy her even more." Dawn worked long hours at the Cleveland headquarters of a national company.

"Are you feeling as liberated as you thought you would?" I queried.

"Well, I'm not sure that's the word. I have more demands on my time. I work nine or ten hours a day and drop off Kerry at preschool at seven. I pick her up, or Edward does, by six. I get to have dinner with her—we use Ready-Dinners, those delivered, healthy packs of pre-measured ingredients that I just assemble fresh and bake. It's like I prepared everything, but I don't have to shop or think about it. Then I read to her—very important—and put her to bed. Then I do some more work on my laptop. That's four nights a week. The other three—Thursday, Friday, and Saturday nights—she's with Edward. That's when I get together with my folks for dinner and take a painting class. On Saturday we try to go to Kerry's ballet with her, alternating weeks."

She'd been looking upward while trying to detail her schedule, but paused to check on Kerry. "To be very honest, my life is much more hectic, and I have to handle it all alone. I tried asking another mom to pick up Kerry with her daughter, but that really didn't save me anything. I ended up working later and then lost a half hour chatting when I came to pick her up. Kerry fell asleep in the car, and I got no time with her at all."

Dawn is the friend of someone I know in Cleveland who thought she'd be a good interview on the topic of the false allure of independence. I already knew that divorce multiplies hassles when there's a child. I wondered if Dawn's career achievement sufficiently made up for that.

"I do get immense satisfaction from my career. I'm recognized as important, and I like being paid well for it. But your question is like asking about apples and oranges. You can't compare watching your child invent a story with her dollies to attending meetings and writing memos. I went to business school, and I'm still paying for it, but I'm starting to recognize after doing this having-it-all thing for a year that it's a lot of stress and pressure."

It didn't surprise me when my Cleveland friend told me the following spring that Dawn got back together with Edward. I don't know the details of their reconciliation, but I suspect it was on terms that Dawn laid out to safeguard her separate identity.

But that's a good outcome.

If you're looking forward to independence and freedom from restriction, before you make the traumatic move out, you might consider three things. (1) The *number* of choices left to no one but you will increase; you'll have the responsibility of many more decisions. (2) The *types* of choices you must make will in large measure be unrewarding necessities rather than opportunities for self-expression. (3) As a single parent, many of your child-related choices will be complicated by requirements from your ex. You can certainly live in your own place (perhaps with less money to do it) and come and go as you please. You'll have "blessed silence," which some people come to see as "cursed loneliness." You may have your children, in which case, scratch the "blessed silence" part for those days of the week and replace it with helping them adjust to mobility and impermanence.

Is that a fresh start? Even if you have no children, even if you change jobs, move to another part of the country, and buy a new condo, you're still carrying with you the baggage of your previous marriage. You're older. You've been through a hellish detangling of assets and emotions. You've left behind half your friendships (who sided with her), half your resources, and when you enter the dating market, you've got to compete with younger people with less history.

And of course no matter where you go, you bring along your own personality. The same characteristics that kept you from getting through your marital problems remain to plague or at least influence your new relationships. You can set off for a fresh start, but it's the same old you lugging your backpack into the sunset. What have you done to change the communication style that didn't work with your spouse? What have you done to change how you deal with conflict?

The kind of people who ditch their marriages for a fresh start are the kind of marriage partners who clam up in a conflict. They're the ones who look at their watches and realize they've gotta go. They're the ones who don't like complications or loud expressions of frustration. Was this your style? Are you the one who's been looking for the door in every disagreement? Now that you're out of the house and down the block, you'll breathe. And repeat the same habits in your next, soon-to-be-dissatisfying relationship.

If your partner rejected you in a chop-and-run dump, you're left befuddled, asking, "What did I do to cause this? What could I have done to prevent it? What is it about me that made him love me once and then stop?" You wonder if you've changed, or he's changed, or if the whole marriage was a charade, a façade hiding something he couldn't tell you. You're left with the same "you" that someone you love deserted.

The erosion of your confidence affects every new relationship. That "fresh start" is really a euphemism for a mere change of scenery. Your view is different, your routine changes, but even with therapy and insight and new friendships, you can't escape the interior you, and you can't stop carrying the familiar baggage.

IT'S ABOUT THAT TIME: VULNERABLE STAGES FOR DIVORCE

Much has been made of two relatively new divorce trends, "Starter Marriages" and "Gray Divorces," a recognition of rising divorce rates among the youngest and the oldest marrieds, the causes of which are quite different. And at the center of the timeline, mid-life-crisis divorces continue to tear families apart.

STARTER MARRIAGES

Angela was a beautiful bride of twenty-one, floating down the aisle of a Los Angeles church. We'd flown down for the wedding, joining two hundred other friends and relatives. A vivacious blonde, she moved smoothly from the arm of her father onto that of her fiancé, who admired her with the too-happy grin of an I-can't-believe-it's-happening groom. She had fallen hard for Mason after he pursued her with determination, and they became engaged after two months of dating and intense online chatting. Today, six months later, they looked so in love, beaming along with their thrilled parents.

I was stunned to hear just a year later that the young couple was divorcing. Angela's dad, a psychologist and a close friend, couldn't bring himself to tell me what went wrong, but after his lengthy efforts to tape together the union, my friend sadly admitted that a divorce was necessary. I'd heard such justifications before, of course—by the time he was flying to L.A. to retrieve his daughter's belongings (many being wedding gifts), he needed to believe that supporting Angela was the only next step. He was mortified that he had failed to protect his little girl, especially given his profession. She had suffered in an emotionally punishing situation from which he might have saved her.

But Angela, meanwhile, was looking forward. She, too, avoided discussing her short-lived marriage, and when she came home for a visit, her divorce was the elephant-in-the-room topic everyone awkwardly ignored.

Pamela Paul's *The Starter Marriage and the Future of Matrimony* (2002) depicted a marriage in one's twenties with no offspring as the increasingly popular first foray into a lifetime of serial monogamy. "With almost twice the time to be adults, should we insist on an entire lifetime of marriage—especially when active parenting only absorbs about twenty years?" she asked. "Or perhaps, given changing biological and social realities, a series of two, three, possibly even four marriages might make more sense."[4]

It's already happening. Multiple marriages are a big yawn, even for presidential candidates. Paul suggests a "new traditional marriage," in which parenthood closely follows matrimony but on a much more leisurely timetable: "We could delay our decisions about what we want to do with our lives, whom we want to marry, and what kinds of families we want to build until our thirties, rather than make such decisions in our twenties, with the expectation that we'll make new decisions in five years' time."[5]

It's easy to forget that the concept of the "teenager"—a developing creature freed from traditional responsibilities to contribute to the family's welfare—arrived only with the automobile and consolidated "high school," which allowed youth to convene and date on their own. The "teenage mindset" appeared in the 1920s, and the word "teenager" followed after World War II.[6] This age of no responsibility—actually a time of expected irresponsibility—eventually stretched into the college years and well beyond. (Some of the most successful high-tech entrepreneurs—Bill Gates and Mark Zuckerberg, for instance—began corporations in their college years and became multi-millionaires before they would have had to leave their parents' health insurance plans under Obamacare.) Pamela Paul would extend those teenesque years of exploration to age thirty.

But is this delayed adulthood good for you? Is it more satisfying to dabble away this time like a dilettante? When you look back, will you wish you'd dedicated your physically prime years—when you had the most endurance and enthusiasm and bravado—to the pursuit of something meaningful?

One of the many sweet things my hubby occasionally says to me is "I wish I'd met you ten years earlier." We regret missing ten years of closeness we might have enjoyed if we'd crossed paths before. Achieving deep satisfaction in your marriage requires experiences over time. For example, an early task is finding the amount of overlap, independence, and interchange that meets each spouse's desires and expectations. It's a trial-and-error process that leads to disagreements, but those clashes bring compromise or capitulation that establishes a hum, a smooth path for the next projects in your relationship. With this expanding backdrop of negotiations, learning unspoken rules, you adjust continually throughout your relationship, and previous success in bridging differences makes the next glitch less difficult to handle.

When you find—or create—your most meaningful relationship, will you join Pamela Paul in expecting its demise in five years? Do you want to assume you'll diverge from this carefully-forged union and discard the investment you've made? Do you think it's helpful or healthy to envision "sets" of children from several spouses? Why set up a disrupted and disjointed life, broken into chunks by one-decade families?

The idea that a "starter marriage" is just another developmental phase undermines couples dedicated to overcoming problems in their young lives together. It dismisses the devastation and disappointment of the youths whose well-intentioned launch soon spiraled into failure, and of their families who perhaps went into debt so that their beloved children might embark on hopeful futures with a beautiful beginning.

I was unimpressed by (though sympathetic to) the view of five young women who met through a divorce support website and decided to write a book on their short-lived connubial experiences. "After reading *The Starter Marriage* by Pamela Paul, we all agreed the term 'starter' was insulting," their volume begins. "We decided to find a name that embodied what our marriages were—real, but short. The term 'mini-marriage' was coined."

Their point is that the flippant moniker "starter marriage" implies just a warm-up to the real thing, but they entered their bonds with the same permanent intent as the rest. "We're here to be a testament to the fact that divorce is a painful experience, no matter your age or the length of your marriage or whether you had children."[7] To my ear, "mini-marriage" also sounds a bit chirpy. Mini-skirts. Mini-series. Mini-*me*. That's the implication—the marriages are of lesser meaning because they're just so small, a miniature form of a serious commitment.

Mini or starter marriages are less consequential because by definition they involve no children. And that allows them to disintegrate leaving only internal traces (and a stack of silver and crystal). Angela's dad, while discomfited by the divorce, expressed what everyone was thinking: "At least she got in and out of it quickly." The less time it lasted, the easier it would be to forget.

I agree that if the marriage was doomed, it's better that no children suffer the breakup for a lifetime. If Mason was physically abusive, Angela needed to leave. But don't call it a "starter marriage." There's no difference in the seriousness of a youthful pledge of conjugal love that endures until death and one that dissolves shortly. This retrospective redefinition of the marriages that go bust as "just" an appetizer before the main meal belittles them and the institution.

Sascha Rothchild proposes the term "learner marriage" in *How to Get Divorced by 30*, the tale of the two-and-a-half-year marriage she began at age twenty-seven.[8] When she entered into that "opposites attract" union with a "stoner" dude, the best man offered a toast to "to the best five years of your life!" She quips, "He was off by two-and-a-half. While I was planning my 30th birthday party, I realized I didn't want my husband on the guest list."

Her label "learner marriage" makes sense, because enduring divorce at least should be educational. "It's true that second marriages have an even higher divorce rate than first marriages," she notes, "but that's because many people don't investigate why things went wrong and instead repeat the same self-destructive patterns."[9] Every bride and groom from a botched no-kids youthful marriage I know blames the dissolution on the other partner. In some cases, no doubt, that's accurate. But in many, I suspect, the same cockiness that led them to ignore red flags because getting married is such an exciting me-focused celebration lets them think the same problems won't arise again.

The concept of the starter marriage prompts twenty-somethings in new, testing-phase marriages to "slip out the back, Jack," too easily. Fitting into an identified "phenomenon" legitimizes their divorce, assuring them they're not at fault because so many of their peers experience the same thing. They're the new wave, the forefront of social innovation. Freeing them from self-examination and remorse, the idea encourages newlyweds confronted with first conflicts to duck out before they learn the skills that might have carried them through a lifetime together.

If you're in a marriage that might turn out to be your "starter," before you storm out, please consider the following:

You are some percentage of the problem. You might be tempted to blame your partner entirely—he's too controlling, she's a shrew, his parents are smothering me, her nagging is incessant—but think about how your own reactions could be exacerbating the problem. Your responses shape what comes next in every interchange. You have the power to turn a nag into something positive if, instead of muttering your resentment to yourself, you stop and look your partner in the eyes (the longer the better) and calmly explain what your reaction tends to be when you hear requests made that way. Enlist your partner in solving the problem; after all, you're still in the formation stages of your relationship.

You'll have to go through this again. I'll assume that if you end this marriage, you'll be hoping to find another candidate and try again. What happens then? You bring your same personality into a new relationship, which you'll have to craft into another two-person entity. You've tried that already, and apparently it isn't going well, but at this point there are fewer surprises to encounter. In a new marriage, you're back at square one. Maybe your down-the-road mate will be a more thoughtful and considerate person, but no matter what, you'll have to negotiate on many points. You're not marrying your clone; there are bound to be conflicts and if you bail out now, you'll never know the satisfaction of transforming a tough relationship into a good one.

You're letting down people who have faith in you. You didn't get married in a vacuum. Everyone who knows you and wished you well has some stake in your relationship. No, you can't stay together just for other people, but their caring about you should motivate you to work it out. Your mom or dad probably has some good advice. Your friends will sympathize and echo whatever you say to them—if you tell them you hate to derail your life so soon after starting out, they'll support you in that. (If you complain about your mate, they'll amplify that, too—warning!) Your siblings don't want you to suffer, and they see your marriage as a barometer of their own. Use this community of support to get through this period with your husband or wife.

Your expectations were wrong. Your new spouse has disappointed you. In fact he really enrages you because he's not acting like the husband you thought you were marrying. We have impossibly high expectations for others and more relaxed standards for ourselves. Maybe your partner never learned the skills you expect him to have (time management, spending prudence, hygiene). Instead of expressing your disgust, educate, in a kindly way. Maybe you expected her to treat you a certain way, but she doesn't. Don't get mad, get talking. Or writing. Send a thoughtful email saying how you feel and the words you'd like to hear. But the first task is to evaluate honestly what your initial expectations were. Perhaps they were ideals that need to be calibrated to the quirks and inadequacies that characterize real people.

You'll never get away unscathed. You may not have many assets to divide, and of course there are no children, but you'll find that divorce is still traumatic. You're staring at evidence that you make poor judgments, that your ability to communicate and resolve conflicts is lacking, that you're impatient. Not so long ago you pledged to love this person forever. In retrospect you'll come up with a hundred excuses for why you couldn't succeed, but in your heart of hearts, you know it wasn't all her, and that is a permanent scar.

Starter marriages aren't supposed to hurt your chances for later relationships, *but they do.* When an attractive potential mate hears you're divorced, he has to assume that something horrible blew up your marriage, and it might have been you. Even in our no-fault culture, a divorce is a strike against you. Anyone attracted to you will ask himself, "If she couldn't make it through with the first guy she committed to, how can I be sure she'll make it with *me*?"

MIDLIFE MADNESS

The reason there's a midlife crisis stereotype is that, like starter marriages, they're common. Chet, fifty-six, worked his way to a comfortable plateau in the Minnesota state planner's office. The job was interesting—sometimes in the field, lots of meetings, conferences three or four times a year. And the family vacationed in Hawaii at Christmas. He was in pretty good shape, working out at the gym with his son, who was in law school, four times a week. Chet's wife and daughter both taught fourth grade.

Then something happened to remind Chet he was mortal. His younger brother, Rick, active and a jogger, was diagnosed with throat cancer. His little brother? The kid? Chet was shaken to see his brother lose all his hair from chemo, to watch him shrivel from a powerful, healthy man to a weakened form barely able to hobble. They'd lost their dad and mom, but the prospect of losing Rick sent Chet into a funk. What did he want to accomplish with his life? Where was he going from here—to the shrunken state of his brother?

Some people coming face to face with mortality for the first time become more spiritual. They feel the pull of time and want to prepare. Others make a bucket list and start ticking off items, mostly as a tourist of the world's sights and sounds.

Then there are the less uplifting responses. Chet had never rebelled. He'd always been the dutiful son, the big brother to roughhouse with, the considerate boyfriend, the participating dad. Suddenly he felt constrained by the predictability of his world. A nice world, to be sure, but all Chet could see from now until retirement—only nine years away—was more of the same. Or less, if he were to be struck by something unexpected, as Rick was.

So he gave himself a little wiggle room. "I wasn't thinking I'd throw away my life," he wrote to me in an email exchange. "I was thinking I'd just let myself follow my feelings." At a conference in Memphis, he decided to sit in a different part of the room, not with the other planners he always saw at these conferences. He liked them; good people. But "good" was not the way he was feeling just then.

Scanning the crowd, he chose a spot toward the back next to an attractive woman seated by herself. "She looked to be about forty, wearing a white tank top with a tan blazer over it," he recalled. "I could see that her chest was tanned." She dropped her pen; they both leaned between their chairs to retrieve it, bumping their arms, pretending they didn't touch. But it was an invitation, and Chet knew it.

He and this woman, Claire, began a correspondence. When their innuendo became clearer, Chet started to take a break at lunch, sitting on a park bench and FaceTiming her. "It felt like we were together." Claire, divorced with no kids after fifteen years of marriage, had recently ended another relationship. "She just wanted someone to appreciate her," and Chet found much to admire.

FaceTiming at lunch with an attractive woman sixteen years younger felt like a tonic. "I had something to look forward to each day," Chet wrote. Claire was a distraction from his brother's depressing condition and from the predictable sex life he had with his wife. He and Claire FaceTimed for nine months and then connived to attend the same conference.

Though he didn't plan to have sex—he was still thinking their relationship was exciting but hadn't crossed the line—when they came together,
electricity returned. "I said goodnight to her and left," Chet remembers.
"But then I went back and knocked on her hotel room door." Once they
made love, the months of intimate talk coalesced. Chet's rebellion felt
exhilarating; liberating.

"I couldn't reconcile cheating with who I was, but I also wasn't going
to give up Claire," he wrote. He reasoned that the kids were grown and his
wife loved her career. She had the support of their daughter and son. If he
didn't take this opportunity now, how would he feel the rest of his life,
knowing there was a beautiful woman in love with him that he let go? And
not just any beautiful woman. Claire understood the intricacies of his work.
She loved the outdoors, as he did. They might even be able to have a family
together. He could start over with none of the loneliness and hassles of the
dating world. "My new life was handed to me on a platter," he said, a gift
he had to take.

Chet didn't expect the reaction he received from his family. "It's true
this seemed out of the blue," he recognized. "Everyone in my family turned
against me." His kids, protective of their mom, wouldn't talk to him. His
brother, now almost recovered, begged him to reconsider, said he was "stupid to do this to the people who loved you." His wife alternated between
outraged and devastated, though most of the time she refused to answer her
phone. She blocked his texts. He had to pay an errand service to pick up his
stuff from the house. He lost access to all but one of their accounts.

"I became a pariah," Chet wrote. "Claire was sympathetic but said I
should have handled it much better." Six months later, Chet was in legal
negotiations over their assets. Was it worth it? "I'm not sure. I absolutely
needed to break out. I needed that reminder I was dynamic and alive." But
is having Claire worth enraging a wife of twenty-six years and two children?
"No. Actually, I took my relationship with my wife for granted, and while
I have a replacement of sorts, I miss her." My last question: could you go
back?

"I can never rebuild the trust we had. I don't think my kids or my wife
would have me back, even with my head down and tail between my legs."

Can you resolve a midlife crisis without destroying your family? Of
course. It's a matter of understanding the causes of your panic. The former

NPR journalist Barbara Bradley Hagerty has written a delightful book on the subject, *Life Reimagined: The Science, Art, and Opportunity of Midlife* (2016), synthesizing two years of research about navigating this feared passage. Some measure of distress about advancing years and mortality, she shows, is natural. In fact, she was inspired to investigate the subject because she was experiencing some angst of her own.

Dumping the relationship you've cultivated for twenty years or more may offer an enormous distraction, but it doesn't make you any younger. An affair fulfills two desires of an anxiety-ridden middle-ager—it's audacious and rebellious, and the sex itself confirms your generative power. Sex, particularly with a nubile partner, contains the potential to thrust your DNA into the future, guaranteeing your immortality. But you can pursue audacity and rebellion *without* upsetting the entire context of your life, i.e., your family. And there's nothing wrong with wanting great sex, but if your marriage isn't providing it, a little novelty or perhaps some therapy might fix the problem. An affair may provide ecstasy and a flurry of extreme emotions that simulate youthful exuberance, but after two or three years, those will subside. Then you're facing aging and death once more—this time with half your wealth, a new spouse, and a lot more complications. Soon it's time to find another way to address your existential issues.

Ms. Hagerty makes the point that midlife now leaves enough time for a whole new career. And of course that means there's time for a whole new family also, but do you really want to start over and become that gray-haired dad getting winded playing basketball with his teen at the park? The one with two sets of kids and two mothers to coordinate?

Maybe you've perendinated in pursuing a passion that will ignite excitement. A career change to something vastly different that intrigues and satisfies you can address the urgency to really live. At the same time you can take on the project of enriching and evolving the marriage in which you've already invested. Career and marriage have different but complementary functions. Career, focused on the outside, lets you make a wider impact on the world. Your marriage meets the private need, it lets you express intimately the deepest doubts of your soul. In marriage you can be vulnerable, emotionally safe within your couple-ness and the coziness of your nuclear family.

Ms. Hagerty has synthesized her wisdom into eight points, which I summarize—guidelines for handling a midlife impulse to break free and tempering the need for destructive grand rebellion:[10]

- "Aim for long-term meaning rather than short-term happiness, and you will likely find both." Focus on the good life— "striving with a purpose"
- "Choose what matters most." You might like the immediate rewards work gives, but investing time in your family brings the higher payoff
- "Lean into fear, not boredom." Hagerty quotes Howard Stevenson of Harvard Business School, who warns about stagnation in one's work—"Ask yourself regularly: How will I use these glorious days left to me for the best purpose?"
- "'At every stage of life, you should be a rookie at something,'" quoting the botanist Chris Dionigi on the importance of trying new things
- "Add punctuation to your life." Punctuate your calendar with goals to achieve. For example, Hagerty entered a bicycling marathon and found daily victories in improving her times
- "A few setbacks are just what the doctor ordered." Calling on your main strengths and letting other people help you through trials will leave you stronger when you bounce back
- "Pay attention: Two of the biggest threats to a seasoned marriage are boredom and mutual neglect." A jaunt out of your comfort zone together can be the time of your lives
- "Happiness is love. Full stop." That's the essential finding of a decades-long study of the Harvard classes of 1939–1944. "The secret to thriving is warm relationships"

Having an affair isn't the only way somewhat immature men are known to combat a midlife crisis. They buy sports cars. Or, like someone I know, hi-fi equipment. They pursue risky, adrenaline-pumping activities like skydiving, bungee jumping, scuba diving at the Great Barrier Reef, hiking the Appalachian Trail alone. I know people who volunteered for the

Israeli army. The key antidote to the fear of death at the center of a midlife crisis is a combination of fear and thrill.

The psychologist Carol Ryff has identified six "dimensions" of psychological well-being: self-acceptance, positive relations with others (primarily one's spouse), autonomy (feeling empowered and independent), mastery of one's environment, having a purpose in life, and personal growth.[11] If we evaluate the effects of an affair according to the Ryff measure, we can see how damaging infidelity is to well-being.

Self-acceptance: Far from fostering self-acceptance, the dishonesty of an affair drives a wedge between what you believe, what you know, and what you feel. The temptation of an affair, in fact, is often strongest when one's self-acceptance is low, not when one feels comfortable with oneself.

Positive relations with others: While a philanderer might say his hanky-panky gives him a positive relationship with his inamorata, its clandestine nature opens up a chasm between him and his spouse, family, and larger circle of friends.

Autonomy: You might say that flouting conventional morality by breaking your wedding vows is a bold gesture of autonomy. But at the same time, sneaking around imposes constraints on lovers; their furtive trysts require planning and deception that impinges on free movement.

Mastery of one's environment: Though following through on an attraction definitely shows will, it's the sense of lacking control over aging and mortality that spurs the need for an affair in the first place. Does an affair fill that need? That might depend on the outcome. If the lover leaves or the marriage disintegrates in ill will, the mid-lifer could end up feeling even less powerful and more subject to fate than before.

Purpose in life: An affair usually sidetracks or undermines grander goals. Dalliances sizzle in the here and now, fueled by hormonal frisson. Purpose, derived from a broader view, often requires deferring immediate wows for something more lasting and substantial.

Personal growth: An affair enhances the very characteristics that spiritual and moral people seek to minimize: overstepping bounds, breaking vows, lying with a straight face.

There is something to be said for passion, titillation, intrigue and pursuit, but none of these requires a marital betrayal that upends your life and destroys the security and trust of your family. Cultivating a more passionate, exciting, sexy, and goal-oriented lifestyle with your spouse checks off all the criteria for well-being. That's the antidote to ennui at any age.

GOING GRAY

An elderly couple hobbles into the swank offices of a divorce attorney. They take a seat. Rarely have such old people sought his services. "What can I help you with?" he asks. "We want a divorce," announces the man.

"A divorce! I see. How long have you been married?"

"Sixty-three years," the woman replies.

"Sixty-three years! That's a long time for any marriage. What's the problem?"

The man looks angrily at his wife and replies, "She nags me to death! I can't stand the sound of her voice! It's been like that for fifty years!"

The attorney's eyes widen. "Fifty years of hating the sound of her voice? Why did you wait this long to come for a divorce?"

The woman answers, "We wanted to wait until the children were dead!"

And indeed, the number of "gray divorces"—those occurring among couples married twenty, thirty, forty, or more years—has escalated considerably. In 1990, the divorce rate was 4.7 per thousand persons aged fifty or older. But by 2010, that rate had climbed to 10.5 per thousand. In absolute numbers, the change is more striking. In 1990, 206,007 people fifty or older divorced. Twenty years later that number was 643,152. The projections for 2030 show the divorce rate holding constant at 10.5 per thousand, representing 828,380 actual divorcees.

Breaking those figures down, we see that the numbers are far higher for the younger segment—persons aged fifty to sixty-four—than for those sixty-five or older. The divorce rate for the younger group soared from 6.90 in 1990 to 13.05 in 2010, or from 175,954 persons in 1990 to 529,842 in 2010. The older group saw a much smaller increase over those twenty years, the rate rising from 1.79 to 4.84, and the number of persons rising from 30,053 to 113,310.[12]

One in ten divorces in 1990 involved spouses aged fifty or older, but by 2009 that proportion grew to one in four, despite declining divorce rates across all age groups. But Baby Boomers are accustomed to forging the lifestyles they want, and with better health and greater longevity, many of them are unwilling to let all those golden years go to waste. Their "start over" mentality has stretched the midlife-crisis phase to age sixty-five.

Donna and Larry were on their second marriage. Divorced in their thirties, they found each other online through OkCupid when Larry was forty-three and Donna forty. Donna's seventeen-year-old daughter, Gina, was still at home; Larry's youngest was eighteen and living with her mom. They both hailed from Astoria, Queens, a happy coincidence, they thought. After they got together, they hit a few bumps in the road with Gina, who wanted to take off on a world adventure rather than college, and they lost a bundle on a bad investment. Then Donna got thyroid cancer. They survived all that, but when things calmed down, they started to diverge.

Larry got intensely involved in politics, listening to radio talk shows incessantly and building his own following contributing to an online newsletter. Donna found political blather irritating, so she devoted more attention to her interior design business, taking on an assistant to expand her brand on social media. You could see it coming: with adversity behind them and interests that seldom overlapped, two years later they felt they'd grown apart.

Larry and Donna are typical of couples filing for a "gray divorce." "Older adults who divorce tend to be in shorter marriages than either those who remain married or become widowed," notes a report by the Center for Family and Demographic Research at Bowling Green State University conducted by Susan L. Brown and I-Fen Lin. They found that "the modal duration for those who divorce is less than 10 years versus 40+ years for those who remain married or become widowed." In other words, the "gray divorce" trend is fueled mostly by second and subsequent marriages that dissolve before their tenth anniversaries. The longer a couple remains married, the smaller their chances of divorce.[13]

Still, "gray divorce" is a real phenomenon, and it is projected to continue. "Assuming the divorce rate remains constant over the next two decades—a conservative assumption based on the recent trend," say Brown and Lin, "the number of persons aged 50 and older who would experience divorce in 2030 would rise by one third."[14]

Why is this happening? "The trend defies any simple explanation," writes Susan Gregory Thomas in the *Wall Street Journal*, "but it springs at least in part from boomers' status as the first generation to enter into marriage with goals largely focused on self-fulfillment." The first generation to enter adulthood with the personal computer, which too soon drew spouses from each other, and toward their own online worlds.

"As they look around their empty nests and toward decades more of healthy life, they are increasingly deciding that they've done their parental duty and now want out," Thomas speculates. But only if they received little satisfaction from the marriage during that time; in a strong marriage, a spouse usually grows in importance, filling the newly empty nest.

Professor Brown agrees with my assessment that oldsters may be victims of what she calls "individualized marriage," where satisfaction of personal needs is the standard for staying together. "Individualized marriage is more egocentric," she says. When one spouse in such a marriage wants to pursue greener grass, no one can contradict him or her.

"Many of those now opting for gray divorces, however, fail to foresee its complications in today's bleak economic landscape," Thomas notes. "This is especially true for women" who may too easily trade financial assets for more custody or just to end discord.

Another downside is loneliness. An AARP-commissioned study found "being alone" was by far the biggest fear of divorced persons over forty, affecting 45 percent of the respondents. Half of the women cited uncertainty about what's ahead as a major difficulty. Those divorced in midlife or later contend with loneliness or depression (29 percent), feelings of desertion or betrayal (25 percent), a sense of failure (23 percent), not having someone to love or to love them (22 percent), and lack of self esteem or self-confidence (20 percent). Not a pretty picture.[15]

How do you stop a gray divorce from happening? The same way you stop any divorce—first, call a truce and express your desire to reconcile. You might try the bonus exercise at the conclusion of this book, which provides two key strategies for achieving a better relationship.

CHAPTER 18

The Grass Isn't Greener on the Singles Side of the Fence

With the number of unmarried people expanding, I'm not going to tell you that there's anything wrong with being single.

In fact, many singles get downright irritated when anyone suggests that married people are any happier, healthier, better connected, or more successful than they are. Bella DePaulo, a psychologist and the author of several books defending the single life, has coined the terms "singlism" for prejudice against the uncoupled and "matrimania" for the "over-the-top hyping of marriage, coupling, weddings, and brides." While she expends quite a bit of effort offering counter-evidence[1] to the studies[2] that suggest benefits of marriage, I'd like to say *stop*. You're both right. If you prefer being single, wonderful. You're probably miffed that I compare your world to a verdant lawn that some marrieds look longingly at over the fence, when you don't see either side as greener. But confirmed singles are the exception.

It's true that more people are prolonging their single years, pushing off marriage to later ages. And singles nowadays want to be farther along in their careers before they make that "forever" commitment. They also have higher expectations for the person they select.[3]

But for all their hesitancy to wed, many young adults are not truly "single." About a quarter (24 percent) of never-marrieds between the ages of twenty-five and thirty-four are living with a partner, and research shows that marriage's benefits accrue to these couples, too.[4] An uncounted number of others, including several twenty-somethings I know, are entrenched in long-term relationships but maintain separate residences. Though these "steadies" may put off marriage for the same reasons as the rest of their cohort—completion of education and launch into a career, financial readiness—when age thirty approaches, they plan their nuptials. So if you're thinking about seeking a new relationship, remember that it's not as easy as you might think to find an unattached candidate with the qualities you require.

There are a couple of facts of dating life you ought to consider before throwing away your marriage. First, *there's a lot of competition out there.* What has this got to do with you? One of the misconceptions that makes the grass look greener is that there are scads of people just waiting for you to become available. Or at least enough to entertain you while you search for a new commitment. Unfortunately, that's not the case. Pew projects that though twenty-somethings want marriage and are dating, 25 percent of those who stay single into their thirties will *never* find a spouse.[5] Soul mates don't grow on trees.

These never-marrieds—*very* few of whom are not looking to wed—are your competition when you emerge, divorced and likely with children, onto the dating scene. And the more time it takes you to find someone new, the fewer high-quality candidates there are. "In 2012, there were 71 first-time newlyweds for every 1,000 never-married adults ages 25 to 34," reports the Pew Research Center. But by the time you get to the age group forty-five to fifty-four, there are only sixteen newlyweds per thousand never-marrieds. And finally, the number of first-timers per thousand never-married adults aged fifty-five and older is just *seven.*[6]

The second fact to face is that *you've got baggage.* If you go ahead with a divorce, it will become your first piece of baggage. Your second piece of luggage is your first child. Each subsequent child is another suitcase that could drag any new relationship down. You can't just say, "Yeah, I have kids," because any potential long-term relationship must include your new spouse as a major fixture in their lives, and they in hers.

The website AskMen.com lists ten reasons why women won't date single dads. Among them are dealing with the ex-wife, a concern that you're "damaged goods," wanting your undivided attention, and a desire to have her own kids, not the ones you already have.[7] These aren't selfish or trivial concerns; they're about the context and ground rules for her future with you. One reader's comments should shatter the illusions of anyone who thinks that if a woman loves the guy she'll love his kids:

> I'm dating a single father and it's difficult. His life has so many more demands than mine. His son is struggling with reading and needs constant help. He spends his weekday evenings doing homework. I come home from work and it's hard to want to take that on every day. He's on an every other week schedule with his kids but now he has his son full time and his ex gets him every other weekend.
>
> I love him and I love his kids but it is hard to put my life on hold for someone else's responsibilities. Especially when there's no end in sight.[8]

If you're a mom looking to remarry, you face the same obstacles, compounded if you're the primary residential parent. If you have fifty-fifty shared custody, then your partner will have to work around those time and attention requirements, coming in second in your priorities.

Children and an ex aren't your only baggage. Suppose you have no kids and get away with a relatively clean divorce. You're not as young as you were when you made your first commitment, and your life experiences and circle of attachments make the "package" that is you more complicated than it was in your younger years. Potential partners are now more likely to come with their own marital mishaps, their own children, and a universe of connections. And with age comes illness. A chronic health problem makes you less desirable, no matter how good-looking, affectionate, and fun-loving you are.

Debra, a sixty-two-year-old freshly divorced from a diabetic husband of thirty-five years, was lonely. A self-starter, she decided to try some matchup websites and received many responses. She'd correspond in a light-hearted way, but as soon as she could inoffensively find out, she asked about their health status. "I met some fabulous men," Debra told me. "Most were funny, many had really illustrious careers and were close to retiring. I know I would have really enjoyed spending time with any one of them, but if I found out they had a chronic health issue, I'd say 'thanks but no thanks.'" Debra said she'd "already had enough of multiple medications, hospitals, and treatment centers." So she screened by health history. But "even if they're healthy," she admitted, "I'm finding I'm just not attracted to them. They can be slim and athletic, but after so many years with the same person, I imagine them without their clothes and instead of exciting, it's a turn-off."

DATING IS NOT FUN

If it weren't entertaining to watch people compete for affection, how could we explain the popularity of so many reality shows about dating? *The Bachelor* and *The Bachelorette* are classics, of course, and the genre is always expanding, usually featuring tropical locales, lots of alcohol, models instead of normal people, jealousy, and heartbreak. Calling these meet-markets "reality shows" doesn't mean they bear any similarity to real life, but they do keep the hormone-driven pursuit of coupling in the public consciousness. If you're weighed down by a troubled marriage, the carefree thrills of a tropical tryst can seem pretty attractive. But despite what you hear about quick-find apps or see on *Coupled*, for most people dating is a mix of fear, embarrassment, hope, and disappointment. Sometimes it's a source of friendship, occasionally sex, and, if you're very lucky, ultimately a long-term partner.

Everyone knows the cliché: "You've got to kiss a lot of frogs to meet a prince." And most people know that kissing frogs is no fun. One dating website, assuring its readers that "it's all about perspective," offers these slightly pathetic suggestions:

- Lighten up: Have *fun* because dating is fun…it's supposed to be
- Think positive: Even if this is your tenth date this month, keep trying

- Experience: Take each date as a learning experience about what is out there and what you're looking for
- Stop being so hard on yourself: There is nothing wrong with you. Repeat after me, "I am a prize"
- Put your best foot forward: Looking good will make you feel good and it will be obvious to everyone around you

I have respect and even sympathy for the millions of people who are seeking someone with whom to complete their lives, but if these are the best suggestions an expert can offer...well, draw your own conclusions.

Brian was normally a quiet guy who loved spending free time looking up stuff on Wikipedia. He and Glynnis had been married sixteen years and their one daughter, Kara, was already in high school when Glynnis took off with her assistant. Brian was devastated, especially after the court decided on shared custody, meaning he'd see his daughter only half the week. An actuary by profession, he wasn't outgoing, but a year after the divorce came through, his co-workers started asking when he was going to begin dating.

Kara made him a Match.com profile, and after weeks of her begging him to sign up, he relented. She kept tabs on his account, and when Sylvia, a thirty-eight-year-old bank manager with a ten-year-old son, expressed interest, Kara told her dad and got them emailing. Trouble was, Brian was terrified to go on a date. He wasn't over Glynnis, and he couldn't imagine trying to be charming with someone unfamiliar. Kara nudged him to "move on," but while he agreed intellectually, the whole dating thing was a complete turn-off.

By the time he and Sylvia met at a coffee shop, he was so tied up in knots that their meeting went like an old Chevy Chase routine. Brian tried to talk too soon after sipping his strawberry frappuccino; the straw stuck to his lip, pulled out of the cup, and dripped all over his pants. He got up to grab some napkins, causing the icy goo to drip all the way down his leg. He turned as pink as his drink. Sylvia was forgiving but skeptical. When she asked about his daughter, he relaxed a bit, but he knew he wasn't open to a relationship. After they parted, neither followed up. This first post-divorce dating experience didn't make Brian want to try again.

Any date can be stressful, as Brian's story shows, but you also have to keep in mind that *some daters are rats*. The hacking of the Ashley Madison website in 2015 opened a window onto a sordid world of cheating that makes "Dating is not fun" a grotesque understatement. In fact, if you trawl singles' websites, you see that the general feeling is more that "dating (pardon the vernacular) sucks." You might retort that this perspective is only half the story—isn't the bad balanced with the good? If there are so many weirdos, creeps, and social maladroits in the dating world, there *must* be an equal number of kind, courteous, and decent people. You'd think. But if that's true, we don't hear about it much. Instead, online complaints fall into several disturbing categories:

- Sexpectations: "The fact I'm an insecure hopeless romantic in a culture of casual sex and friends with benefits"
- Social media woes: "Social media seem to be the only way people want to meet or converse. Why can't I just meet a nice girl at a book store or something?"
- Emotional cruelties: "The rush of everything. How quickly you could be all over each other and the next thing, everyone becomes Houdini, gone before you know it"

SINGLES' SEX

For all the talk about the hookup culture, the average number of sexual partners for Americans is still surprisingly low. The lifetime average for women is about four partners and between six and seven for men, according to the National Center for Health Statistics. Media make much of hooking up, but only a small fraction of Americans, mostly a subset of college students, actually live in that culture.[9]

Chances are, if you divorce you'll be prudent—but if you choose to partake in those options (swipe right!), the person who pleasures you will have less investment in your satisfaction than your spouse did. "We've been sold this bill of goods that we're in an era where people can be sexually free and participate equally in the hookup culture," says Justin R. Garcia of the Kinsey Institute. "The fact is that not everyone's having a good time."[10] In casual sexual encounters, the man is often concerned about the pleasure of only one of the participants—himself. Who'd have believed it?[11]

If you go on the prowl, prepare to meet some unusual breeds. Writing in *New York* magazine in 2005, Amy Sohn observed, "Young people might think they are the only ones out there having casual encounters, but it turns out the most enthusiastic sex freaks these days are the newly single thirty- and forty-somethings who are reentering the dating world with a gusto they've never known before." You might run into someone like "Jefferson," a divorced father of three. "Half the week, he's taking care of his kids. The other half, he goes out with friends or on dates with what he calls 'vanilla' women. And twice a month, he hosts orgies at his apartment for a group of men and women he met on the swingers scene." After his divorce, he found that a sedate sex life didn't express who he "actually was." "I can be polygamous and bisexual, do all the stuff I did when I was in my mid-teens. I don't want to put all my stock in this one other person," he says.[12]

Maybe you'd like to revisit your teens with "Jefferson," but having been married before, chances are your ultimate goal is not a life of meaningless sexual exchanges with strangers. Most people, *especially* those who have seen the potential for a really close connection (even if that ultimately fizzled or fractured), retain the ideal of a true love for life, an "other half" who can keep you interested and also fulfill the roles of sex playmate and reliable companion. Perhaps no one can serve all those needs, but a quickie hookup barely meets one. It's fleeting and leaves you with sheets to wash and having to start the whole process again.

MEETING ONLINE

If these sex-and-singles experiences aren't daunting enough, wait till you "put yourself out there" on dating sites like Match, OkCupid, eHarmony, Plenty of Fish, Zoosk, and Badoo. Acceptance of online dating is growing quickly, surveys show. The percentage of those surveyed who agree that "online dating is a good way to meet people" rose from 44 in 2005 to 59 in 2015. Those who think users of the sites are "desperate" declined in the same period from 29 percent to 23 percent. In the two years from 2013 to 2015, the percentage of singles between eighteen and twenty-four who used dating sites nearly tripled, from 10 to 27. In those same two years, the percentage of people between fifty-five and sixty-four years old who used those sites doubled, from 6 to 12.[13] If you're a Boomer, you're in the fastest-growing singles market, with a third of your cohort never married and another fourth divorced.[14] Even the American Association of Retired Persons has launched its own dating site, "ideal for seniors who are tired of being crammed up at home.... "[15]

Dating sites, which charge from about twenty-five to sixty dollars per month (and renew automatically with a charge to your credit card),[16] apply sophisticated computer algorithms to answers on questionnaires and use behavioral data to predict how users will respond to proposed matches.[17] In a popular TED talk, Amy Webb tells how she "hacked" these algorithms through careful data analysis and developed an irresistible "super-profile"—"still me," she says, "but me optimized now for this ecosystem."[18]

The hitch in outsmarting the system is that enrollees simply lie about themselves, causing the algorithms to backfire. Greg Hodge, tired of rejecting dishonest applicants for his "exclusive" dating site Beautiful People, commissioned a survey to find out the prevalence of "exaggeration." Fifty-three percent of Americans responding to the 2011 OpinionMatters poll admitted prevaricating, with women ten points more likely to fib. Items most likely to be fudged included weight (38 percent of women and 22 percent of men), outdated photo (21 percent of women, 15 percent of men), and physique or body shape (20 percent of men and 14 percent of women). Twenty-two percent of men lied about their height, and 11 percent of women lied about their breast size. Men's most common falsehood was their job description, followed by money and looks. Women's top four untruths were physical; the fifth was money.[19]

Hodge asks, "Do women really think that when they finally encounter their date in person, it won't be immediately obvious that they are two cup sizes smaller, two inches shorter and 20 pounds heavier than they claimed online?" He wonders why daters defeat the purpose of finding a true match by submitting a false profile. "Perhaps they assume their personalities will magically make up for the fact they do not look anything like the picture that was posted online."

The most important question is: does it work? Keep in mind that a third of the people who go to online dating sites never actually go on a date with anyone they meet there. And there is evidence that online dating rarely leads to a lasting relationship. "Even among Americans who have been with their spouse or partner for five years or less," Pew researchers note, "fully 88% say that they met their partner offline—without the help of a dating site."[20]

The Pew findings contradict a survey commissioned by the dating site eHarmony (ostensibly according to strict scientific guidelines) that found more than a third of U.S. marriages started with online introductions. This figure was confirmed in separate research by Eli Finkel, a professor of social psychology at Northwestern University. The nationally representative eHarmony survey of nineteen thousand people who married between 2005 and 2012 also found that couples who met online were a bit happier than those who met in other ways, though Dr. Finkel doubts there's a difference.[21]

Back to you. You do have some post-divorce options. You can be one of those divorced singles who cultivate their own contentment, not seeking another relationship. You don't *have* to be lonely, and in fact singles tend to maintain connections with family and friends. A Cornell study of how marriage affects happiness found that "entering into any union improved psychological well-being" but at the same time "reduced contact with parents and friends."[22] So you may be happier if you find a new love, but if you don't, you can reach out to others.

Another option is to engage in your life *without* actively seeking another partner, though you might desire one. If you're a college-educated woman, that option might be the most realistic. Jon Birger, who specializes in the math of dating, says, "Because women have been graduating from college in 30-plus percent greater numbers than men for years, there are now four women for every three men nationally in the marriage-age, college-educated dating market." The author of *Date-Onomics: How Dating Became a Lopsided Numbers Game* (2015), Birger advises these diploma-toting ladies to relocate to parts of the country with better odds and choose a career in a male dominated field. And relax the religiosity: "'People who leave organized religion are disproportionately male,' Birger says. 'Atheists and agnostics are also disproportionately male. An atheist meet-up would be a really good place to meet men.'" You'll have to be aggressive as well. He cites a study finding that 60 percent of married couples solemnized their union because the woman issued an ultimatum.[23]

Does this seem distasteful to you? Rather sexist? Then again, don't you know some incredible, intelligent, achieving women who can't seem to find a mate? And women's difficulties rise as they age, since older men tend to prefer younger women—an age gap of fifteen or twenty years is common-place. Women who click with notably younger men—"cougars," we call them—are simultaneously admired and reviled.

COMMITMENT PHOBIA

Even if you do find the perfect spousal replacement, a person you enjoy and respect and who seems dedicated to you, your search for lasting love may run aground on "commitment phobia"—the fear of making a binding promise to another person. Also called "relationship anxiety," it's often a reaction to parental divorce (another reminder that if *you* divorce, you may foist this disability onto your children).

"People with a commitment phobia," writes John Grohol, Psy.D., "*want a long-term connection* with another person, but their overwhelming anx-iety prevents them from staying in any relationship for too long. If pressed for a commitment, they are far more likely to leave the relationship than to make the commitment. Or they may initially agree to the commitment, then back down days or weeks later, because of their overwhelming anxiety and fears."[24]

I maintain that with so many adults bearing the psychological scars of their parents' divorce and so many options for coupling without marriage, commitment phobia is on the rise, encouraging the delay of marriage and out-of-wedlock births. More partners who desire a marriage are willing to accept a relationship without it now that they suffer no stigma, sacrificing security to keep the person they love.

This leaves lots of commitment-phobes simply ignoring the problem. They're often urged by their accountants to take advantage of tax breaks and other financial benefits of marriage, but the fear of committing is so strong that they're willing to take the economic hit. If you met and wanted to marry a commitment-phobe, would the heartache and uncertainty be worth it?

Consider that should your divorce turn acrimonious, *you* might emerge fearing remarriage. With your first alliance folding and children, perhaps, still dependent on you emotionally, you might reserve your own feelings to avoid exposure to hurt a second time. Or to keep your life uncomplicated and well-controlled.

After imagining the effort and frustrations of finding a new spouse, while dealing with the aftermath of the marriage you're leaving, doesn't it make sense to skip the uncertainty and discomfort and take another look at the spouse to whom you've already committed yourself? The person with whom you once had happy times and with whom you likely have a family (even if they're grown). Yes, if you make the split, you'll valiantly make lemonade, but you can make lemonade *right now*. If reading about the singles' world kindles equal parts fear and hope, harness those same motivational emotions to conquer your fear and dedicate yourself to reviving, or perhaps building for the first time, the marriage you wish you had. It's so much easier than devising your own algorithm.

CHAPTER 19

Rebuilding Trust
after Betrayal

"It feels so good to be desired."
"For the first time in twenty years, I feel alive!"
"I don't know what came over me—it just happened."
"I can't go back to my marriage when I've met the love of my life."
Four excuses for affairs, four potential reasons for divorce.

The last one is the toughest to refute, because it suggests that (1) the affair is prolonged, (2) there's a deep emotional bond, and (3) the other party shares an investment in the relationship. You can be sure the paramour knows her (could be "his") lover is married. Not only doesn't that stop her, it might motivate her to "win" your spouse away. In fact, your mate may have implied or promised that he'll forsake you. In this case, the lure to leave is powerful, as it's a choice between the "same old" and this new siren song. But you're still married, you still have your family, and if your partner is conflicted at all, you still have hope.

The other three excuses for affairs are variants on the same theme—"follow your heart" to an exciting, romantic destination. Of course it feels good to be desired! The coy cat-and-mouse game of flirtation, tentative connection, uncertainty, and actualization are so beguiling that hormones take over. Your mind races with interpretations and possibilities, and soon you're plotting the consummation. The throbbing, consuming headiness of it all overtakes everything. The affair blooms with increasing emotional connection, and fantasy is as seductive as reality. Keeping your attraction secret increases its allure and, with all that blood pumping, *makes you feel alive*. There's nothing normal or predictable with an affair; its very naughtiness and danger, imperiling your staid life, give it power over you and draw you away from your moral code. All that you learned from your parents and your church, everything you've read in newspapers and magazines about the heartbreak of broken homes—it all recedes as desire pumps adrenalin through your system. That's what overcomes you—a combination of attraction, sexual energy, and the thrill of the illicit— and you have an accomplice to fan the flames.

When approached by a distinctly unsexy researcher, Americans overwhelmingly nix affairs. Seventy-four percent of the 5,738 respondents between eighteen and sixty in an Austin Institute representative sample disagreed with the proposition "It is sometimes permissible for a married person to have sex with someone other than his/her spouse," and most of the rest said they weren't sure.[1] A whopping 84 percent of Americans say "married people having an affair is morally unacceptable," according to a 2013 Pew Research Center poll.[2]

Nevertheless, says Esther Perel in a TED talk on infidelity, "We are walking contradictions.... [S]o 95 percent of us will say it is terribly wrong for our partner to lie about having an affair, but just about the same amount of us will say that that's exactly what *we* would do if we were having one." Sexual "alchemy" drives us to acts that are compelling yet destructive.[3] Can you think of anything more fundamental to a strong marriage than *trust*? Without it, what's your vow worth?

Maybe less than before the betrayal—but it's still worth *a lot*. There's the family you built, the history you've shared, the promise of a restored future together. Even the process of recovery can teach you, individually and together, new skills that enliven your relationship, enhancing communication, restoring purpose, perhaps bringing you even closer together than before.

In a book with the astonishing title *My Husband's Affair Became the Best Thing that Ever Happened to Me*,[4] Anne Bercht explains how that's possible. Of course, when you discover a betrayal, you've got to get through the bad stuff first. That took two and a half years for Mrs. Bercht and included a suicide attempt by her daughter in reaction to the affair. She came to realize that her own insecurity had contributed to her husband's acts by subtly conveying that his efforts to show his love weren't enough to satisfy her.

When Anne Bercht understood her feelings of inadequacy, she was able to emerge from a difficult rebuilding period—she was immobilized for eight months—as a stronger, more confident person. Once able to return to work, "Within a couple of months my income doubled! I look after my health better now. I actually look and feel better than I did 20 years ago, have more energy, more zeal and more enthusiasm for life. Since I have gotten over my insecurities, I experience far better relationships including my marriage, but with my children and others as well." Today she is the director of the Beyond Affairs Network.[5]

Lying and cheating are wrong and devastating. But they don't have to mean the end of your marriage. In every marriage, both spouses contribute to a climate that affects how each one behaves, but in most cases the betrayal is not "about" you, the faithful spouse, but about a need or insecurity in the betrayer. It's also about that person's willingness to allow distance and deception in the marriage—and in his own character. If you were hurt, remember that a cheater's cruel behavior is hardly ever intended to hurt his spouse. Instead, it fills his need for reassurance of his desirability, excitement, vengeance, or freedom. The innocent spouse is collateral damage. A weak or arrogant spouse responds to an invitation, can't refuse an opportunity, or craves validation so much that he'll override his marriage, getting drawn into an ever more complicated situation. Sometimes he's brazen enough to think he's above rules of honesty and decency. Sometimes he subconsciously wants to be caught and becomes careless about his concealment. Other times, he's so skilled at prevarication that his lies integrate into his life without detection. Then he gets found out. (I'm using the masculine pronoun though of course women and men both cheat.)

The National Science Foundation's General Social Survey found that self-reported infidelity among men had actually declined in 2010 to 19 percent, down from 21 percent in 1991. Meanwhile, women's reported unfaithfulness increased from 11 percent in 1991 to 14 percent in 2010—a rate still substantially lower than men's. Naturally, researchers view self-reports with suspicion. After all, these people are lying to their partners, so why not on a survey? But they're likely not far off, since the research isn't linked to specific names, and there's nothing to lose in being truthful.

It is possible for the perpetrator to re-stabilize and improve not only his marriage but also his own direction by understanding what he's done to his spouse and to himself. The first key is his remorse and willingness to repent. Some say "once a skunk, always a skunk—once a liar, always a liar." Without real regret, that may be true. Liars and cheaters won't change without an internal evaluation that usually results from hitting bottom. The deceiver must become detestable in his own eyes—considering his behavior a moral violation—if he is to avoid subsequent temptation.

The other key is his willingness to involve outsiders, primarily you, and likely a therapist, in his vigilant effort to preserve an honest and loving marriage.

CHEATING AND LYING: SEXUAL AND OTHERWISE

Most infidelity in some way involves sex, imagined or real.

There's the betrayal of a long-term affair, a one-night fling, and everything in between. Most stupefying are the cases where a man leads a double life, sometimes with two separate families. Donna Anderson married her husband after responding to an online dating profile that was all lies. "My ex-husband, James Montgomery, cheated with at least six different women during our 2.5-year marriage," she writes on Lovefraud.com, a site for victims of sociopaths. "He had a child with one of the women. Ten days after I left him, he married the mother of the child, which was the second time he committed bigamy. And of course, he took a quarter-million dollars from me—spending much of the money entertaining these other women."[6]

Some infidelities are nearly entirely physical. Some involve fantasy and emotional connections not even based in reality. Others, mostly or completely emotional, may run deeply into the consciousness and even identity of the perpetrator. In six states, the painful loss of a spouse to another person, traditionally called "alienation of affections," remains an actionable claim against the wife- or husband-stealer. Between 2000 and 2007, an average of 230 alienation of affections tort claims were filed per year in North Carolina.[7] Adultery, condemned by the Ten Commandments, carries the biblical punishment of death—it's that serious.[8]

The most hurtful aspect of an affair is the "tangled web" of misrepresentations, exaggerations, and outright falsehoods to cover the liaison, deceit that can make the dalliance more thrilling. The reason it's so difficult to rebuild trust is that an affair is not a single blow but death by a thousand cuts. Initiating, actualizing, and continuing infidelity require many individual decisions, and each one that furthers the affair is a separate choice, a betrayal in itself. Each phone call, text, exaggeration, and lie takes a momentary brain flash when the person formulates a statement or reply. Patterns of lying may come "naturally," but they are within a person's control and become easier with practice.

Do you smile back? Do you return the text? Do you say something suggestive? Do you answer the email? Do you make a date? Do you show up for the date? Do you enter the restaurant? Do you enter the apartment? Do you sit down? Do you go into the bedroom? Do you kiss back? Each small step closer to an emotional involvement and then to sexual contact is a point at which the unfaithful spouse might stop—but chooses to continue. This is what gnaws at the betrayed partner—the hundreds, even thousands of deliberate steps that the husband or wife took to advance the extramarital relationship to the next level. That's why recovering from an affair requires such diligence and transparency.

Infidelity might not even involve a real human being—pornography offers an alternative world populated by actors and personas in videos that might have been created years before. Porn is so easy to come by and so easy to hide that it can become addictive, taking over someone's life and encouraging other addictions, often to alcohol. And yet most people dismiss porn as a harmless private indulgence. In a survey of two thousand teens and adults in 2016, respondents ranked viewing porn as less immoral than wasting electricity or water, overeating, or harboring antipathy toward someone else.[9]

Trust can be destroyed by actions that are not even sexual. The intentional betrayal of a confidence or the blatant breaking of a bargain that you and your partner consider sacrosanct to the duo you've formed undercuts the foundation of your life together.

A trust-killing relationship may be romantic and even sexual but not physical. Email, Skype, WhatsApp, and other forms of communication make flirtation easy and enticing. "It's nothing serious" is a common protest when emotionally the connection *is* serious. The excitement of sexually-tinged communication, even with no physical presence, can be just as hurtful as a sexual fling. Texting and sexting, video-making, and even plain old phone sex make a hot and heavy relationship possible anywhere in the world. The harm is so widespread that Amazon offers more than three dozen books on recovery from affairs.

It's so easy to slip from an attraction into something deeper. It can start with a compliment. Hoping to boost her business through a bit of networking, Sarah emailed Brett to praise his presentation at the national conference for car dealerships. She had no ulterior motive. Brett remembered her from the crowd that surrounded him after his talk, and he remembered handing her his business card. Both were married with children, busy lives, and a million interests. Sarah attended church with her family every week. She never expected anything to happen, but Brett returned her compliments, noting that her dealership was the leading earner in Oregon. What were her secrets in staying top earner for four years running? He loved her succinctly-worded reply and asked permission to send it to the entire association. How about a photo with her staff to go along with it? Oh, and here's me with my vintage Corvette. Hope you have a great weekend; I'm heading to Aspen to ski.

You can see how it shaped up. Their relationship took a couple months to move into flirtation and a couple more to become more personal. Brett and Sarah were never in the same state, but soon they were exchanging selfies. Nothing really suggestive, just doing the things they loved. After five months, they arranged to meet at another conference.

Neither wanted to leave his or her marriage. Neither wanted to disrupt a rewarding and busy life, but the outside "friendship" progressed. Brett was perhaps the more persistent, but nothing unreasonable. They didn't remember when they crossed the line—was it the goodnight kiss at the conference? His arm around her on the walking tour that cold afternoon? But when they parted, the relationship was on a different footing.

Brett and Sarah were good people, but they moved to a level that could have ruined two families. Happily, it didn't. Sarah started feeling deeply guilty about her feelings for Brett and about hiding part of her life from her husband. She felt like a hypocrite going to church with her family and behaving in a way that she would be ashamed of were her children to find out. Because Brett lived across the country, she had an easy out. Explaining directly that the relationship was causing her anguish, she ended it immediately. She then blocked his number from her phone, un-friended him on Facebook, stopped following his Twitter feed, and erased every trace of him from her emails and photos.

Finally she felt somewhat better. Sarah decided not to tell her husband, because the admission would hurt him. That was her punishment—keeping the knowledge of her temporarily distracted affection locked within her soul. Though infidelity often kills a marriage, Sarah ended her dangerous liaison before doing irreparable harm. But the diversion of her attention and emotions left a scar, and she'll carry the memory of her lapse forever as a secret that she can't share.

HOW DO INFIDELITIES START?

Cheating doesn't just "happen," insists Dr. John Gottman, the author of *What Makes Love Last? How to Build Trust and Avoid Betrayal.* It's not the result of hapless persons being thrust into unexpected circumstances. Cheaters "head down the path unwittingly and at a slow, undetected pace," he writes, drawing on forty years of studying couples in his "Love Lab" at the University of Washington. Preceding the betrayal are small withdrawals, retreats to individual corners, and quick affronts that go unrepaired in the marriage. Conflicts fester, hurts go unreported, and while this doesn't always mean an affair is imminent, in 70 percent of such cases "at least one partner's trustworthiness metric plummets. He or she no longer considers the relationship sacred and is not willing to put it first."[10]

You begin, Dr. Gottman suggests, by making invidious comparisons— your mate seems less admiring than a co-worker, needs and respects you less than a friend does, looks a lot older than the client who wants to take you to lunch. Such comparisons lead to speculation about how much happier, sexier, exhilarated you might feel if you were with that other person, even if only for a short time. Once an affair becomes possible, fantasizing becomes conniving. You start hiding things, you become complicit with the new person. Then your allegiance shifts, and you rationalize your behavior, even justify it. Eventually you consider your *spouse* to be the untrustworthy one.

IT'S NOT ABOUT YOU

While many couples have traveled the path to infidelity that Dr. Gottman describes, I've found that even partners with real closeness and excellent communication can fall to the lure of extramarital involvements. As the marriage hums along in devotion, a partner can succumb to flattery and his own insecurity, compartmentalizing a flirtatious emotional connection, sabotaging trust, and hurting his "soulmate," the outcome Sarah avoided by breaking off her communication with Brett.

In a comprehensive review of research on infidelity in 2010, a team of psychologists and anthropologists identified the factors that drive people into affairs, ranging from brain architecture and chemistry (tested in prairie voles!), genes that attract us to potential partners with odors that differ from our own (which help divert us from incest), and a multitude of psychological and social determinants. One finding stands out especially: for a majority of men, dissatisfaction with their marriage was *not* the problem. Fifty-six percent of men (and 34 percent of women) who had affairs rated their marriages as "happy" or "very happy."[11]

Family therapist Esther Perel says in her TED talk, "Affairs are an act of betrayal, but also an expression of longing and loss." They reflect a yearning for novelty, freedom, autonomy, sexual intensity, or youthful liberation never experienced. "An affair isn't always turning away from our partner, but the person that we have ourselves become."

And then of course, some people just crave sex. The continuum of sexual desire is a bell-shaped curve. Most couples enjoy sex with each other somewhere between four times a week and a couple times a month.[12] A November 2015 meta-study of thirty thousand people over a forty-year period found that contrary to popular wisdom, more frequent sex doesn't make a marriage happier. Couples' peak happiness occurred when they had intercourse just once a week, as long as they maintained other types of close physical connection.[13] More frequent sex didn't diminish the couple's well-being but didn't increase it either.

But then there are those on the right-hand slope of the bell curve, whose sexual needs run higher than most people's. And some pairs face a mismatch in desires, leaving one craving more sex than he receives at home. The sex-seeker might simply repress that urge, or he might resort to internet porn and stop there. He might hire prostitutes or "swipe right" on women with suggestive profiles.

Any sexual act with another person violates the trust on which committed marriage relies. But trust-busting behavior may not necessarily involve sex. John Gottman lists ten: conditional commitment, a non-sexual affair, lying, forming a coalition against the partner, absenteeism or coldness, withdrawal of sexual interest, disrespect, unfairness, selfishness, and breaking promises.[14] Less serious trust-degraders may occur in the normal ebb and flow of a relationship. In a strong marriage, they're quickly repaired by apology, discussion, and demonstrating constancy. But when any of them becomes a pattern, the marriage is in trouble.

Some of the items on Gottman's non-sex betrayal list, like lying and emotional affairs, seriously crack the trusses undergirding marriage. Nearly everyone weds with the expectation of sexual and emotional exclusivity and fidelity. Trust forms the foundation of *any* solid relationship, but especially marriage, the connection involving greatest vulnerability and investment.

The late Peggy Vaughan, author of *The Monogamy Myth*[15] and the founder of the Beyond Affairs Network, maintained that affairs result from a mixture of three factors—a person's *pushes* toward the affair (excitement, attraction, curiosity), his internal *pulls* (boredom, relief from something in the marriage, need for validation), and societal conditions that glamorize sex and promote a code of secrecy about illicit liaisons. She called monogamy a "myth," incorrectly asserting that 80 percent of marriages will suffer from the infidelity of at least one partner.

But monogamy is *not* a myth if you look beyond Ms. Vaughan's so-called "conservative estimates" to real data. In a reliable meta-analysis published in 2005, Adrian J. Blow and Kelley Hartnett concluded that "over the course of married, heterosexual relationships in the United States, [extra-marital] sex occurs in *less than 25%* of committed relationships, and more men than women appear to be engaging in infidelity...."[16] That's still a lot of marriages suffering from sexual betrayal, and undoubtedly many more face emotional infidelity.

A 2011 study headed by Kristen Mark of Indiana University found a small difference between men's and women's infidelity, with 23 percent of men and 19 percent of women reporting affairs. The study of nine hundred subjects, half of them married, found that neither marital status nor religion correlated with affairs. Instead, the researchers found that men and women differ in their *reasons* for cheating, with men responding to cues of arousal, and women seeking a closeness that's missing in their marriages. Not a surprise. "Women reporting low relationship happiness were 2.6 times more likely to report having engaged in infidelity," says an Indiana University release. "Women who perceived low compatibility in terms of sexual attitudes and values were 2.9 times more likely to cheat."[17]

Psychiatry professor Peggy Drexler of Weill Cornell Medicine, observing that women are having more affairs than they used to, writes, "Their reasons are familiar: validation of their attractiveness, emotional connection, appreciation, ego—not to mention the thrill of a shiny new relationship, unburdened by the long slog through the realities of coupledom." She suggests that greater exposure to straying women on TV, on the internet, and in movies conveys "a feeling that infidelity has become more acceptable." And of course more frequent interactions with men in the workplace add to the temptations.[18]

Some argue that affairs are the result of "transitions" that bring on a midlife or life-cycle crisis. Rona Subotnick and Gloria Harris, the authors of *Surviving Infidelity: Making Decisions, Recovering from the Pain,*[19] say the birth of a child, a graduation or a death, and the problems of aging— among other causes—can prime someone for an affair. Willard F. Harley Jr., in *His Needs, Her Needs: Building an Affair-Proof Marriage,* blames husbands' and wives' conflicting, unmet needs (men need sex, women need affection).[20]

I suspect affairs result from a combination of factors, chief among them the dangerous duo of *opportunity* and *excitement.* The excitement of feeling desired or being attracted to another has to be triggered. One of the side effects of women's integration into formerly male-dominated careers is an increase in such opportunities. While the benefits of women's achievement surely outweigh this downside, the politically incorrect truth is that *the opportunity for affairs increases with greater exposure to potential partners.* Proximity breeds familiarity, as the maxim goes.

Conscious of this reality, a vulnerable spouse can, with a little prudence, avoid situations in which temptations might arise. Don't meet off-premises. Keep the office door open. Ask a third party to stick around. Choose to collaborate with no-risk colleagues. Work in groups. Copy others on your emails. Schedule through an assistant or open calendar app. Shake hands rather than greet with a hug. Wear a wedding ring. Make your spouse's photo the wallpaper on your phone and computer. Put family photos on your desk.

And try the suggestion below.

VULNERABLE TO AFFAIRS? TRY THIS PREVENTATIVE

If there are problems in your marriage, yes, you need to come clean and face them. But many affairs occur when the marriage is not only serviceable but also satisfying. I'd guess that most affairs come "out of the blue" for the unsuspecting spouse, who may feel the marital sex life is great and the relationship close. In those cases—a majority!—one of the best anti-affair preventatives is for a person vulnerable to affairs (you know who you are) to *devise patterns and rituals that constantly bind your partner to you, that require you to give him or her your attention.* You feel closest to the people and things in which you have invested the most. If you give to someone, you feel connected.

Evan was a married professor of education whose students often came to office hours asking for advice on their papers, ideas for their classrooms, and recommendations for graduate work. Meetings were businesslike, but Evan was a healthy male and did occasionally notice an attraction. How could he avoid a coed's made-up eyes, lush lipstick, or low-cut outfit? Nevertheless, happily married for fifteen years, with two kids and no intention of straying, he certainly considered it unethical to have a relationship with a student.

But his resolve slipped with a woman, not his student, who made an appointment to explore grad school options in the department. She was at a crossroads, recently divorced and looking for ways to increase her income. Perhaps it was the combination of her neediness and her looks that led Evan to accept her follow-up invitation for coffee. Their affair had gone on for a month when his wife, Kelly, found a telltale text. The affair hurt her to the core, and Evan felt awful. After buying my book, he came to me for advice on repairing the breach he'd created.

I wanted to speak separately to each of them. Broadsided when she found the text, Kelly would have packed up and left if it weren't for the children, ages five and nine. Having taken time out from her career to stay at home while the children were young, she didn't have an income at the moment. And Evan's pleading and remorse suggested that leaving might be throwing away her marriage just to salve her devastated pride.

The repairs began with Evan incorporating phone calls to Kelly throughout his day. When he got to work, he'd phone. When he left his office to head to class, another call. After class, a third call, and before coming home, another phone call. Evan volunteered to touch base with Kelly like this to prove that he cared enough to connect, to reassure her that she was his first priority, and to confirm that he wasn't where he shouldn't be. These calls became part of his wife's and his daily routines. Even if all he said in one of these calls was, "This morning I read two journal articles and prepared for my afternoon class," connection to Kelly shaped Evan's day. With a quick "Hey, Kel, how was your yoga class?" he showed that he remembered his wife's schedule and cared about her life.

Evan reinforced these calls with other gestures of devotion. He knew Kelly loved Trader Joe's ginger cookies, so he'd bring some home. He'd stop at the supermarket for flowers, cut out an article he thought she'd like, or write her a note. These physical tokens, which required his planning and consideration, along with the phone calls gradually reassured Kelly that Evan put her first.

Evan and Kelly also worked through their feelings about the affair in counseling. Confirming honesty was essential. Evan's stealth and the violation of trust had hurt Kelly. But before this lapse, the relationship was solid, and since deception wasn't an ingrained pattern, rebuilding was easier.

Some relationships are tougher to recover. Sometimes an affair is the product of a spouse's history, an inherited predisposition, rather than a willful violation. Does that mean you can't blame a man for replicating the pattern he learned from his father? That you can't blame a wife for faltering when she witnessed or, worse, suffered molestation in her youth? No, of course not. But these unfortunate facts of history may shape

wounded by infidelity, but it can become rock-solid and rewarding. As the pain of the incident fades, the relationship can regain its playfulness and sexuality and grow with greater communication.

The circumstances of the betrayal affect the reconciliation. Was this a one-night fling with little emotional attachment? Or was it prolonged, involving a series of lies? Is the cheating spouse completely committed to monogamy, or has this happened before? How likely is this to occur again? The deeper the wound, the longer the healing and the more the offender must repent and atone.

If the affair was prolonged or there were multiple affairs, the questions go beyond "Why did you do it?" and there is more ground to cover on the way to reconciliation. Also, there are differing requirements for proving the return is sincere, depending on the transgression. No errant spouse just falls back into the pre-affair relationship he violated. The very basis of the relationship is shaken—a betrayed spouse will be wary, distant, and suspicious until enough time and faithfulness allay these feelings. The distrust may *never* go away entirely, even if the marriage endures and improves. With terms of the marriage dashed, new, more guarded grounds need to be established.

Some friends with only your welfare in mind might suggest you shouldn't tolerate infidelity. But insisting "once a cheater, always a cheater" excuses "being a cheater." The misbehavior is out of the cheater's control; it's an inherited trait or learned from early examples and now it's *internalized*, never to be cleansed. This is also an exit line for the wounded party, because the prognosis is already set—he's going to cheat again sometime. There's no room for rehabilitation; no room for sincere regret and demonstration of trustworthiness.

But it's just not true that "once a cheater, always a cheater." Maybe "once" happened, but the "always" part is mere speculation that cruelly cuts off the possibility of happiness in the future. If a cheater is "always a cheater," you're wasting your time and emotion by sticking around. With this neat little rationalization, the marriage is doomed.

Some feminists derided Hillary Clinton when she endured the humiliation of her husband's oh-so-public affairs—but she remains married, which is admirable. California Governor Arnold Schwarzenegger fathered a baby in 1998 with the family housekeeper, leading to his divorce. Later the

Terminator star called his dalliance "the stupidest thing I've ever done."[22] Imagine how the son of that liaison feels.

Your friends might tell you that your self-respect demands that you leave your cheating spouse. Your self-respect needs to remain intact *with or without* your cheating spouse. It's a blow when one you trusted acts like scum, to be sure, but your self-respect is not dependent on how outsiders view your marriage or your choices. After that kind of kick in the gut, your self-respect likely needs revitalization, but that must come from within and from surrounding yourself with people and activities that bring you satisfaction and pleasure. The trauma of betrayal is bad enough without subjecting yourself to the complete re-set of divorce. Much better to stay in the relationship in which you've invested your heart. If your partner regrets his misdeeds and values you and your family, casting him off because of others' indignation is a big mistake. If your friends start egging you on to leave because they believe the insult of infidelity is too great for you to bear, excuse yourself from their company. Their views are based on their own values and on their experiences in their own marriages. Don't let them impose those views on you.

You'll find lots of advice from support groups, websites, and self-help books for rebuilding your marriage after betrayal, all of which I have boiled down to six points:

(1) The offender needs to *come completely clean and purge* every remnant of the affair and every connection with the paramour. That means cutting off all lines of communication with the source of betrayal, whether that's an individual, prostitutes, pornography, or some other temptation.

(2) The guilty spouse needs to show remorse and affirm his commitment to the marriage. He must admit wrongdoing and humbly accept any emotions his spouse expresses.

(3) You should *wait*. The initial wound is so deep that it disables rational decision-making, and most experts say to wait *months* before deciding to end the marriage, even if the urge is to flee immediately. You may want to avoid talking about the affair during this waiting period, allowing emotions to cool, or you may wish to talk.

(4) When the initial trauma subsides, *talk it through*. If the marriage is to survive, the partners need to be direct in asking and answering questions about the betrayal. Be aware that some lines of inquiry might exacerbate

pain rather than resolve it. But if the wounded spouse requires information, it is pertinent.

(5) Build *transparency* into the marriage. To reconstruct trust, the unfaithful party (and ideally both partners) must not just be honest, but transparent. Honesty is what couples expect when their relationships maintain their original high level of trust. Honesty is simply describing events and feelings completely and accurately. Once that has been violated, something more is needed.

Transparency allows the hurt partner, if she chooses, to corroborate her spouse's assertions. For example, an errant husband could give his wife passwords and access to his cell phone, calendar, and credit card purchases. More important than her actually checking these sources is the offender's willingness to open up every corner of his communication, time, and expenditures. Her ability to spot-check at will allows her to rebuild confidence in her partner's truthfulness.

(6) At some point—perhaps after the marriage regains its equilibrium—the couple needs to *address the problems* in the relationship and in the straying individual that led to the betrayal. This is best done with a therapist or a support network. Sorting through deeper problems is not a do-it-yourself project.

Dr. John Gottman and his psychologist wife, Dr. Julie Gottman, have a catchy three-word summary of tasks to overcome infidelity. The partners must *atone, attune,* and *attach*. Atonement is likely the most difficult, as the wrongdoer responds to his spouse's need for information about the affair. One area of discussion is off-limits: sexual details. This, the professors believe, can cause post-traumatic stress and impede the third phase, reestablishing physical attachment. The middle phase, attuning, is the emotional reconnecting (or perhaps creation) of empathy, the feeling that both partners "get" the essence and values of the other.

CHAPTER 20

No Marriage Is Perfect: How to Be Happy Anyway

THE GLASS IS HALF FULL

W e can choose our responses to events and stimuli, though usually we're not even aware we're making those choices. When reactions become habit, they can form the backdrop for an entire relationship, for good or for ill.

You know the joke: two people come upon a room filled with manure. One of them says, "Ugh! Look at all that disgusting…stuff!" The other one claps gleefully, squealing, "There must be a pony in there somewhere!"

If your room is filled with poop, you have a choice. You can walk away in revulsion or start looking for the pony.

The author of another book about divorce tells about a successful businesswoman, married with a daughter, who came to her for therapy for workaholism and anxiety. As the therapy unfolded, it became clear that the woman's husband was "an angry, withholding, unbending and passionless man," and that her immersion in work was her way of avoiding him, leaving their daughter bereft of motherly presence and affection. A sad scenario. But instead of tackling the marital problems head-on, the therapist directed her client to "accept the realities of her marriage," redirecting her attention toward the needs of the daughter. How heartwarming to read how the mom, realizing her neglect, cultivated a close relationship with the girl, now a teenager.

And the marriage? Well, our heroine "decided it was not viable" and broke up.

That's it? She up and left? I kept reading, hoping to learn the husband's side of the story. I wanted to know if the businesswoman's perceptions of her mate and marriage were somehow distorted by role models from her youth or attributable to some event, bad habits formed in the relationship, or her pervasive anxiety. I wanted to know the steps the therapist took to bring husband and wife closer, to offer them more loving habits and new communication skills, and to address each of the problems that for years kept them together and functioning but distant. After all, they had a daughter to consider. From the author's description of the couple, it appeared that they had a "low-conflict" marriage, the type that when ended shatters a child's secure if imperfect world. The type that after divorce leaves young adults skittish to commit, fearing that what they perceive as a good relationship is really doomed by an invisible fatal flaw.

To my disappointment, the author omitted any mention of the husband's further role in the story. But "deciding the marriage isn't viable" should be a two-person process at the least. Instead, the implication was that the newly-enlightened businesswoman unilaterally dumped her spouse, forming a cozy and important but fatherless relationship with the daughter, rather than using her new insights to revamp her marriage.

This is only an anecdote in a self-help book, but readers looking for help will notice the implications. The subtle instruction is to focus on your own needs; look at what's holding you back and remove those barriers. But what about the *family*? The "get outta my way, I'm gonna please myself!" approach sounds inspirational coming from Oprah, but it smacks of destructive narcissism. A family was at stake here, and the question wasn't only about whether the mom might stop working so hard and notice her child, but how each member of the family could gain skills and motivation to form a harmonious whole.

Lots of people see the glass of lemonade and swear it's half empty. Pessimists tend to be contrary and unhappy, and the psychologist Martin

Seligman, famous for his studies of pessimists, finds that they usually learned this habit of mind from their parents. If the family style is to assign fault and blame, or even to push it off onto somebody else, children learn that when something's not right or someone forgets or doesn't succeed (like everyone, every day), it's not just a shortfall by a fellow team member but a mean-spirited failure. The world is populated with incompetents, and should anything excellent slip by, well, that's the exception.

I learned how deflating a pessimist can be when I was in graduate school, sharing a cubicle with Darlene. Though her snide jokes were often hilarious, her consistently gloomy outlook wore me down.

> *Me* (entering the cubicle): Wow, what a beautiful day out there! The clouds were amazing, and the sky was just cerulean!
>
> *Darlene*: I heard it's going to rain.
>
> *Me* (next day, entering the cubicle): Wow, did you see the rainbow out there? I stopped and snapped a photo.
>
> *Darlene*: Yeah, all this rain flooded my carport.
>
> *Me* (next day, entering the cubicle): Hi, Darlene, did you get your carport drained?
>
> *Darlene*: Yes, but it left my car covered with mud and now I need to get my car washed.

It took me far too long to catch on. I kept wondering why I was leaving work in a funk. Then it dawned on me: Darlene was *contrary*. Constantly battling her cynicism was exhausting. I decided to check my hypothesis, and my opportunity arrived the next day as Darlene sat at her desk eating lunch.

> *Darlene*: This sandwich is so fattening. I'm going to blow up like a beach ball.
>
> *Me*: Hope not. I just got on the scale and lost two pounds!
>
> *Darlene*: Maybe you didn't, and your scale is off. Did you check it first?
>
> *Me*: It was on the zero.

Darlene (falling into my trap): Maybe it was just water weight, and you'll gain it back tomorrow.

Me: What if I get on the scale again, and I'm still down two pounds?

Darlene: Maybe it's just an aberration. You're probably just the same.

Me: What if I get on the scale for two more days and I'm still two pounds lower?

Darlene: First calibrate your scale; it's probably off kilter.

Me: What if I calibrated my scale, and it was right and showed I lost two pounds for three days in a row?

Darlene: Maybe you weighed yourself right after peeing and before breakfast, and you'll gain it back during the day.

Me: What if I weighed myself at night too and it *still* said I lost two pounds?

Darlene: Did you pee first?

Me: No.

Darlene: Well, there must be some reason....

Me: Couldn't I have just lost the two pounds?

Darlene (exasperated): Well...well ...

She couldn't bring herself to say it. She was contrary and a pessimist. Once I figured that out, I left work much happier each day. All the negativity floating around that cubicle belonged to *her*.

Some people don't want to face their downbeat attitude and end up wallowing in it. Or more commonly, denying it. *This alone can poison a marriage.* In fact, when I'm asked for the most important quality to look for in a mate, I say optimism. Just as a pessimist grinds down those around him, an optimist can lift them up. Pessimism is as powerful as gravity, so it takes more to lift a pessimist off the ground than it does to tether a joyful person.

Smiling is a reaction to perceiving something positive; a "serious" face is the default. Note that I said *perceiving* something positive. Optimists, people habituated to awe and amazement, will interpret people, comments, and events through the lens of their optimism and perceive them in a positive light, while people habituated to disgruntlement and skepticism will spin those same stimuli into reason to scoff.

These patterns of perception have enormous effects on your marriage. One partner can undermine the mood of the couple or the family with a sense of gloom. James, like many a pessimist, *chose* his mate, Kimberly, because her upbeat, ebullient affect contrasted with his usual scowl. Kimberly thought her highly-achieving mathematician husband was so accomplished, always dashing off to conferences and writing journal pieces way beyond her comprehension. They were the odd couple, and yet their mutual respect and sexual chemistry somehow clicked. Kimberly loved to cook and kept their home buzzing with Sunday brunches and Bible classes and birthday parties for their friends, and soon, their friends' children. Their own two sons had their dad's cerebral abilities and their mom's good looks.

Their younger boy, however, took after James and was quiet and brooding, while the elder shared Kimberly's sense of fun and adventure. And it's true; research confirms that children are born with emotional proclivities. Studying twins and siblings in the 1970s, Jerome Kagan found that different "temperaments" appeared to be innate.[1] Follow up studies showed these qualities usually remained throughout development.

More recent research points to a genetic basis for temperament, which interacts with experience to shape personality.[2] This is the old "nature versus nurture" question that applies to spouses wondering if they're stuck with someone who can never change.

The practical answer to that question is that nature is the set-up, nurture shapes it, but will and determination can conquer all. As in the children's game of rock-paper-scissors, each of these factors can predominate under certain circumstances. Many who simply observe personalities in action don't realize the extent that controllable intent and tenacity can subdue the other two influences.

James and Kimberly, over the years, developed affinities for their kids based on their outlooks. Although Kimberly tried to encourage the younger boy to see the bright side of things, he emulated his father's somber outlook. Eventually, James's demeanor became so difficult that Kimberly just let him stew and developed a life of her own. This divergence and her disgust with her husband's grumpy withdrawal eventually brought her to my office. As James was unwilling to participate, we looked for strategies that could improve both their relationship and the way Kimberly viewed his behavior. After several months of dialogue, James finally agreed to discuss change.

If there's a James or Darlene in your relationship, even if programmed by depressive parents' examples and similarly tilted genetic material, there are strategies and tools to revise that person's outlook. In teaching optimism, Dr. Seligman builds on Albert Ellis's "ABC" description of the way people respond to problems. "A" is the introduction of some *adversity*—a challenge or a problem. "B" is the *belief* according to which the person responds to the adversity—in other words, an internal overlay that frames how the event is viewed. "C" is the *consequence*—what the person says or does that follows from applying his belief to the adversity.[3]

For example, Darlene hears it's a beautiful day outside and applies to that news her belief that beauty is a brief illusion and that life will inevitably return to its unpleasant norm. Her response, therefore, is, "It's supposed to rain tomorrow." When a happy sucker like me retorts "No, the forecast is for sunshine tomorrow!" Darlene is in the position to respond, "Well, today's paper says rain." When I turn on the radio and she hears the revised forecast for sunshine, she's forced to answer, "Well, things change so fast they never know for sure."

And so it goes, in the gloomy groove. But that's where Dr. Seligman's learned optimism comes in, adding "D" and "E" to Ellis's "ABC." "D" is for *disputation*, an internal conversation by which Darlene intentionally revises her belief. For example, after dismissing the sunny forecast with "It's supposed to rain tomorrow," she might dispute her original belief by saying to herself, "But maybe that forecast is right, given how the weather changes so quickly. And the trees and flowers love the rain. And maybe we'll have rain in the night time and sunshine in the daytime."

Disputations stop the old negative belief patterns in their tracks, replacing them with evidence-based positivity. Every time she counters her reflexive pessimism with an acknowledgment that things might go well instead, she is practicing and reinforcing an appreciative, positive outlook. She is "learning" optimism.

The "E" in Dr. Seligman's alphabetical antidote is for *energizing*, the result of successfully applying the disputation. The kick you get from actually making a change in yourself is enhanced by the positive content of the replacement sentiment. Disputing negativity requires a search for evidence of inspirational and expansive truth.

I rarely hear anyone discussing temperament and personality as the root problems in a marriage, but if you dig beneath many of the usual items in those lists of the top ten sources of conflict, you'll often find telltale patterns in the ways spouses approach their problems.

In my speeches over the years, I've found myself returning to research conducted decades ago by one of my professors, Dr. Linda Beckman of the UCLA Neuropsychiatric Institute. She interviewed and administered questionnaires to childless women and mothers between the ages of sixty and seventy-five looking for differences in how they perceived their lives. At that time, women in that age group without children were the rare exception and had probably experienced infertility. Dr. Beckman wanted to test the stereotype of older, childless women as "lonely, unhappy, maladjusted, unlikable, unsatisfied with later life, insensitive, unloving and unable to get along."[4]

Her findings have stuck with me. Some of the women were indeed dissatisfied and pessimistic, but others were upbeat. When teased out, however, the differences didn't fall along the line between mothers and non-parents. Instead, the differences were in outlook. The non-mothers who were pessimistic said, "I lost so much. I have no one now to love me, to take care of me. I have no grandchildren, and I just watch from the sidelines while everyone else gets attention from her family." The pessimistic mothers said, "My kids give me so much worry! They know I need to know they're all right, but they never call me! They don't come visit, either. They're too busy to have time for their mother!"

At the other end of the continuum, the optimistic non-mothers said, "I may not have had children, but I've had time to pursue my career and travel. And I had wonderful relationships with my nieces and nephews." The mothers said, "Yes, my children are the lights of my life. It wasn't always easy, but at every phase they added so much to my happiness."

By observing your immediate reactions to events (or asking your partner to let you know), you can discern if your glass is half empty or half full. If it's the former, try using Dr. Seligman's ABCDE process to revise the beliefs that thwart you. It's crucial to counter a pessimistic belief with a robust, buoyant disputation.

When James and Kimberly understood the damage James's habits caused their marriage, they invented "Project Happiness," a joint effort to elevate the joy quotient in their relationship. James realized that much of the "work" would entail his adjusting the ambiance by ramping up his positive attitude. Every time he responded to a remark by Kimberly or the kids with negativity or blame, Kimberly signaled him by tracing a smile on her grinning lips. The boys soon joined in the "project" and as the family mood was elevated, their bond strengthened.

Before you reject the idea that you and your partner can change the tenor of your marriage, try to identify the beliefs that inform your responses to challenges. Talk about them, ideally with each other, but if necessary with a friend or relative who knows each of you well. You might want the trained contribution of a therapist. But be aware that your problems might be caused or inflamed by a broader outlook or tendency. Realizing that could be the pony in the poop.

"PUT A RUBBER BAND ON IT"—ANTICIPATE AND STRETCH WITH CHANGE

The singer Beyoncé suggested that "if you liked it then you shoulda put a ring on it," and whattaya know: you *did*. Once, you fell in love, and you decided your relationship was so compelling that you made a declaration before God to yourselves, your family, and witnesses (required by law to emphasize the importance of your marriage to your community). You promised to love and stay with this person through all the trials life might throw at you until one of you dies.

How's that working out for you? Well, something changed along the way, didn't it?

Change is inevitable. In the throes of "matrimania," people suspend logic and misgivings, just wanting with all their hearts to don that long mermaid bridal dress with the flowing train and walk up the aisle toward their one true love, where the officiant will pronounce how significant their love is as they proclaim their fealty in good times and bad, in sickness and in health.

Beyoncé says "put a ring on it," but I think it's a better idea to "put a rubber band on it," because marital love needs to be *elastic*. Your relationship must stretch over time to accommodate added stresses—like children, each of whom is an amalgam of idiosyncrasies and needs. It will have to give when a partner is sick, and unfortunately, that's sure to happen. Your ring should allow for experimentation—a new career, a move, changing schools, and enlarging friendships—but it must have the capacity to return to a snug fit when the two of you can be close.

YOUR "CHEESY" MARRIAGE

Speaking of change, let's move from stretchy wedding rings to stretchy cheese.

The parable *Who Moved My Cheese* by Spencer Johnson (1998) was a mega-bestseller because it cleverly and succinctly summarized the constructive and destructive ways we view and deal with change. You remember it is the story of two mice, Sniff and Scurry, and two mini-humans, Hem and Haw, placed in a maze looking for cheese, which represents whatever it is they most want (in your case, a happy marriage). They come upon a large quantity at Cheese Station C.

Every day, the mice and little humans eat some of the cheese. The mice keep tabs on their cheese supply, but Hem and Haw grow complacent, assuming it will be replenished and even that they are entitled to it. They don't notice that it's decreasing, and they get lazier about going to get it.

Then one day the cheese is gone.

The mice are ready. Without analyzing or hesitating, they leap into their jogging suits and tennis shoes and run off to find new cheese somewhere else in the maze. After much searching, they find plenty at Cheese Station N.

Hem and Haw, however, respond with denial then move into analysis, which keeps them from action. Determined not to budge, they even try digging in the wall behind where their cheese had been, hoping to find more.

Finally, Haw reluctantly realizes he'll have to brave the maze in search of cheese. Conquering his inertia is exhilarating, and in his search he gains insights he scribbles on the maze walls. After returning and unsuccessfully urging Hem to overcome his fears and join him, Haw hopes "the handwriting on the wall" will eventually help Hem find the cheese. Haw had learned to anticipate change and stay alert for it, to adapt quickly as circumstances shift, and to enjoy responding.

What's that got to do with your marital problems? Everything. As I said, your "cheese" is a fulfilling marriage, those same feelings of love and possibility you felt on your wedding day. Most people hope, as they recite their vows, that their love and devotion will expand and deepen, but love can be nibbled away, too, by neglect or unkindness. Married people who sustain their cheese expect their feelings for each other and their relationship to change, and they pay attention to those changes.

To refresh your memory of the cheese you crave, recall the vows you and your spouse made to each other on your wedding day. I hope you can still taste the tang of your cheese. Now analyze how the cheese in your marriage moved. Did you have a child and focus your attention there, assuming your relationship would adapt? Did your interests diverge? Did one partner turn toward an affair? In each of these scenarios, *both parties missed something*. The cheese was being depleted, and you were like Hem and Haw, unrealistically confident that it would magically replenish.

You may be able to pinpoint when your marriage started to dissolve. Or perhaps, looking back, you now see that you or your partner developed a hurtful communication pattern with one or more of what Dr. John Gottman calls the "four horsemen": criticism, contempt, defensiveness, and stonewalling (withdrawal).[5] Contempt is the opposite of respect, and "teasing" is contempt disguised as humor.

If you wed very young, you may have unknowingly reproduced the marriage of your parents, all or parts of which may have been dysfunctional or at least inappropriate for the spouse you chose. That's what happened to Anne and Dean. Believing that a wife's role is caring for children and placating her husband, Anne replicated her own mom's passivity, allowing Dean to get away with hoarding all her cheese.

Dean was the oldest by six years of three sons born to Rosalie and Ted in the 1960s. Ted was in the Navy, and Rosalie worked in her family's furniture retail business, but as the boys needed more attention, she left her job and became a full-time mom. Ted was discharged from the military when

Dean was six and earned a law degree at night while working at a car dealership. Rosalie bragged that Dean was so inquisitive that he'd go to his room, shut the door, and spend hours reading. By the time her youngest left the nest, Rosalie returned to the family business. But it was hardly fulfilling. She decided to take some art courses.

This is the backstory that Anne, whom Dean married when he was twenty-three and working toward his own law degree, told me when she eventually became my client. Dean's isolation growing up had been a response to his mom's alcoholism. He shut himself away, meeting his intellectual needs, because Rosalie was unavailable emotionally and Ted was seldom home. So Dean learned to withdraw into his own world. Anne accepted his lack of communication and distance, rationalizing that he developed it as a form of self-defense against the pain of his mom's addiction.

Anne recalled times when one of their three kids would have a mishap. As she, distressed, tried to address the blood or tears, Dean would smirk, "Don't worry about them. Let them cry. It'll toughen them up." She was still resentful over the day their four-year-old, walking along the beach, tripped and fell face-first into a sandcastle, layering sand into his mouth, eyes, and nose. While the boy bawled, barely able to breathe, Dean stood there laughing and taking a video of Anne's frantic effort to clean up her son. "What kind of dad thinks it's okay for his child to endure pain from sand in his eyes?" she demanded, still emotional about the event.

Though Dean could be harsh and uncommunicative, Anne thought they had a happy marriage and a close family. Their sex life was excellent, and their bright kids excelled in school. Dean traveled some, occasionally taking several days to consult on cases in Las Vegas and Chicago. When his brother had heart surgery, Dean spent two weeks in Phoenix.

As the couple approached their fifteenth wedding anniversary, Anne asked Dean how he wanted to celebrate. She thought they might take a special vacation, maybe to Costa Rica, where she wanted to see the sea turtles at Tortuguero. Dean said he was too busy; he was preparing a case that he had to present in Las Vegas then. Anne was disappointed but accepting. Her business selling button-art for baby nurseries on Etsy certainly wasn't earning enough to sustain the family.

Right before the Las Vegas trip, Anne was in the kitchen and heard Dean's car pull into the driveway. He didn't come in for ten minutes, so she went out to greet him. He was in his car talking on his cell phone with the windows closed, and when Anne surprised him with a tap on the glass, he looked up suddenly with the most peculiar, panicked look and quickly ended the call. He got out angrily. "Don't you ever do that to me again!" he railed. "I was having a very important conversation! Why did you disturb me? You're always trying to investigate what I'm doing!"

Anne felt like a five-year-old scolded by a parent, this time unfairly. "I just saw you in our driveway and wanted to welcome you," she began defensively.

"You could *see* I was on the phone but had to interrupt me anyway! Don't you *ever* do that to me again!" He stormed into the house, leaving Anne standing there incredulously. Then came tears.

She was crying as she recounted the incident. It took her five minutes and four tissues before she could continue. "It was that first look he gave me," she said, and the tears flowed again. "It wasn't so much his attack— he'd snapped at me many times before, and I always chalked it up to stress on the job. But that look was as if he got caught. And it planted a seed in my mind, and I started to get suspicious where I never was before."

Her suspicion increased because after that Dean started hiding his cell phone instead of leaving it on the nightstand. She decided to try something she would never have done before. While Dean was in Las Vegas, she called the firm there and asked the secretary who answered if he was available. She said no. Anne asked when he was expected and was told he wasn't expected at any time on their calendar.

"I didn't know where he was, but I did know he was lying to me," Anne explained. "That opened my eyes, though at first I denied it was possible. I thought I must have made a mistake. I thought our marriage was good."

Anne's "cheese" was closeness and communication with her husband, but she had *never tasted it*. Rather than tell Dean about her longing for attachment, she explained away his distance as a logical response to Rosalie's alcoholism. She tolerated her "hunger" because she was afraid of change, afraid to discuss Dean's recollections of his mom's drinking lest she anger him. And Dean continued to keep her at bay, sequestering his thoughts and creating a chasm to fill with a second life.

Sometimes you have to search for cheese in the maze of your own thought patterns. The "writing on the wall" that Haw left for Hem helps you find where your marriage became too rigid; where you refused to notice your cheese was depleting and failed, unlike the mice, to lace up your tennis shoes.

This is what the elders in the Cornell Legacy Project mean when they say "marriage is hard" and it "takes discipline and work."[6] You need the discipline to "monitor" your marriage and anticipate change—if you know it's coming, then you're ready to adapt. You need to summon the energy to accept it and without pausing to look backward, jump into your tennis shoes and scoot to new cheese.

That's the basic message of *Who Moved My Cheese* as applied to *any* aspect of life. Change is inevitable, partially because (deny if you must) change is inevitably occurring in *you*.

As you age, you're changing, even if you never read a newspaper or expand your knowledge or leave your house. Your relationship changes with every interaction; with every sweet remark you improve it, and with every cutting insinuation you eat away at the cheese you could savor and that you need for sustenance to go forward. Dr. Gottman, by the way, says you need five positive comments or gestures to balance a single negative one.

Okay, you might say this advice is cheesy, but if it prevents you from being mousy about your relationship....

I used to tell my clients that I enjoyed my profession because each person was like a puzzle—I gained one or a few pieces at a time, and eventually I could fit them together and make out part of the picture they formed. But that's somewhat inaccurate, because an individual and a marriage contain pieces fitting into *ever-changing* pictures. Every day we add another piece of experience and information to the collection. At some times they fit cleanly together, and their design is discernable; at other times their edges clash and some pieces must be discarded. If we keep observing the shapes of our puzzle pieces, with enough artistry, we can continue arranging them to express most elegantly the beauty of our totalities.

THE JOYS OF AN ADEQUATE MARRIAGE

I've been emphasizing that people, and therefore relationships, constantly change. That's why a happily-ever-after wedding day can give way to boredom and separation and why the sexual excitement of the honeymoon slips into predictable monotony. Perhaps you were initially attracted to your spouse's caring nature, but later it came to seem hovering, then cloying, and eventually smothering. I frequently hear the complaint that the one characteristic that most drew a partner to the other is precisely the characteristic that becomes unbearable.

But if you look at your marriage not so much as stable and constant but as continuously adapting and adjusting, you can more easily understand that even if you endure *years* of a particular trial, you can at the same time receive other types of satisfactions. And even as one aspect of the relationship diminishes, others brighten. Later you might regain the faded connection and at the same time initiate *new* directions. An attitude of ongoing exploration, appreciating the ever-expanding possibilities, is what keeps a relationship vital. And an attitude is a choice.

In marriage and family life, simultaneous challenges pull our attention in different directions. A child may have special gifts or needs that require an extra time commitment for one or both of you. An aging parent may need care. Your spouse may have a professional opportunity that's exciting but demanding, or your family may face financial struggles. These are occasions to more fully contribute to the great enterprise that is your family, and we love most those in whom we have made the greatest investment.

As you and your partner pursue these adventures and grapple with difficulties, if one of you makes a mistake, reveals a cranky side, or gives vent to irritation, the other can respond in kind or choose to soothe; each moment offers an opportunity. It is in scaling an obstacle together that couples often find the most comfort in each other and find their bond strengthening. Each member of your family is a package of experiences, expectations, values, intentions, and emotions. We can shape them and try to control them. We can respond to them and manipulate them, we can allow external influences to act upon them and bend them in one direction or another. *Nobody's perfect.* But some are more willing than others to try to improve.

Sometimes you need to put up with imperfections or annoyances—and sometimes much worse—for a greater good, like your children's welfare, or because you know you'll eventually get through this phase and can resume the smooth relationship you once enjoyed, or because you don't want to be alone, and there are some characteristics of your mate you do appreciate.

Almost any reason you could name to stay together is a *good* reason to stay together. (Okay, if you want to stay just to beat up the other person, get out.) But assuming you want to ride it out, there are things you can do.

In their 2002 study of spouses who described themselves as unhappy in their marriages, Linda Waite and her team of researchers wanted to test the popular belief that divorce makes unhappily married people happier. What they found was astonishing. Aside from answering the question "No, it doesn't," they also examined spouses who initially described themselves as unhappy but rated themselves as happily married five years later. What happened to turn them around? The researchers found that three "ethics" were behind these marital rebounds:

1. The "marital endurance ethic": Simply remaining together for those five years allowed problems to resolve themselves.

2. The "marital work ethic": Partners worked on marital problems, "with wives especially often enlisting the help of outside others to change their husbands' bad behavior." In these marriages, husbands tended to "see marriage-and-fatherhood as an important marker of successful manhood."

3. The "personal happiness ethic": Rather than the marriage changing, "persons in the marriage changed their lives in ways that made them personally happier in spite of ongoing marital problems."[7]

Dr. Waite and her colleagues found in focus group interviews that the unhappy couples whose marriages became happy often faced serious problems, "including alcoholism, infidelity, verbal abuse, emotional neglect, depression, illness and work reversals." So why did they survive? "Spouses who stay married often described marital unhappiness as caused by outside tensions, rather than internal relationship dynamics, even when those outside tensions caused considerable marital friction, thoughts of divorce and marital unhappiness." In other words, they were able to *see their problems as separate from their marriages.* "Many spouses said their marriages got happier, not because they and their partner resolved problems, but because they stubbornly outlasted them," the researchers reported, underscoring *the power of commitment.* Few credited counseling for improving the situation.

The psychologist Joshua Coleman develops these notions in his book *The Marriage Makeover: Finding Happiness in Imperfect Harmony* (2003),[8] suggesting that troubled couples understand, attempt to address, and, if that fails, *live with* characteristics in each other or their marriage that may be uncorrectable. He offers a process for not only coming to peace with a marriage that may never rise to your original expectations but for coming to appreciate its strengths. And if your marriage cannot fulfill every need, he says, those needs can be met in other ways. This approach allows you to honor your values and preserve for your children the united home they deserve without resigning yourself to a depressing, never-satisfied future. A marriage doesn't have to be all things to both spouses all the time. *You can be happy in an adequate marriage.*

A marriage is largely what the spouses make of it. If you choose to view a particular stretch of time as its "friendship" segment or the years when children are living at home as its "child-centric" segment, you have precluded nothing else. Within the child-centric period you can make a romantic weekend escape. If you find your division of labor or scheduling unrewarding, you can always re-negotiate. That's why I introduced this section with the cheese-moving discussion of *change.* Your marriage isn't static, and Dr. Coleman offers a way to take advantage of that.

Parents who are committed to staying together "for the sake of the children," can enjoy a stable and pleasant family life, Dr. Coleman insists, even if they never recapture the original zest of their marriage. An intact family confers pleasures and gratification that cannot survive divorce. After reading this far, I'm sure you're aware that maintaining a low-conflict home, even if unexciting to the parents, offers children the greatest opportunity for well-being and their own healthy marriages. That's the very best gift you can give your children, even if offering it means some sacrifice to you.

Two responses to that: it's possible you are not sacrificing anything, because you just don't know that you could ever find what you're looking for in marriage. You can, however *refuse to believe* you are sacrificing. Just waking up in the same house with your children, watching them develop from one day to the next, overhearing their banter and tucking them in every night offers greater joy than many people ever experience. And were you to leave this marriage (and allow whatever collateral damage accrues to your kids), a subsequent marriage, as we have seen, is unlikely to make you happier. As a divorcee, especially if you have children, you'll never begin with a "clean slate," and you'll always have a set of standards for a new mate to meet.

Dr. Coleman finds most disgruntled couples' expectations unrealistic. "Highly educated people come into my office every day with the same script of marriage that is being recited by the actors in the romantic movie at the cineplex down the street," he tsks. "Their expectations of themselves, their spouses, and their marriages have little to do with what is reasonable to expect from a long-term relationship."[9]

So his first task is teasing out the history that creates these wild expectations, followed by "getting really clear on whom you married and what expectations, problems and conflicts *you* bring to the party."[10] There's usually a list of desires and myths operating in the background, like "My partner should be able to anticipate my needs," "My partner should be emotionally available to me whenever I need him or her," and "Love is a feeling that can't be forced or manufactured. It either exists or it doesn't."[11]

"As a rule, expecting to find happiness in marriage is a bad idea," Coleman warns.[12] That's because your basic attitude about your whole life will encompass how you view your marriage.

Once clients get their expectations straight, then they can look at obstacles and attempt to address them. In many of Dr. Coleman's cases and probably in the majority of cases I've seen in my professional career, one person (usually the wife) is dedicated to working on the marriage, while the other person blames problems solely on the first. It's in these cases that Dr. Coleman's perspective is most useful. As he says, many books will tell you how to have a great marriage. He's more concerned with how to have a great *life*.

This is where I emphasize the importance of *family* rather than simply marriage. The Legacy Project elders and anyone who's survived a life-threatening illness can tell you that family, spouse included, is ultimately your most precious asset and enduring accomplishment. How do you retain that even with an imperfect spouse and an incomplete relationship? Or, as Dr. Coleman puts it, how do you live in "imperfect harmony"?

The first step is to do whatever you can to revitalize your marriage. Try to recall the routines of your happier days together. What did you include in your relationship that has crept out of the mix today? If you can't recall a time of harmony, I suggest you try the exercise at the conclusion of this book, an experiment in behavior that will let you know if you can once again, or for the first time, gain pleasure from your marriage.

Step two is to recognize each person's limitations. If your partner clings stubbornly to behavior or characteristics that preclude his meeting your desires, accept them—and possibly *grieve* for the loss of the ideal you held. Though it means working around an undesirable trait, you can recognize the futility in insisting that he conform to your expectations.

Forgiveness can bring a measure of peace. Researchers at the University of Missouri found that "forgiving others helped protect older women from depression, even when they felt unforgiven by others." Dr. Amit Sood of the Mayo Clinic says "forgiveness is acknowledging that you have decided to forgo anger and resentment, and that any future relationship with the offending party will be on your own terms."[13]

Troy, a salesman for a line of pottery, had pretty traditional ideas about the roles of husbands and wives, and he expected his wife, Louise, to take care not only of all the kids' needs but of his as well. After driving hundreds of miles across his sales territory, he expected her to have dinner ready when he got home. Sometimes he'd enter the house to find that their two boys, at the chaotic ages of three and five, had left toys all over the living room. Irritated by traffic and tired of being deferential to his customers, he'd "let go," yelling at the kids and even at Louise. Troy's temper could mean a string of expletives at peak volume, and Louise would shepherd the boys into their bedroom, then just take his venting.

Anger management therapy would have been helpful, but Troy wouldn't hear of it. After Louise had been coming to therapy for about two months, Troy finally agreed to show up, but of course it was only to help Louise. Troy was a small man, little more than five feet tall, but he had a presence. He fairly swaggered into my office and sat in the middle of the couch, legs crossed as widely as possible, arms folded and ready for combat.

Of course I took him on his terms, asking him to describe the problem from his perspective. "Louise is messy, she can't get control of the boys. She knows I want dinner when I get home, and it's not early, it's 6:30 at night, for crying out loud! There are blocks all over the carpet, and what has she done all day? She has no paid employment; her only job is to take care of the boys and the house!"

As any mom knows, responsibility for two boys those ages is more than a full-time job, but Troy couldn't cut her any slack. "It's my home; I pay for everything. She has no worries! I don't ask that much, just a neat home and my dinner on the table! Is that asking too much?"

He had New York bluster and the accent to go with it. I could imagine that in the lower-middle-class neighborhood where he grew up, he must have needed to be tough, given his small stature. "Do you think you might help Louise a little bit? She's got so much laundry and the kids are constantly making a mess, even right after she cleans up when you're coming home."

I knew already that Troy didn't listen to Louise, and I hoped he'd listen to someone he was paying to dispense expertise. But he looked at me as if I were bonkers. "I don't change diapers," he scowled. Taking another tack, I diplomatically asked about the temper. Troy shrugged, "I yam what I yam!" he replied, and I thought to myself, "He's Popeye the Sailor Man!"

I did learn a lot about Troy in that meeting. Foremost, that on his own, he wouldn't change.

The Marriage Makeover had not been published when I was working with Louise and Troy, but looking back, I found that *six tactics* aligned with Dr. Coleman's approach helped Louise improve her lot. First, she *accepted Troy's temper* and tried to understand the context of his outbursts. They weren't an attack against her personally but rather a way for a "little guy" to feel powerful in a safe milieu with no repercussions.

Understanding Troy's outbursts would not excuse them, of course. No husband should raise his voice to his wife in such an abusive way. Louise's second tactic was to assure herself that Troy was behaving unacceptably and to express that at the right time (doing so in the midst of his wrath probably would have backfired).

Third, Louise also *established her own authority* in the home. She learned how to stand her ground when Troy requested something unreasonable, calmly asserting her own view. This was a difficult one, because Louise recoiled at Troy's volume. He would never physically abuse her, but he needed to understand that his noise level caused fear and was a form of verbal abuse. Louise learned to withdraw emotionally from the scene by imagining herself as an objective observer standing at the doorway. From that vantage, she could see clearly that Troy was a bully, and she the peacekeeper. This empowered her.

Fourth, Louise built protections for the boys' sensitivities. Afraid to broach the topic of his anger, Louise usually just removed the boys from their father when she saw his irritation escalate. Learning how to *discuss their sons' wellbeing* when he was not inflamed helped her identify their welfare as a worthwhile goal for Troy. With practice and encouragement in counseling, she even learned how to speak up during an anger episode in order to spare the children.

Fifth, Louise developed a program of *self-care*. Troy's repeated accusations of incompetence penetrated her soul, even though she was internally strong. She began work to complete her bachelor's degree, taking one class per semester at the community college, where a daycare program assisted with the boys. She got involved with the women's center there and organized a group for other students married to men with anger problems.

Finally, Louise focused inward through cognitive therapy, examining the beliefs and assumptions that had tamped down her assertiveness and allowed her to absorb Troy's rage all these years. For example, the house *was* a mess, so she believed she deserved his scoldings. Dinner *was* sometimes late or cold or not complete, and she accepted fault for that. She realized that she was caught in a vicious circle, accepting Troy's insults, which fed her own feelings of inadequacy. She learned to *replace them with appropriate truths* in her mind and to respond evenly when Troy exploded. The change in her reactions transformed the character of their home.

Louise couldn't make Troy over, but with her unilateral actions and responses, she could reduce the friction in her home. She pursued enriching outside activities and friendships. She was able to deflect Troy's ire and step away from personal responsibility for it. Troy's anger was a serious problem, but it did not define him. Less bothered by outbursts, Louise could open herself to his finer qualities and more freely give to him. And in the end, Troy could continue to say, "I yam what I yam."

CHAPTER 21

Life's Finest
Accomplishment

We've seen that there's plenty wrong with divorce. It doesn't solve many of the problems plaguing you and creates its own set of headaches. It doesn't bring happiness and in fact many spouses who report unhappiness five years later say they're happy with their marriages.[1] Divorce scars children for life, even if they do overcome it, and 20 percent of them carry dysfunction rooted in their parents' divorce forever.[2] Blended families face a passel of special problems, and dating after divorce to find a new mate is awkward and emotionally perilous.

Yes, there's plenty to dislike about divorce. Yet it's one alternative you're considering.

Now it's time for the balance, the good stuff about marriage. We know that marriage isn't a static state; we know not every phase is perfect, just as neither spouse can be perfect. But throughout a lifetime, marriage offers an ideal context, a *unique* context, for some of life's peak experiences, as well as the opportunity to bond with another in the deepest, most significant union possible.

BRINGING HAPPINESS INTO MARRIAGE

Marriage is the chief source of happiness for many people, but even if it's not the chief source of *your* happiness, it does a pretty good job of increasing the happiness of those who stick with it. In *For Better: The Science of a Good Marriage*, Tara Parker-Pope summarizes the effects of marriage on everything from sex, children, and career to meeting the need for attachment. After reviewing hundreds of studies she concludes, "The struggle is well worth it. We are hardwired for love and long-term partnership. And, by every measure, ranging from better sleep to more sex, it's clear that a good marriage is good for you."[3]

Arthur Brooks, an economist and president of the American Enterprise Institute, has made the study of happiness a science. In *Gross National Happiness*, he writes, "For most men and women, matrimony brings far more happiness than the alternatives. The evidence is that humans are designed for long-lasting monogamous relationships, and they are happiest when they are in these relationships—even if they sometimes fight like little children when they're stressed out."[4]

Then Mr. Brooks asks,

> But can we say marriage *brings* happiness? Research suggests that it does. One study followed 24,000 people over more than a decade and documented a significant increase in happiness after people married. For some of these people, the happiness increase wore off in a few years and they ended up back at their premarriage happiness levels. But for others, it persisted for a long time. This is evidence that marriage does bring happiness— and in some cases, long-term happiness.[5]

A 2015 study led by John F. Helliwell of the Vancouver School of Economics analyzed international data about well-being, finding that "marital happiness long outlasted the honeymoon period. Though some social scientists have argued that happiness levels are innate, so people return to their natural level of well-being...the researchers found that the benefits of marriage persist."

Importantly, "those who consider their spouse or partner to be their best friend get about twice as much life satisfaction from marriage as others," Helliwell adds. "Maybe what is really important is friendship, and to never forget that in the push and pull of daily life." But even if the spouses' friendship is strained, marriage retards typical dips in happiness that occur in middle age. "The biggest benefits come in high-stress environments, and people who are married can handle midlife stress better than those who aren't, because they have a shared load."[6]

In 2002, thirteen leading marriage scholars, in a summary of the scientific research on "the importance of marriage in our family and social system," announced this "fundamental conclusion: *Marriage is an important social good, associated with an impressively broad array of positive outcomes for children and adults alike.*" Among their findings are the following:

- Marriage increases the likelihood that fathers have good relationships with their children
- Marriage is a virtually universal human institution
- Married couples seem to build more wealth on average than singles or cohabiting couples
- Married men earn more money than do single men with similar education and job histories
- Children who live with their own two married parents enjoy better physical health, on average, than do children in other family forms
- Marriage is associated with reduced rates of alcohol and substance abuse for both adults and teens
- Married people, especially married men, have longer life expectancies than do otherwise similar singles
- Marriage is associated with better health and lower rates of injury, illness, and disability for both men and women[7]

But you don't have to take the researchers' word for it. Married people themselves report their satisfaction. "When, in 2012, we asked married people whether they would remarry their current spouses, 81% said yes," reports Helen Fisher of her representative national survey of five thousand Americans. "Seventy-five percent also reported they were still in love. Moreover, 89% of single people believe you can stay married to the same person forever."[8]

The 2015 American Family Survey, a nationwide study by the *Deseret News* and the Center for the Study of Elections and Democracy, found that a whopping "92% of married respondents say their marriage is the same or stronger than two years earlier."

Nevertheless, pollsters regularly find a discrepancy between individuals' reports about their own experience and their perceptions of general social conditions. Although 92 percent of married persons attest to the strength of their own marriages, 83 percent of them say "marriages generally" have stayed the same or grown *weaker* in the last two years. Asked about the importance of marriage on that intangible societal level, only 62 percent agree that "marriage is needed to create strong families," only 60 percent agree that "marriage makes families and kids better off financially," and only 52 percent agree that "society is better off when more people are married." And yet most still want to be married. Seventy-one percent disagreed with the idea that "marriage is old fashioned and out of date."[9]

This discrepancy between personal experience and impressions of society at large is the result of news stories ("We don't have a news business; we have a *bad* news business," as my husband likes to say) and by politicians preying on constituents' fears. In a 2015 Gallup poll, 85 percent of respondents said they were satisfied "with the way things are going in [their] personal life at this time," a number roughly consistent with measurements of satisfaction since 2000. But when asked about satisfaction "with the way things are going in the United States at this time," just 21 percent were satisfied.[10]

Okay, let's talk about the content of these happy marriages. Eli J. Finkel, a psychologist at Northwestern University, describes a dramatic change in the way most people conceive of marriage: "Since around 1965, we have been living in the era of the self-expressive marriage. Americans now look to marriage increasingly for self-discovery, self-esteem and personal growth...less as an essential institution and more as an elective means of achieving personal fulfillment."[11] With marriage less about "do your duty" and more about "follow your heart," what makes an enduring marriage possible? If feelings can shift when a sexy alternative presents itself, what is the glue that keeps couples together?

Cultivating the ethereal rewards that people now expect from marriage—"self-discovery, self-esteem, and personal growth"—requires a huge investment of time. Dr. Finkel cites a study showing "spouses who spent 'time alone with each other, talking, or sharing an activity' at least once per week were 3.5 times more likely to be very happy in their marriage than spouses who did so less frequently."[12]

That's why marital satisfaction dips during the child-rearing phase, returning to pre-parental levels when the kids leave. Time. The more of your life you invest in something, the more it means to you. So the more you invest in your spouse and in the unique dynamic that is the combination of the two of you, the stronger your marriage will be.[13] That doesn't mean you should be clones of each other. Differences of sex and personality contribute to marital success.

Perhaps you've heard the adage "happy wife, happy life." A survey of nearly four hundred couples married an average of 38.5 years confirms that bit of folk wisdom, concluding that "women are the ones that drive the emotional climate of the relationship." The researchers found that "married men tend to be a lot happier when their wives rate their marriage more highly—even if the men don't rate the marriage very highly themselves." Why? "Women satisfied in their marriages tend to do a lot more for their husbands."[14]

The late Judith Wallerstein summarized her decades of research on families in *The Good Marriage: How and Why Love Lasts*. She started out asking, "What do people define as happy in their marriages?" The answer "turned out to be straightforward," she found. "For everyone, happiness in marriage meant feeling respected and cherished." Referring to the couples interviewed over the years, she said "all felt that they were central to their partner's world and believed that creating the marriage and the family was the major commitment of their adult life. For most, marriage and children were the achievements in which they took the greatest pride." She concluded, "Above all, they shared the view that their partner was special in some important regard and that the marriage enhanced each of them as individuals."[15]

If marriage is the life "achievement in which people take most pride," why are twenty-somethings waiting so long to embrace it? Perhaps a tectonic shift from community and other-directedness (of the 1960s) to our current, isolated individualities partly explains it. Offering "Advice for a Happy Life," Charles Murray tells millennials, "Consider marrying young." "If you wait until your 30s, your marriage is likely to be a merger. If you get married in your 20s, it is likely to be a startup." And a startup has advantages. "For one thing," he asserts, "you will both have memories of your life together when it was all still up in the air. You'll have fun remembering the years when you went from being scared newcomers to the point at which you realized you were going to make it."

"Even more important," he adds, "you and your spouse will have made your way together. Whatever happens, you will have shared the experience. And each of you will know that you wouldn't have become the person you are without the other."[16]

Shared experience. Mr. Murray and many others writing on happy marriage emphasize being picky in choosing a mate, but my perspective is that *love can be learned*, even if you and your partner are not well matched at all. Remember, we're all constantly evolving. In good marriages there are times when the spouses move apart and times when they reunite. It's the rubber wedding band, accommodating and encouraging stretching and contracting.

A study at the University of Texas at Austin asked students to rate the romantic appeal of classmates at the beginning of the semester and again three months later. "Perceptions of mate value change the more time that people spend together," said Lucy Hunt, research co-author. "Sometimes you get that Seth Rogen happy story, where an unattractive person comes to seem more attractive to one person in particular. But the opposite is just as likely to happen, too. Someone can become less attractive."

A second study, at Northwestern University, also found that familiarity fosters attraction. People videotaped talking about their relationships were rated on their appearance by an objective panel. The couples who knew each other before becoming lovers were more mismatched in looks, while those who started dating shortly after meeting tended to be similarly attractive, suggesting that a connection with the other person plays a greater role in falling in love than physical appearance.

A third study, by Helen Fisher at the Kinsey Institute, asked respondents if they had ever fallen in love with someone they initially thought unattractive. The ones who answered affirmatively said that "great conversations," "common interests," and "appreciation of his/her sense of humor" were what did the trick.[17]

These studies show that people can learn to love if they invest the time to share experiences and to understand and appreciate each other. Despite our sophisticated evaluations of compatibility on questionnaires and fact-checking, writes Alain de Botton in a column titled "Why You Will Marry the Wrong Person," "Marriage ends up as a hopeful, generous, infinitely kind gamble taken by two people who don't know yet who they are or who the other might be, binding themselves to a future they cannot conceive of and have carefully avoided investigating." When we marry, we are ostensibly seeking happiness, but we are really seeking familiarity and an end to loneliness. "Finally, we marry to make a nice feeling permanent," he says. That's the Romantic ideal. "[I]t doesn't matter if we find we have married the wrong person." Instead of discarding the spouse or the marriage, "we need to swap the Romantic view for a tragic (and at points comedic) awareness that every human will frustrate, anger, annoy, madden and disappoint us—and we will (without any malice) do the same to them."

"The person who is best suited to us is not the person who shares our every taste (he or she doesn't exist) but the person who can negotiate differences in taste intelligently—the person who is good at disagreement." He concludes, "Rather than some notional idea of perfect complementarity, it is the capacity to tolerate differences with generosity that is the true marker of the 'not overly wrong' person. Compatibility is an achievement of love; it must not be its precondition."[18]

In fact, given the right kind of interaction, anyone can fall in love. At least that's the premise of an exercise devised by the psychologists Elaine and Arthur Aron to develop closeness among subjects in another study.[19] The method received wide attention after it was featured in an article in the *New York Times* "Modern Love" column, "To Fall in Love with Anyone, Do This." In the exercise, two persons alternately answer thirty-six increasingly personal questions, topped off with four straight minutes of eye-gazing. The questions begin innocuously with "Given the choice of anyone in the world, whom would you want as a dinner guest?" and build in intensity ("Of all the people in your family, whose death would you find most disturbing?"). The author of the column did fall in love with her subject, and she comments, "I've begun to think love is a more pliable thing than we make it out to be. Arthur Aron's study taught me that it's possible—simple, even—to generate trust and intimacy, the feelings love needs to thrive."[20] If this process works with a stranger, just think how it might warm up the relationship to which you've already vowed your life. The technique underscores that vulnerability and transparency create intimacy. The more open and exposed you are to your *mate*, the more of your *soul* you share.

THE FIVE UNIQUE REWARDS OF MARRIAGE

Finally, I'd like to offer my list of rewards uniquely characteristic of marriage. Oh, perhaps you can find one or two in a long-term relationship or in cohabitation. You might be able to squeeze a couple out of a good friendship. But it is the permanent bond, the lifetime pledge of marriage in body and soul that ties these five benefits together in a package unlike any other.

(1) *Marriage is a safe place to grow.* Every psychologist (including me) tells you that out of pain comes growth, and in marriage, you are sure to encounter some degree of emotional pain. The most in-sync couples may seldom fight or experience deep division, but as the years continue, misfortunes and calamities befall everyone. When my husband was diagnosed with throat cancer, I felt weak and incompetent facing distasteful medical realities. I had to face aspects of his treatment that under normal conditions made me squeamish and faint. I lost the unshakeable rock to whom I naturally turned for support, as his treatment required pain medications that altered his mind. During the weeks of his hospitalization, I felt immobilized and helpless. I arrived early and was the last one to leave his floor other than the medical staff, and the sun moved across the window, the darkness arrived, and the blinking red glow of two nearby radio broadcast towers illuminated his room.

With God's help, he recovered—slowly but bravely and determinedly. Listeners to his radio show often ask him what he learned from his ordeal. Why would God choose to give someone whose calling and passion require his voice *throat cancer*? What is the message? He always responds that as much as he had appreciated us before, the lesson he carries is continual gratitude for his marriage and children. It is in times of crisis that appreciation for life—and loyal family—swells.

With the protection of marriage, we can afford to make some mistakes. We can venture out on a new career, relocate, or embark on the grandest adventure of all, having a child, and confront any resultant difficulties in tandem. In a good marriage, you can count on your partner for encouragement and consolation. You can bare your feelings and in the best cases know your partner's empathy will lead her to your vantage point (even if she disagrees with your conclusions).

The permanence of your relationship removes any constriction. If we can't afford a house this year, we can plan and save for one several years in the future. We can envision seeing our children through elementary school, high school, even the expense of college, as a team, sharing our resources and making joint decisions. We can expand our horizons because the vista in married life is expansive.

(2) *Marriage is a celebration of opposites.* Traditionally, marriage is the combination of two individuals, male and female, with divergent backgrounds, perspectives, habits, and desires into a single unit, a special combination that fuses their facets in a union designed to form a whole. Now that same-sex marriage is the law of the land, two men or women, often of contrasting characteristics, pledge their lifelong devotion.

I'd like to remind you of what I wrote earlier about the essential nature of the marital merge. In the book of Genesis, God presents the creation of man and woman in the Garden of Eden. You'd think God could have just set them both down there together. Why the description of Adam's searching through animals for a partner, failing, and then separately generating Eve? Some feminists might bristle at the notion that woman is an afterthought who emerges from man, but that is misinterpreting the traditional meaning of the story.

God made Eve not of Adam's *rib*, as you usually see the Hebrew "tsela" translated, but from his *side*. God separated the masculine "side" of human behavior from the feminine "side." Joining together these opposites benefits them both, because now they can act together from a fuller perspective than either would have alone. Woman, according to the Bible, is man's *eizer kenegdo*, or "helper, opposite him." That's why marriage to someone too similar, who mirrors all one's qualities, becomes predictable and boring. The joy of marriage is that surprising remark, that novel idea, that contrasting view that clarifies the thinking of both.

"Vive la différence!" isn't just a French recognition of male-female contrast. It's a hope that those differences live on, kept alive and not disparaged or diminished. It is difference united in a common purpose and shared goals—like the "family project"—that make a relationship innovative and interesting. Polarity allows for varying roles according to inclination and ability.

Noting distinctions is central to the Jewish faith that I live. We demarcate the Sabbath from the rest of the week, day from night, kosher from non-kosher, and even permissible relationships from forbidden ones. Awareness of borders and contrasts lets you live a more observant and mindful life, because you're always thinking about your position in relation to the world around you. When I first took on Jewish observance, I was asked why I would submit to so many restrictions. My response was that though my life had been delightful, it now seemed like a black-and-white movie in which so many contrasts and distinctions were smudged. Because the rules and guidelines of Jewish law come into play in every area of life, I was forced to think about and really notice what surrounded me. Bringing all of that into focus was like the moment when Dorothy opens the door of her tornado-transported farmhouse in the Land of Oz—suddenly everything was in Technicolor.

It's something like that when you live with your spouse. Your differences bring your own preferences into sharp focus, and if you are unclear how to respond, you have a loving helper right there, opposite you.

(3) *Marriage is the ultimate commitment.* You wonder: why is marriage universal across cultures? Why do men and women (mostly) promise to stay together until death? Perhaps marriage historically served the aristocracy—combining kingdoms, providing heirs. But why would anyone else make a commitment, a public display? Evolutionists suggest that though men wanted to spread their seed, women required a reliable source of protection and food. Men, caring about their own offspring, stuck around to claim them as their proud accomplishments.

That doesn't make sense to me. If men want to spread their seed, why would they make any commitment? Only women require protection when pregnant or nursing. There's no need for a man to proclaim ownership of a woman by promising anything; his strength alone should be enough to keep her close by.

But human beings are not animals, and marriage is one proof. Marriage elevates and sanctifies what would otherwise be a merely physical, reproductive act or an act of aggression, joining opposites who assume equal though differing roles. Marriage uses the most human of faculties—language—to form a binding contract. No animal could comprehend an agreement or contract, which deals in intangibles like loyalty, faithfulness, and even money (which is merely a symbol for what it can buy), binding the parties into a future they cannot see. What could be more spiritual than the combination of words, ideas, and time? By making a commitment, we raise our partnership above the practical and approach the divine, we project our existence onto a plane we can't now envision and yet confidently and willfully guarantee our role.

When a marriage begins to unravel, partners "forget" the promise they made in the marital contract. In a sense, they commit fraud, the honorable persons whose sincere intent was to fulfill their commitment having proved themselves false. It's sad that it's easier to get a divorce than to violate a business contract. Nothing is more precious than the bond a couple makes that can echo through generations.

(4) *Marriage is a chance to emulate God.* Most of the time we human beings feel pretty puny. We look up at the night sky and, if we're not in New York or L.A., see the welkin dotted with stars. We're at the mercy of weather, and a big storm can change the plans of millions of people. We're drawn to beaches and find the colors of sunsets majestic and magical.

But marriage gives us a chance to emulate God.

In generations past, that statement would have been understood to mean procreating children within the sacred framework of matrimony. Certainly no other moment in a parent's life compares to the birth of a child. All you can do is melt in awe that a complete, self-contained person has emerged from your union and in great humility realize the potential that your simple and presumably delightful act of love produced. When your child is born, you feel like a partner with God as well as with your spouse; you sense the possibility and the fulfillment of past, present, and future in this tiny creature you now fiercely protect.

At a time when 40 percent of babies are born to unmarried parents and some women deal with that proverbially ticking clock by electing to experience motherhood on their own, it is no longer taken for granted that procreation is reserved exclusively for marriage. Nevertheless, marriage is a unique opportunity to behave as God did. This gets a little deep, but did you ever wonder why he would create the world? It's an interesting question even if you're an atheist. He certainly has everything he needs. If he didn't, he wouldn't be God. Why go to the trouble of making dinosaurs and continents and atmosphere, plants, animals, and man? The traditional Jewish answer is that one of God's characteristics is the desire to give, the desire to offer kindness just because that's rewarding in itself. The Hebrew word for it is *chesed* (pronounced "*hess*-edd"). It's the desire to serve one's country, to volunteer for charity, to give your bus seat to a tired mom, to help your neighbor with her groceries.

Even without marriage, our daily lives offer endless opportunities to satisfy this altruistic desire. But the kind of *chesed* you offer in marriage is unique. It's not a one-shot occasion. It's not a promise to work at the homeless shelter every Thursday night. It's a vow to give to your other "side" 24/7, whenever needed and, especially, whenever not. You've heard the expression that marriage isn't a fifty-fifty endeavor; a *good* marriage is two people each giving 100 percent all the time. Part of exercising *chesed* is that you expect your partner to fail in that; when inevitably he does, you willingly fill in. *Chesed* is cheerfully doing the other's assigned chores (something the Legacy Project elders mentioned). *Chesed* is noticing that your partner is tired or down or in need of bolstering. And *chesed* is boosting and expressing appreciation even when it's not filling a need.

This is how you emulate God. You give without expectation of return. You give with joy, and you give because your partner's well-being is yours.

(5) *Marriage makes soul mates.* The minute you emerge from under the wedding canopy, leave the church, or stroll away from the seaside collection of folding chairs, you gain the benefit of the four aforementioned rewards of marriage. You've made the commitment and signed the contract that binds you and your love until death. You've formally declared that your marriage will be the repository for your deepest desires and the cushion for your most disappointing failures. You've recognized and embraced your differences, and you've pledged to be kind and supportive, starting right this minute.

What you can't have on your wedding day is a soul mate.

I can hear your objection. You knew "at first sight" that this person clicked with you, that he was the "other half" you'd been craving all your life. You even said right there in your vows, "you are my soul mate." No one could feel closer than you and your spouse, no one has ever seen into the depths of your being like this one person.

But a real soul mate is something you gain only over time. If you're reading this book, you may feel you've lost the chance to *ever* recapture the empathy you had before, much less become so close that your spouse parallels your soul. Again, your partner is and should be different; a soul mate is not a duplicate of yourself. Instead, a soul mate *understands you.*

Your soul mate knows what you like and can anticipate it. Your soul mate understands how your dad treated you and suffers along with you. Your soul mate would never want to change you, and instead allows you room to express yourself—messy desk, spilled hair gel, dirty clothes pile and all.

As I was finishing this book, my husband returned from speaking (three times!) at a conference in Las Vegas. While he was gone and I was concentrating on finishing, I wasn't attentive to much else. Don't tell: I wore the same yoga pants and t-shirt three days in a row. I never showered, even after I sneaked out for the yoga class feeling very, very guilty. When he came home at five in the evening, I hadn't brushed my teeth or eaten all day. My hair was a stringy blob clipped to my head. He walked in, and I apologized. His first words? "Congratulations on finishing the book! You look beautiful!" That's my soul mate. Now go make yours.

Epilogue

Truce: How to Stop the Momentum of Divorce

Thwarting divorce requires more than just holding back anger or taking a hiatus from harm. It means replacing bad habits and negative feelings with *positive* ones. I'm going to talk to you now as if you were a client seeking advice on how to stop a divorce.

Even if you are completely unwilling or unable to reconcile with your spouse, just *reading* these last few pages might shed some light on your relationship. No matter how you feel about divorcing, you'll benefit from *envisioning* the following process.

This truce, this divorce turn-around, concerns *behavior*, not emotions. *Divorce is driven by emotions.* Don't let them get in the way. Put your emotions in an imaginary box and set it on a shelf in your closet. Close the door. I'm offering you a temporary brain Band-Aid, and it's concerned only with behavior. Later, you can explore the emotions that brought you to the "D-word."

THE EXPERIMENT: A "NO DUMPING ZONE"

As a test of whether you can sustain your marriage, your assignment is to suspend anger, hurt, and conflicts and to relate to each other positively. I call this exercise creating a "No Dumping Zone." No dumping your old garbage. No dumping *on* each other. No dumping *of* the other.

You're skeptical. But it works. If you haven't completely given up on your marriage, just checking off this box—meaning this exercise—can pay off. You may not believe it's possible to revive your feelings. I dare you to try.

Remember that advertising relies on repetition. And if you (or your partner) feel like withdrawing, or reverting to your past habits, well, you've got a *marriage* at stake. And more importantly, a *family*.

Ideally, I'd like you to try this experiment for three months, but if that seems like too much, start with a week. This is your turning point, starting right now. This is the day you recognize and push away the Divorce Industry that hovers at your door, the day you fight and win against the forces conspiring to destroy your marriage.

The goal is just to *turn toward your partner*. Simple. Write this goal on several pieces of paper and tape them where you'll see them—your bathroom mirror, your computer screen frame, the dashboard of your car, the refrigerator door. The act of writing "Turn toward so-and-so" plants the goal in your mind.

To establish your No Dumping Zone, you need to do two things: (1) win by letting go and (2) behave as if you were happily married.

1. WIN BY LETTING GO.[1]

Most important and fundamental to heading off conflict is the strategy of "winning by letting go," formulated in 1985 by the communications expert Elizabeth Brenner Danziger. The prize you "win" immediately is conflict-avoidance. The bigger prize, the reward for letting go habitually, is a revived and satisfying relationship. When you let go, you're not giving in but taking control of your position. You're assessing the situation, perceiving a hurt or a conflict and choosing to let it melt out of the picture, opting not to let this moment's disagreement obstruct or impede your relationship.

So simple, so powerful. When you start feeling angry or irritated, breathe deeply and say aloud, "I'm going to let this go." The first time you say it, your difficulty in actually letting go will be offset by your partner's surprise that you're willing to try. Letting go puts your partner in the position of receiving your gift. When you offer it repeatedly and avoid conflict, he will learn to loosen a habit of control. When you let go, you're no longer adversaries. You've calmly and openly used a strategy to sidestep a potentially explosive situation.

I'm not suggesting a blanket surrender or relinquishing your views or values. Just decide to let this issue or this reminder of hurt or betrayal go for now.

What if you don't want to let go—what if you're clearly right, or if your way is really better? Consider that your spouse holds a point of view that he believes is more right than yours. Or your spouse might oppose you just to be contrary. Or to test you. The reason for your conflict is irrelevant. This is a test to see if you fall back into confrontational habits. Dump your need to control outside your marital No Dumping Zone.

Many spouses—men in particular—don't even realize they're being controlling. They believe their stance is just factual and based in reality, that their perspective is clearly the most useful and correct. But is your "factual" insistence perceived by your mate as controlling or manipulating? That perception determines how your interchange goes, not the "reality" you see. Most women understand that letting go allows conflict to pass, and usually a wife backs down when her husband asserts himself. In this experiment, both parties should let go, and see what emerges.

Maybe in your heart of hearts you realize you can be "insistent" (i.e., stubborn), but that very stubbornness keeps you clinging to "who you are." Maybe letting go is "not you." Maybe it violates your need for honesty and order. Stubborn people tell themselves that letting go would be so "inauthentic," so "phony." Right now, intentional phoniness is okay. Your previous style—however authentic it may be—is irrelevant to this task of setting up a No Dumping Zone. The task is to see if you (and your spouse) can do things differently to point your relationship in a new direction. Let yourself let go.

One tool for accomplishing this is something you're doing anyway: breathing. The pause while you breathe changes the dynamic of the conflict, allowing you to reset. Another tool for letting go is talking your way through the process: "I will let this go, right now. We can discuss my position later, but in the interest of our family, marriage, and future, I will let go now."

Dr. John Gottman dissected the communication patterns of troubled couples, finding a deadly pattern he calls "flooding,"[2] when something triggers a fight-or-flight instinct. Flooding shuts down everything. The tools of distraction, breathing, and talking your way through those moments can hold back a flood. His research also inspired the goal of "turning toward your partner."

2. BEHAVE AS IF YOU WERE HAPPILY MARRIED.

"Winning by letting go" clears out the "bad" of the past and the present conflict. The next step is to make your marriage feel good. You do that by fostering positive experiences shared by you and your spouse.

Obviously, you're not happily married, or you wouldn't be thinking about divorce. But since your ultimate goal is to build a constructive, rewarding relationship with your spouse, the most efficient approach is to behave as if you were happily married.

What does this mean? Setting aside the marriage's physical aspects, on a deeper level, happily married people give their partners three basics: respect, acceptance, and affection. Dr. Gottman calls this "attunement," which he defines as "the ability to understand and respect your partner's inner world."[3]

As we know from studies of arranged marriages,[4] love can be learned. Behaving as if you are happily married can become a self-fulfilling prophecy of the best kind.

Even if at this moment you are insincere, even if you feel the opposite of affectionate, fake it till you make it. Model the characteristics you'd wish to see in your spouse. Put yourself in your partner's place—what does he or she want? Answer: reassurance of your respect, acceptance, and affection. Displaying these three attitudes is behaving as if you're happily married.

Respect: Acknowledge your partner's talents and good qualities. Even if a partner's characteristics are not all honorable, for the present, focus on the positives and explain away or just ignore the bad stuff. Ask yourself, "How can I respond right now with respect?"

Acceptance: As Ingrid Michaelson sings, "You take me the way I am." It's good that your partner is not you and does not do everything the same way you do. Each of us needs a "complement," another person to provide support and encouragement—and sometimes correction—because human beings never forfeit the potential to improve and grow. So accept and appreciate your partner's individuality.

Affection: A relationship will go flat and sad without expressed love and appreciation. Commonly, men crave respect, and women crave affection, but a happy marriage (which you're behaving as if you had) contains both. In these ninety days, recall your past if necessary as the basis of that expression, but say something you know your partner would want to hear.

Nancy Dreyfus's book *Talk to Me Like I'm Someone You Love: Relationship Repair in a Flash* (2009),[5] provides 127 messages just the way you should say them. Leafing through this book can help you verbalize what you wish you'd said. Here are some examples:

4. All I want is for you to listen to me with an open heart.

57. You don't have to agree with me, but it hurts when you don't take me seriously.

75. I'm sorry that I've been acting as if everything's all your fault.

109. I know you like to verbally process what's going on in our relationship first—but right now, if we could just touch each other, it could help me be more present with you.

If hostility or anger blocks communication, come up with a silly, smile-inducing code word to jar yourselves out of bad patterns. (One woman says "squatty potty," and that jolts her into a smile.)

During this test period, resolve to be positive. This may require *practicing* an attitude that, the first time or two or three, seems completely unnatural. Pretend you're an observer watching yourself, someone who would assume you're in love. Grab some flowers at the supermarket. Enter the house with a cheerful, "Hi, honey! How was your day?" Put your clothes in the hamper instead of leaving them on the floor. Replace the roll of toilet paper you just used up. This is how lovers behave.

Write a note expressing appreciation for one aspect of your life together and leave it where your partner will see it. For example, "I appreciate that you do the laundry and am grateful to have clean t-shirts to wear." "I appreciate that you work so hard each day." "I'm grateful you're willing to test the possibilities for our future." Something mundane or something deeper—surely there is one aspect of your married life that you can write a note to appreciate. Writing the note is for *you* as much as for your partner; you can improve your own attitude by composing and especially by writing down a positive thought.

Even a week of this managed turnaround will let you know if it's possible to rebuild your marriage (longer is better). If you have children, this can save their lives. Unless you try the No Dumping Zone test, you have not treated your marriage with the respect such a weighty and important enterprise deserves. Look at your wedding photographs—remember your hopes and expectations on that day. Don't undervalue the lofty aspirations with which you started your marriage—a commitment *for life* to form a loving, dedicated partnership.

What about sex? It could be a complication during this special evaluation period. This timeframe isn't your "normal" relationship, and you need to negotiate the level of intimacy you would like *before* you start the process. If either of you feels that sexual contact would interfere in any way with other dynamics of your relationship, refrain. You might decide that even hugging, kissing, and touching could be a distraction. I've seen partners use sex and seduction to manipulate the other into investing more, or submitting, or otherwise subverting attention and the issues. Be careful.

The No Dumping Zone stays clean and repels pests of all sorts. Ideally, this time will interrupt bad patterns, like a need to control. You'll give the other person space and accept what he does with it. You'll put everything into the relationship, as you did when you started out. You'll go the extra mile, offering a nice gesture and feeling even better when you get a surprised and pleased reaction.

After this type of break in a bored, stale, controlling, or hurtful relationship, you reset. Start with an hour. Add another. Build to a day. And another day. Get to a week. With each hour and each day that you win by letting go and behave as if you're happily married, you should congratulate each other. Talk about your efforts; remark on the efforts of your partner. No dumping, just offering your personal feelings and reactions with the goal of rebuilding your trust and love.

David Skinner, writing in the *Weekly Standard*, described the many things he "gives up" in order to nurture his marriage by pleasing his wife. She went on the Paleo diet, which isn't an easy one. Skinner had fantasies of sabotage, offering her a plate of cream-sauced pasta and her favorite IPA. Instead, he joined her.

> It fits with my sense of what keeps a marriage going in the hard spots: a will to submit, to surrender, to give up, as in giving up being right. Giving up being indifferent to issues that your spouse is passionate about. Giving up the possibility of giving up, because people are depending on you to earn a living, to come home, to be around, to be the person you are....
>
> There's a 70 times 7 logic to marriage. How many times should I try to put my wife's feelings first? The answer is not 490. To me, the answer is something like, as many times as you possibly can.

Skinner is one bright fellow: "When you think you've been humble enough, when you think you've been on your knees all day long and deserve to stand up, that's when you have to remember that your spouse has to put up with you all the time. The least you can do is let this one thing go. And the next. And, if you can, the one after that."[6]

Your marriage is significant. You knew that when you decided to marry. You knew that when you applied for your marriage license, and when people who love you surrounded you in joy on your wedding day. Just as your wedding was a blessing to those around you, your divorce would be a misfortune—and probably to a larger circle of people than celebrated your marriage.

Imagine yourself in ten or fifteen years. If you stay with your partner, you'll look back at this as a rough patch (or even one of several) in a long-term, stable, satisfying marriage. If you split, you'll have pain, mopping up and starting again as a major phase of your life.

"Winning by letting go" might clash with your usual approach, or you might think this strategy is wimpy or weak. You might say you've just got exacting standards, high expectations for your partner's behavior. In many cases, that can be appropriate. In other cases, expectations can ruin you.

The strategy here is to make the relationship inviting and rewarding for your partner, and with that, for yourself, by evaluating each difficulty on a case-by-case basis—and whenever feasible avoiding conflict. When your partner understands and believes that you can sincerely offer this gift, the usual reaction with time is softening and gratitude. This strategy works cumulatively—one "letting go" leads to another. As magnanimity and peace replace conflict and hurt as the norm, you and your partner will remember your relationship is worthwhile.

Acknowledgments

Before all, I must thank God for granting me the opportunity, ability, and inspiration for this project. Of course I was aided by many more human supports, certainly my merciful and talented editor, Tom Spence, and Regnery's wise publisher, my friend Marji Ross, and the many staff members who designed and promoted this book.

Many friends indulged and encouraged my writing process, especially my irreplaceable "Twinny" Terri Schneeweiss, and our dear friends Kim and Mark Weinstein. Laura Macht, Nika and David Klinghoffer, and Rabbi Daniel and Susan Lapin, among many beloved friends, cheered me on. The Jewish community of Island Synagogue, led by Rabbi Yechezkel and Devorah Kornfeld, provided a solid spiritual backdrop. My friend and teacher Rabbi Hanoch Teller, a prolific author in his own right, kept me going with Proverbial sustenance.

I owe grounding and joy to my family: our eldest, Sarah, a brilliant teacher who lives too far away in New York City; Shayna, also an educator, and her polymath fiancé, Mark Giuliano, who expand my life with their insights and exploits; and Danny and his delightful wife, Richelle, who have enlivened our existence as they live with us awaiting the birth of their first child (while remodeling a newly-purchased house). I love each of them with the kind of boundless envelopment only a mother can understand. My brother-in-law Harry (the most considerate person on the planet) and his wife, Michele, also contributed to my well-being during this project.

And of course most credit is due to my most intimate advisor and booster, the one I call "my heart," my husband, Michael, who produced his marvelous and significant book *The American Miracle: Divine Providence in the Rise of the Republic* while I labored on *Don't Divorce*. We've shared a most blessed life, and I cannot adequately express my gratitude for his protection and partnership through all of the adventures we've enjoyed and are yet to embrace.

Notes

Why You Need to Read This Book

1. US Census Bureau, "Median Age At First Marriage, 1890 to Present," Figure MS 2, https://www.census.gov/hhes/families/files/graphics/MS-2.pdf.
2. Pew Research Center, Pew Research Center analysis of U.S. decennial census (1960–2000) and American Community Survey data (2008, 2010–2014), Data Trend, "Marriage," http://www.pewresearch.org/data-trend/society-and-demographics/marriage/.
3. Pew Research Center, "U.S. Public Becoming Less Religious," November 3, 2015, Report from the Religious Landscape Study, http://www.pewforum.org/2015/11/03/u-s-public-becoming-less-religious/CHAPTER ONE.
4. Diane Medved, *The Case Against Divorce*: *Discover the Lures, the Lies, and the Emotional Traps of DivorceDiscover the Lures, the Lies, and the Emotional Traps of Divorce—Plus the Seven Vital Reasons to Stay Together* (New York: Ivy Books, 1990).

Chapter One: Stop the Divorce Momentum

1. Carol Tavris, *Anger: The Misunderstood Emotion* (New York: Simon & Schuster, 1989).
2. A central Jewish concept is the strong aversion to speaking about others (except under certain specified circumstances). "Motzi shem ra" is the name of such speech when it's malicious; "lushon ha ra" is its name when the contents of the communication are true. Both terms contain the Hebrew word for evil, "ra," because the outcome of this behavior can only be to everyone's detriment.
3. M.C. Black, et al., *The National Intimate Partner and Sexual Violence Survey (NISVS): 2010 Summary Report* (Atlanta: National Center for Injury Prevention and Control, Centers for Disease Control and Prevention, 2011), http://www.cdc.gov/ViolencePrevention/pdf/NISVS_Report2010-a.pdf.
4. Hawkins, Alan J. et al., *What Are They Thinking? A National Survey of Married Individuals Who Are Thinking about Divorce* (Provo, UT: Family Studies Center, Brigham Young University, 2015), https://www.researchgate.net/publication/283329227_What_Are_They_Thinking_A_National_Survey_of_Married_Individuals_Who_Are_Thinking_About_Divorce.
5. D'Vera Cohn et al., "Barely Half of U.S. Adults Are Married—A Record Low," Pew Research Center, December 14, 2011, http://www.pewsocialtrends.org/2011/12/14/barely-half-of-u-s-adults-are-married-a-record-low/ .
6. Obergefell v. Hodges, 576 U.S. ___ (2015), http://www.supremecourt.gov/opinions/14pdf/14-556_3204.pdf.
7. Jan Jarboe Russell,, *Lady Bird: A Biography of Mrs. Johnson* (New York: Simon & Shuster, 1999), 8–36; Betty Boyd Caroli, *Lady Bird and Lyndon: The Hidden Story of a Marriage that Made a President* (New York: Simon & Schuster, 2015).
8. Dana Mack and David Blankenhorn, eds., *The Book of Marriage: The Wisest Answers to the Toughest Questions* (Grand Rapids, MI: William B. Eerdmans Publishing Company, 2001), 21.
9. Graff, E. J., *What is Marriage For: The Strange Social History of our Most Intimate Institution*, 2004, Boston: Beacon Press, p.251.
10. Brooks, David, "Three Views of Marriage," *New York Times*, Tuesday, February 25, 2016, page A27
11. Andrew Cherlin, *The Marriage-Go-Round: The State of Marriage and the Family in America Today* (New York: Random House, 2009).
12. Analysis and Gary Langer, "Poll: Most Americans Say They're Christian," ABC News Poll, July 18, 2015, http://abcnews.go.com/US/story?id=90356.

13. "Barack Obama on Gay Marriage," YouTube video, posted by GLASSBOOTHdotORG, October 28, 2008, https://www.youtube.com/watch?v=N6K9dS9wl7U.

14. Ezriel Gelbfish, "Study on Arranged Marriages Reveals that Orthodox Jews May Have it Right," July 6, 2012, *The Algemeiner*, http://www.algemeiner.com/2012/07/06/study-on-arranged-marriages-reveals-that-orthodox-jews-may-have-it-right/# .

15. Danielle Crittenden, *What Our Mothers Didn't Tell Us: Why Happiness Eludes the Modern Woman* (New York: Simon & Schuster, 1999).

Chapter Two: The Three Divorce Magnets

1. Hannah Schacter, "Love Me Tinder: A Psychological Perspective on Swiping," Psychology in Action, April 16, 2015, http://www.psychologyinaction.org/2015/04/16/love-me-tinder-a-psychological-perspective-on-swiping/.

2. Craig Smith, "By the Numbers: 37 Impressive Tinder Statistics," DMR website (accessed May 16, 2016), http://expandedramblings.com/index.php/tinder-statistics/.

3. Justin R. Garcia et al., "Sexual Hookup Culture: A Review," Rev Gen Psychol. 16(2) (June 1, 2012): 161–176. Available through the US National Library of Medicine, National Institutes of Health: https://www.ncbi.nlm.nih.gov/pmc/articles/PMC3613286/.

4. Pornography Addiction Survey (conducted by Barna Group), 2014, ProvenMen.org., www.provenmen.org/2014pornsurvey/pornography-use-and-addiction. Another study, for the Austin Institute, reports similar results: David Gordon et al., "How Much Pornography are Americans Consuming?" in *Relationships in America Survey*, The Austin Institute for the Study of Family and Culture, February 17, 2014, http://relationshipsinamerica.com/relationships-and-sex/how-much-pornography-are-americans-consuming.

5. Kirsten Weir, "Is Pornography Addictive?" *Monitor on Psychology* 45, no. 4 (April 2014) American Psychological Association, http://www.apa.org/monitor/2014/04/pornography.aspx.

6. Peg Streep, "What Porn Does to Intimacy," *Psychology Today*, July 16, 2014, https://www.psychologytoday.com/blog/tech-support/201407/what-porn-does-intimacy.

7. Nathaniel M. Lambert, et al., "A Love That Doesn't Last: Pornography Consumption and Weakened Commitment to One's Romantic Partner," *Journal of Social and Clinical Psychology* 31, no.4 (2012): 410–438, http://www.docslides.com/pasty-toler/journal-of-social-and-clinical-psychology-vol-31-no-4-2 .

8. Andrea Marie Gwinn et al., "Pornography, Relationship Alternatives, and Intimate Extradyadic Behavior," *Social Psychological and Personality Science* 4, no. 6, (2013): 699–704.
9. Peg Streep, op. cit.
10. Amanda Maddox, Galena K. Rhoades, and Howard J. Markman, "Viewing Sexually-Explicit Materials Alone and Together: Associations with Relationship Quality," *Archives of Sexual Behavior* 40 no. 2 (April 2011): 441–448, http://www.ncbi.nlm.nih.gov/pmc/articles/PMC2891580/.
11. Jill C. Manning, MS, Testimony, *Hearing on Pornography's Impact on Marriage and the Family, Subcommittee on the Constitution, Civil Rights and Property Rights, Committee on Judiciary, United States Senate,* November 10, 2005, http://s3.amazonaws.com/thf_media/2010/pdf/ManningTST.pdf. See also Manning, "The Impact of Internet Pornography on Marriage and the Family: A Review of the Research," *Sexual Addiction & Compulsivity* 13 no. 2–3 (2006).
12. Jacque Wilson, "Viagra: The Little Blue Pill that Could," CNN, March 27, 2013, http://www.cnn.com/2013/03/27/health/viagra-anniversary-timeline/.
13. Meghan O'Dea, "Transcript: Sheryl Sandberg at the University of California at Berkeley 2016 Commencement," May 14, 2016, *Fortune*, http://fortune.com/2016/05/14/sandberg-uc-berkley-transcript/.
14. Robin J. Ely, Pamela Stone, and Colleen Ammerman, "Rethink What You "Know" About High-Achieving Women," *Harvard Business Review*, December, 2014, https://hbr.org/2014/12/rethink-what-you-know-about-high-achieving-women.
15. Anne-Marie Slaughter, "Why Women Still Can't Have it All," *The Atlantic*, July–August 2012, http://www.theatlantic.com/magazine/archive/2012/07/why-women-still-cant-have-it-all/309020/.
16. Anne-Marie Slaughter, *Unfinished Business* (New York: Random House, 2015).
17. Rebecca J. Rosen, "The Evolution of Anne-Marie Slaughter," *The Atlantic*, October 16, 2015, http://www.theatlantic.com/business/archive/2015/10/anne-marie-slaughter-evolution/410812/.
18. PR Newswire, "Elle and MSNBC.com's 'Office Sex and Romance' Survey Asks 31,207 People What Really Goes on in Today's Workplace," May 13, 2002, press release, http://www.prnewswire.com/news-releases/elle-and-msnbccoms-office-sex-and-romance-survey-asks-31207-people-what-really-goes-on-in-todays-workplace-77385087.html.
19. Christina Pesoli,"Flirting With Disaster: How Your 'Harmless' Intrigue Is Undermining Your Marriage," November 3, 2014, Huffington Post, http://

www.huffingtonpost.com/christina-pesoli/flirting-with-disaster-ho_b_3853755.html.

Chapter Three: The Danger of Detaching Marriage from Parenthood

1. Centers for Disease Control and Prevention, National Center for Health Statistics, "National Survey of Family Growth, 2011–2013," http://www.cdc.gov/nchs/nsfg/key_statistics/a.htm#marriage.

2. Sammy Cahn and Jimmy Van Heusen, "Love and Marriage," recorded in 1955 by Frank Sinatra.

3. The Bundy Cheer mirrors a technique I'd occasionally suggest as a therapist to couples with patterns of escalating irritation. Pre-select a tension-breaking phrase—like "Whoa Bundy!"—as a signal to reset the ambiance. The phrase is an instant reminder to step back, cut the tension, and remember the underlying connection in the marriage.

4. Galena K. Rhoades, Scott M. Stanley, and Howard J. Markman, "The pre-engagement cohabitation effect: A replication and extension of previous findings," *Journal of Family Psychology* 23 no. 1 (February 2009): 107–111, http://dx.doi.org/10.1037/a0014358. Quotation is from the abstract: http://psycnet.apa.org/journals/fam/23/1/107/.

5. Megan Cassidy, "Study Finds Living Together Before Marriage Leads to Greater Chance of Divorce," *Her*, October 2016, http://www.her.ie/life/study-finds-living-together-before-marriage-leads-to-greater-chance-of-divorce/286438.

6. Centers for Disease Control and Prevention, National Center for Health Statistics, "National Survey of Family Growth, 2006–2010," http://www.cdc.gov/nchs/nsfg/key_statistics/c.htm#chabitation.

7. Centers for Disease Control and Prevention, 2011–2013. http://www.cdc.gov/nchs/nsfg/key_statistics/a.htm#marriage.

8. Mike Stobbe, "Americans growing less comfortable with divorce, survey shows," Associated Press, March 16, 2016.

9. Quentin Fottrell, "America's falling fertility rate explained in four charts," Market Watch, August 18, 2015, http://www.marketwatch.com/story/americas-falling-fertility-rate-explained-in-four-charts-2015-08-18.

10. Catherine Rampell, "Americans are becoming more socially liberal—except when it comes to divorce," *Washington Post*, April 18, 2016, https://www.washingtonpost.com/opinions/socially-liberal-except-on-the-question-of-divorce/2016/04/18/f431f716-05a2-11e6-b283-e79d81c63c1b_story.html.

11.   U.S. Census Bureau, U.S. Decennial Census (1890–2000); American Community Survey (2010). For more information on the ACS, see http://www.census.gov/acs. This info from a graph at https://www.census.gov/hhes/socdemo/marriage/data/acs/ElliottetalPAA2012figs.pdf.

12.   Centers for Disease Control and Prevention, "Infertility FAQs," April 14, 2016, http://www.cdc.gov/reproductivehealth/infertility/.

13.   Lise Brix, "Childless couples have more divorces," ScienceNordic, February 14, 2014, http://sciencenordic.com/childless-couples-have-more-divorces.

14.   Brix, "Childless couples have more divorces."

15.   Mark Banschick, "The High Failure Rate of Second and Third Marriages," *Psychology Today*, February 6, 2012, https://www.psychologytoday.com/blog/the-intelligent-divorce/201202/the-high-failure-rate-second-and-third-marriages.

16.   Alison Aughinbaugh, Omar Robles, and Sun Hugette, "Marriage and divorce: patterns by gender, race, and educational attainment," U.S. Bureau of Labor Statistics, *Monthly Labor Review* (October 2014), http://www.bls.gov/opub/mlr/2013/article/marriage-and-divorce-patterns-by-gender-race-and-educational-attainment.htm.

17.   Maggie Scarf, *The Remarriage Blueprint: How Remarried Couples and Their Families Succeed or Fail* (New York: Scribner/Simon & Schuster, 2013).

Chapter Four: The Divorce Industry: Friends and Helpers You Never Wanted to Know

1.   Vikki G. Brock, *Grounded Theory of the Roots and Emergence of Coaching*, Ph.D. dissertation, International University of Professional Studies, Maui, 2008. Available online at https://www.nobco.nl/files/onderzoeken/Brock_Vikki_dissertatie__2_.pdf.

2.   IBIS World, "Life Coaches in the U.S.: Market Research Report," February 2016, http://www.ibisworld.com/industry/life-coaches.html.

3.   A site for "Expertlifecoach" offers many assurances and then a button to "buy expertlifecoach certification—$69.99." http://www.expertrating.com/certifications/Life-Coach-Certification/Life-Coach-Certification.asp.

4.   Genevieve Smith, "50,000 Life Coaches Can't Be Wrong," *Harper's*, May 2014, https://harpers.org/archive/2014/05/50000-life-coaches-cant-be-wrong/?single=1.

5.   Sam Margulies, "Marriage Counseling and the Decision to Divorce: Can marriage counseling make things worse?" *Psychology Today*, April 12, 2009, https://www.psychologytoday.com/blog/divorce-grownups/200904/marriage-counseling-and-the-decision-divorce.

6. Jed Diamond, "Why Marriage Counseling Leads to Divorce," The Good Men Project, February 22, 2015, http://goodmenproject.com/featured-content/why-marriage-counseling-leads-to-divorce-wcz/.

7. Divorce Care website: http://www.divorcecare.org/ . Seventeen thousand churches are part of this network, and the site provides links to help divorcing individuals connect with a local group, as well as descriptions of their programs.

8. Penelope Green, "Divorced, but Not from Life," *New York Times*, July 19, 2015, Sunday Styles, 1.

9. Martha C. White, "The Booming Business of 'Divorce Parties,'" *Time Magazine*, October 15, 2012, http://business.time.com/2012/10/15/the-booming-business-of-divorce-parties/.

10. Sin City Parties website, Las Vegas, Nevada (accessed May 25, 2016), http://www.mysincityparty.com/divorce-parties-las-vegas/ .

11. The Sapphire Strip Club, Las Vegas, Nevada, website accessed May 25, 2016, http://www.sapphirelasvegas.com/las_vegas_vip_services/sapphire_divorce_party/.

12. Bartz's, the party stores, website (accessed May 25, 2016), http://www.ebartz.com/divorce-party-supplies-s/3178.htm.

13. Café Press website (accessed May 26, 2016), http://www.cafepress.com/mf/50941840/not-with-stupid-anymore_invitations?productId=507121064.

14. Michelle Ruiz, "How Divorce Parties Became the New Bachelorettes," *New York*, October 12, 2012, http://nymag.com/thecut/2012/10/how-divorce-parties-became-the-new-bachelorettes.html.

15. Tia Ghose, "Awkward! How Facebook Complicates Breakups," LiveScience, August 21, 2014, http://www.livescience.com/47471-facebook-causes-breakup-stress.html#sthash.JcZex8Be.dpuf.

16. Emanuel Maiberg, "I paid this company $30 to break up with my girlfriend," Motherboard, November 12, 2015, http://motherboard.vice.com/read/i-paid-this-company-30-to-break-up-with-my-girlfriend. This post even includes the audio for the breakup phone call, and an astute analysis of its content.

17. Aimee Lee Ball, "Breaking Up? Let an App Do It," *New York Times*, December 27, 2015, Sunday Styles, 1.

18. Maiberg, "I paid this company $30 to break up with my girlfriend."

19. Rx Breakup website (accessed May 26, 2016), https://itunes.apple.com/us/app/rx-breakup/id971720226?mt=8.

20. Mend website (accessed May 26, 2016), https://www.letsmend.com/.

21. Divorce360 website: http://www.divorce360.com/ ; So You've Been Dumped website: http://www.soyouvebeendumped.com/blog/; Splitsville website: http://www.splitsville.com/.

22. Maureen O'Connor, "Winning the Breakup in the Age of Instagram," *New York*, December 2, 2014, http://nymag.com/thecut/2014/12/winning-the-breakup-in-the-age-of-instagram.html.

23. Agent Broker Training Center offers at-home study with exams: http://www.abtrainingcenter.com/CFDP.asp.

24. Website for the Association of Divorce Financial Planners: https://divorceandfinance.site-ym.com/. In comparing these divorce financial planning groups, I noticed a similarity in website wording. IDFA says it's "the premier national organization..." and ADFA says it's "the premier professional membership organization for divorce financial planners, allied divorce professionals, and students seeking advancement and development in a growing, dynamic profession." The site continues, "ADFP members are held to high educational, professional, licensing, ethical, and compliance standards, demonstrating a true commitment to professional client service." Their standards, as posted on their website, require that members must not have had licenses revoked or been convicted of a felony.

25. Jeff Landers, "The Four Divorce Alternatives," *Forbes*, April 24, 2012, http://www.forbes.com/sites/jefflanders/2012/04/24/the-four-divorce-alternatives/#279f733c1df3.

26. Avvo is an online legal service that independently rates attorneys. Users can research and post legal questions for free, get a fifteen-minute consultation for thirty-nine dollars, and use Avvo's ratings and descriptions without charge to select an attorney. The site says it was founded "in 2006 in Seattle, WA by tech-savvy attorney Mark Britton," and that 97 percent of U.S. lawyers are rated by the firm's algorithm. Site address: https://www.avvo.com/.

27. www.Legalzoom.com and www.nolo.com are two sites offering forms and articles to assist do-it-yourself divorce.

28. Salary info from "How, and How Much, Do Lawyers Charge"?, http://research.lawyers.com/how-and-how-much-do-lawyers-charge.html.

Chapter Five: Hazardous to Your Health

1. David A. Sbarra, Karen Hasselmo, and Widyasita Nojopranoto, "Divorce and Death: A Case Study for Health Psychology," *Social and Personal Psychology Compass*, 6(12) (December 1, 2012): 905–919. Available online at http://www.ncbi.nlm.nih.gov/pmc/articles/PMC3532853/.

2.   Eran Shor et al., "Meta-analysis of Marital Dissolution and Mortality: Reevaluating the Intersection of Gender and Age," *Social Science and Medicine*, 75(1) (July, 2012): 10.1016/j, available online at http://www.ncbi. nlm.nih.gov/pmc/articles/PMC3881174/ .

3.   Matthew E. Dupre et al., "Association Between Divorce and Risks for Acute Myocardial Infarction," *Circulation: Cariovascular Quality and Outcomes* 9 no. 6 (April 14, 2015), http://circoutcomes.ahajournals.org/content/ early/2015/04/13/CIRCOUTCOMES.114.001291.abstract.

4.   Ian Sample, "Marriage may improve chances of surviving a heart attack, say researchers," *The Guardian*, June 7, 2016, http://www.theguardian.com/ society/2016/jun/08/marriage-may-improve-chances-of-surviving-a-heart-attack-say-researchers.

5.   Tara Parker-Pope, "Divorce, It Seems, Can Make You Ill," *New York Times*, August 4, 2009, D5.

6.   Johan L. Vinther et al., "Marital transitions and associated changes in fruit and vegetable intake: Findings from the population-based prospective EPIC-Norfolk cohort, UK," *Social Science & Medicine* 157 (May 2016): 120–126, http://www.sciencedirect.com/science/article/pii/S0277953616301642.

7.   Alexis Blue, "Losing Sleep Over Your Divorce? Your Blood Pressure Could Suffer," UA News (press release), July 16, 2014, https://uanews.arizona.edu/ story/losing-sleep-over-your-divorce-your-blood-pressure-could-suffer.

8.   Edward Farber, *Raising the Kid You Love with the Ex You Hate* (Austin, TX: Greenleaf Press, 2013).

9.   US National Library of Medicine, "Munchausen syndrome by proxy," July 10, 2015, Medline Plus, https://www.nlm.nih.gov/medlineplus/ency/ article/001555.htm.

Chapter Six: "I Got the Shaft": The Financial Cost of Divorce

1.   Jeffrey Dew, Sonya Britt, and Sandra Huston, "Examining the Relationship Between Financial Issues and Divorce," *Family Relations* 61 no. 4 (October 2012): 615–628.

2.   Andrew M. Francis, and Hugo M. Mialon, " 'A Diamond is Forever' and Other Fairy Tales: The Relationship between Wedding Expenses and Marriage Duration," *Economic Inquiry* 53 no. 4 (October 2015), http:// onlinelibrary.wiley.com/doi/10.1111/ecin.12206/abstract.

3.   Sun Trust Bank, "Love and Money: People Say They Save, Partner Spends, According to SunTrust Survey," publicity release from PR Newswire, February 4, 2015, http://www.prnewswire.com/news-releases/

love-and-money-people-say-they-save-partner-spends-according-to-suntrust-survey-300030921.html.

4. TMZ staff, "Arnold Schwarzenegger Dragging Feet in Divorce with Maria," TMZ, October 10, 2015, http://www.tmz.com/2015/10/10/arnold-schwarzenegger-maria-shriver-divorce/.

5. Emily Jane Fox, "Rupert Murdoch, the Greatest Romantic of our Time," *Vanity Fair*, January 13, 2016, http://www.vanityfair.com/news/2016/01/rupert-murdoch-the-greatest-romantic-of-our-time.

6. Katie Kindelan, via Good Morning America, "Mel Gibson Loses Half of His $850 Million Fortune to Ex-Wife in Divorce," ABC News, December 26, 2011, http://abcnews.go.com/blogs/entertainment/2011/12/mel-gibsons-loses-half-of-his-850-million-fortune-to-ex-wife-in-divorce/.

7. "Camille Grammer Divorce Settlement Details Emerge, 'Housewives' Star Gets $30 Million," HuffPost Celebrity, September 6, 2012, http://www.huffingtonpost.com/2012/09/06/camille-grammer-divorce-settlement-30-million_n_1860913.html.

8. Pete Norman,"Heather Mills 'So Happy' with $50M Divorce Settlement," *People*, March 17, 2008, http://www.people.com/people/article/0,,20184578,00.html.

9. Brandi Fowler, "Mel Gibson Isn't the Only One: Five Other Pricey Hollywood Divorces," E Online News, December 26, 2011, http://www.eonline.com/news/282875/mel-gibson-isn-t-the-only-one-five-other-pricey-hollywood-divorces.

10. Brian Orloff, "Rep: Madonna to Pay Guy Ritchie $76 Million in Divorce Settlement," *People*, December 15, 2008, http://www.people.com/people/article/0,,20246841,00.html.

11. Dotson Rader, "Robin Williams on Returning to TV, Getting Sober, and Downsizing in His 60s," *Parade*, September 12, 2013, http://parade.com/154817/dotsonrader/robin-williams-on-returning-to-tv-getting-sober-and-downsizing-in-his-60s/.

12. Lenore Weitzman, *The Divorce Revolution: The Unexpected Social and Economic Consequences for Women and Children in America* (New York: Free Press, 1987).

13. Richard R. Peterson,"A Reevaluation of the Economic Consequences of Divorce," *American Sociological Review* 61 (June 1996): 528–536, http://boydetective.net/docs/Peterson-Weitzman-Peterson%20-%20FullASRDebate.pdf.

14. P. J. Smock, W. D. Manning and S. Gupta, "The effect of marriage and divorce on women's economic well-being," *American Sociological Review*

64, no. 6 (December 1999): 794–812, https://www.jstor.org/
stable/2657403?seq=1#page_scan_tab_contents.

15.   Jay L. Zagorsky, "Marriage and Divorces Impact on Wealth," *Journal of Sociology* 41, no. 4 (November 2005): 406–424, https://www.researchgate. net/publication/249674022_Marriage_and_Divorces_Impact_on_Wealth. Quotations are from Ohio State's press release about the study: https:// researchnews.osu.edu/archive/divwlth.htm.

16.   Robert I. Lerman, "Married and Unmarried Parenthood and Economic Well-Being: A Dynamic Analysis of a Recent Cohort," Urban Institute and American University (July 2002), http://www.urban.org/research/publication/ married-and-unmarried-parenthood-and-economic-well-being/view/full_ report.

17.   George Erb, "Mercer Island woman finds out she's financially lost after divorce," *Seattle Times*, June 28, 2015, D6.

Chapter Seven: Bad for Your Spirit

1.   Wendy Paris, *Splitopia: Dispatches from Today's Good Divorce and How to Part Well* (New York: Atrium Books, 2016),154.

2.   Nehami Baum, "The Male Way of Mourning Divorce: When, What, and How," *Clinical Social Work Journal* 31 no. 1(March 2003: 37–50.

3.   David Sbarra et al., "Divorce Elevates Risk for Depression, But Only for Some People," *Clinical Psychological Science*, August, 2013, , http://www. psychologicalscience.org/index.php/news/releases/divorce-elevates-risk-for-depression-but-only-for-some-people.html?utm_source=pressrelease&utm_ medium=vocus&utm_campaign=divorcedepression.

4.   Briefly summarized from the *DSM-5, for Major Depressive Disorder*, fifth ed. (Arlington: American Psychiatric Publishing, 2013).

5.   "Many View Depression as Weakness," *New York Times*, December 11, 1991, http://www.nytimes.com/1991/12/11/health/many-view-depression-as-weakness.html; and Lauren Pelly, "Mental illness still viewed as a sign of weakness," *Toronto Star*, June 7, 2016, https://www.thestar.com/life/health_ wellness/2016/06/07/mental-illness-still-viewed-as-a-sign-of-weakness.html.

6.   An excellent discussion of efforts to question the usefulness of antidepressants appeared July 9, 2011 in the *New York Times* by Peter D. Kramer, author of *Listening to Prozac*: http://www.nytimes.com/2011/07/10/opinion/ sunday/10antidepressants.html?_r=0.

7.   Anonymous, "What it feels like to have an affair," *Thought Catalogue*, July 3, 2014, http://thoughtcatalog.com/anonymous/2014/07/what-it-feels-like-to-have-an-affair/.

8.   Jeff Landers, "How 'Conflicting Out' Top Divorce Attorneys Can Impact Your Divorce," *Forbes*, April 17, 20012, http://www.forbes.com/sites/jefflanders/2012/04/17/how-conflicting-out-top-divorce-attorneys-can-impact-your-divorce/#52fda9b5a850.
9.   Dennis Prager, *Happiness is a Serious Problem: A Human Nature Repair Manual* (New York: William Morrow, 1998).

Chapter Eight: A Crucial Difference: Divorce with and without Children

1.   Pamela Paul, *The Starter Marriage and the Future of Matrimony* (New York: Villard Books, 2002).
2.   Mike McManus, *How to Cut America's Divorce Rate in Half: A Strategy Every State Should Adopt*, Foreword by Gov. Mike Huckabee (Potomac: Marriage Savers, Inc., 2008).
3.   Paul Edwards et al., *Summary Report: Marriage and Family—Attitudes, Practices & Policy Opinions*, The American Family Survey, Deseret News and the Center for the Study of Elections and Democracy, Brigham Young University, November, 2015, Executive Summary, 46, http://national.deseretnews.com/files/american-family-survey.pdf.

Chapter Nine: If You Love Your Children

1.   Penelope Leach, *When Parents Part: How Mothers and Fathers Can Help Their Children Deal with Separation and Divorce* (New York: Alfred A. Knopf, 2015).
2.   Leach, 15.
3.   Ibid., 35.
4.   J. E. McIntosh, "Infants and Overnights: The Drama, the Players and Their Scripts," Plenary paper, Association of Family and Conciliation Courts Forty-Ninth Annual Conference, Chicago, 2012.
5.   Leach, *When Parents Part*, 34.
6.   Ibid., 43.
7.   Ibid., 46.
8.   Ibid., 49.
9.   Ibid., 71.
10.   Edward Farber, *Raising the Kid You Love with the Ex You Hate* (Austin: Greenleaf Book Group, 2013).

11. Andrew Cherlin, *The Marriage-Go-Round: The State of Marriage and the Family in America Today* (New York: Alfred Knopf/Random House, 2009), 6.
12. Judith S. Wallerstein, Julia M. Lewis, and Sandra Blakeslee, *The Unexpected Legacy of Divorce: The 25-year Landmark Study* (New York: Hyperion Books, 2000), 6.
13. Sara McLanahan, and Gary Sandefur, *Growing Up with a Single Parent: What Hurts, What Helps* (Cambridge, MA: Harvard University Press, 1994), 1.
14. Barbara Dafoe Whitehead, *The Divorce Culture* (New York: Alfred A. Knopf, 1997).
15. David Blankenhorn, *The Future of Marriage* (New York: Encounter Books, 2007), 155.
16. Paul R. Amato and Alan Booth, *A Generation at Risk: Growing Up in an Era of Family Upheaval* (Cambridge, MA: Harvard University Press, 1997); L. Strohschein, "Parental Divorce and Child Mental Health Trajectories," *Journal of Marriage and Family* 67 (2005):1286–1300.
17. Constance Ahrons, Ph.D., *We're Still Family: What Grown children Have to Say About Their Parents' Divorce* (New York: HarperCollins, 2004, HarperCollins), 52-61. Only her "high conflict" marriages were so dysfunctional or harmful that the children were relieved upon their dissolution.
18. Divorcesource website (accessed April 20, 2016), http://www.divorcesource.com/ds/considering/most-marriages-and-divorces-are-low-conflict-483.shtml.
19. Elizabeth Marquardt, *Between Two Worlds: The Inner Lives of Children of Divorce* (New York: Three Rivers Press, 2005).
20. Elisabeth Joy LaMotte, MSW, LICSW, AAMFT, *Overcoming Your Parents' Divorce: 5 Steps to a Happy Relationship* (Far Hills, NJ: New Horizon Press, 2008).
21. Lamotte's steps are (1) Rewrite your history (look back with adult eyes), (2) face the mirror (note the effect of divorce on yourself), (3) confront your commitment phobia, (4) calculate your dividend (i.e., the good that came from the divorce), and (5) forge healthy relationships.
22. Paul R. Amado, Jennifer B. Kane, and Spencer James, "Reconsidering the 'Good Divorce,'" *Family Relations*, 60 no. 5 (December, 2011): 511–524, https://www.ncbi.nlm.nih.gov/pmc/articles/PMC3223936/.
23. Cherlin, *Marriage-Go-Round*.

24. L. Laumann-Billings and R. E. Emery, "Distress among young adults from divorced families," *Journal of Family Psychology* 14 no. 4 (December 2000): 671–687.

25. Esme Fuller-Thomson, J. Fillippelli, and C. A. Lue-Crisostomo, "Gender-specific association between childhood adversities and smoking in adulthood: findings from a population-based study," *Journal of Public Health* 127 no. 5 (May, 2013): 449–460, http://www.publichealthjrnl.com/article/S0033-3506(13)00007-3/abstract.

26. Jane Mauldon, "The Effect of Marital Disruption on Children's Health," *Demography* 27 no. 3 (August 1990), http://link.springer.com/article/10.2307%2F2061377#page-1.

27. Hyun Sik Kim, "Consequences of Parental Divorce for Child Development," *American Sociological Review* 76 no. 3 (June 2011): 487-511, http://asr.sagepub.com/content/76/3/487.short.

28. Lisa Strohschein, Noralou Roos, and Marni Brownell, "Family Structure Histories and High School Completion: Evidence from a Population-Based Registry," *Canadian Journal of Sociology* 34, no. 1 (2009), https://ejournals.library.ualberta.ca/index.php/CJS/article/view/1331/5152.

29. S. Alexandra Burt, Ph.D. et al., "Parental Divorce and Adolescent Delinquency: Ruling out the Impact of Common Genes," *Developmental Psychology* 44 no. 6 (November, 2008): 1668–1677, http://www.ncbi.nlm.nih.gov/pmc/articles/PMC2593091/.

30. Grechen Livingston, "Fewer than half of U.S. kids today live in a 'traditional' family," Pew Research Center, December 22, 2014, http://www.pewresearch.org/fact-tank/2014/12/22/less-than-half-of-u-s-kids-today-live-in-a-traditional-family/.

31. McLanahan, and Sandefur, *Growing Up with a Single Parent*, 24.

32. Nicholas Wolfinger, *Understanding the Divorce Cycle: The Children of Divorce in Their Own Marriages* (New York: Cambridge University Press, 2005).

33. Dana, G. Thompson Alonso, Ph.D., Malka Stohl, MS, and Deborah Hasin, Ph.D., "The Influence of Parental Divorce and Alcohol Abuse on Adult Offspring Risk of Lifetime Suicide Attempt in the United States," *American Journal of Orthopsychiatry* (May 2014).

34. Thomas DeLeire and Leonard M. Lopoo, "Family Structure and the Economic Mobility of Children," The Economic Mobility Project, an initiative of the Pew Charitable Trusts, 2010, http://www.pewtrusts.org/~/media/legacy/uploadedfiles/pcs_assets/2010/familystructurepdf.pdf.

35. Linda J. Waite, and Maggie Gallagher, *The Case For Marriage: Why Married People Are Happier, Healthier, and Better Off Financially* (New York: Doubleday, 2000), 118. Italics added.

36. Rachel Emma Silverman, and Michelle Higgins, "When the Kids Get the House in a Divorce," *Wall Street Journal*, September 17, 2003, D1.

37. Anna Davies, "Is Birdnesting the stupidest—or smartest—divorce trend yet?" *New York Post*, April 28, 2016, , http://nypost.com/2016/04/28/is-birdnesting-the-stupidest-or-smartest-divorce-trend-yet/.

38. Lara Adair, "When parents divorce and the house gets the children," *San Francisco Chronicle*, August 10, 2005, http://www.sfgate.com/homeandgarden/article/When-parents-divorce-and-the-house-gets-the-2648936.php.

39. Eleanor E. Maccoby, and Robert H. Mnookin, *Dividing the Child: Social and Legal Dilemmas of Custody* (Cambridge, MA; Harvard University Press, 1998).

40. Ronnie Koeni, "Divorced Parents, Living Close for the Children's Sake," *New York Times*, January 15, 2016, http://www.nytimes.com/2016/01/17/realestate/divorced-parents-living-close-for-the-childrens-sake.html?_r=0.

41. Ibid.

42. E. Mavis Hetherington and John Kelly, *For Better or for Worse: Surprising Results from the Most Comprehensive Study of Divorce in America* (New York: Norton, 2002).

43. Martin Seligman, Ph.D., "Resilience Training for Educators," University of Pennsylvania Authentic Happiness, https://www.authentichappiness.sas.upenn.edu/learn/educatorresilience.

44. Anthony Scioli and Henry B. Biller, *Hope in the Age of Anxiety* (New York: Oxford University Press, 2009); Scioli and Biller, *The Power of Hope: Overcoming Your Most Daunting Life Difficulties—No Matter What* (Deerfield Beach, FL: Health Communications, Inc., 2010).

45. Therese J. Borchard, "5 Ways to Build and Sustain Hope: An Interview with Anthony Scioli," Psychcentral.com, January 17, 2010, http://psychcentral.com/blog/archives/2010/01/17/5-ways-to-build-and-sustain-hope-an-interview-with-anthony-scioli/.

46. Scioli and Biller, *The Power of Hope*, 57.

47. Ahrons, *We're Still Family*, 199.

48. An excellent collection of essays about childhood temperament is available online: Mary K. Rothbart, "Temperament," Encyclopedia on Early Childhood Development, June 2012, http://www.child-encyclopedia.com/sites/default/files/dossiers-complets/en/temperament.pdf.

49. Rosalind Sedacca, "Depression and Divorce: Helping Your Children Cope With Both," The Huffington Post, August 11, 2012, http://www. huffingtonpost.com/rosalind-sedacca/depression-and-divorce-he_b_1582445.html.

50. "An Overview of the Psychological Literature of the Effects of Divorce on Children," American Psychological Association, May 2004, http://www.apa. org/about/gr/issues/cyf/divorce.aspx.

51. Diane N. Lye, Ph.D., "What Parents Say: Washington State Parents Talk About the Parenting Act," Report to the Washington State Gender and Justice Commission and Domestic Relations Commission, June 1999, https://www. courts.wa.gov/committee/pdf/parentingplanstudy.pdf.

52. Dennis Prager, "The Fallacy of 'White Privilege,'" *National Review Online*, February 16, 2016, http://www.nationalreview.com/node/431393/print.

53. Robert E. Emery, "How Divorced Parents Lost their Rights," *New York Times Sunday Review*, September 7, 2014, SR5.

54. Ruth Teichroeb, "One Size Doesn't fit all Families in Divorce, Study Says," *The Seattle Post-Intelligencer*, October 4, 1999, B1.

55. Kim Parker, "Five Facts About Today's Fathers," Pew Research Center Fact-tank June 18, 2015, http://www.pewresearch.org/fact-tank/2015/06/18/5-facts-about-todays-fathers/.

56. Many studies document the decline in marital satisfaction occasioned by the birth of the first child, and continuing its descent through the following fifteen years. For example, see Gilad Hirschberger et al., "Attachment, Marital Satisfaction, and Divorce During the First Fifteen Years of Parenthood," *Personal Relationships* 16 no. 3 (September, 2009): 401–420, http://www. ncbi.nlm.nih.gov/pmc/articles/PMC3061469/.

57. Ana Swanson, "144 Years of Marriage and Divorce in the United States in One Chart," *Washington Post*, June 23, 2015, https://www.washingtonpost. com/news/wonk/wp/2015/06/23/144-years-of-marriage-and-divorce-in-the-united-states-in-one-chart/.

58. David Blankenhorn, *Fatherless America: Confronting Our Most Urgent Social Problem* (New York: Basic Books, 1997), 117.

59. Woody Allen on Wikiquotes: https://en.wikiquote.org/wiki/Woody_Allen.

60. Paul Raeburn, *Do Fathers Matter? What Science Is Telling Us About the Parent We've Overlooked* (New York: Scientific American/Farrar, Straus and Giroux, 2014), 227. Italics added.

61. Anthony DeBenedet, M.D., and Lawrence J. Cohen, Ph.D., *The Art of Roughhousing* (Philadelphia: Quirk Books, 2011), 13.

62.   Bruce Sallan, *A Dad's Point of View: We ARE Half the Equation*, with a foreword by Diane and Michael Medved (Los Angeles: Bruce Sallan publisher, 2011). Bruce's website is http://www.brucesallan.com/.

63.   Branislaw Malinowski, *Argonauts of the Western Pacific: An Account of Native Enterprise and Adventure in the Archipelagoes of Melanesian New Guinea* (London: Routledge and Kegan Paul, 1922). Enhanced Edition reissued by Waveland Press, 2013.

64.   David Blankenhorn, *The Future of Marriage* (New York: Encounter Books, 2007), 70–71.

65.   Gretchen Livingston, and Kim Parker, "A Tale of Two Fathers: More Are Active but More Are Absent," Pew Research Center, June 15, 2011 , http://www.pewsocialtrends.org/2011/06/15/a-tale-of-two-fathers/. Data for 2011 are from Kim Parker, "6 Facts about American Fathers," FactTank, Pew Research Center, June 18, 2015, http://www.pewresearch.org/fact-tank/2015/06/18/5-facts-about-todays-fathers/.

66.   Parker, "6 Facts about American Fathers."

67.   Ibid.

68.   Dr. Lawrence Birnbach, and Dr. Beverly Hyman, *How to Know If It's Time to Go: A 10-Step Reality Test for Your Marriage* (New York: Sterling Ethos, 2010).

69.   Max Sindell, *The Bright Side: Surviving Your Parents' Divorce* (Deerfield, FL: Health Communications, Inc., 2007).

70.   Michael Medved, and Diane Medved, Ph.D., *Saving Childhood: Protecting Our Children from the National Assault on Innocence* (New York: HarperCollins, 1998).

71.   Dr. John Gottman is famous for recording and decoding couples' interactions, and he might have given this family little hope. Nevertheless, his typology of couples includes "volatile" couples who chew on problems and accept head-on confrontation. "They seem to love to debate and argue," Dr. Gottman notes in *Principia Amoris* (New York: Routledge, 2015), 118, but do so without disrespect. They, like two other types of couples he describes, are "Happy-Stable" and do "just fine." However, hostile-detached couples have a poorer prognosis.

72.   Ann Lukits, "Children Have the Power to Change Parents' Habits," *Wall Street Journal*, April 19, 2016, D4.

Chapter Ten: The Ruinous Ripples of Divorce

1.   Carol Tavris, *Anger: The Misunderstood Emotion* (New York: Touchstone/Simon and Schuster, 1989).

2. Brad J. Bushman, "Does Venting Anger Feed or Extinguish the Flame? Catharsis, Rumination, Distraction, Anger, and Aggressive Responding," *Personality and Social Psychology Bulletin* 28 no. 6, (June 2002): 724–731.
3. Elizabeth Bernstein,"Venting Isn't Good for Us," *Wall Street Journal*, November 11, 2015, D1.
4. Slater and Gordon, "Social Media is the New Marriage Minefield," press release, April 30, 2015, http://www.slatergordon.co.uk/media-centre/press-releases/2015/04/social-media-is-the-new-marriage-minefield/.
5. American Academy of Matrimonial Lawyers, "Big Surge in Social Networking Evidence Says Survey of Nation's Top Divorce Lawyers," press release, February 10, 2010, http://www.aaml.org/about-the-academy/press/press-releases/e-discovery/big-surge-social-networking-evidence-says-survey-.
6. Sebastian Valenzuela, Daniel Halpern, and James E. Katz, "Social network sites, marriage well-being and divorce: Survey and state-level evidence from the United States," *Computers in Human Behavior* 36 (July 2014): 94–101, http://www.sciencedirect.com/science/article/pii/S0747563214001563.
7. D. J. Kuss and M. D. Griffiths, "Online social networking and addiction: A review of the psychological literature," *International Journal of Environmental Research and Public Health* 8 (2011): 3528–3552.
8. Keith Hampton et al., "Social networking sites and our lives," Pew Research Center, June 16, 2011, pewinternet.org/Reports/2011/Technology-and-social-networks.aspx.
9. Nicoletta Balboa and Nicola Barban, "Does Fertility Behavior Spread among Friends?" *American Sociological Review* 79, no. 3 (2014): 412–431, http://www.asanet.org/sites/default/files/savvy/journals/ASR/Jun14ASRFeature.pdf. Using data from the National Longitudinal Study of Adolescent Health, researchers followed an American female cohort of 1,726 girls from middle and high school into their late twenties and early thirties (1995–2009), identifying pairs of long-term friends and controlling for factors like race, location, and marital status.
10. Balboa and Barban, "Friend and Peer Effects on Entry into Marriage and Parenthood: A Multiprocess Approach," Dondena Working Papers No. 056., 2013, https://ideas.repec.org/p/don/donwpa/056.html.
11. Rose McDermott, Ph.D., James Fowler, Ph.D., and Nicholas Christakis, M.D., Ph.D., M.P.H., "Breaking Up Is Hard to Do, Unless Everyone Else is Doing it Too: Social Network Effects on Divorce in a Longitudinal Sample," *Social Forces* 92, no. 2 (December 2013): 491–519, http://www.ncbi.nlm.nih.gov/pmc/articles/PMC3990282/. These researchers studied parents and their children participating in the longitudinal Framingham Heart Study—a total

of ten thousand subjects—involving several check-back re-examinations over thirty-two years.

12. McDermott, Fowler and Christakis, "Breaking Up is Hard to Do."

13. Ibid.

14. Alan Booth, John N. Edwards, and David R. Johnson, "Social Integration and Divorce,"*Social Forces* 70, no. 1 (1991): 207–224.

15. "Grandparents' Rights in Custody and Visitation," Divorce Source, Inc., http://www.divorcesource.com/ds/grandparentsrights/grandparent-s-rights-in-custody-and-visitation-566.shtml.

16. "Parent and Grandparent Animosity in Custody Issues," Divorce Source, Inc., http://www.divorcesource.com/ds/grandparentsrights/parent-and-grandparent-animosity-in-custody-issues-567.shtml.

17. Steve Salerno, "Not All in the Family," *New York Times* magazine, November 17, 2003, 60.

18. McDermott, Fowler, and Christakis, "Breaking Up Is Hard to Do."

19. Donna Bobbitt-Zeher, Douglas Downy, and Joseph Merry, "Are There Long-Term Consequences to Growing Up Without Siblings? Likelihood of Divorce Among Only Children," presented on Tuesday, August 13, 2013, at the American Sociological Association's 108th Annual Meeting, New York.

20. Ann Patchett, "My Despised Family Party," *New York Times* March 15, 2016, D6.

21. M. Christian Green, " 'There but for the Grace': The Ethics of Bystanders to Divorce," *Propositions*, July 2012, Institute for American Values, http://americanvalues.org/catalog/pdfs/2012-07.pdf.

22. Sue Shellenbarger, "Co-Workers Can Wreck a Marriage: At the Office, Divorce Is Contagious," *Wall Street Journal*, November 13, 2003, D1, http://www.wsj.com/articles/SB10686862404494500.

Chapter Eleven: When Divorce Is Necessary: How to Know When to Quit

1. Austin Institute, "Divorce in America: Who Wants Out and Why," February 17, 2014, http://www.austin-institute.org/research/divorce-in-america/.

2. National Institute on Drug Abuse, "How Many People Abuse Prescription Drugs?" November, 2014, https://www.drugabuse.gov/publications/research-reports/prescription-drugs/trends-in-prescription-drug-abuse/how-many-people-abuse-prescription-drugs.

3. National Institute on Drug Abuse, "Popping Pills: Prescription Drug Abuse in America," January, 2014, https://www.drugabuse.gov/related-topics/

trends-statistics/infographics/popping-pills-prescription-drug-abuse-in-america.

4. Al-Anon Family Group Message Board, "The topic: Divorce," November 29, 2010, http://alanon.activeboard.com/t39610454/divorce/.

5. Susan Pease Gadoua, "So You're Married to An Addict: Is Divorce Inevitable?" *Psychology Today*, September 11, 2011, https://www.psychologytoday.com/blog/contemplating-divorce/201109/so-youre-married-addict-is-divorce-inevitable.

6. Gregory Jantz, Ph.D., with Ann McMurray, *Healing the Scars of Emotional Abuse*, 3rd ed. (Grand Rapids, MI: Revell, 2009), 12.

7. Patricia Evans, *The Verbally Abusive Relationship* (Avon, MA: Adams Media, 1992, 2010), 228.

8. Louise Rafkin, "Booming: Lessons Learned When It's All Over," *New York Times*, August 9, 2013, Style Section.

9. Rafkin, "A Doctor Who Played Gigs, Until the Music Stopped," *New York Times*, January 10, 2016, ST 13.

10. Bruce Derman and Wendy Gregson, "Are You Really Ready for Divorce? The 8 Questions You Need to Ask," Mediate.com, http://www.mediate.com/articles/dermanGregson1.cfm. Mediate.com, a commercial website, "serves as a bridge between professionals offering mediation services and people needing mediation services."

Chapter Twelve: It's About *You*

1. Eileen Patten and Kim Parker, "A Gender Reversal On Career Aspirations," Pew Research Center, April 19, 2012, http://www.pewsocialtrends.org/2012/04/19/a-gender-reversal-on-career-aspirations/.

2. Mark Banschick, M.D., "The High Failure Rate of Second and Third Marriages," *Psychology Today*, February 6, 2012, https://www.psychologytoday.com/blog/the-intelligent-divorce/201202/the-high-failure-rate-second-and-third-marriages.

3. Kalman Heller, "Improving the Odds for Successful Second Marriage," *Psych Central*, October 30, 2015, reprinted from ParentTalk online column, http://psychcentral.com/lib/improving-the-odds-for-successful-second-marriages/?all=1.

4. Fiona Macrae, "Couples in second marriages are 'less likely to get divorced' because they benefit from experience of the first," *The Daily Mail*, April 29, 2013, http://www.dailymail.co.uk/news/article-2316323/Couples-second-marriages-likely-divorced-benefit-experience-first.html.

5. Cclowe12345, "Children Divide and Conquer Parents," MD Junction, June 30, 2010, http://www.mdjunction.com/forums/blended-families-stepparenting-discussions/general-support/1640904-children-divide-and-conquer-parents.

6. Elizabeth Bernstein, "Secrets of a Second Marriage: Beat the 8-Year Itch," *Wall Street Journal*, September 20, 2011, D1.

7. Austin Institute, "Divorce in America: Who Wants Out and Why," February 17, 2014, http://www.austin-institute.org/research/divorce-in-america/.

8. 8   Francesca Di Meglio, "Top 10 Signs of a Meddling Mother-in-law," About.com, Relationships, http://newlyweds.about.com/od/familyfriends/tp/Top-10-Signs-Of-A-Meddling-Mother-In-Law.htm.

9. Carolyn Hax, "A mother-in-law won't take 'no' for an answer" *Washington Post*, May 4, 2015, https://www.washingtonpost.com/lifestyle/style/carolyn-hax-a-mother-in-law-wont-take-no-for-an-answer/2015/05/03/b5d476bc-e918-11e4-9a6a-c1ab95a0600b_story.html#comments.

10. Melissa R. Fales et al., "Mating markets and bargaining hands: Mate preferences for attractiveness and resources in two national U.S. studies," *Personality and Individual Differences* 88, no. 78 (January, 2016), 10.1016/j.paid.2015.08.041.

Chapter Thirteen: "It's All About *Me*"

1. Austin Institute, "Divorce in America: Who Wants Out and Why."

2. Mark D. White, "Serial Adultery: Is It Chance or Character?" *Psychology Today*, April 19, 2010, https://www.psychologytoday.com/blog/maybe-its-just-me/201004/serial-adultery-is-it-chance-or-character.

3. Tara Parker-Pope, "Divorcing a Narcissist," *New York Times*, August 24, 2015, http://well.blogs.nytimes.com/2015/08/24/divorcing-a-narcissist/?_r=0.

4. Susan Krauss Whitbourne, "Two Warning Signs that Your Relationship May Not Last," *Psychology Today*, June 11, 2013, https://www.psychologytoday.com/blog/fulfillment-any-age/201306/two-warning-signs-your-relationship-may-not-last.

5. National Alliance for Borderline Personality Disorder, http://www.borderlinepersonalitydisorder.com/what-is-bpd/bpd-overview/.

6. For the research Dr. Whitbourne discusses, see K. L. Disney, Y. Weinstein, and T. F. Oltmanns, "Personality disorder symptoms are differentially related to divorce frequency," *Journal of Family Psychology* 26 no. 6 (2012): 959–965.

7. Austin Institute, "Divorce in America: Who Wants Out and Why."

8. Lara Bazelon, "From Divorce, a Fractured Beauty," *New York Times*, September 27, 2015, ST6.

Chapter Fourteen: "It's *Nobody's* Fault"

1. Esriel Gelbfish, "Study on Arranged Marriages Reveals Orthodox Jews May Have it Right," *The Algemeiner*, July 6, 2012, http://www.algemeiner.com/2012/07/06/study-on-arranged-marriages-reveals-that-orthodox-jews-may-have-it-right/#.
2. Utpal M. Dholakia, "Why Are So Many Indian Arranged Marriages Successful?" *Psychology Today*, November 24, 2015, https://www.psychologytoday.com/blog/the-science-behind-behavior/201511/why-are-so-many-indian-arranged-marriages-successful.
3. "Indians Swear by Arranged Marriages," *India Today*, March 4, 2013, http://indiatoday.intoday.in/story/indians-swear-by-arranged-marriages/1/252496.html.
4. Dholakia, "Why Are So Many Indian Arranged Marriages Successful?"
5. Gelbfish, "Study on Arranged Marriages Reveals Orthodox Jews May Have it Right."
6. Aron Moss, "Why Get Married?" *Chabad.org*, http://www.chabad.org/library/article_cdo/aid/482475/jewish/Why-Get-Married.htm.
7. Stanley Fish, "Marital Disputes: A Survival Guide," *Wall Street Journal*, July 2–3, 2016, C3.
8. Ibid.
9. Michael Fulwiler, "The 5 Types of Couples," The Gottman Institute, November 22, 2014, https://www.gottman.com/blog/the-5-couple-types/.
10. Rabbi Joseph Telushkin, *A Code of Jewish Ethics, Volume I, You Shall Be Holy* (New York: Bell Tower/Crown/Random House 2006),339.
11. Kristin Wong, "The 8 Most Common Reasons for Divorce," MSN Survey, July 24, 2014, http://www.msn.com/en-us/lifestyle/marriage/the-8-most-common-reasons-for-divorce/ss-AA3gtcM.

Chapter Fifteen: There's No Such Thing as a Good Divorce

1. Constance Ahrons, Ph.D., *The Good Divorce: Keeping Your Family Together When Your Marriage Comes Apart* (New York: Quill/HarperCollins, 1994)
2. Ahrons, *The Good Divorce*, 3.
3. Ibid., 51.
4. Constance Ahrons, Ph.D., *We're Still Family: What Grown Children Have to Say About Their Parents' Divorce* (New York: HarperCollins, 2004).

5. Ahrons, *We're Still Family*, 44.
6. Ibid., 235.
7. Ahrons, *The Good Divorce*, 250.
8. Norval Glenn, "How good for children is the 'good divorce'?" *Propositions* 7, The Institute for American Values, April 2012.
9. Paul Amato and Alan Booth, "Parental Pre-Divorce Relations and Offspring Post-Divorce Well-Being," *Journal of Marriage and Family* 63, no. 1(February, 2001): 197–212.
10. Belinda Luscombe, "Why 25% of Millenials Will Not Get Married," Time, September 24, 2014, http://time.com/3422624/report-millennials-marriage/.
11. Wendy Paris, *Splitopia: Dispatches from Today's Good Divorce and How to Part Well* (New York: Atria/Simon and Schuster, 2016).

Chapter Sixteen: "Do Your Duty" or "Follow Your Heart"?

1. Esther Perel, "Why Happy Couples Cheat," TED Talks, May 21, 2015, YouTube access at https://www.youtube.com/watch?v=P2AUat93a8Q.
2. Karl Pillemer, "Seven Things Elders Want to Tell You About Marriage," The Legacy Project, Lessons for Living from the Wisest Americans, July 6, 2015, http://legacyproject.human.cornell.edu/category/love-and-marriage/.
3. Zach Brittle, "Turn Towards Instead of Away," The Gottman Institute blog, April 1, 2015, https://www.gottman.com/blog/turn-toward-instead-of-away/.

Chapter Seventeen: Divorce Won't Make You Happier

1. Linda J. Waite et al., *Does Divorce Make People Happy? Findings from a Study of Unhappy Marriages* (New York: Institute for American Values, 2002), 4–5, http://americanvalues.org/catalog/pdfs/does_divorce_make_people_happy.pdf.
2. Jason Taylor, "Baby, come back! Most people regret getting divorced," *Express* (London), August 17, 2014, http://www.express.co.uk/news/uk/500492/Most-divorcees-regret-marriage-break-up.
3. Gemma Gillard, "Do you regret getting divorced? Astonishing 50 per cent of people wish they had never ended their marriage," The Daily Mail.com, August 18, 2014, http://www.dailymail.co.uk/femail/article-2727716/Is-going-separate-ways-really-good-idea-Astonishing-50-divorcees-regret-breaking-partner.html.
4. Pamela Paul, *The Starter Marriage and the Future of Matrimony* (New York: Villard Books, 2002), 251.
5. Paul, *The Starter Marriage and the Future of Matrimony*, 252.

6.   "The Invention of the Teenager," UShistory.org, Independence Hall Association, copyright 2016, http://www.ushistory.org/us/46c.asp.

7.   Karen Jerabeck et al., *The Mini Marriage: 5 Bite-Sized Memoirs of Young Divorce* (CreateSpace Independent Publishing Platform, 2010), 8.

8.   Sascha Rothchild, *How to Get Divorced by 30: My Misguided Attempt at a Starter Marriage* (New York: Plume, 2010).

9.   Sascha Rothchild, "In Defense of Starter Marriage," *Your Tango*, June 9, 2010, http://www.yourtango.com/201072875/in-defense-of-starter-marriage.

10. Barbara Bradley Hagerty "8 Ways You Can Survive—And Thrive In—Midlife," NPR, March 26, 2016, http://www.npr.org/2016/03/17/469822644/8-ways-you-can-survive-and-thrive-in-midlife.

11. Carol D. Ryff and Corey Lee M. Keyes, "The Structure of Psychological Well-Being Revisited," *Journal of Personality and Social Psychology* 69 no. 4 (1995): 719–727.

12. Susan L. Brown, and I-Fen Lin, "The Gray Divorce Revolution: Rising Divorce Among Middle-Aged and Older Adults, 1990–2010," *Journal of Gerontology, Psychological Science and Social Sciences* 67 no. 6 (November 2012); 731–741. Published online October 18, 2012. DOI: 10.1093/geronb/gbs089.

13. Susan L. Brown, and I-Fen Lin, *Divorce in Middle and Later Life: New Estimates from the 2009 American Community Survey*, Center for Family and Demographic Research, Bowling Green State University, 2010, http://paa2011.princeton.edu/abstracts/110947.

14. Brown and Lin, "The Gray Divorce Revolution," 731–741.

15. Xenia P. Montenegro, Ph.D., "The Divorce Experience: A Study of Divorce at Midlife and Beyond," Knowledge Networks, Inc., Commissioned by *AARP* the magazine, May 2004, http://assets.aarp.org/rgcenter/general/divorce.pdf
.

Chapter Eighteen: The Grass Isn't Greener on the Singles Side of the Fence

1.   Bella De Paulo, "Everything You Think You Know About Single People is Wrong," *Washington Post*, February 8, 2016, , https://www.washingtonpost.com/news/in-theory/wp/2016/02/08/everything-you-think-you-know-about-single-people-is-wrong/. See also DePaulo, *Marriage vs. Singles' Life: How Science and the Media Got it so Wrong*, CreateSpace Independent Publishing Platform February 24, 2015.

2. Linda Waite and Maggie Gallagher, *The Case for Marriage: Why Married People are Happier, Healthier and Better Off Financially* (New York: Doubleday, 2000).
3. Wendy Wang and Kim Parker, "Record Share of Americans Have Never Married," The Pew Research Center, September 24, 2014, http://www.pewsocialtrends.org/2014/09/24/record-share-of-americans-have-never-married/.
4. Kelly Musick and Larry Bumpass, "Reexamining the Case for Marriage: Union Formation and Changes in Well-being," *Journal of Marriage and Family* 74 no. 1 (2012), http://www.ncbi.nlm.nih.gov/pmc/articles/PMC3352182/.
5. Wang and Parker, "Record Share of Americans Have Never Married."
6. Frank Newport and Joy Wilke, "Most in U.S. Want Marriage, but Its Importance Has Dropped," Gallup, August 2, 2013, http://www.gallup.com/poll/163802/marriage-importance-dropped.aspx.
7. Emily Miller, "Top 10: Reasons Why Women Won't Date Single Dads," AskMen, April 19, 2010, http://www.askmen.com/top_10/dating/top-10-reasons-why-women-wont-date-single-dads.html.
8. Miller, "Top 10: Reasons Why Women Won't Date Single Dads."
9. Centers for Disease Control and Prevention, Center for National Health Statistics, "Number of Sexual Partners in Lifetime, 2011-2013," National Survey of Family Growth, http://www.cdc.gov/nchs/nsfg/key_statistics/n.htm#numberlifetime.
10. Natalie Kitroeff, "In Hookups, Inequality Still Reigns," *New York Times*, November 11, 2013, D1, http://well.blogs.nytimes.com/2013/11/11/women-find-orgasms-elusive-in-hookups/?_php=true&_type=blogs&_php=true&_type=blogs&_r=2.
11. Kitroeff, "In Hookups, Inequality Still Reigns."
12. Amy Sohn, "Back in the Saddle Again," *New York*, May 16, 2005, http://nymag.com/nymetro/nightlife/sex/columns/mating/11927/.
13. Aaron Smith and Monica Anderson, "5 facts about online dating," Pew Research Center, February 29, 2016, http://www.pewresearch.org/fact-tank/2016/02/29/5-facts-about-online-dating/.
14. Quentin Fottrell, "10 things dating sites won't tell you," Market Watch, August 19, 2015, http://www.marketwatch.com/story/10-things-dating-sites-wont-tell-you-2013-02-08?page=1.
15. AARP, "Top 20 Senior Dating Sites," http://www.top20seniordatingsites.com/product/aarp-dating/.
16. Fottrell, "10 things dating sites won't tell you."

17. Jessica Shambora, "eHarmony's algorithm of love," *Fortune*, September 23, 2010, http://fortune.com/2010/09/23/eharmonys-algorithm-of-love/.

18. Amy Webb, "How I Hacked Online Dating," TED Talks, October 2, 2013, https://www.youtube.com/watch?v=d6wG_sAdP0U; see also Webb, *Data, A Love Story*: *How I Cracked the Online Dating Code to Meet My Match* (New York: Plume, 2014).

19. Greg Hodge, "The Ugly Truth of Online Dating: Top 10 Lies Told by Internet Daters," Huffington Post, October 10, 2012, http://www.huffingtonpost. com/greg-hodge/online-dating-lies_b_1930053.html. Direct link to survey: https://beautifulpeoplecdn.s3.amazonaws.com/studies/usa_studies. pdf#page=2.

20. Smith and Anderson, "5 facts about online dating."

21. "One-Third of Married Couples Meet Online: Study," *Daily News*, June 4, 2013, http://www.nydailynews.com/life-style/one-third-u-s-marriages-start-online-dating-study-article-1.1362743.

22. Kelly Musick, and Larry Bumpass, "Re-Examining the Case for Marriage: Union Formation and Changes in Well-Being," *Journal of Marriage and the Family* 74 no. 1 (February 1, 2012):.1–18, http://www.ncbi.nlm.nih.gov/pmc/ articles/PMC3352182/.

23. Reed Tucker, "Sorry, ladies, there really is a man shortage," *New York Post*, August 25, 2015, http://nypost.com/2015/08/25/hey-ladies-here-are-8-reasons-youre-single/; Jon Birger, *Date-Onomics: How Dating Became a Lopsided Numbers Game* (New York: Workman, 2015).

24. John M. Grohol, Psy.D., "What is Commitment Phobia & Relationship Anxiety?" *Psych Central*, January 8, 2015, http://psychcentral.com/blog/ archives/2015/01/08/what-is-commitment-phobia-relationship-anxiety/.

Chapter Nineteen: Rebuilding Trust after Betrayal

1.   Austin Institute for the Study of Family and Culture, "Relationships in America" 2014, http://relationshipsinamerica.com/.

2.   Richard Wike, "5 ways Americans and Europeans are different," Pew Research Center Fact Tank, April 19, 2016, http://www.pewresearch.org/ fact-tank/2016/04/19/5-ways-americans-and-europeans-are-different/.

3.   Esther Perel, "Why Happy Couples Cheat," TED talks, YouTube, May 21, 2015, https://www.youtube.com/watch?v=P2AUat93a8Q.

4.   Anne Bercht, *My Husband's Affair Became the Best Thing That Ever Happened to Me* (Victoria, Canada: Trafford Publishing, 2004).

5.   Anne Bercht, "How Could I Choose Such an Outrageous Title for My Book?" Beyond Affairs Network October 22, 2013, http://beyondaffairs.com/20-top-articles/how-could-i-choose-such-an-outrageous-title/.

6.   Donna Anderson, "Sociopaths and Double Lives," LoveFraud.com, March 26, 2012, http://www.lovefraud.com/2012/03/26/sociopaths-and-double-lives/.

7.   Eugene Volokh, "The First Amendment protects a right to engage in adultery?" *Washington Post*, June 16, 2014, https://www.washingtonpost.com/news/volokh-conspiracy/wp/2014/06/16/the-first-amendment-protects-a-right-to-engage-in-adultery/.

8.   Deuteronmy 22:22 and Leviticus 20:10.

9.   "Porn in the Pulpit and the Pews," study conducted by the Barna Group, commissioned by Josh McDowell's ministry, April, 2016, published in *Christianity Today*, 24–25.

10. John Gottman, Ph.D. and Nan Silver, *What Makes Love Last? How to Build Trust and Avoid Betrayal* (New York: Simon & Schuster, 2012), 80.

11. Irene Tsapelas, Helen E. Fisher, and Arthur Aron, "Infidelity: When, Where, Why," in William R. Cupach and Brian H. Spitzberg, *The Dark Side of Close Relationships II* (New York: Routledge, 2010), 175–196. Available online at http://www.helenfisher.com/downloads/articles/INFIDELITY.pdf.

12. Elizabeth Bernstein, "How Often Should Married Couples have Sex?" *Wall Street Journal*, April 22, 2013, http://www.wsj.com/articles/SB1000142412 7887324874204578438713861797052.

13. A. Muise, U. Schimmack, and E. A. Impett, "Sexual frequency predicts greater well-being, but more is not always better," *Social Psychological and Personality Science* (2015). Advanced online publication.

14. Gottman and Silver, *What Makes Love Last?*

15. Peggy Vaughan, *The Monogamy Myth: A Personal Handbook for Recovering from Affairs* (New York: HarperCollins, 2003).

16. Adrian J. Blow, and Kelley Hartnett, "Infidelity in Committed Relationships II, A Substantive Review," *Journal of Marital Family Therapy* 31 no. 2 (May 2005); 217–33.

17. Kristin Mark, Erick Janssen, and Robin Milhausen, "Infidelity in Heterosexual Couples: Demographic, Interpersonal and Personality-Related Predictors of Extradyadic Sex," *Archives of Sexual Behavior* (June 2011) , http://citeseerx.ist.psu.edu/viewdoc/download?doi=10.1.1.437.1327&rep=re p1&type=pdf. Press release by Indiana University, June 24, 2011, http://newsinfo.iu.edu/news-archive/18977.html.

18. Peggy Drexler, *Wall Street Journal*, "The New Face of Infidelity," *Science* (October 20–21, 2012) 1.

19. Rona B. Subotnik, and Gloria Harris, *Surviving Infidelity: Making Decisions, Recovering from the Pain* (Avon, MA: Adams Media, 2005).

20. Willard F. Harley, *His Needs, Her Needs: Building an Affair-Proof Marriage* (Grand Rapids, MI: , Revell, 2011).

21. Wendy Plump, "A Roomful of Yearning and Regret," *New York Times*, December 12, 2010, http://www.nytimes.com/2010/12/12/fashion/12Modern.html?_r=0.

22. Leslie Stahl, "Arnold Schwarznegger, Success and Secrets," *60 Minutes* transcript, September 30, 2012, http://www.cbsnews.com/news/arnold-schwarzenegger-success-and-secrets/.

Chapter Twenty: No Marriage is Perfect: How to Be Happy Anyway

1.   A transcript of Dr. Kagan's contribution to a panel on "The Affect of Emotions: Laying the Groundwork in Childhood," entitled "Understanding the Effects of Temperament, Anxiety, and Guilt" describes his basic concept at this website: http://loc.gov/loc/brain/emotion/Kagan.html.

2.   John J. Medina, "The Genetics of Temperament—An Update," *Psychiatric Times*, March 10, 2010, http://www.psychiatrictimes.com/articles/genetics-temperament%E2%80%94-update.

3.   Dartmouth College offers a useful description of Albert Ellis's ABC concepts: http://www.dartmouth.edu/~eap/abcstress2.pdf.

4.   While I was unable to find Dr. Beckman's study dissecting life satisfaction by outlook, I'm sure it was derived from the data reported here: Betsy Bosak Houser, Sherry L. Berkman, and Linda J. Beckman, "The Relative Reward and Costs of Childlessness for Older Women," *Psychology of Women Quarterly* 8 no. 4 (Summer 1984), https://www.researchgate.net/publication/247643272_The_Relative_Rewards_and_Costs_of_Childlessness_for_Older_Women.

5.   Ellie Lisitsa, "The Four Horsemen: Recognizing Criticism, Contempt, Defensiveness, and Stonewalling," The Gottman Institute relationship blog, April 24, 2013, https://www.gottman.com/blog/the-four-horsemen-recognizing-criticism-contempt-defensiveness-and-stonewalling/.

6.   Karl Pillemer, *30 Lessons for Loving* (New York: Avery, 2015), http://legacyproject.human.cornell.edu/.

7.   Linda J. Waite et al., *Does Divorce Make People Happy? Findings from a Study of Unhappy Marriages*, Institute for American Values, 2002, http://americanvalues.org/catalog/pdfs/does_divorce_make_people_happy.pdf.

8.   Joshua Coleman, *The Marriage Makeover: Finding Happiness in Imperfect Harmony* (New York: St. Martin's Griffin, 2003).

9.   Coleman, *The Marriage Makeover*, 12.

10. Ibid., 13.

11. Ibid., 14.

12. Ibid., 16.

13. Diane Cole, "The Healing Power of Forgiveness," *Wall Street Journal*, March 21, 2016, R8.

Chapter Twenty-One: Life's Finest Accomplishment

1.   Linda J. Waite et al., *Does Divorce Make People Happy? Findings from a Study of Unhappy Marriages*, 2002, Institute for American Values, http://www.americanvalues.org/search/item.php?id=13.

2.   E. Mavis Hetherington and John Kelly, *For Better or for Worse* (New York: Norton, 2002). In their long-term follow up of children of divorce, they found "three quarters developing within the normal range" (p. 149) and have stated that up to 25% experience divorce-related problems throughout life.

3.   Tara Parker-Pope, *For Better: The Science of a Good Marriage* (New York: Dutton, 2010), 21.

4.   Arthur C. Brooks, *Gross National Happiness: Why Happiness Matters for America—and How We Can Get More of It* (New York: Basic Books, 2008), 60.

5.   Brooks, *Gross National Happiness*, 62.

6.   Claire Cain Miller, "Study Finds More Reasons to Get and Stay Married," *New York Times*, January 8, 2015, A3, http://www.nytimes.com/2015/01/08/upshot/study-finds-more-reasons-to-get-and-stay-married.html?_r=0.

7.   Norval Glenn et al., *Why Marriage Matters: Twenty-One Conclusions from the Social Sciences* (New York: Institute for American Values, 2002), http://www.americanvalues.org/search/item.php?id=728.

8.   Helen Fisher, "Love in the Time of Neuroscience," *New York Times Book Review*, February 9, 2014, 20.

9.   "Findings from new nationwide survey of family-related attitudes, values and experiences," *Deseret News National*, November 16, 2015, http://national.deseretnews.com/files/american-family-survey.pdf.

10. Justin McCarthy, "Americans' Personal and U.S. Satisfaction on the Upswing," Gallup, January 15, 2015, http://www.gallup.com/poll/181160/americans-personal-satisfaction-upswing.aspx.

11. Eli J. Finkel, "The All-or-Nothing Marriage," *New York Times*, February 16, 2014, SR1.

12. Finkel, "The All-or-Nothing Marriage."

13. Kayla M. Sanders, *Marital Satisfaction Across the Transition to Parenthood*, Masters Thesis, University of Nebraska, 2010, http://digitalcommons.unl. edu/cgi/viewcontent.cgi?article=1001&context=sociologydiss.

14. Daniel Akst, "Dear Sir, Cheer Up Your Wife," *Wall Street Journal*, September 20–21, 2014, C4.

15. Judith S. Wallerstein and Sandra Blakeslee, *The Good Marriage: How and Why Love Lasts* (Boston: Houghton Mifflin, 1995).

16. Charles Murray, "Advice for a Happy Life," *Wall Street Journal*, March 29–30, 2014, C1, adapted from *The Curmudgeon's Guide to Getting Ahead: Dos and Don'ts of Right Behavior, Tough Thinking, Clear Writing, and Living a Good Life* (New York: Crown Business, 2014).

17. John Tierney, "Love at Gradually Evolving Sight," *New York Times*, June 29, 2015, http://www.nytimes.com/2015/06/30/science/for-couples-time-can-upend-the-laws-of-attraction.html.

18. Alain de Botton, "Why You Will Marry the Wrong Person," *New York Times* May 29, 2016, 1.

19. Elaine Aron, Ph.D., "36 Questions for Intimacy, Back Story," Huffington Post, March 18, 2015, http://www.huffingtonpost.com/elaine-aron-phd/36-questions-for-intimacy_b_6472282.html.

20. Mandy Len Catron, "To Fall in Love With Anyone, Do This," *New York Times*, January 9, 2015, http://www.nytimes.com/2015/01/11/fashion/modern-love-to-fall-in-love-with-anyone-do-this.html.

Epilogue

1. Credit for the formulation of this most valuable concept goes to my longtime friend Elizabeth Brenner Danziger, whose book *Winning by Letting Go: Control without Compulsion, Surrender Without Defeat* (San Diego: Harcourt Brace Jovanovich, 1985) has helped innumerable couples throughout the years of my psychology practice and lecturing.

2. John Gottman, Ph.D., and Nan Silver, *What Makes Love Last: How to Build Trust and Avoid Betrayal* (New York: Simon and Schuster, 2012), 31.

3. Ibid.

4. Ezriel Gelbfish, "Study on Arranged Marriages Reveals Orthodox Jews May Have it Right," *The Algemeiner*, July 6, 2012, http://www.algemeiner. com/2012/07/06/study-on-arranged-marriages-reveals-that-orthodox-jews-may-have-it-right/#.

5.   Nancy Dreyfus, Psy.D., *Talk to Me Like I'm Someone You Love*: *Relationship Repair in a Flash* (New York: Jeremy Tarcher/Penguin, 1993, 2013).

6.   David Skinner, "Got To Give It Up," *Weekly Standard*, March 28/April 4, 2016, 5.

Index

379

Ellis, Albert, 308
Emery, Robert, 131
Emory University, 74
emotions, xvii, xx–xxi, 4–6, 13, 15, 17,
    21, 24, 48, 55, 61, 64, 68, 83, 97, 99,
    102–3, 116, 144, 155, 174, 180–81,
    195, 201, 203, 206, 210, 216, 229,
    236, 248–50, 258, 267, 283, 291,
    300, 316, 337
  "emotions trump logic," xxi, 13, 21,
    24, 155, 181
  stopping the internal conversation, 5
engagement, 36–37, 169. *See also* pro-
  posing
  engagement rings, 84
Epstein, Robert, 216, 218
Erhard, Werner, 48
Erickson, Milton, 49
Esalen Institute, 48
"Eugenio: Till Death Do You Part," 243
Evans, Patricia, 175
Eve (first woman), 207, 218, 331
"Every Other Weekend," 68–69
expectations, 12–13, 17–20, 94, 110,
    134, 144, 154, 161, 176, 187, 190,
    192, 217, 221, 229, 237, 241, 260,
    263–64, 274, 278, 293, 316, 318–20,
    334, 342–43
  unmet expectations, 154, 187

F

Facebook, xii, 24, 30, 53, 55–57, 148–
    50, 291
  the breakup flow, 55
Facebook Addictive Disorder, 150
FaceTime, 133, 137, 256, 265
family. *See also* binuclear families;
  blended families; children
  decline of the, 44
  extended family, 159–60, 163–65,
    231, 237
  as the traditional purpose of mar-
    riage, 16–17, 20

Family Ties (TV show), 36
family values, xiv, 40
Farber, Edward, 102–3
fatherhood, fathers, 101, 105, 114, 121,
    132–38, 143, 160, 182, 211, 231,
    235, 241, 267, 275, 324, 335
  the importance of dads, 132–38
Fatherless America (Blankenhorn), 134
fear, 7–8, 21, 60, 63, 79, 110–11, 124,
    142, 158, 174–75, 182, 199, 231,
    267–69, 272, 276, 282–83, 304, 312,
    321, 326
Feminine Mystique, The (Friedan), 18
feminism, feminists, xii, 13, 17–19, 26,
    32, 134, 299, 331
fertility treatments, 41. *See also* infertility
Fiddler on the Roof (film), 201
finances, xiii, 20, 42, 68, 73–74, 80, 84,
    87, 119, 131, 171, 181–82, 228. *See
    also* money
Finkel, Eli, 281, 326–27
Fish, Stanley, 220, 223–24
Fisher, Helen, 325, 328
"flooding" (relationship pattern), 340
For Better (Parker-Pope), 324
Ford, Harrison, 85
forgiveness, 223, 320
freedom, 130, 132, 139, 209, 257, 287,
    292
Friedan, Betty, 18
friends, friendships, xi–xii, xiv–xv, xvii,
    4, 10, 15, 18–19, 21, 24, 26–27, 31,
    43, 47, 50, 54–56, 74, 89, 92–94,
    100, 105, 107, 115–17, 122, 139–40,
    148, 150, 153–59, 163, 165–66, 170,
    173, 185–86, 190, 195–96, 206, 209,
    215, 217, 228, 237, 242, 244, 256,
    258–59, 263, 269, 276, 278–79, 281,
    290, 298–300, 307, 311, 318, 322,
    325, 330
  advice from friends during divorce,
    159

as emotional baggage of spouses, 195–96
friendships between opposite sexes, 32–34, 166, 288–92
loyalty when friends divorce, 153
within marriage. *See* marriage: friendship in
Full House (TV show), 36

G

Gadoua, Susan Pease, 174
Gallagher, Maggie, 114
Garcia, Justin R., 278
Garden of Eden, 207, 331
Gates, Bill, 260
gay marriage, 12–17. *See also* same-sex marriage; homosexuality
gender identity, 16
gender roles, 18–20, 136
Genesis (book of the Bible), 331
Genovese, Kitty, 165
ghosting, 56
Gibson, Mel, 75
Gitti, Cristina, 119
Glenn, Norval, 239
God, xviii, 5, 14–16, 18, 30, 52, 54, 59, 81, 94, 160, 192, 207–8, 218–19, 250, 310, 330–31, 333–34
Good Divorce, The (Ahrons), 48, 122, 227
"good divorces," 48, 73, 87, 112, 122, 227–38
children of good divorces, 234–35
choosing a good marriage over a good divorce, 235–38
good marriages. *See* marriage: good marriages
Good Marriage, The (Wallerstein), 327
"Good Part, the," 52
Google, 30
Gordon, Jane, 255–56
Gottman, John, 220, 247, 291–93, 301, 312, 315, 340

Gottman, Julie,
Graff, E. J., 14
Grammer, Camille, 75
Grammer, Kelsey, 75
grandparents, xvii, 122, 142, 160–62, 164, 241
"gray divorces," 139, 259, 270–72
Great Barrier Reef, 268
Greater Good Science Center, 55
Green, M. Christian, 165
Gregson, Wendy, 179–82
Grigorieva, Oksana, 82
Grohol, John, 282
Gross National Happiness (Brooks), 324
"growing apart," 10, 213–16, 271
guilt, xiii, xviii, 6–7, 19, 23, 27, 78–79, 100, 177, 194, 197, 198, 208, 291, 300, 335

H

Habitat for Humanity, 163
habits, xx, 26, 45, 47, 80–81, 84, 120, 145, 178–79, 185–90, 201, 225, 243, 245, 247, 258, 303–5, 307, 310, 331, 337, 339
bad habits, 80, 188–89, 201, 304, 337
eight suggestions regarding bad habits, 188–90
Hagerty, Barbara Bradley, 267–68
Hall, Jerry, 75
happiness, xiv, 14, 81, 94–95, 98, 101, 131, 138, 242, 251, 253–54, 268, 281, 292, 294, 299, 309, 317, 319, 323–30
Harley, Willard F., Jr., 294
Harper's Bazaar, 185
Harper's magazine, 49
Harris, Gloria, 84
Hartnett, Kelley, 293
Harvard, 30–31, 104, 268
Harvard Business School, 31, 268
Hax, Carolyn, 194–95

as a "home for the heart," 14
how to be happy in an imperfect marriage, 303–22
joys of an adequate marriage, 315–22
low-conflict marriages, 106, 111, 114,
234, 304, 318
mending marriage good for you and
for your spouse, xvi, 239–335
partners sharing the blame for breakdown of, xix
as primary gateway to adulthood, xii
remarriage. *See* remarriage
as a ritual, 12, 219, 295
and shared experience, 108, 328
a source of happiness, 324–30
three trends affecting perception of,
xii
three types of modern marriage, 14
traditional marriage, 16, 18–20, 260
traditional purpose of marriage, xv,
16–17, 20
traditional versus redefined, 20
why stay married, 6–7
Marriage Makeover, The (Coleman),
317–18, 321
Married…with Children (TV show), 36
Martin, Chris, 117
Match.com, 277
Mathison, Melissa, 75
"matrimania," 273, 310
Mayo Clinic, the, 320
McBride, Karyl, 205
McCartney, Paul, 75
McDermott, Rose, 156
McEntire, Reba, 68
McGill University, 69
McLanahan, Sarah, 104, 113
MD Junction, 193
"Me Decade," the, 242
media, the, xiv, 10, 53, 57, 104, 227
mediation, 47, 51, 60, 62, 76, 84, 117,
126, 129–31, 178, 256
Medicaid, 49
Medicare, 49

medication, 8, 29, 48, 77, 206,233, 276,
330
Medved, Michael, xviii, 30, 140
men, xii, 13, 16, 18–19, 26, 28, 31–35,
38–39, 42, 52, 69, 75–76, 80, 88,
112, 136, 171, 196–98, 200, 207,
241, 246, 268, 276, 278–82, 287,
292–94, 298, 322, 324–35, 327, 331–
32, 339, 341
and affairs, 287–301. *See also* adultery; affairs; infidelity; cheating
benefits of marriage for, 325, 327
and desire for physical attractiveness,
196, 198, 200
health risks as result of divorce,
69–70
median age for marriage, xii
porn use, 26–28
men's roles, 17–20, 134–36, 246
response to emotional pain of divorce,
75–76
Mend (app), 57
Mercer Island, 89
Michael Medved Show, The, 30
Michaelson, Ingrid, 340
micro-aggressions, 16, 203
midlife crises, 264–72, 294, 325, 370
millennials, 16, 118, 327
Mills, Heather, 85
mini-marriage, 261
"Modern Love" (column), 210, 297, 329
money, 10–11, 14, 47, 57–58, 83–84,
86–87, 89, 93, 114, 140, 176, 178,
224, 244, 246, 253, 258, 275, 280,
288, 304, 325, 333. *See also* finances
monogamy, 33, 107, 163, 165, 242, 260,
293, 299. *See also* marriage
serial monogamy, 107, 163, 165, 242,
260
Monogamy Myth, The (Vaughan), 293
Montgomery, James, 288
Moore, Robyn Denise, 85

revenge, 181, 205, 208
Rhoades, Galena, 37
Rice University, 217
Ringer, Robert, 242
Ritchie, Guy, 86
romance, ix, 14, 33, 58, 86, 141, 155, 188, 191, 241
"Roomful of Yearning and Regret, A," 297
Rosie the Riveter, 241
Rothchild, Sascha, 262
Rx Breakup, 57
Ryff, Carol, 269

S

Sabbath, the, 214, 332
Salerno, Steve, 162
Sallan, Bruce, 136
same-sex marriage, 12, 14, 17, 331. *See also* gay marriage; homosexuality
Sandberg, Sheryl, 30–31
Sandefur, Gary, 104, 113
San Francisco Chronicle, 117
Sapphire, 54
Saving Childhood (Medved), 140
Sbarra, David, 71
Scarf, Maggie, 44
Schmidt, Lone, 41
Schwarzenegger, Arnold, 75, 299
Scioli, Anthony, 121–22
Scott, Adam, 242
self, elevation of, 241–42
self-esteem, xvi, 27, 113, 121, 138, 199, 209, 235, 253–54, 326
self-expression, 257, 326
self-help books, 52, 223, 300, 304
Seligman, Martin, 31, 120, 305, 308–10
serial monogamy, 107, 163, 165, 242, 260
settlement, 47, 59, 61–62, 79, 83–87, 115, 233
settlement conference, 47, 62–63

sex, xv, 12, 14, 17–18, 20, 24–30, 32–34, 40, 69, 74, 78–79, 81, 130, 140, 166, 171, 186–87, 197, 199–200, 218, 220, 224, 242, 248, 265–67, 276, 278–79, 286–88, 292–95, 297, 313, 324, 327, 331, 342
"sexpectations," 278
sexting, 290
sexuality, 16, 18, 30, 53, 140, 298, 208, 299
sexual revolution, the, 17. *See also* 1960s, the
Shakespeare, William, 14
Shellenbarger, Sue, 165–66
Shriver, Maria, 75
Simon, Paul, 9
Sinatra, Frank, 35
Sindell, Max, 139
single dads, 275
singlehood, single life, xii, xv, 10, 25, 31, 41, 43, 48, 52, 55–56, 69–70, 75, 88–89, 101, 104–5, 113, 124, 131, 140, 142, 158, 163, 166, 235, 244, 257, 273–83, 325
single moms, 43, 88, 163
"singlism," 273
Skinner, David, 343
Skype, 133, 149, 290
Slater and Gordon (law firm), 149
Slaughter, Anne-Marie, 32
smiling, 307
Smith, Genevieve, 49
smoking, 69, 80, 112
Snapchat, 149
"social contagions," 53
social media (a. k. a. online social networks), xii, 10, 16, 24, 55–56, 148–50, 271, 278
   as doorway to divorce, 148–50
social workers, 48–49, 111, 157, 174
Sohn, Amy, 279
Sood, Amit, 320
soul mates, ix, 199, 242, 274, 292, 334–35

and "happy wife, happy life" concept,
   200, 327
income, 88–89, 133, 272
median age for marriage, xii
porn use, 28
response to emotional pain of divorce,
   75–76
women's movement, 18, 133. *See also*
   feminism, feminists
women's roles, 17–20, 136, 246
and work-home balance, 19, 30–32,
   105
workplace affairs, 30–34. *See also* co-
workers
World War II, 133, 241, 260
Wynette, Tammy, 67

Y
Yiddish, 221, 223

Z
Zicherman, Stuart, 106
Zoosk, 279
Zuckerberg, Mark, 260